Corporate Acquisitions and Mergers in the European Union

Corporate Acquisitions and Mergers in the European Union

Fifth Edition

Riccardo Celli
Philippe Noguès
Christian Peeters
Rebecca Evans

O'Melveny & Myers LLP

This book was originally published as a chapter in Corporate Acquisitions and Mergers.

General Editor: Peter Begg

Wolters Kluwer

Published by:
Kluwer Law International B.V.
PO Box 316
2400 AH Alphen aan den Rijn
The Netherlands
E-mail: lrs-sales@wolterskluwer.com
Website: www.wolterskluwer.com/en/solutions/kluwerlawinternational

Sold and distributed by:
Wolters Kluwer Legal & Regulatory U.S.
920 Links Avenue
Landisville, PA 17538
United States of America
E-mail: customer.service@wolterskluwer.com

ISBN 978-94-035-2058-2

e-Book: ISBN 978-94-035-2068-1
web-PDF: ISBN 978-94-035-2078-0

Contents

O'Melveny & Myers LLP

O'Melveny & Myers LLP has one of the world's pre-eminent Antitrust and Competition practices. Ian Simmons, former attorney of the Department of Justice, and Ben Bradshaw head the practice group. With more than seventy experienced antitrust and competition lawyers based in offices across the United States (Washington D.C., New York, Los Angeles, Austin, Dallas, Houston, and San Francisco), Asia (Tokyo, Beijing, Hong Kong, Seoul, Singapore, and Shanghai), and Europe (Brussels and London), few firms can match its consistent strength across these three major economic areas.

The Brussels office, headed by Riccardo Celli, head of the firm's European Antitrust and Competition Practice, specialises in European Union (EU) and European national competition, regulatory and international trade law. The lawyers in our Brussels office are experienced practitioners of EU law as well as the key national laws and procedures, speak the local languages, work closely with local authorities, and are accustomed to coordinating complex cross-border projects. These strengths enable O'Melveny to represent clients in multi-jurisdictional proceedings with resource, efficiency and shared expertise.

O'Melveny is recommended as a leading antitrust and competition law practice in the prestigious Global Competition Review's 100, and several of its partners are recognised globally as leading experts in competition law, including Riccardo Celli in the Brussels office.

Authors[1]

Riccardo Celli is a partner at O'Melveny and head of the firm's European Antitrust and Competition Practice. Riccardo's thirty-year expertise in competition law covers the entire range of antitrust issues faced by companies, including: competition clearances for acquisitions and joint ventures (notifying and dealing with regulators, advising and coordinating multi-jurisdictional filings, advising on optimal transaction structures to achieve clearances, including assisting in preparing and negotiating possible commitments with regulators); anticompetitive practices, cartels and abuse of dominance (avoiding competition infringements in contracts and general commercial behaviour, helping clients deal with competition investigations, 'dawn raids' and infringement proceedings, assisting companies that are victims of anticompetitive practices in making complaints to the competition authorities and preparing compliance programmes); and competition litigation. As for antitrust merger control, Riccardo has been involved in advising on the application of the EU Merger Regulation since its original implementation in 1990. Since those early days, he has represented dozens of multinational corporations in securing clearances for hundreds of transactions as well as in opposing third-party mergers. He holds a dual qualification as an Italian Avvocato and Solicitor of the Supreme Court of England and Wales. Riccardo is recognised as one of

[1] The authors wish to express their gratitude to Katharina Weiss, associate at O'Melveny & Myers LLP, who assisted in the preparation of this fifth edition.

the world's leading lawyers in the field of competition law in many specialised publications, including *Chambers*, *Legal 500*, *Global Competition Review*, *Practical Law* and *International Who's Who of Competition Lawyers*.

Philippe Nogués is a counsel in O'Melveny's Brussels office. He focuses on EU and French competition law as well as on the coordination of multi-jurisdictional matters. Philippe advises in the fields of mergers and acquisitions, anticompetitive agreements, concerted practices and abuse of dominance in relation to various industry sectors such as energy, aviation, mineral resources, automotive, pharmaceuticals, as well as in high-tech industries and intellectual property rights. Philippe has authored a number of articles on competition law, especially in the field of leniency and in the energy sector. Philippe is a member of the Paris and Brussels bars.

Christian Peeters is a Partner in the O'Melveny's Brussels office. Qualified as a German Rechtsanwalt, his competition law practice specialises in multi-jurisdictional merger cases as well as defences in complex abuse of dominance and cartel investigations, representing clients before the European Commission, the German Federal Cartel Office and other agencies around the world. Christian has counselled some of the world's leading businesses on their headline-grabbing transactions and bet-the-company litigation. Several of these cases serve as precedents for the way antitrust is practised today.

Rebecca Evans is an associate working with the O'Melveny Brussels competition team from the firm's London office. She is a solicitor of the Senior Courts of England and Wales, focusing on UK and EU competition laws and advising on multi-jurisdictional matters regarding both merger control and antitrust compliance. Rebecca has worked with clients across various sectors, including technology, aviation, consumer goods and basic industry.

O'Melveny & Myers LLP

Blue Tower

Avenue Louise 326

1050 Brussels, Belgium

Tel.: +32-2-642-4100

Fax: +32-2-642-4190

Email: brussels@omm.com

Web: www.omm.com

1 INTRODUCTION & GENERAL REMARKS

[01] Originally established by Council Regulation 4064/89 on the control of concentrations between undertakings ('the 1989 Regulation'),[2] today's merger control regime of the European Union (EU) is governed by Council Regulation 139/2004 (the 'Merger Regulation') which replaced the 1989 Regulation on 1 May 2004.[3]

[02] European merger control is relatively young in comparison to other systems in force in the United States (US) and in Germany. The European Commission's (the 'Commission') desire to introduce specific merger rules at the Community level dates from 1966 as the regulator rightfully considered that Articles 101 and 102 of the Treaty on the Functioning of the European Union (TFEU) were not suitable and reliable tools to monitor the increasing concentration activity in Europe. However, it was not until the European Court of Justice's (ECJ) judgment in the Continental Can case of 1973 that the Commission submitted its first draft of a merger regulation to the European Council (the 'Council').[4] Until the late 1980s, little progress was made on this draft, primarily due to disputes on the jurisdictional scope of the regulation and the extent to which non-competition related factors, such as regional restructuring and social policies, should be taken into account – themes that would resurface decades later during the 2008–2009 financial crisis as well as in 2019 in the aftermath of the Commission's prohibition of the *Siemens/Alstom* transaction.[5]

[03] Ultimately, it was the business community's desire for a clear-cut system of merger control at the EU level that prevailed over the reluctance of Member States to grant specific merger control powers to the Commission. In order to allocate competencies between the Commission and the national Member State authorities, the new regime introduced quantitative (revenue-based) thresholds in order to define those concentrations that have a 'Community dimension' and that are, therefore, in principle, best dealt with by the Commission, leaving smaller transactions to the Member States' jurisdiction.[6] This 'one-stop-shop' principle under which the Commission has exclusive competence to deal with large transactions of Community dimension is a key characteristic of European merger control still today.

[04] That said, since its inception in 1990, the EU merger control regime has undergone significant changes over time. In 1997, the first notable round of

[2] Council Regulation (EEC) 4064/89 of 21 Dec. 1989 on the control of concentrations between undertakings; OJ L 395, 30.12.1989; corrected version OJ L 257, 21.9.1990, p. 13 with amendments introduced by Council Regulation (EC) 1310/97 of 30 Jun. 1997 in OJ L 180, 9.7.1997, p. 1, Corrigendum OJ L 40, 13.2.1998, p. 17. The 1989 Regulation entered into force on 21 Sep. 1990.

[3] Council Regulation (EC) 139/2004 of 20 Jan. 2004 on the control of concentrations between undertakings; OJ L 24, 29.1.2004, pp. 1–22.

[4] Commission Proposal for a Regulation of the Council on the control of concentrations between undertakings; OJ C 92/1, 1973.

[5] *See* case M.8677 *Siemens/Alstom*.

[6] In 1990, when the 1989 Regulation entered into force, only three Member States, France, Germany and the United Kingdom (UK), had developed systems of merger control.

revisions to the 1989 Regulation brought about three important changes to the system. First, the amended regulation eliminated the complex distinction between 'cooperative' and 'concentrative' joint ventures. Second, an additional, lower set of jurisdictional thresholds intended to give the Commission competence over a greater number of cases was adopted. These revised thresholds targeted concentrations that affected three or more Member States but fell below the original thresholds of the 1989 Regulation. Third, the Commission introduced a 'simplified procedure' for unproblematic transactions.

[05] In 2004, the Merger Regulation introduced another set of critical changes that reflected the Commission's experience from dealing with concentrations for more than a decade. Most importantly, the substantive test against which mergers are examined – compatibility with the Internal Market – is no longer based on the creation or strengthening of a dominant position but on whether competition in the Internal Market is significantly impeded as a result of the notified 'concentration' (the term used in the Merger Regulation in place of 'merger').

[06] With twenty-seven Member States in the EU today, the above-mentioned 'one-stop-shop' principle has great importance for fostering procedural efficiency and jurisdictional certainty, but it has suffered some erosion. In keeping with the principle of decentralisation, which is a feature of the modernised approach to enforcing Articles 101 and 102 of the TFEU, there is now greater flexibility as to whether notifications are handled by the Commission or Member States. The reform has also introduced greater procedural flexibility, particularly with the ability to extend the procedural review deadlines and to notify proposed concentrations before any binding agreement exists or a bid is launched. There have also been changes to the internal organisation of the Competition Directorate of the Commission ('DG Comp'). The Merger Task Force has been disbanded, and merger work is spread across DG Comp's industry sector units. With a view to moving EU merger control towards a more effects-based analysis, the post of Chief Economist was created to provide independent guidance on methodological issues of economics and econometrics in the application of EU competition rules.[7]

[07] These changes are a response both to criticisms from the European General Court regarding the overall rigour and quality of the Commission's decision-making and to the perennial (but hitherto unheeded) complaint that the Commission effectively acts as investigator, prosecutor, judge and jury in merger proceedings.[8]

[7] First employed in *Carnival/P&O* [2003] OJ L 79/27.

[8] During 2002, the Commission's application of the 1989 Regulation came under considerable additional scrutiny as a result of the General Court's judgments overturning the Commission's decisions in three separate merger cases, *Airtours/First Choice* (T-342/99, judgment of 6 Jun. 2002); *Schneider/Legrand* (T-77/01, judgment of 22 Oct. 2002) and *Tetra Laval/Sidel* (case T-80/2, judgment of 25 Oct. 2002). The Commission also controversially prohibited the proposed acquisition of Honeywell by General Electric, which had been cleared by the US department of Justice. More recently, a new set of judgments from the General Court (*UPS v. Commission* and *CK Telecoms UK Investments Ltd v. Commission*) overturning Commission merger decisions have fuelled criticism of the Commission's investigations and theories of harm.

[08] The Merger Regulation sets forth the legal framework and principal provisions of EU merger control. It is based on the following four main principles:

(1) the 'one-stop-shop' principle, i.e., the exclusive competence of the Commission to review concentrations that have a Community dimension;
(2) the mandatory notification of such concentrations and their suspension until clearance is obtained;
(3) the consistent application of market-oriented competition-based criteria; and
(4) the provision of legal certainty through decisions adopted pursuant to short and strict deadlines.

[09] The Merger Regulation is supplemented by the Commission's Regulation implementing the Merger Regulation (the 'Implementing Regulation') containing details on relevant procedures, including the Form CO, the Short Form CO, the Form RS and the Form RM. The Implementing Regulation outlines the standard information required from the parties for their notification.

[10] To complement the Merger Regulation and Implementing Regulation, the Commission issued various notices and guidelines over the years in order to streamline its decision-making process and make it more transparent as well as to strengthen the economic analysis and protect applicants' rights more effectively.[9]

[11] The EU merger review package is composed of the following main elements:[10]

(a) A Merger Regulation.
(b) An Implementing Regulation.[11]
(c) A Consolidated Jurisdictional Notice (the 'Consolidated Notice').[12]
(d) A Commission Notice on remedies acceptable under the Merger Regulation and the Implementing Regulation (the 'Remedies Notice').[13]
(e) A Commission Notice on a simplified procedure for treatment of certain concentrations under the Merger Regulation.[14]
(f) Guidelines on the assessment of horizontal mergers (the 'Horizontal Guidelines')[15] and Guidelines on the assessment of non-horizontal mergers under the Merger Regulation (the 'Non-horizontal Guidelines').[16]
(g) Best Practice Guidelines on the conduct of merger control proceedings.

---

[9] *See* IP/02/1856 of 11 Dec. 2002.

[10] For a more exhaustive list of the EU merger review package, please refer to s. 3.1 of this contribution.

[11] Commission Implementing Regulation (EU) No. 1269/2013 of 5 Dec. 2013 amending Regulation (EC) No. 802/2004 of 21 Apr. 2004 implementing Council Regulation 139/2004, OJ L 336/1, 14 Dec. 2013.

[12] Commission Consolidated Jurisdictional Notice under Council Regulation (EC) 139/2004 on the control of concentrations between undertakings, OJ C 95/1, 16 Apr. 2008.

[13] OJ C 267/1, 22 Oct. 2008.

[14] Commission Notice on a simplified procedure for treatment of certain concentrations under Council Regulation (EC) No. 139/2004, OJ C 366/5, 14 Dec. 2013.

[15] OJ C 31/5, 5 Feb. 2004.

[16] OJ C 265/6, 18 Oct. 2008.

[12] As new technologies and business models emerge, the Commission continues to closely monitor the efficacy of its regulatory toolkit in order to assess whether existing instruments should be revised or new ones should be adopted. In 2020, for example, the Commission launched its long-awaited public consultation on the 23-year-old Market Definition Notice. While the notice continues to provide a solid methodological framework, Commissioner Vestager noted that clarity is needed with respect to two main issues: globalisation and digitalisation.[17] The Market Definition Notice needs to find the delicate balance between flexibility to deal with markets across all sectors, which are evolving at different rates and legal certainty. Revising the notice now can also act as a release valve in response to calls for radical reforms to the merger review process in the wake of its controversial *Siemens/Alstom* prohibition, without regulation or treaty change, which could open a Pandora's box for the Commission. On 8 November 2022, the Commission released its draft revised Market Definition Notice ('Draft Notice') and invited all interested parties to submit their comments. The Draft Notice raises various topics. In particular, it emphasises that the outcome of market definition may differ, even when the products and geography concerned are the same, depending on the parameters of competition, the enterprises involved and the time period considered. Regarding the last aspect, the Commission refers to its *Metso/Svedala* decision, where the geographic market for crushers was defined as EEA-wide.[18] In its subsequent *Outotec/Metso* decision,[19] the Commission concluded that the relevant geographic market for the supply of mining capital equipment was global in scope. The Draft Notice also provides that expected structural market transitions may be taken into account when the case calls for a forward-looking assessment. The structural market transitions can affect the product market definition – for example, when there is sufficient probability that new types of products are about to emerge on the market – or the geographic market definition, for example, when there are impending technological changes or imminent changes in the regulatory framework. With respect to the types of evidence that the Commission can rely on in its definition of the relevant market, the Commission acknowledges that it shall not apply a rigid hierarchy of different sources of information or types of evidence. That being said, the Commission also indicates that a higher probative value is attributed to evidence that cannot have been influenced by the Commission's investigation, such as evidence pre-dating discussions of a concentration or conduct and pre-dating the Commission's investigation. For instance, internal documents of relevant entities that are prepared in the ordinary course of business are more relevant than those prepared in view of or during the Commission's merger investigation.[20] The Commission's consultation ended on 13 January 2023, and the Commission expects to adopt and publish the final version in the second half of 2023.

[17] *See* https://ec.europa.eu/commission/commissioners/2019-2024/vestager/announcements/defining-markets-new-age_en.

[18] Case M.2033 *Metso/Svedala*.

[19] Case M.9585 *Outotec/Metso*.

[20] *See*, https://competition-policy.ec.europa.eu/public-consultations/2022-market-definition-notice_en.

[13] Potentially more transformative for EU merger control was the Commission's March 2021 guidance on the application of the referral mechanism between Member States and the Commission set out in Article 22 of the Merger Regulation (the 'Article 22 Guidance').[21] The Article 22 Guidance aims to address concerns that an increasing number of transactions are escaping appropriate regulatory scrutiny (including by national competition authorities (NCAs)) as they involve target companies whose revenues are too low to meet applicable jurisdictional thresholds. Since these low revenues may not always reflect a company's high competitive potential, there is arguably a risk of regulatory underenforcement in particular in the digital and pharmaceutical sectors where innovation is an important parameter of competition. The Commission considers that encouraging and accepting more referrals under Article 22 of the Merger Regulation would be the best means of enabling it to target transactions that merit review at the EU level (even if such transactions are not reportable under any national merger control legislation). Accordingly, the Article 22 Guidance clarifies the categories of cases which may be suitable for an Article 22 request in situations where the transaction is not notifiable in the referring Member State(s), and it identifies the criteria that the Commission may take into account in exercising its discretion to accept such referrals. In December 2022, the Commission complemented its existing Article 22 Guidance by publishing a 'Frequently Asked Questions and Answers ("Q&A") document' which aims to provide practical information with respect to the application of its recently revised Article 22 referral policy. The Q&A addresses how transaction parties can approach the Commission for 'early indications' whether a transaction is a candidate for referral under Article 22 (please refer to section 5 below for more detailed information in this regard).

[14] With a view to simplifying the procedures for unproblematic mergers, in April 2023, the Commission adopted a package of legal texts aimed at simplifying the EU merger review process. The package expands the categories of cases that may be eligible for the simplified procedure, and streamlines the review of simplified cases. It also reduces certain information requirements in notifications subject to the ordinary (non-simplified) review procedure. The package includes a revised set of filing forms (Form CO, Short Form CO, Form RS and Form RM), applicable as of 1 September 2023. The revisions include a number of welcome changes that will reduce the burden on notifying parties in transactions with no substantive concerns. However, some of the issues with the previous information requirements remain, and, contrary to its aim, the package also introduces additional requirements for notifying parties even in cases with no substantive concerns.

[15] Overall, the successive reforms and the Commission's consideration of comments to its proposed reforms have created a European merger regime which is widely admired for its efficiency, flexibility and openness in the assessment of mergers. However, the Commission's new policy approach in relation to the above-mentioned Article 22 referrals has sent a worrying message to both the legal and

---

[21] *See*, https://ec.europa.eu/competition/consultations/2021_merger_control/guidance_article_22_referrals.pdf.

business communities by creating a new level of uncertainty which can deeply affect the efficiency of the Merger Regulation.

[16] This contribution has been updated until 1 June 2023. Following a year of record-level M&A deal activity in 2021 in the aftermath of the COVID-19 pandemic, 2022 saw the European M&A market settle back into a more familiar pace totalling approx. EUR780 bn, down 39% from 2021. Yet, in terms of the absolute number of cases reviewed, 2021 and 2022 were both relatively busy years for the Commission (with 405 concentrations notified in 2021 and 371 in 2022). With 309 cases reviewed under the simplified procedure in 2021, the Commission reached another record-breaking figure, representing a 10% increase compared to the 278 simplified cases reviewed in 2020. This trend has continued in 2022 which saw the Commission deal with 291 simplified cases in line with its continued efforts to further simplify the merger control procedures and focus its resources on transaction raising substantial concerns.

[17] The year 2022 also saw the Commission block two transactions in the shipbuilding[22] and pharmaceutical[23] industries, and while the Commission did not prohibit any transactions in 2021, this should not be interpreted as a softening of the Commission's appraisal after the Covid-19 pandemic. Indeed, the *Nvidia/Arm*, the *Kronospan/Pfleiderer Polska,* the *Kingspan Group/Trimo* and the *IAG/Air Europa* and *Air Canada/Transat* transactions were all abandoned in 2021 due to Commission concerns and possibly anticipated prohibitions.

[18] Indeed, 2021, 2022 and the first half of 2023 were characterised by a number of clear enforcement trends.

Commission's new Article 22 referral policy

[19] First, the above-discussed Article 22 Guidance, issued by the Commission in early 2021 to encourage referrals by Member States of concentrations that fall below their domestic jurisdictional thresholds, signals the Commission's willingness to assert jurisdiction over non-reportable transactions. While the Article 22 Guidance applies to all industries, it identifies the digital and pharmaceutical sectors as primary targets. The Commission has announced that it will monitor transaction activity in publicly available sources and cooperate closely with Member States to identify suitable referral candidate transactions. Moreover, the Article 22 Guidance invites third parties, such as competitors and customers of merging parties, to bring referral candidate cases to the Commission's attention. While most Member States are cooperating with the Commission under the new referral policy, some, notably Austria and Germany, have declared they will adhere to the old policy and only consider referring cases that meet national filing thresholds. Illumina's acquisition of Grail is the first transaction captured by the new policy. Announced in September 2020, the acquisition was not filed to the Commission or in any Member State. However, actively encouraged by the Commission, France made a referral request in March 2021 and was subsequently joined by Belgium,

[22] Case M.9343 *Hyundai Heavy Industries Holdings/Daewoo Shipbuilding & Marine Engineering*.
[23] Case M.10188 *Illumina/Grail*.

Greece, Iceland, the Netherlands, and Norway. The new referral policy can have a major impact on deal timing and deal certainty. If triggered pre-closing, an Article 22 referral may delay closing significantly, and merging parties may have to agree to remedies to address substantive concerns or, in an extreme case, face a prohibition decision. A post-closing review entails the risk of post-closing remedies or dissolution of the transaction.

[20] That said, so far, the number of Article 22 referral requests launched after the Commission's policy shift does not suggest that the procedure will be used in as many cases as many commentators may have initially feared. Between 2021 and June 2023, Article 22 referrals were only made in the following five transactions: *Illumina/Grail, Meta/Kustomer, Viasat/Inmarsat, Adobe/Figma* and *Cochlear/Oticon*. Moreover, out of these five transactions, only *Illumina/Grail* involved a transaction of the type directly targeted by the Article 22 Guidance, i.e., those that do not require a filing in any Member State. By contrast, all other transactions met the filing thresholds of at least one Member State.

[21] However, in light of its first instance victory in the *Illumina/Grail* appeal (where the General Court confirmed that the Commission has jurisdiction to review transactions that were referred to it under Article 22 even if the referring Member State does not have jurisdiction to review the proposed transaction),[24] the Commission may be encouraged to make more active use of this enforcement tool in the future.

Additional transaction reporting obligations in Europe

[22] Since the turn of the decade, Europe has witnessed the emergence of additional transaction reporting obligations and enforcement activity due to national foreign direct investment (FDI) legislation (and the related Foreign Direct Investment Regulation (the 'FDI Regulation') of the EU), the Digital Markets Act (the 'DMA'), and the Foreign Subsidies Regulation (the 'FSR').

[23] The FSR introduces a system for screening subsidies by foreign (non-EU) governments that may distort competition within the Internal Market, including the M&A market.[25] This subsidy control system, which is separate from and a complement to existing merger control and FDI control regimes, gives the Commission powers to review and potentially prohibit foreign-subsidised transactions. To this end, the FSR introduces a mandatory, suspensory FSR filing pursuant to which transactions need to be notified to the Commission if:

- the European turnover of the target (in case of an acquisition), one of the merging parties (in case of a merger) or the joint venture itself has an EU-wide turnover of at least EUR500 m; and

[24] Judgment by the General Court of 13 Jul. 2022 in Case T-227/21, *Illumina, Inc. v. European Commission* [2022] ECLI:EU:T:2022:447.

[25] *See* Regulation (EU) 2022/2560 of the European Parliament and of the Council of 14 Dec. 2022 on foreign subsidies distorting the internal market; OJ L 330, 23.12.2022, pp. 1–45.

- the combined foreign financial contributions (i.e., subsidies) of the parties involved in the deal are at least EUR50 m in the three years prior to the signing of the deal.

[24] Many procedural aspects of the FSR review regime have been modelled on the Merger Regulation. For example: (i) the Commission's review entails a first review phase of twenty-five working days and potentially a second, in-depth review phase of ninety working days; (ii) the parties are not allowed to close before the Commission has issued a decision, (iii) the Commission has wide-ranging investigative powers, and (iv) the Commission can impose fines on companies for procedural breaches, up to 10% of their aggregated turnover for a failure to notify, or up to 1% of the aggregated turnover for providing incorrect information. The FSR adds another layer of complication and uncertainty for dealmakers in Europe as companies will need to collect the FSR-relevant data on an ongoing basis (and for the preceding three years) in order to determine and manage their FSR exposure.

[25] On 14 September 2022, the Commission adopted the DMA with the aim of regulating digital platforms more effectively.[26] The DMA aims to address concerns about 'contestability' and 'fairness' in the digital economy by introducing a number of per se prohibitions and obligations for those systemically important big tech companies that meet certain quantitative and/or qualitative criteria and that the Commission has, therefore, designated as so-called gatekeepers. While the DMA grants the Commission very similar powers as in the antitrust area (the Commission can carry out inspections, send requests for information, interview employees of the relevant companies, impose interim measures, conduct market investigations, and, more significantly, impose fines and periodic penalty payments), the notification regime for transactions covered by the DMA is much less far-reaching. Indeed, the DMA only imposes on gatekeepers the obligation to 'inform' the Commission of acquisitions 'where the merging entities or the target of concentration provide core platform services or any other services in the digital sector or enable the collection of data' irrespective of any other threshold requirements beyond the acquirer's designation as gatekeeper. The DMA also does not create any review or decision-making powers for the Commission or Member States with regard to transactions that are subject to this information obligation. However, the information provided to the Commission under the DMA may well be used in conjunction with the referral mechanism pursuant to Article 22 of the Merger Regulation to 'call in' even non-reportable transactions by gatekeepers.

[26] Another addition to the regulatory maze that deal makers have to navigate in Europe is FDI screening. While the competence for vetting FDI remains with the EU Member States applying their national laws, enforcement policy has been steered by the Commission's April 2019 FDI Regulation.[27] The FDI Regulation does not oblige Member States to adopt an FDI screening mechanism, nor does it

[26] *See* Regulation (EU) 2022/1925 of the European Parliament and of the Council of 14 Sep. 2022 on contestable and fair markets in the digital sector and amending Directives (EU) 2019/1937 and (EU) 2020/1828 (Digital Markets Act).

[27] *See* Regulation (EU) 2019/452 of the European Parliament and of the Council of 19 Mar. 2019 establishing a framework for the screening of foreign direct investments into the Union.

seek to achieve full harmonisation in this field. It does, however, provide for information sharing and cooperation between Member States and the Commission. This involves the mandatory notification to the Commission and other Member States of any FDI scrutinised at the national level, including the provision of certain specified information. The FDI Regulation also requires that existing (and any new) regimes comply with a minimum set of requirements while also encouraging those Member States that do not yet have an FDI regime to adopt relevant rules.

[27] The triggering criteria for FDI filings differ significantly among Member States but typically relate to: (i) whether and to what extent the target has a local presence (e.g., via local assets or subsidiaries); and (ii) whether the economic sector that the national target is engaged in is considered strategic or sensitive. In several Member States, the acquisition of a fairly small interest in a target company (e.g., 10%) can trigger an FDI filing. FDI notifications typically are less data intensive when compared to merger control filings, although that may be different in individual cases depending on the complexity of the case. Some Member States, such as Austria, Germany and Italy, require FDI filings to be made quickly after signing the transaction agreement, which can lead to timing pressure. A failure to make a required filing can trigger significant fines or even criminal sanctions, including imprisonment of companies' decision-makers. On 1 September 2022, the Commission published its Second Annual Report under Article 5(4) of the FDI Regulation which covers the 2021 period and provides an overview of FDI trends and screening in the 27 Member States, as well as emerging developments in national screening mechanisms.[28] One notable feature mentioned by the Annual Report is that informal review remains prevalent: the Member States reported that of all the cases submitted to their authorities, 71% were deemed not to require formal screening, for example, because they were deemed to fall outside the scope of the Member State's screening regime or to lack impact on national security. There are very few instances of prohibitions due to FDI concerns. Notable examples are, however, Italy's veto in April 2021 concerning the attempted indirect acquisition by a Chinese state-owned company of an Italian microchip company,[29] or Germany's effective prohibition of Taiwanese company GlobalWafers' attempted acquisition of Germany-based chip supplier Siltronic in early 2022 (when the FDI approval process was delayed until the deal collapsed). These examples show that Member State FDI reviews can derail transactions, even if the transactions had been cleared by merger control authorities, as was the case in the *GlobalWafers/Siltronic* case.[30]

[28] Antitrust merger control and FDI review are separate regimes that in principle apply in parallel, but there are important interdependencies as can also be attested by the *VIG/Aegon CEE* transaction which was unconditionally cleared by the Commission under the Merger Regulation[31] but was later blocked by the Hungarian

[28] *See*, https://ec.europa.eu/transparency/documents-register/detail?ref=COM(2022)433&lang=en.

[29] *See* Reuters article: Reuters, 'Italy vetoes takeover of semiconductor firm by Chinese company Shenzhen', 9 Apr. 2021.

[30] The transaction had obtained merger control approvals in Austria, China, Germany, Japan, Singapore, South Korea, Taiwan, and the United States.

[31] Case 10102 *VIG/Aegon CEE*.

government pursuant to its FDI regime. In February 2022, the Commission issued a decision finding Hungary's FDI veto to be in breach of Article 21 of the Merger Regulation which allows Member States to block a transaction that the Commission is competent to review under the Merger Regulation for reasons of 'legitimate interest' and generally only subject to prior consultation with the Commission. The Commission ultimately found that these conditions were not present in this case and ordered Hungary to withdraw its veto. While cases in which Member States infringed Article 21 of the Merger Regulation have been rare (there have been only three since 1990), it is well possible that they arise more often in the future given the proliferation of FDI review in Member States.

Fines for procedural infringements

[29] The Commission has continued to be particularly vigilant and aggressive with regard to procedural infringements of its merger control regime and has to date imposed fines in seven cases where companies had implemented their transactions prior to obtaining regulatory clearance.[32] In April 2018, the Commission fined Altice EUR125 m for breaching EU rules by controlling PT Portugal before obtaining merger approval. In that case, the Commission found that Altice had: (i) implemented the transaction prematurely through obtaining the veto rights contained in the pre-closing covenants in the sale and purchase agreement; (ii) actually exercised decisive influence over PT Portugal by intervening in its day-to-day business prior to clearance; and (iii) prematurely exchanged a considerable amount of competitively sensitive information with PT Portugal. The General Court later dismissed Altice's appeal against the Commission's decision in 2021[33] (most recently, Advocate General Collins recommended that Altice's appeal be dismissed in its entirety).[34] General Electric was fined EUR52 m in April 2019 for providing incorrect information in relation to its acquisition of LM Wind,[35] and Canon was fined EUR28 m in June 2019 for 'gun jumping'.[36] Also, in May 2021, the Commission fined Sigma-Aldrich EUR7.5 m for three infringements in providing incorrect or misleading information in its replies to two requests for information made pursuant to Article 11(2) of the EU Merger Regulation during the official investigation into its acquisition by Merck KGaA in 2015. Specifically, Sigma-Aldrich failed to disclose the existence of the iCap innovation project, which was closely linked to the businesses it divested to Honeywell in order to address competition concerns in

[32] *See* cases M.920 *Samsung/AST*, M.969 *A.P. Moller*, M.4994 *Electrabel/CNR*, M.7184 *Marine Harvest/Morpol*, M.7993 *Altice/PT Portugal*, M.8179 *Canon/Toshiba Medical Systems*, and M.10483 *Illumina/Grail*.

[33] *See Altice Europe v. Commission*, Case T-425/18, judgment of 22 Sep. 2021.

[34] *Altice Group Lux v. Commission*, Case C-746/21 P, Opinion of Advocate General Collins, 27 Apr. 2023.

[35] Case COMP/M.8436 *General Electric Company/LM Wind Power Holding*, where the Commission found that General Electric's initial notification of its then-proposed acquisition of LM Wind contained incorrect or misleading information concerning its research and development activities.

[36] Case COMP/M.8006 *Canon/Toshiba Medical Systems Corporation*, where the Commission found that Canon had acquired control of Toshiba Medical Systems through a 'warehousing' structure involving an interim buyer that acquired 95% of Toshiba Medical Systems' shares prior to receiving Commission approval.

the markets for specific laboratory chemicals. In addition, it continued to withhold information about iCap in replies to specific requests for information.[37]

2 RELATIONSHIP BETWEEN THE MERGER REGULATION AND ARTICLES 101 AND 102

2.1 Application of Articles 101 and 102 to Concentrations Prior to the Adoption of the 1989 Regulation

[30] Prior to the adoption of the 1989 Regulation, several mergers and acquisitions were investigated by the Commission under Articles 101 and 102. The inadequacies of these instruments for merger control purposes ultimately led to the adoption of the 1989 Regulation.[38]

[31] For a long time, the Commission took the view that Article 101 of the TFEU was not applicable to mergers or *'concentrations'*.[39] While this view of the law arguably remains intact, it had to be read in the light of the judgment of the ECJ in the *Philip Morris* case.[40] Following an agreement in 1981, Philip Morris Inc. ('Philip Morris') of New York purchased 50% of the shares in Rothmans Tobacco (Holding) Ltd ('Rothmans Tobacco (Holding)') from the Rembrandt Group Ltd of South Africa which held a controlling interest in Rothmans International plc ('Rothmans International'), the cigarette manufacturer. Following complaints by competitors,

[37] *See* https://ec.europa.eu/commission/presscorner/detail/en/ip_21_2181.

[38] Article 101(1) of the TFEU prohibits all agreements, decisions and concerted practices which may affect trade between Member States and which have as their object or effect the prevention, restriction or distortion of competition within the Internal Market. Article 101(2) of the TFEU provides that any arrangements prohibited under Art. 101(1) of the TFEU are automatically void. Article 101(3) of the TFEU provides in effect that such arrangements may be exempted from the prohibition of Art. 101(1) of the TFEU where they contribute to improving the production or distribution of goods, or to promoting technical or economic progress, provided: (a) that they also allow consumers a fair share of the resulting benefit, (b) that they only impose restrictions indispensable to achieving those objectives and (c) that they do not permit the elimination of competition in the relevant market. Agreements which are in breach of Art. 101 cannot be enforced. In addition, the parties involved incur the risk of substantial fines and third-party claims for compensation. Article 102 of the TFEU prohibits the abuse of a dominant position within the Internal Market (or in a substantial part of it) insofar as it affects trade between Member States, for example, by refusal to supply, or by unfair or discriminatory pricing.

[39] This position was first adopted in the Commission's 1966 *'Memorandum on the Problem of Concentrations in the Internal Market'* on the basis that: *'It is not possible to apply [Article 101 of the TFEU] to agreements whose purpose is the acquisition of total or partial ownership of enterprises or the reorganisation of the ownership of enterprises (merger, acquisition of holdings, purchase of part of the assets).'* If after the concentration process, several independent enterprises exist (e.g., in the case of joint ventures) it will be necessary to examine carefully whether, apart from the changes in ownership, the participating enterprises did not enter into agreements or concerted practices within the meaning of Art. 101(1) of the TFEU.

[40] *BAT and Reynolds v. Commission,* Joined cases 142 and 156/84 [1987] ECR-4487 [1988] 4 CMLR 24.

the Commission intervened, and the parties renegotiated the agreement to bring it into line with EU competition law. Under the new agreement, Philip Morris abandoned its 50% shareholding in Rothmans Tobacco (Holding) in exchange for a direct shareholding in Rothmans International, accounting for 30.8% of the total shares of Rothmans. This represented only 24.9% of the voting rights in the company. Philip Morris also gave undertakings to the Commission which were intended to prevent Philip Morris from being able to influence the behaviour of its competitor. These included, *inter alia*, undertakings that Philip Morris would not be represented on the board of Rothmans International and would not receive information of a sensitive competitive nature. This solution was not satisfactory to Philip Morris' competitors who appealed the Commission's decision to the ECJ. The judgment of the ECJ makes it clear that Article 101 of the TFEU can apply to shareholdings acquired from competitors because it could be a means of influencing their commercial conduct, thereby restricting or distorting competition.[41]

[32] The true meaning of the judgment gave rise to a substantial degree of controversy. One school of thought interpreted the judgment as confirming that all acquisitions whereby legal control passes (whether by virtue of a 51% or a 100% shareholding) potentially fall within the prohibition of Article 101(1) of the TFEU where the parties are competitors. The Commission interpreted the case as providing it with greater control over acquisitions than is explicitly provided in the judgment itself. In particular, the then Competition Commissioner, Peter Sutherland, stated that it provided *'unambiguous confirmation ... that Articles 81 and 82 apply to transactions relating to changes in corporate ownership'*. However, the transaction under consideration in the *Philip Morris* case was an acquisition of a *minority shareholding* in a competitor company, and the ECJ failed to draw any specific conclusions as to the applicability of Article 101 of the TFEU to transactions leading to a change in control. Despite the Commission's claims that Article 101 of the TFEU could apply to concentrations, there has been no instance of it being successfully applied to anything other than minority shareholdings, non-concentrative joint-venture relationships and consortium bidding arrangements.

[33] Although not expressly dealing with merger control, Article 102 of the TFEU has been used by the Commission to control mergers. The Commission considers Article 102 of the TFEU to be applicable to mergers which would result in a dominant undertaking increasing its market share in such a way that it would be abusing its dominant position. However, the mere existence (as opposed to the improper exploitation) of a dominant position is not in itself prohibited.

[41] The main principle laid down by the ECJ at paras 37 and 38 of the judgment was as follows: *'Although the acquisition by one company of an equity interest in a competitor does not in itself constitute conduct restricting competition, such an acquisition may nevertheless serve as an instrument for influencing the commercial conduct of the companies in question so as to restrict or distort competition on the market on which they carry on business. That will be true in particular where, by the acquisition of a shareholding or through subsidiary clauses in the agreement, the investing company obtains legal or de facto control of the commercial conduct of the other company – or where the agreement provides for commercial co-operation between the companies or creates a structure likely to be used for such co-operation.'*

[34] This use of Article 102 of the TFEU to control acquisitions was first applied by the Commission and supported by the ECJ in *Continental Can Company v. Commission*.[42] In that case, Continental Can acquired control of a German company which controlled a substantial share of the German market for metal tins and containers. Two years later, the same American company tried to obtain control of a Dutch company which was the largest manufacturer of the same product range in the Benelux countries. The Commission argued that the subsequent acquisition of the Dutch company was an abuse of Continental Can's already dominant position, insofar as it would effectively eliminate all future competition between the companies and would appreciably affect trade between Member States. The ECJ upheld the Commission's interpretation of Article 102 of the TFEU, although it did in fact allow the merger to proceed on other grounds. It stated that:

> Abuse may...occur if an undertaking in a dominant position strengthens such position in such a way that the degree of dominance substantially fetters competition, i.e. that only undertakings remain in the market whose behaviour depends on the dominant one.

[35] The ECJ's case law on Article 102 of the TFEU developed after *Continental Can*, and the definition of abuse was widened in *United Brands v. Commission*[43] and *Hoffman La Roche v. Commission*.[44] In those cases, the ECJ held that behaviour can infringe Article 102 of the TFEU if it has an *'appreciable effect on competition'* rather than the more stringent criterion of *'a substantial fettering of competition'* used in *Continental Can*. As a result, where a dominant position in a substantial part of the EU already exists, any advantageous structural change brought about by the undertaking holding the dominant position could have been considered to adversely affect market conditions and thereby risked an action under Article 102 of the TFEU.[45] The Commission used its powers under Article 102 of the TFEU to investigate a number of mergers prior to the adoption of the 1989 Regulation.[46]

---

[42] Case 6/72 [1973] ECR-215.

[43] Case 27/76 [1978] ECR-207.

[44] Case 85/76 [1979] ECR-461.

[45] In the Tenth Report on Competition Policy (1980), the Commission stated: *'A dominant position can generally be said to exist once a market share in the order of 40 per cent to 45 per cent is reached. Although this share does not in itself automatically give control of the market, if there are large gaps between the position of the firm concerned and those of its closest competitors...a dominant position may well exist. Strengthening [of a dominant position] by means of a merger is likely to constitute an abuse if any distortion of the resulting market structure interferes with the maintenance of remaining competition (which already has been weakened by the very existence of the dominant position), or its development. Such an effect depends, in particular, on the change in the relative market strength of the participants after the merger,* i.e., *the position of the new unit in relation to remaining competitors.'*

[46] *Pilkington/BSN-Gervais-Danone*, *Michelin/Kleber-Colombes*, and *Baxter Travenol Laboratories/SmithKline RIT* all referred to in the Tenth Report on Competition Policy (1980); *Amicon/Fortia/Wright*, Eleventh Report on Competition Policy (1981); *Irish Distillers Group*, Eighteenth Report on Competition Policy (1988). The Commission allowed other concentrations to proceed subject to certain conditions, including *British Airways/British Caledonian*, Eighteenth Report on Competition Policy (1988); *Consolidated Gold Fields/Minorco and Stena/Houlder Offshore* referred to in the Nineteenth Report on Competition Policy (1989).

2.2 Application of Articles 101 and 102 to Concentrations Following the Adoption of the 1989 Regulation

[36] Article 22(1) of the 1989 Regulation provided that the merger regulation alone will apply to concentrations as defined in Article 3[47] and that the various implementing regulations for Articles 101 and 102 (depending on the industry sector) will not apply (except in relation to joint ventures that do not have a Community dimension and which have as their object or effect the coordination of the competitive behaviour of the joint venture's parent companies).[48] The effect of Article 22(1) was to prevent the Commission from using its powers under Articles 101 and 102 of the TFEU to challenge concentrations. The question remained as to whether transitional competition rules set out in Articles 104 and 105 of the TFEU applied to concentrations without a Community dimension.[49] In practice, application of Article 101 or 102 of the TFEU by the Commission (or Member States) to mergers without a Community dimension was very unlikely. The Commission had stated that it did not intend to take action in respect of concentrations with a worldwide turnover of less than EUR2 bn or below a turnover in the Community of less than EUR100 m, or which fell within the two-thirds thresholds exception in Article 1(2) because they would not normally have a significant effect on trade between Member States. Of course, and as will be explained in more detail below, this view now needs to be balanced with the Commission's novel application of Article 22 of the Merger Regulation which allows the Commission to review concentrations that fall below the filing thresholds of the Merger Regulation, if asked to do so by one or more Member States, and provided certain conditions are met. Indeed, in 2021, in a major shift in its policy, the Commission started accepting Article 22 referrals in relation to transactions that were not notifiable under the national merger control regimes of any EU Member State (previously, it only accepted referrals if the concentration was notifiable in at least one Member State). While five transactions have been referred to the Commission under Article 22, *Illumina/Grail* was the only transaction not requiring a filing in any Member State.

[37] The Merger Regulation adopts a similar approach in Article 21(1). According to this provision, Regulation 1/2003 and its implementing regulations are inapplicable to concentrations as defined in Article 3 of the Merger Regulation.[50]

---

[47] Article 3 does not distinguish between concentrations with a Community dimension and those without.

[48] *See also* Recital 7 of the Merger Regulation.

[49] Article 103 of the TFEU does not apply to concentrations with a Community dimension which fall under the Merger Regulation procedure as the Merger Regulation is adopted under Arts 83 and 308 of the TFEU. However, for concentrations without a Community dimension (other than joint ventures which have a coordinative object or effect) there are no implementing provisions as required by Art. 103 of the TFEU and therefore Art. 105 of the TFEU may apply which enables the Commission to investigate a transaction on an application from a Member State. Member States may apply Art. 101 and Art. 102 of the TFEU in accordance with Art. 104 of the TFEU.

[50] Council Regulation (EC) 1/2003 of 16 Dec. 2002 on the implementation of the rules on competition laid down in Arts 81 and 82 of the Treaty, OJ L 1/1, 4 Jan. 2003.

[38] The position is different for full-function joint ventures of a coordinative nature without a Community dimension. The exception in Article 21(1) provides that Regulation 1/2003 and the other implementing regulations continue to apply to full-function joint ventures falling below the thresholds of the Merger Regulation and which have as their object or effect the coordination of the competitive behaviour of undertakings that remain independent. However, the Commission has emphasised that under normal circumstances, it is for the NCAs to deal with such joint ventures, and it will not allow Article 101(3) of the TFEU to be used in an attempt to override the domestic control of such joint ventures.[51]

[39] Notwithstanding the above, in its *Towercast* judgment of 16 March 2023, the ECJ clarified that Article 21(1) of the Merger Regulation does not preclude NCAs or courts from reviewing acquisitions of control by dominant undertakings under abuse of dominant rules that fall below the Merger Regulation's and national merger control thresholds.[52] Even though the *ex post* review of deals has not been present in practice since the introduction of the first Merger Regulation in 1989, the ECJ's ruling to open the door for an Article 102-based merger review in exceptional cases fits into recent developments that provide competition authorities with additional review powers for non-reportable acquisitions. These powers mainly address a recent concern, which is especially strong in the tech and pharma industries, that incumbent firms arguably acquire innovative start-ups or nascent competitors solely to discontinue their business and pre-empt future competition ('killer acquisitions').

[40] The *Towercast* case related to such a scenario of killer acquisition. In October 2016, the French broadcaster Telediffusion de France (TDF) acquired its rival Itas. The transaction was not reviewed under either the Merger Regulation or the French merger control rules as it did not meet the respective jurisdictional thresholds, and the French Competition Authority did not refer the case to the Commission under Article 22 of the Merger Regulation. Nearly a year later, Towercast complained to the French competition authority that the transaction amounted to an abuse of TDF's dominant position in the digital terrestrial television sector, in breach of Article 102 of the TFEU. Following an investigation, the French competition authority closed its procedure on the grounds that it had no power to apply the abuse of dominance rules to a merger. Towercast appealed the French competition authority's conclusion before the Court of Appeal of Paris which sought guidance from the ECJ as to whether Article 21(1) of the Merger Regulation precluded NCAs from reviewing mergers under Article 102 of the TFEU, even where those mergers have never been notified or reviewed under the Merger Regulation or any national merger control regime.

[41] In its judgment of 16 March 2023, the ECJ clarified that Article 21(1) of the Merger Regulation does not categorically preclude the review by NCAs of mergers

[51] Notes for the Council Minutes on the amendment of the Merger Regulation. *'Where a national authority intends to prohibit a case on the grounds of the creation of a dominant position by the joint-venture itself, whether on the basis of the national rules on merger control or on restrictive practices, there is no scope for an exemption to be granted by the Commission under Article [101(3)]of the TFEU.'*

[52] Case C-449/21, *Towercast SASU v. Autorité de la concurrence and others*, para. 53.

that fall below the national or European thresholds. However, as Regulation 1/2003 does not apply, such reviews must be carried out on the basis of national procedural rules. The ECJ also outlined the relevant test for a finding of an abuse. It stated that the mere finding that a dominant undertaking's position has been strengthened by a merger is not sufficient for a finding of abuse. Rather, it must be established that '*the degree of dominance thus reached would substantially impede competition, that is to say, that only undertakings whose behaviour depends on the dominant undertaking would remain in the market*'. From a practical standpoint, this judgment leads to considerable legal uncertainty as the substantive test remains somewhat vague. This carries the risk that any transaction carried out by an (alleged) dominant company might be challenged under dominance rules without any time limit, even long after closing (like in the *Towercast* case). Indeed, less than a week after the *Towercast* judgment, the Belgian Competition Authority opened an ex officio investigation into a possible abuse of dominance by Proximus' (non-reportable) acquisition of Edpnet, which could pave the way for other NCAs to follow suit.[53] It remains to be seen how the new referral policy under Article 22 of the Merger Regulation will interact with this *ex post* tool to review below-threshold mergers under Article 102 TFEU.

3 THE MERGER REGULATION

3.1 The Merger Regulation and Supporting Documents

[42] The Merger Regulation is the central pillar of merger control under the TFEU and supersedes the application and effectiveness of Articles 101, 102 and, in cases where the concentration has a Community dimension, national merger control rules. The Merger Regulation lays down the main substantive provisions for Community merger control and is supplemented by other instruments adopted by the Commission in order to facilitate its implementation and interpretation. In particular, the Implementing Regulation sets out important procedural aspects regarding the application of the Merger Regulation, including: the mechanism and content of notifications; the formal forms of notification – the Form CO, the Short Form CO, the Form RM and the Form RS; the calculation of time limits and their suspension; and the provision for hearings and representations of undertakings concerned and third parties. The Implementing Regulation was revised in April 2023 and includes a revised set of filing forms (Form CO, Short Form CO, Form RS and Form RM), applicable as of 1 September 2023. The revisions include a number of welcome changes that will reduce the burden of notifying parties in transactions with no substantive concerns. The new Short Form CO, for example, introduces various sections to be filled in by ticking relevant boxes (on points such as basic jurisdictional details and details of the transaction). Both the Form CO and the Short Form CO also contain various tables and template language aimed at

[53] *See* press release 10/2023 dated 22 Mar. 2023 – '*The Belgian Competition Authority opens an ex officio investigation into a possible abuse of dominance by Proximus in the context of the takeover of edpnet, in application of the Towercast case law.*'

streamlining the information to be provided by the parties – including a template table for information on horizontal overlaps and vertical relationships.[54] The main innovation appears to be the electronic submission of documents, which is now compulsory.

[43] In order to provide transaction parties and stakeholders with guidance and transparency, the Commission has issued a number of notices, guidelines and best practices regarding its interpretation and enforcement policy concerning the Merger Regulation.

Notices, Guidelines and Communications:

- Commission Notice on the definition of the relevant market for the purposes of Community competition law (the 'Market Definition Notice').[55] Market definition is crucial to assess whether competition is significantly impeded by a merger under the Merger Regulation. This notice sets out the approach of the Commission to market definition in all competition cases but recognises that under the Merger Regulation, this is essentially a prospective analysis. As will be explained in more detail below, further to a public consultation initiated in June 2020 to evaluate whether to update the Market Definition Notice, the Commission published its Staff Working Document in July 2021 summarising the findings of its evaluation,[56] and prepared the Draft Notice published for consultation on 8 November 2022.[57] The Draft Notice provides updated guidance on the methodology used for market definition but does not curb the Commission's substantial flexibility in the application of the rules it sets out. The Commission targets to adopt its updated market definition notice in the second half of 2023.
- Consolidated Jurisdictional Notice.[58] As explained above, on 10 July 2007, the Commission adopted a Consolidated Jurisdictional Notice which replaced the previous four jurisdictional notices which were all adopted by the Commission in 1998, i.e.: (i) the Notice on the concept of concentration;[59] (ii) the Notice on the concept of full-function joint ventures;[60] (iii) the Notice on the concept of undertakings concerned;[61] and (iv) the Notice on calculation of turnover.[62] The Consolidated Jurisdictional Notice therefore covers a wide range of jurisdictional issues relevant for establishing the Commission's competence under the Merger Regulation. It adapts the existing texts in the light of recent judgments of the European courts in addition to the reformed Merger Regulation. It also provides up-to-date guidance on the

[54] *See*, https://ec.europa.eu/transparency/documents-register/detail?ref=C(2023)2400&lang=en.

[55] OJ C 372/5, 9 Dec. 1997.

[56] *See*, https://competition-policy.ec.europa.eu/system/files/2021-07/evaluation_market-definition-notice_en.pdf.

[57] *See*, https://ec.europa.eu/commission/presscorner/detail/en/ip_22_6528.

[58] OJ C 95/1, 16 Apr. 2008.

[59] OJ C 66/5, 2 Mar. 1998.

[60] OJ C 66/1, 2 Mar. 1998.

[61] OJ C 66/14, 2 Mar. 1998.

[62] OJ C 66/25, 2 Mar. 1998.

Commission's competence to review a transaction under the Merger Regulation.

- Commission Notice on a simplified procedure for treatment of certain concentrations under the Merger Regulation (the 'Simplified Procedure Notice').[63] As part of its initiative to further simplify EU merger control procedures, the Commission adopted a new Notice on Simplified Procedure on 20 April 2023. It replaces previous guidance from 2013 concerning certain types of transactions that are generally considered unlikely to raise competition concerns and where a market investigation may seem unnecessary.
- Remedies Notice.[64] Parties may offer commitments to modify a notified concentration in order to alleviate concerns identified by the Commission. The Remedies Notice sets out the Commission's approach to the type of commitments that will be necessary to obtain clearance. Originally adopted in 2008 and revised in 2013, the Remedies Notice also provides template texts for the engagement of trustees and guidance on how to monitor compliance with commitments that are given to address competition concerns and secure merger control approval. As a result of the revised Implementing Regulation, a new Form RM will enter into force on 1 September 2023.
- Commission Notice on restrictions directly related and necessary to concentrations (the 'Ancillary Restraints Notice').[65] Decisions under the Merger Regulation declaring a concentration compatible with the Internal Market also cover restrictions that are 'directly related and necessary to the implementation of the concentration'. This notice sets out guidance on which restraints are likely to be considered ancillary and a revised approach to the assessment of these provisions by the parties.
- Commission Notice on Case Referral in respect of concentrations (the 'Referral Notice').[66]
- Commission Notice on the internal rules of procedure for access to file (the 'Notice on access to file').[67] This is a fundamental procedural safeguard which ensures the rights of defence of companies. Access to the file is an important procedural step in all contentious antitrust and merger cases. It allows the companies or organisations that receive a Statements of Objections (i.e., the Commission's explanation as to why it has reached the preliminary view that the addressees may have breached the competition rules) to see all of the evidence, whether it is incriminating or exonerating, in the Commission's file.
- Horizontal Guidelines, as mentioned above,[68] which explain how the Commission will apply its compatibility test to concentrations which involve undertakings having activities which overlap effectively or potentially.

[63] OJ C 160/1, 5 May 2023.
[64] OJ C 267/1, 22 Oct. 2008.
[65] OJ C 56/24, 5 Mar. 2005.
[66] OJ C 56/2, 5 Mar. 2005.
[67] OJ C 325/7, 22 Dec. 2005.
[68] OJ C 31/5, 5 Feb. 2004.

- Non-Horizontal Guidelines, as mentioned above,[69] which explain how the Commission will apply its compatibility test to concentrations which raise vertical or conglomerate issues.
- Decision of the President of the Commission on the function and terms of reference of the hearing officer in certain competition proceedings.[70]
- DG Competition Information note on Article 6(1) c 2nd sentence of Regulation 139/2004 (abandonment of concentrations).
- Commission Guidance on the application of the referral mechanism set out in Article 22 of the Merger Regulation to certain categories of cases (Communication from the Commission).[71]

Best Practices:

- Best practices on merger control proceedings.[72]
- Best practices on the submission of economic evidence.[73]
- Best Practices on divestiture commitments.[74]
- Guidance on the preparation of public versions of merger decisions.[75]
- Best Practices on the disclosure of information in data rooms.[76]

[44] The main purpose of these interpretative notices, guidelines and best practices is to set out as comprehensively as possible the principles built up by the Commission through its practice since the adoption of the 1989 Regulation. Further guidance is also drawn from the Commission's interpretation laid down in its decisions, as non-confidential versions of Phase II merger decisions are published in the Official Journal in all the official languages of the EU, while non-confidential versions of all decisions taken after Phase I are available in their original language on the Commission's website.[77]

[45] Over the years, the Commission explored various options of refining and expanding the scope of its merger review powers, including the power to review certain acquisitions of non-controlling minority shareholdings (triggered by the Commission's experience in the *Ryanair/Aer Lingus* case, in which it was unable to review Ryanair's acquisition of 29.8% of the shares of its rival airline Aer Lingus, on the grounds that the shareholding did not confer decisive influence). However, many of these initiatives were ultimately abandoned as changes to the Merger Regulation were deemed unlikely to secure the required unanimous backing from the EU Member States.

[69] OJ C 265/6, 18 Oct. 2008.
[70] OJ L 275/29, 13 Oct. 2011.
[71] *See,* https://ec.europa.eu/competition/consultations/2021_merger_control/guidance_article_22_referrals.pdf.
[72] Published on 20 Jan. 2014.
[73] Published on 17 Oct. 2011.
[74] Published on 5 Dec. 2013.
[75] Published on 26 May 2015.
[76] Published on 2 Jun. 2015.
[77] http//ec.europa.eu/competition/merger/cases/.

[46] Ultimately, a March 2021 Commission Staff Working Document concluded on its evaluation of procedural and jurisdictional aspects of EU merger control that there is no need (after all) to amend the merger control thresholds (for the time being)[78] because the Commission considers that the current available system of referrals from NCAs should be sufficient to allow the Commission to review high-value transactions concerning targets that have low turnover or even no turnover at all in the EU, if necessary. A case in point in this regard is the *Illumina/Grail* transaction, where the Commission on 6 September 2022 prohibited the US life sciences firm Illumina, a supplier of NGS systems for genetic and genomic analysis, from acquiring its customer Grail, a biotechnology company.[79] The case was referred to the Commission under Article 22 of the Merger Regulation, and the proposed transaction was not notifiable in the referring Member States (and was not notified in any other Member States as Grail did not generate any revenues in Europe). Following the Commission's prohibition, Illumina will have to divest Grail. Illumina completed the deal in August 2021 while the Commission's review was still ongoing, which resulted in an order to keep Grail separate from Illumina and to appoint independent managers to run Grail until the investigation was finished.[80] In parallel, on 12 July 2023, the Commission imposed a record-breaking fine against Illumina for unlawfully closing its acquisition of Grail, saying it was an 'unprecedented' breach of EU merger control rules to do so before the end of its probe. An EU official said the authority had initially arrived at a confidential figure, which it lowered to around EUR540 m because the companies followed the agency's hold separate measures. The commission reduced that amount again to EUR432 m, which was 10% of Illumina's annual turnover – the maximum allowed under the Merger Regulation. In (another) unprecedented move, the Commission also issued a 'symbolic' penalty of EUR1 000 against Grail as it was the first time the agency has punished a target company for gun-jumping. The company was 'fully aware' of the standstill requirement but nonetheless took legal steps to enable the transaction, the Commission said.[81]

3.1.1 A Summary of the Main Features of the Merger Regulation

[47] The basic concept underlying the application of the Merger Regulation is that the notification of mergers falling within the scope of the Merger Regulation is compulsory. A merger, or, using the terms in the Merger Regulation, a *'concentration'*, falls within the scope of the Merger Regulation when it has a *'Community dimension'*, that is, when it satisfies either of the two turnover tests set out in Article 1(2) of the Merger Regulation. Such concentrations must be notified to the Commission prior to their implementation, i.e., ahead of the implementation of a

[78] *See*, https://ec.europa.eu/competition/consultations/2021_merger_control/SWD_findings_of_evaluation.pdf.

[79] Case M.10188 *Illumina/Grail*.

[80] Cases M.10493 *Illumina/Grail* and M.10938 *Illumina/Grail*.

[81] *See*, https://ec.europa.eu/commission/presscorner/detail/en/ip_23_3773.

public bid, the completion of a legally binding agreement, or acquisition of a controlling interest.[82]

[48] Before the reform of 1 May 2004, notifications had to be filed with the Commission within one week of the announcement of a public bid or the entering into of a legally binding agreement to acquire a controlling interest. To provide greater flexibility, the Merger Regulation now expressly permits notifications to be made where the undertakings can demonstrate a *'good faith intention'* to conclude an agreement or to make a public bid, the intention of which must have been publicly announced. Furthermore, the obligation to file within a specific time period has been abolished since the merger transaction may not be closed before such notification is made nor before any decision has been taken to clear it, or before the time periods within which such decision has to be taken have lapsed. Implementing a transaction before notifying it or before obtaining clearance from the Commission carries the risk not only of the imposition of fines but also of the unwinding of the transaction where the Commission would have ultimately declared the concentration *'incompatible'* with the Internal Market.

[49] Once a concentration is notified, the Commission is required to examine it and decide whether it is compatible with the Internal Market. Such an assessment, which is predominantly concerned with the outcome of the concentration on effective competition, is procedurally a two-stage process. In an initial examination, the Commission must determine within a period of twenty-five working days following notification (extended to thirty-five working days if the parties have submitted remedies to DG Comp for consideration) whether the notified transaction falls within the scope of the Merger Regulation and, if so, whether it raises serious doubts about its compatibility with the Internal Market. The principal criterion in this respect is whether the transaction will *'significantly impede effective competition, in the Internal Market or in a substantial part of it, in particular as a result of the creation or strengthening of a dominant position'*. If the Commission finds that the transaction raises 'serious doubts' as to its compatibility with the common market, it will open an in-depth investigation (Phase II) and will normally take a final decision as to the compatibility of the proposed transaction with the Internal Market within ninety working days from the initiation of the Phase II proceedings. However, this basic ninety-day period can be extended for certain reasons. First, the deadline can be extended to one hundred and five working days in cases where the parties offer remedies to the Commission after the fifty-fifth working day from the initiation of Phase II proceedings in order to solve the competition problems raised by the Commission in its Statement of Objections. Second, the Merger Regulation also provides the possibility for the parties to request, within fifteen working days of the initiation of the Phase II proceedings, an extension of the Commission's investigation period. Such an extension can be up to a maximum of twenty working days and must be assessed in conjunction with the Commission's ability to extend their Phase II review also up to a maximum of twenty working days with the agreement

[82] Article 4(1) of the Merger Regulation.

of the parties. The duration of any extension or extensions in this manner must not exceed twenty working days in total.

[50] According to Article 10(4) of the Merger Regulation, the investigation periods of Phase I and Phase II proceedings can also exceptionally be suspended when undertakings have failed to reply to the Commission's formal requests for information pursuant to Article 11 of the Merger Regulation (also called 'stop the clock' provision), or where the Commission orders an on-site inspection pursuant to Article 13 of the Merger Regulation. As will be explained in more detail below, in recent years, the Commission has issued an increasing number of 'stop-the-clock' decisions after making requests for internal documents that require the merging parties and their advisors to identify, review and submit thousands of documents under strict deadlines. Indeed, in Phase II cases, one or more stop-the-clocks have become the norm rather than the exception.

[51] Merging parties also have the ability to 'pull and refile' their notification during the Phase I review in an attempt to prevent the opening of an in-depth Phase II investigation by the Commission. Unlike the US Hart-Scott-Rodino Act, the Merger Regulation does not specifically foresee the 'pull and refile', but it is today commonly used in cases that transaction parties and Commission agree can benefit from a rerun of Phase I.[83] In these cases, parties can withdraw their notification from DG Comp and refile it shortly after with any additional documents and information required to be included with the new filing. This practice benefits both DG Comp and the merging parties. It restarts the initial statutory Phase I waiting period, allowing DG Comp more time to evaluate the transaction and possible commitments offered by the parties, which often works to avert a Phase II, thus saving the parties the considerable costs associated with a Phase II and the even longer delays in closing the transaction. While the decision whether or not to pull and refile a transaction in Phase I ultimately rests with the notifying party/parties, the Commission is likely to discourage this strategy in cases that it feels require a full-blown market investigation that cannot be carried out in Phase I. As of 1 January 2021, the notifying party decided to pull and refile their transaction in thirty-six cases. For example, in *DIC/BASF Colors & Effects* the notifying party withdrew its notification after failing to convince the Commission that its Phase I remedy package was sufficient to remedy its concerns. The notifying party re-filed its notification almost four months afterwards and was granted conditional clearance by the Commission in Phase I.[84]

[52] The parties may offer commitments to modify the notified transaction either during Phase I or Phase II to alleviate concerns raised by the Commission. If such commitments address the concerns, the Commission can impose obligations on the merging undertakings as the price for declaring the merger to be compatible

[83] It is understood that the COVID-19 pandemic also resulted in a steep increase of such 'pull and refile' cases due in part to the Commission's inability to conduct proper market investigations as a result of many economic sectors being shut down, and because the competitive landscape in certain economic sectors had significantly evolved which meant that the description initially provided by the parties was no longer accurate and needed to be resubmitted.

[84] Case M.9677.

with the Internal Market and allowing it to be implemented. At the expiration of its investigation period, the Commission will have to determine whether or not the concentration significantly impedes effective competition in the Internal Market or in a substantial part of it, in particular as a result of the creation or strengthening of a dominant position. If this is the case, despite taking account of any remedies offered by the parties, the Commission is required to declare the concentration incompatible with the Internal Market and further prohibit it.

[53] Where a notified full-function joint venture raises the risk of coordination of competitive behaviour between the undertakings which remain independent, the Commission will analyse whether the transaction significantly impedes effective competition in the Internal Market or in a substantial part of it. This analysis is particularly in relation to the creation or strengthening of a dominant position, and whether the coordination of the parent companies' behaviour would lead to a restriction of competition.

[54] Since 1 May 2004 it is no longer possible to notify joint ventures which do not amount to concentrations under Article 101(3) of the TFEU. Undertakings have to rely on self-assessment in order to determine whether any restrictions concerning the activities of the joint venture are contrary to Article 101(1) of the TFEU or can be considered as ancillary to the concentration (Please refer to the chapter on Ancillary restraints). In practice, a joint-venture arrangement will be likely to give rise to possible coordination of competitive behaviour if two or more parent companies remain active in the market of the joint venture or if the creation of the joint venture may lead to a restriction of competition between the parent companies in upstream, downstream or neighbouring markets.

[55] Where a concentration falls within the scope of the Merger Regulation, the EU Member States are precluded from applying their domestic merger control laws to it (except in very limited and specified circumstances which will be explained in further detail below). Since 1 January 2021, parties to a transaction also need to consider a potential UK filing requirement even if their transactions fall within the scope of the Merger Regulation. Indeed, as a result of Brexit, the UK is no longer part of the EU, and, therefore, the Merger Regulation no longer applies there. This means that for transactions that are caught by the Merger Regulation, the UK Competition and Markets Authority now has concurrent jurisdiction to review transactions which meet the UK notification thresholds.[85] Since Brexit, a larger number of transactions have required a parallel review from the UK CMA and the Commission, and while most of these cases have seen similar conclusions from the authorities, there is an ever-growing number of cases where both authorities have diverged in the outcome of their analysis including in the *ALD/LeasePlan, Veolia/Suez, Facebook/Kustomer, Cargotec/Konecranes* and *Microsoft/Activision* cases.

[56] In *ALD/LeasePlan* and *Veolia/Suez*, the divergence is at most notional and easily explained by the different competitive dynamics in the sub-national markets in question. For *ALD/LeasePlan*, the CMA found the merged entity would continue to be constrained by a large number of competitors in the UK leasing services market,

[85] *See*, https://ec.europa.eu/info/sites/default/files/brexit_files/info_site/eu-competition-law_en_0.pdf.

whereas the EC found that there would be limited competitive constraints facing the merged entity in markets for operational leasing in the Czech Republic, Finland, Luxembourg, Ireland, Norway and Portugal, so divestment remedies were offered and accepted. Similarly, *Veolia/Suez* was cleared by the EC with Phase 1 remedies but was effectively unwound in the UK after the parties appeared not to be willing or able to offer satisfactory remedies to address the CMA's concerns regarding the overlap in the parties' competing operations in the UK.

[57] The same notional divergence point can be made for another ongoing case – *Korean Air Lines/Asiana Airlines* – which the CMA has recently cleared in Phase 1 with commitments (so-called undertakings in lieu (UILs)), while the Phase II review process before the Commission remains ongoing at the time of writing. In this airline merger, the CMA and Commission consider different routes and in the case of the CMA, only a single city-pair (London-Seoul) while the Commission is investigating four different routes between Seoul and each of Paris, Rome, Frankfurt and Barcelona.

[58] Most interesting are the cases where the CMA and Commission considered the same supra-national markets, but reached different conclusions. To date, this has only happened in three post-Brexit cases where the issue of remedies was potentially determinative.

[59] First, in *Facebook/Kustomer*, the CMA cleared the transaction unconditionally in Phase I despite, among others, two input foreclosure theories of harm. The Commission initiated a Phase II investigation and ultimately cleared the concentration further to behavioural remedies for similar input foreclosure concerns. Second, in *Cargotec/Konecranes*, the CMA blocked the deal in Phase II as the CMA was not satisfied with the remedy package offered by the parties, and accepted by the Commission. Third, in *Microsoft/Activision*, while the Commission conditionally cleared the transaction on 15 May 2023 further to licensing commitments on the cloud gaming market offered in Phase II, in April 2023, the CMA blocked the transaction, saying the deal raises competition concerns in the same nascent cloud gaming market and after rejecting the similar commitments previously accepted by the Commission.

[60] Overall, the Commission and the CMA appear to have aligned procedures where possible. In some instances, they have coordinated even with regard to substantive requests for information where parties granted confidentiality waivers. That said, there can be no doubt that both authorities will investigate according to their own rules and time schedules and reach their own conclusions even if that will lead to significant diverging review timelines or decision outcomes. Parallel Commission and CMA investigations may well, therefore, require additional planning and coordination by the merging parties.

3.1.2 The European Economic Area Agreement

[61] Following the entry into force of the European Economic Area (EEA) Agreement on 1 January 1994, the Commission's competence over concentrations was extended to the territory covered by the EEA Agreement. Article 57 of the EEA

Agreement[86] provides that mergers and full-function joint ventures which impede effective competition, in particular as a result of the creation or strengthening of a dominant position within the territory covered by the EEA Agreement, shall be declared incompatible with the functioning of the Agreement. The Commission has sole competence to take decisions on concentrations with a Community dimension (as defined in the Merger Regulation) in cooperation with the EFTA (European Free Trade Association) Surveillance Authority (ESA).[87] The ESA is competent where there is no Community dimension and the relevant EFTA thresholds in the EEA Agreement are met.[88] However, this is without prejudice to the competence of EU Member States to apply their national merger control rules to the transaction.[89]

[62] The Commission and the ESA have established rules for consultation and exchange of information in cases where either the parties have a combined turnover in the EEA countries that equals 25% or more of their total turnover or at least two parties achieve a turnover of EUR250 m in the territory of the EEA Agreement, and the transaction is likely to create or strengthen a dominant position in the EEA territory or a substantial part thereof.[90]

3.1.3 Territorial Scope of the Merger Regulation

[63] As EU competition law applies to conduct that has effects within the EU, the Merger Regulation may apply, in the same way as Articles 101 and 102 of the TFEU, to transactions involving undertakings originating from non-EU countries. Under the Merger Regulation the Commission has exclusive jurisdiction (as opposed to EU Member States) over mergers that have a 'Community dimension', i.e., those that satisfy the worldwide, EU-wide and national turnover criteria in the Merger Regulation, irrespective of where the mergers take place. Applying these turnover criteria, a separate question can arise as to whether it would be legitimate in terms of public international law for the Commission to take jurisdiction over a purely non-EU merger as it has done in the past. The Commission has generally claimed competency over transactions satisfying the relevant turnover criteria on the basis of the impact of the operation upon competition conditions in the Internal Market by reference to Recital 10 of the Merger Regulation which provides *'that is the case irrespective of whether or not the undertakings effecting the concentration have their seat or their principal fields of activity in the Community, provided they have substantial operations there'.*[91]

[86] *See* Decision 78/2004 and 79/2004 of the EEA Joint Commission, OJ L 219/13 and 24, 2004.

[87] Protocol 24 to the EEA Agreement; *see* case M.582 *Orkla/Volvo.*

[88] There have been no cases decided by the EFTA Surveillance Authority, and it is unlikely that a merger will fulfil the thresholds in the EEA countries (Norway, Iceland and Liechtenstein).

[89] Article 57(2)(b) of the EEA Agreement.

[90] Article 2 of Protocol 24 to the EEA Agreement. Important examples of this cooperation are case M.1157 *Skanska/Scancem*; case M.1439 *Telia/Telenor*; case M.1578 *Sanitec/Sphinx* and case JV.1 *Telia/Telenor/Shibsted.*

[91] XXVIIth Report on Competition Policy (1997).

[64] The Commission's jurisdiction was challenged in case M.619 *Gencor/Lonrho*[92] where the Commission prohibited the merger of the South African platinum interests of a British Company and a South African company because it would have created a situation of collective dominance in the platinum and rhodium markets. The General Court in *Gencor v. Commission*[93] rejected the argument that the term '*substantial operations*' in Recital 10 of the Merger Regulation requires the location of production facilities within the Community. The Court stated that according to the *Woodpulp* judgment, the criterion as to the implementation of an agreement is satisfied by mere sales within the Community, irrespective of the location of the sources of supply and the production plant. The General Court did not actually analyse the impact of the operation on conditions of competition in the Internal Market.[94] Instead, the Court stated that '*the application of the Regulation is justifiable under public international law when it is foreseeable that a proposed concentration will have an immediate and substantial effect in the Community*'.

[65] While it is questionable whether the creation of a joint venture that does not have any actual or future sales in the EU can be considered to meet the Court's effects threshold, it is clear from the Implementing Regulation that the Commission considers itself to have jurisdiction also over these kinds of transactions – albeit under the Short Form CO procedure.[95]

[66] Other examples of the application of the Merger Regulation to non-EU transactions include case M.877 *Boeing/McDonnell Douglas,*[96] case M.2220 *General Electric/Honeywell,*[97] case M.5181 *Delta Air Lines/Northwest Airlines,*[98] case M.6266 *J&J/Synthes,*[99] case M.6410 *UTC/Goodrich,*[100] case M.6765 *Precision Castparts/Titanium Metals,*[101] case M.7932 *Dow/DuPont,*[102] case M.8492 *Quaker/Houghton,*[103] case M.9424 *Nvidia/Mellanox,* case M.9489 *Air Canada/Transat,* case M.9343 *Hyundai Heavy Industries Holdings/Daewoo Shipbuilding & Marine Engineering,* M.10059 *SK Hynix/Intel's NAND and SSD business,* M.10149 *Korean Air Lines/Asiana Airlines* or case M.10188 *Illumina/Grail*. In *Gencor/Lonrho*, the Commission concluded that any impact on the world market for platinum group metals would be fully reflected in the EEA because: sales were made into Europe via a Belgian subsidiary of one of the parties; European consumption accounted for 20% of worldwide demand; a

---

92 Case M.619 *Gencor/Lonrho.*

93 Case T-102/96 *Gencor v. Commission* [1999] ECR II-879.

94 Case 48/69 *ICI v. Commission* [1972] ECR-619; Joined cases 89, 104, 114, 116, 117 and 125-129/85 *Ahlström Oy and Others v. Commission* [1988] ECR-5193 and Joined cases 48, 49, 51-57/69 *Dyestuffs* [1972] ECR-619.

95 *See* Implementing Regulation, Annex II Short Form CO for the Notification of a Concentration Pursuant to Regulation (EC) No 139/2004, s. 1.3.a.

96 Case M.877 *Boeing/McDonnell Douglas.*

97 Case M.2220 *General Electric/Honeywell.*

98 Case M.5181 *Delta Air Lines/Northwest Airlines.*

99 Case M.6266 *J&J/Synthes.*

100 Case M.6410 *UTC/Goodrich.*

101 Case M.6765 *Precision Castparts/Titanium Metals.*

102 Case M.7932 *Dow/DuPont.*

103 Case M.8492 *Quaker/Houghton.*

major competitor of the parties sold a significant proportion of its product in the EEA through an exclusive agent in the UK; and a downstream fabricator industry had a significant presence in the EEA. In *Boeing/McDonnell Douglas*, the Commission stated that the concentration had a significant effect in the EEA because the EEA accounted for a significant part (30%) of the world market for large commercial jet aircraft and because both parties enjoyed significant market shares in the EEA. In *General Electric/Honeywell*, the Commission for the first time blocked a merger between two US companies which had already been cleared by the US competition authorities.

3.1.4 International Cooperation

[67] In an increasingly global market, international mergers frequently fall within the jurisdiction of several competition authorities. In an attempt to avoid disputes with other countries concerning the assessment of international transactions, the EU has signed cooperation agreements with several countries (including the US,[104] Canada,[105] Japan,[106] Korea,[107] China[108] and Switzerland[109]).

[68] The most comprehensive of these is the agreement with the US. The agreement contains six principal obligations on the parties:

(1) to notify the other where its enforcement activities may affect the activities of the other (Article 2);
(2) to exchange information (Article 3);
(3) to provide assistance (Article 4);
(4) to cooperate in the enforcement of the other's competition laws, positive comity (as a result of the mandatory and time-limited obligations placed on the Commission under the Merger Regulation, the positive comity obligation does not apply to mergers) (Article 5);
(5) to have regard to the important interest of the other (traditional or negative comity) (Article 6); and
(6) to respect the confidentiality of information rules (Article 7).

[69] In practice, there are a large number of cases where the US and the EU authorities have cooperated and coordinated their assessments, such as case M.9660 *Google/Fitbit*, case M.9434 *UTC/Raytheon*, case M.9234 *Harris Corporation/L3 Technologies*, case M.9076 *Novelis/Aleris*, case M.7932 *Dow/DuPont*, case M.8451 *Tronox/Crystal*, case M.7555 *Staples/Office Depot*, case M.7477 *Halliburton/Baker*

[104] OJ L 95/47, 27 Apr. 1995 and OJ L 131/38, 15 Jun. 1995.
[105] OJ L 175/49, 10 Jul. 1999.
[106] OJ L 183/12, 22 Jul. 2003.
[107] OJ L 202/35, 4 Aug. 2009.
[108] Memorandum of Understanding signed on 20 Sep. 2012 and Practical guidance for merger cooperation between DG COMP and Mofcom (now State Administration for State Regulation) signed on 15 Oct. 2015. *See also* the Terms of Reference of the EU-China Competition Policy Dialogue, April 2019, https://ec.europa.eu/competition/international/bilateral/agreement_tor_china_2019.pdf.
[109] OJ L 347/3, 3 Dec. 2014.

Hughes, case M.7265 *Zimmer/Biomet*, case M.6944 *Thermo Fisher Scientific/Life Technologies*, case M.6827 *Honeywell/Intermec*, case M.6410 *UTC/Goodrich*, case M.6203 *Western Digital Ireland/Viviti Technologies*, case M.5181 *Delta Air Lines/Northwest Airlines*, case M.6844 *General Electric/Avio*, case M.2220 *General Electric/Honeywell*, case M.10149 *Korean Air Lines/Asiana Airlines*, or 10646 *Microsoft/Activision*. Cooperation has involved discussions on the relevant product and the geographical market, the potential anticompetitive effects of the transaction, ascertaining law and fact in the other jurisdiction and avoiding conflicting remedies. Most recently, this occurred in the *Zimmer/Biomet* case, where the Commission worked closely with the US Fair Trade Commission and the Japan Fair Trade Commission at key decision-making stages of the case. Aligning the timing of key decision-making stages of the case as well as regular discussions pursuant to waivers of confidentiality enabled effective collaboration between the Commission and the US Federal Trade Commission (FTC) in relation to remedy design and implementation issues. From an early stage, the agencies discussed issues faced in relation to product market definition and the theories of harm, as well as the general views of market participants regarding the transaction. The agencies also kept each other informed about process in their respective jurisdictions. The Commission exchanged views with its counterparts on the types of remedies needed to address common concerns as well as the potential scope of the remedies, including the need for and duration of transitional arrangements. In designing the remedy package, the Commission discussed the viability of the business proposed for divestiture and implementation risks, in particular the risks relating to the identification of a suitable purchaser, and possible ways to mitigate such risks. Ultimately, the parties proposed different buyers for the US and EEA divestment businesses, respectively. However, such cooperation sometimes fails, for example, in *Boeing/McDonnell Douglas*. In this case, following intensive discussions between the EU and US authorities, the Commission and the US FTC reached different conclusions. The FTC decided not to oppose the merger, whereas the Commission was concerned about its effect in the larger commercial jet aircraft market, and made clearance of the merger subject to wide-ranging conditions. In *GE/Honeywell*, the Commission prohibited the transaction after it had been cleared by the US authorities.[110] An important factor in many of these cases is the discrepancy between the timetable for assessment of a transaction in the US and the EU. As a result, there is not always a simultaneous negotiation between the parties and the relevant authorities.

[70] In 2002, the Commission and US competition authorities jointly issued a set of best practice guidelines which they later strengthened in October 2011.[111] The revised practice guidelines provide guidance to merging companies about how to work with the agencies to coordinate and facilitate the reviews of the proposed transactions. They confirm the role played by the other agencies around the world, place greater emphasis on coordination among agencies at key stages of their

[110] Both parties appealed to the General Court, case T-209/01 *Honeywell v. Commission* and case T-210/01 *GE v. Commission*, which upheld the Commission's decision.

[111] Commission Best Practices on Cooperation in Merger Investigations, 14 Oct. 2011 http://ec.europa.eu/competition/mergers/legislation/best_practices_2011_en.pdf.

investigations (specifically the final stage in which the agencies consider potential remedies to address the competitive concerns raised), and finally underline the role that waivers of confidentiality may play in facilitating efficient communication between the reviewing agencies and the merging parties. In particular, they set out the following areas for coordination:

- *Timing*. The guidelines recommend that the EU and US agencies keep each other informed of important developments relating to the timing of their respective investigations throughout the review process in order to allow meaningful communication at the key decision-making stages. In appropriate cases, the authorities should offer to the parties a joint meeting with EU and US officials to discuss timing issues.
- *Collection and evaluation of evidence*. The agencies will endeavour to coordinate the sharing of information to the extent that such sharing is consistent with confidentiality obligations. The authorities will generally request the execution of waivers of confidentiality by the merging parties to enable a more complete communication of confidential information.[112] The information shared would include market definitions, competitive effects, efficiencies, economic theories and empirical evidence. The guidelines also provide, where consent is given, that joint interviews of the parties and third parties would be encouraged. Requests for information and responses would also be shared when confidentiality has been waived by the parties.
- *Communication between the agencies*. The guidelines suggest that the reviewing agencies should contact one another promptly upon learning of any transaction that appears to require a review by both the EU and US agencies. Where it appears at the start of an investigation that substantial cooperation between the authorities may be beneficial, each agency should designate a 'contact person' responsible for coordinating conference, investigation timetables and information-gathering and sharing.
- *Remedies/settlements*. The guidelines consider cooperation to be beneficial throughout the remedial process and suggest that cooperation on the design of the possible remedies may result in a single package that addresses the concerns of both reviewing agencies. In this respect, reviewing agencies should keep one another informed of remedy offers being considered and, where appropriate, share draft remedy proposals.

[71] The impact of multi-jurisdictional cooperation in the field of merger control has become increasingly evident in recent years. For instance, the transaction parties in *Applied Materials/Tokyo Electron* ultimately abandoned the transaction following the regulatory headwinds from the US Department of Justice which had been coordinating closely with other agencies in Europe and Asia. In *Office Depot/Staples*, the FTC and the Canadian Competition Bureau cooperated, and both jurisdictions brought suits to block the transaction (although the Commission had also cooperated on this transaction, it ultimately accepted the undertakings offered by the parties). In the *GE/Alstom* transaction, the US and the Commission coordinated throughout, including at the remedies stage. Additionally, in the *Halliburton/Baker*

[112] Case M.6765 *Precision Castparts/Titanium Metals*, case M.6827 *Honeywell/Intermec*.

Hughes transaction, the US and the EC coordinated their investigations, with the US suing to block the transaction while the Commission's investigation continued. Also, the *Air Canada/Transat* transaction saw the Commission closely cooperate with its Canadian counterpart on assessing the impact of the proposed transaction on the transatlantic routes between Europe and Canada. As a general point, parties to a global transaction which requires merger control filings to both the EU and US authorities, as well as other authorities worldwide, should expect that these authorities will cooperate closely with one another while reviewing the impact of the transaction in the various jurisdictions.[113]

[72] It has increasingly been recognised that there is a need for an international forum to forge closer international cooperation between national and regional competition authorities and provide for a pragmatic and effective regulatory response to the integration of markets. A working party on competition was created within the context of the World Trade Organization. In addition, at the initiative of both the EU and the US, a Global Competition Forum (GCF) was established to discuss all aspects of competition policy.[114] The GCF is open to all countries with a competition regime or those that are in the process of establishing competition rules.

[73] In 2001, the International Competition Network (ICN)[115] was launched. The ICN aims to provide a venue within which antitrust officials from developed and developing countries can work to address practical enforcement and policy issues of common concern. The ICN also aims to facilitate procedural and substantive convergence in antitrust enforcement. Membership of the ICN expanded from the initial fourteen competition agencies to eighty members in less than a year and includes many of the younger, developing competition authorities.

[74] The first official meeting of the ICN was hosted by the Italian Antitrust Authority in the autumn of 2002. Discussions centred around the proposed Guiding Principles for Merger Notification and Review, which was drafted by one of the ICN's working groups. At the ICN's second annual conference in Mexico in June 2003, the ICN members adopted seven non-binding recommended practices in the field of merger control. These provide that competition authorities should:

- only examine a deal if it has a real impact on their national market;
- adopt clear and objective notification thresholds;
- allow for flexibility in the timing of notification (the European Commission believes that the removal of the one-week filing deadline under the 2004 Merger Regulation will bring the EU merger control regime fully in line with the ICN's recommendations);
- require only the information strictly necessary for a proper assessment of the concentration;
- ensure that the investigation timetables are predictable and no longer than necessary;

[113] Speech – *EU competition policy, relations with the US, and global business*, Speech/13/749 of 25 Sep. 2013.
[114] Commission press releases IP/00/1230 and IP/01/147.
[115] *See*, http://www.internationalcompetitionnetwork.org/.

- provide for transparency in their laws, procedures and individual decisions; and
- periodically review their merger control systems.

[75] The ICN has been focusing on the merger control process as it applies to multi-jurisdictional mergers and upon the competition advocacy role of antitrust agencies, particularly in emerging economies. The network will continue to develop non-binding recommendations for consideration by individual enforcement agencies. Where the ICN reaches consensus on particular recommendations, it is left to governments to implement them voluntarily.

[76] In 2012, the ICN's Merger Working Group identified the following immediate priorities:

- promote better understanding of the role of economic analysis in merger review;
- continue to promote familiarity, use and implementation of existing ICN work products;
- establish a framework for merger review cooperation among interested member agencies. Working Group members responded favourably to pursuing the idea. The non-binding framework is intended to facilitate effective and efficient cooperation between and among ICN member agencies reviewing the same merger through the identification of agency liaisons and possible approaches for information exchange among agency case teams.[116]

[77] In 2017, the ICN's Merger Working Group amended the Recommended Practices for Merger Notification and Review Procedures[117] and the Recommended Practices for Merger Analysis[118] to address four main topics: (1) the types of transactions subject to merger review; (2) nexus and thresholds; (3) merger remedies; and (4) the role of efficiencies. Also, in 2017, the ICN's Merger Working Group organised a seminar on investigative techniques and began the process of updating its Investigative Techniques Handbook.[119] In April 2019, the ICN's Steering Group approved an international framework on Competition Agency Procedures aimed at promoting fair and effective antitrust enforcement and merger control processes.[120] The framework governs cooperation between antitrust agencies and sets out common principles to be adhered to, such as non-discrimination, transparency and predictability, and confidentiality, as well as respect for rights to legal representation, good administration, and judicial review.[121]

[78] The long-term goals of the ICN, as indicated in their 2020–2023 Merger Working Group structure and three-year plan, are to:

---

[116] ICN Mergers Working Group – 2012–2013 Work Plan, http://www.internationalcompetitionnetwork.org/uploads/library/doc801.pdf.

[117] *See*, http://www.internationalcompetitionnetwork.org/uploads/library/doc1108.pdf.

[118] *See*, http://www.internationalcompetitionnetwork.org/uploads/library/doc1107.pdf.

[119] *See*, http://www.internationalcompetitionnetwork.org/uploads/library/doc1100.pdf.

[120] *See*, https://www.internationalcompetitionnetwork.org/wp-content/uploads/2019/04/CAP_PR.pdf.

[121] *See*, https://www.internationalcompetitionnetwork.org/wp-content/uploads/2019/04/ICN_CAP.pdf.

- promote greater international cooperation and convergence in merger review standards;
- enable ICN members to improve the quality of their merger review and reduce both 'type 1 errors' (prohibiting a pro-competitive transaction) and 'type 2 errors' (failing to challenge or remedy an anticompetitive transaction);
- assist ICN members in finding ways to avoid imposing unnecessary burdens on agencies and businesses; and
- increase transparency in agency practice in order to minimise uncertainty and increase predictability in merger review.[122]

4 SCOPE OF APPLICATION: CONCENTRATION

4.1 Concentration (Article 3(1))

[79] The Merger Regulation seeks to regulate transactions which have a structural impact on the market. Such transactions will give rise to a concentration, and Article 21(2) of the Merger Regulation gives the Commission exclusive competence, subject to limited exceptions, over concentrations which have a Community dimension in the sense of Article 1(1) of the Merger Regulation. Recital 20 of the Merger Regulation describes concentrations as transactions *'bringing about a lasting change in the control of the undertakings concerned and therefore in the structure of the market'*. Article 3 defines more precisely the nature of the changes which will bring about a concentration within the meaning of the Merger Regulation. Article 3(1) provides that a concentration will arise where:

(a) two or more previously independent undertakings merge (Article 3(1)(a)); or
(b) one or more undertakings (or persons controlling an undertaking) acquire, whether by the purchase of shares or assets, by contract or any other means, direct or indirect control of the whole or parts of one or more other undertakings (Article 3(1)(b)).

[80] Furthermore, Article 3(4) states that the 'creation of a joint-venture performing on a lasting basis all the functions of an autonomous economic entity shall constitute a concentration within the meaning of paragraph 1(b)'.

[81] The Commission's Consolidated Notice explains how it interprets and applies the concepts of concentration, control and full-function joint venture. As regards the concept of a concentration, the Consolidated Notice clearly focuses on certain practical issues which the Commission has faced in its casework in recent years and those which have come under judicial scrutiny since the enforcement of merger control rules in the EU.

[122] *See*, https://www.internationalcompetitionnetwork.org/wp-content/uploads/2020/09/Workplan2020-23MWG.pdff.

[82] In a 2013 consultation paper, the Commission raised the question as to whether the Merger Regulation should be amended to allow the Commission to also look at non-controlling minority shareholdings. The Commission's decisional practice shows that it has dealt in many cases with minority shareholdings. However, the scrutiny of such structural links under the Merger Regulation has important limitations, and the Regulation does not allow the Commission to deal with all the transactions involving potentially problematic minority shareholdings. First, the Commission's scrutiny is limited because many transactions do not fall within the scope of the Merger Regulation, and the Commission is limited to reviewing pre-existing structural links of the parties to a notifiable transaction. This is because the creation of a structural link itself without a change of control is not a notifiable transaction under the Merger Regulation. Second, as demonstrated by the *Ryanair/Aer Lingus* case, the Commission's power to order the unwinding of a concentration declared incompatible with the internal market is limited as the Commission has no means to request the undertakings to fully or partially divest a minority shareholding.[123]

[83] In its proposals, the Commission considered introducing either a mandatory notification system or a 'selective' system where there would be no filing obligation, but the Commission would have the possibility to assert jurisdiction over problematic cases. The Commission's proposals gave rise to a large number of comments, several of which were critical of the Commission's extension of jurisdiction to cover the acquisition of non-controlling shareholdings. In light of these critics, Margrethe Vestager, Commissioner of Competition, concluded recently that the balance between the concerns that this issue raises and the procedural burden of the proposal in the White Paper may not be the right one and that the issues need to be examined further. She indicated that there is no need to rush and that it will be essential for the new rules, as the case may be, to work well and to be proportionate to the problem.

4.1.1 Undertakings

[84] Undertakings are normally commercial, profit-making businesses operating on the market. This concept of *'undertaking'* is similar to that defined by the Community Courts under Article 101 of the TFEU. A change in control over assets may also constitute a change in control over an undertaking where the assets constitute a business to which a turnover is clearly attributable,[124] i.e., sale of a brand, licence, goodwill or customer lists.[125]

[85] The Merger Regulation is also applicable if one or more natural persons acquire control over an undertaking, provided that they already control at least one other undertaking and therefore are considered themselves to be undertakings

123 Case M.4439 *Ryanair/Aer Lingus*.

124 Consolidated Notice at para. 24, and cases M.286 *Zürich/MMI* and M.3867 *Vattenfall/Elsam and E2 Assets*.

125 In case M.890 *Blokker/Toys 'R' Us*, the Commission treated the acquisition of assets coupled with a right to sell toys under a franchise agreement as a concentration.

because they have their own commercial activities. In case M.82 *Asko/Jacobs/Adia*, Asko, a German holding company, and Mr Jacobs, a private Swiss investor, acquired joint control of Adia, a Swiss company. Jacobs was considered an *undertaking concerned* because of the commercial interests he held in other businesses, in particular, chocolate.[126] Management buy-outs are treated as the acquisition of control by individuals and therefore only constitute a concentration where the individuals already control another undertaking. However, the Commission will also look carefully at the rights given to investors in order to finance the operation to establish whether or not they have obtained control of the undertaking.[127]

[86] In case M.3762 *Apax/Travelex*, for example, a private individual acquiring joint control was not considered as an undertaking concerned.[128]

[87] The term *'person'* in Article 3(1)(b) also covers public bodies, including the state itself. In cases M.157 *Air France/Sabena*, M.562 and M.616 *Swissair/Sabena*, the Commission concluded that Sabena was to be treated as a joint venture of the Belgian state and Air France, and the Belgian state and Swiss Air, respectively.[129] In case M.6812 *SFPI/Dexia*, the Commission considered that the Société Fédérale de Participations et d'Investissement was controlled by the Belgian State and that the proposed concentration de facto resulted in an acquisition of Dexia by the Belgian State. Similarly, sovereign wealth funds, which are state-owned investment funds composed of financial assets such as stocks, bonds, property, precious metals or other financial instruments, will also be considered to constitute *'undertakings concerned'* within the meaning of Article 3(1)(b) of the Merger Regulation.[130]

4.1.2 Independent Undertakings

[88] As set out in Article 3, a concentration may arise as a result of a merger between independent undertakings. A concentration could also occur as a result of the change of control of one or more undertakings or parts of one or more undertakings. As set out in paragraph 51 of the Consolidated Notice, internal

---

126 *See also* case M.400 *Allied Lyons/HWE-Pedro Domecq* (where the acquired company was previously jointly controlled by Allied Lyons and Mr Mora Figueroa) and case M.2416 *Tetra Laval/Sidel.*

127 In case M.395 *CWB/Goldman Sachs/Tarkett* a management buy-out of the Tarkett Group was financed through two funds managed by CWB and Goldman Sachs. A new company was set up to hold the shares of the target companies in which the majority of the shares would be held by the different investor group. CWB and Goldman Sachs were to manage the voting rights of the investor group and would also have specific veto rights. The Commission concluded that CWB and Goldman Sachs rather than the management team were acquiring control of the Tarkett group.

128 Pursuant to the shareholders agreement subscribed by Apax and Travelex shareholders, Travelex was to be jointly controlled by Apax and Mr Dorfman. However, given that Mr Dorfman was an individual who did not carry out any economic activities other than in Travelex, he was not considered an *'undertaking concerned'* under the Merger Regulation. *See also* cases M.5734 *Liberty Global Europe/ Unitymedia* and M.7000 *Liberty Global/Ziggo* where the Commission concluded that, although John Malone (a large shareholder in Liberty Global) exercised 'significant influence' over Liberty Global, he did not wield 'decisive influence' and, therefore, did not exercise control over the company as he could not determine the company's behaviour.

129 *See also* Consolidated Notice at para. 12.

130 *See* case M.5528 *Mubadala/UTC/JV.*

restructuring within the same group of companies will not constitute a concentration.[131]

[89] Where a merger or acquisition of control is contemplated between two public companies owned by the same state, the Commission takes the view that the mere fact that the two companies are both owned by the same state does not necessarily mean that they are not independent undertakings. The analysis depends upon whether both public companies are part of the same economic unit (or whether they have the power to make independent decisions) within the meaning of Recital 22 of the Merger Regulation.[132]

[90] Moreover, paragraph 194 of the Consolidated Notice also states that 'where a State-owned company is not subject to any co-ordination with other State-controlled holdings, it should be treated as independent for the purposes of Article 5, and the turnover of other companies owned by that State should not be taken into account. Where, however, several State-owned companies are under the same independent centre of commercial decision-making, then the turnover of those businesses should be considered part of the group of the undertaking concerned for the purposes of Article 5'. It follows that independence does not normally exist where the undertakings are within the same holding company and are therefore subject to a coordinated strategy.

[91] In case M.308 *Kali + Salz/MdK/Treuhand,* the Commission treated former state enterprises in East Germany as part of one economic unit where they were supervised by the same administrative division within the Treuhand (Anstalt).

[92] In case M.511 *Texaco/Norsk Hydro,* the Commission took the view that although the Norwegian state owned 51% of Norsk Hydro, it did not take part in decisions regarding commercial activities and that there were no formal or informal relations between Norsk Hydro and the 100% state-owned oil company, Statoil. The commercial activities of the companies were therefore found not to be coordinated through their common shareholder. This was confirmed in the later *Statoil/Hydro* transaction.[133] In case M.4180 *Gaz de France/Suez,* the Commission did not take into account the other French state-owned companies for the calculation of the relevant turnover and its competitive assessment of the case, despite the fact that Gaz de France was wholly controlled by the French state.[134] Likewise, in case M.6812 *SFPI/Dexia,* while SFPI was an investment company fully owned by the Belgian State, the Commission did not consider other companies controlled by the Belgian state in its competitive assessment of the transaction.

---

131 Case M.1172 *Fortis AG/Generale Bank.*

132 Recital 22 sets out the principle of non-discrimination between the public and the private sectors: *'The arrangements to be introduced for the control of concentrations should, without prejudice to Article 86(2) of the Treaty, respect the principle of non-discrimination between the public and the private sectors. In the public sector, calculation of the turnover of an undertaking concerned in a concentration needs, therefore, to take account of undertakings making up an economic unit with an independent power of decision, irrespective of the way in which their capital is held or of the rules of administrative supervision applicable to them.'*

133 Case M.4545 *Statoil/Hydro.*

134 *See also* cases M.216 *CEA Industry/France Telecom/SGS-Thomson*; M.496 *Marconi/Finmeccanica* and M.931 *Neste/IVO.*

4.1.3 Plurality of Concentrations

[93] Where a company demerges or a joint venture is broken up, there will usually be more than one concentration due to the acquisition of control by each of the parties over the relevant activities.[135] Similarly, a transaction involving asset swaps will normally be considered as two separate concentrations.

[94] The question of plurality of concentrations which may arise from a series of transactions has come under particular scrutiny further to the *Cementbouw judgments*.[136] In this case, the Commission required notification of a series of transactions which together led to the creation of a dominant position, held jointly by Cementbouw and the German building materials conglomerate Haniel in the Dutch market for sand-lime-based building products. The first transaction between the two companies did not meet the Community thresholds and had been notified and approved by the Dutch competition authority. The second transaction which concerned the subsequent termination of a joint venture created in 1999 by Cementbouw and Haniel was authorised by the Commission using an Article 8(2) procedure further to the commitment from the parties to break up their monopoly. This Commission decision was challenged on the ground that the European regulator did not have jurisdiction over the transactions concerned. The General Court's decision, upheld by the ECJ, found that the Commission was entitled to treat the transactions as involving a single concentration with Community dimension, notwithstanding their approval in part by the Netherlands' NCA (the Autoriteit Consument & Markt) and the fact that they were sequential rather than simultaneous. The courts agreed that the Commission had applied the correct test, namely, whether the transactions were interdependent, either legally (being explicitly inter-conditional) in their economic effect or in fact (e.g., by being simultaneous, near contemporaneous, or clearly part of a single overall plan), and thus essentially unitary in nature.

[95] For two (or more) transactions to constitute a single concentration, the transactions must therefore be interdependent and involve the acquisition of control by the same person or undertaking. Recital 20 of the Merger Regulation explains that it is appropriate to treat transactions that are closely connected, in that they are *'linked by condition'* as a single concentration. This conditionality implies that the transactions would not take place without the others, and they are consequently

---

[135] Case M.197 *Solvay/Laporte*. In exceptional circumstances, the Commission has treated the division of an undertaking as one concentration. In case M.138 *Campsa* the Commission stated that *'exogenous constraints falling outside the scope of the control of the owners (a political decision that the petrol monopoly be broken up in accordance with the act of accession of Spain to the EU) was imposed on the parties or products concerned. and conferred a unity on the division'*. *See also* cases M.3293 *Shell/BEB*; M.3294 *ExxonMobil/BEB* and cases M.5461 *Lyonnaise des Eaux/Sociétés de distribution d'eau et d'assainissement*; M.5464 *Veolia Eau/Sociétés des Eaux de Marseille/Société des Eaux d'Arles/Société Stéphanoise des Eaux*; M.8016 *Sanofi Pasteur/Vaccines of Sanofi Pasteur MSD* and M.8083 *Merck/Sanofi Pasteur MSD*.

[136] Case M.2650 *Haniel/Cementbouw/JV(CVK)* and case T-282/02 *Cementbouw v. Commission* [2006] ECR II-319.

seen as constituting a single transaction.[137] However, where several companies form a consortium to acquire the shares of an undertaking which, as agreed, will then be divided between the parties in accordance with a pre-existing plan, the Commission analyses the operation as two (or more) distinct concentrations. This means that each of the acquiring companies is treated as acquiring sole control over the part of the target undertaking that it will ultimately hold,[138] unless the two operations are clearly conditional upon each other.[139]

[96] The Commission considers that the first transaction does not constitute a concentration in itself, and instead only examines subsequent acquisitions of control by the ultimate acquirers, provided a number of conditions are met:

- first, the subsequent break-up must be agreed between the different purchasers in a legally binding way; and
- second, it must be certain that the second step, the division of the acquired assets, will take place within a short time period after the first acquisition.

[97] The Commission considers that normally the maximum time frame for the division of the assets should be one year.[140]

[98] However, if these conditions are not fulfilled, particularly if it is not certain that the second step will proceed within a short time frame after the first acquisition, the Commission will consider the first transaction as a separate concentration involving the entire target undertaking. This will be the case if the first transaction also proceeds independently of the second transaction[141] or if a longer transitory period is needed to divide up the target undertaking.[142]

[99] Even where two or more transactions do not fulfil the conditions for being treated as one concentration according to *Cementbouw*, the anti-avoidance provision in Article 5(2) of the Merger Regulation may still come into play to require them to be treated as one transaction. This article provides that where two or more transactions between the same persons or undertakings take place within a two-year period, they are to be treated as one and the same concentration occurring on the date of the last transaction.[143]

---

137 Cases M.4028 *Flaga/Progas/JV*; M.4146 *GE/Bayer/OSi Europe Business;* M.5993 *Securitas/Reliance Security Services/Reliance Security Services Scotland* and M.6151 *PetroChina/Ineos/JV*. Also, in M.6123 *ArcelorMittal Bremen/Kokerei Prosper/Arsol Aromatics*, the Commission treated the acquisition of sole control of one entity and a minority shareholding in another as a single concentration where the transactions were conducted simultaneously between the same purchaser and the same seller and were legally and economically interdependent.

138 *See* paras 30–35 of the Consolidated Notice.

139 Case M.1188 *Kingfisher/Wegert/Promarkt* and case M.1006 *UPN-Kymmene/April*.

140 *See* cases M.3779 *Pernod Ricard/Allied Domecq* and M.3813 *Fortune Brands/Allied Domecq*, where the split-up of the assets was foreseen to become effective within six months after the acquisition.

141 *See* case M.2498 *UPM-Kymmene/Haindl* and case M.2499 *Norske Skog/Parenco/Walsum*.

142 *See* case M.3372 *Carlsberg/Holsten*.

143 Please also refer to para. [175] below.

4.2 Mergers (Article 3(1)(a))

[100] The term *'merger'* is undefined in the Merger Regulation and is intended to refer to the concept of 'fusion' familiar to civil law jurisdictions, namely the transfer of all the rights and liabilities of the company to be purchased into another company, as a result of which the acquired company ceases to exist. The Consolidated Notice confirms this interpretation:[144] it considers *'mergers'* to occur either when two or more independent undertakings amalgamate into a new undertaking and cease to exist as different legal entities[145] or when an undertaking is absorbed by another, the latter retaining its legal identity while the former ceases to exist as a legal entity.[146] Full legal mergers, however, are fairly rare.

[101] A merger within the meaning of Article 3(1)(a) may also occur in a situation of a de facto amalgamation. This may arise where two or more previously independent undertakings, while retaining their individual legal personalities, contractually establish a common economic management, which results in the creation of a single economic unit. The Commission considers that a prerequisite for the determination of a common economic unit is the existence of a permanent, single economic management. Other factors, such as internal profit and loss compensation as between the various undertakings within the group, and their joint liability externally, are also considered relevant. The existence of cross-shareholdings between the undertakings forming the economic unit reinforces the de facto amalgamation.[147] In *Carnival Corporation/P&O Princess (II),* the Commission required a second notification in relation to an acquisition of P&O Cruise Liners effected through the creation of a dual-listed company. While the companies would have identical boards and senior management, in addition to being managed and operated as if they were a single economic enterprise pursuant to contractual arrangements and amendments to their constitutional documents, each company would continue to exist as a distinct entity.[148] The Consolidated Notice states that the critical factors of common economic management will be established contractually.

---

[144] *See* para. 9 of the Consolidated Notice.

[145] *See,* for example, case M.1846 *Glaxo Wellcome/SmithKline Beecham* and case M.5221 *Kenwood/JVC/HoldCo.*

[146] *See* cases M.2681 *Conoco/Philips Petroleum;* M.5762 *Innolux/Chi Mei/TPO* and M.5804 *Samsung Electronics/Samsung Digital Imaging Co.* A merger in the meaning of Art. 3(1)(a) is not deemed to occur if a target company is merged with a subsidiary of the acquiring company to the effect that the parent company acquires control of the target undertaking under Art. 3(1)(b), *see* cases M.2510 *Cendant/Galileo* and M.5611 *Agilent/Varian.*

[147] Cases M.660 *RTZ/CRA* and M.3071 *Carnival Corporation/P&O Princess II.*

[148] In contrast, in case 36.111 *Northwest Airlines/KLM* the Commission concluded that the cooperation between the two airlines did not constitute a concentration of their transatlantic businesses and emphasised the fact that the airlines continued to operate separately on the market and remained separate legal entities despite their arrangements operating on the basis of shared economic interests.

4.3 Acquisition of Control (Article 3(1)(b))

4.3.1 Definition of Control

[102] The key criterion in determining whether the Merger Regulation may apply to a transaction is whether the transaction leads to an acquisition or change of control. Article 3(2) of the Merger Regulation provides that control consists of:

> rights, contracts or any other means which, either separately or in combination and having regard to the considerations of fact or law involved, confer the possibility of exercising decisive influence on an undertaking, in particular by:
>
> (a) ownership or the right to use all or part of the assets of an undertaking; and
>
> (b) rights or contracts which confer decisive influence on the composition, voting or decisions of the organs of an undertaking.

[103] The General Court has confirmed that the Commission has jurisdiction under the Merger Regulation only in respect of concentrations that involve the acquisition of control.[149] The concept of control is interpreted broadly. The central issue is whether the rights which one undertaking acquires in another are sufficient to confer the possibility of exercising *'decisive influence'* over that undertaking. The Commission thereby considers the possibility of determining the business strategy of an undertaking given that the Merger Regulation is concerned with lasting market changes which affect business activities and competition.[150] The Commission is not concerned with rights regarding the day-to-day management of an undertaking or those which have the limited purpose of protecting the financial interests of minority shareholders. These rights will be ignored in determining control for the purpose of the Merger Regulation.[151] Further, it is irrelevant whether the acquirer of control will actually exercise the decisive influence or whether this was the intended result of the contractual arrangement. However, the possibility of exercising such decisive influence must be effective.[152] For example, in case M.330 *McComick/CPC/Rabobank/Ostmann*,[153] one of the three shareholders of Rabobank had only an investment interest and said it would not participate in major business decisions. The Commission however found that despite this, it retained the *'legal right to exert a decisive interest on the joint-venture'*, and therefore considered that it exercised control.

---

[149] Case T-411/07R, *Aer Lingus Group plc v. Commission*, Order of the Court of First Instance, 2008 ECR II-411. The Order was upheld by the General Court in case T-411/07, *Aer Lingus Group plc v. Commission*, 2010 ECR II-3691.

[150] Recital 20 of the Merger Regulation.

[151] Consolidated Notice at paras 16–23.

[152] Case T-282/02 *Cementbouw v. Commission*, para. 58 [2006] ECR II-319. *See also* cases M.2016 *France Telecom/Orange* and M.430 *Procter & Gamble/Shickedanz* where rights capable of conferring control were acquired but the acquirer will not be in a position to exercise the rights and therefore control will not result.

[153] *See also* case M.157 *Air France/Sabena*.

[104] Finally, the notion of control under the Merger Regulation includes not only positive rights to manage another undertaking (positive control) but also veto rights over another undertaking's commercial policy (negative control).[154]

[105] The means by which an undertaking is able to exercise decisive influence over another is irrelevant and can result from a combination of legal and other factors. Nevertheless, control will often be achieved through the acquisition of the key assets or the shares of the target undertaking. In addition, economic relationships (such as long-term supply agreements or credit arrangements) may also be relevant since they may lead to economic dependence resulting in de facto control.[155]

[106] Control may be acquired either by an undertaking acting alone (sole control) or by a number of undertakings acting jointly (joint control). Normally, control is acquired by the persons or undertakings which hold or are entitled to hold the right conferring control (e.g., ownership of shares with voting rights). In rare cases, the formal holder of the controlling interest differs from the persons or undertakings who actually exercise the rights arising from that interest. This type of control is typically established by identifying the source of finance or the family link. In these circumstances, control is acquired by the person who, in reality, has the power to control the target undertakings and not the formal holder of control.

[107] According to the Consolidated Notice, this can be the case, for example, where an undertaking uses another person or undertaking for the acquisition of a controlling interest and retains the ability to exercise the rights conferring control through this person or undertaking.[156] In this scenario, the holder of the rights acts as a mere vehicle. Control is acquired by the undertaking which in reality is behind the vehicle and which enjoys the ability to exercise decisive influence over the target undertaking. In *Cementbouw*, the General Court concluded from this provision that *'control held by commercial companies can be attributed to their exclusive shareholder, their majority shareholders or to those jointly controlling the companies since these companies comply in any event with the decisions of those shareholders'*.[157]

4.3.2 Sole Control

[108] Sole control arises if one undertaking alone can exercise decisive influence over another undertaking. Normally, this results from the acquisition of positive

[154] In case M.1920 *Nabisco/United Biscuits* a joint venture between Nabisco and three financial institutions acquired United Biscuits but the Commission concluded Nabisco would exercise sole control because it alone *'would have veto rights over decisions regarding the appointment of senior management and business plan and budget'*. *See also* cases M.5148 *Deutsche Telekom/OTE* and M.5496 *Vattenfall/Nuon*. In case M.5949 *Deutsche Bank/Actavis* the Commission determined that Deutsche Bank would exercise negative sole control because it was entitled to appoint three of seven members of the board and could alone block the appointment of the chairman of the board. Also, in case M.6282 *Südzucker/ED&F Man* the Commission considered that the acquisition of a 24.9% shareholding in ED&F Man conferred negative sole control as Südzucker secured veto rights over ED&F Man's annual budget and business plan, and the appointment of directors.

[155] Case M.4225 *Celsa/Fundia*.

[156] *See* Consolidated Notice at para. 13.

[157] Judgment in case T-282/02 *Cementbouw v. Commission*, para. 72 [2006] ECR II-319.

rights to manage another undertaking, but it may also result from veto rights to block strategic commercial decisions (so-called *negative sole control*).[158] The Consolidated Notice deals with sole control in paragraphs [54]–[62].

Sole Control by Majority Shareholding

[109] Sole control often results from the acquisition of a majority of the capital and voting rights of another undertaking. Where an undertaking holds an absolute majority of the shares of the target undertaking, there will generally be no question as to where decisive influence lies. However, where there are no other elements of fact or law, in order for sole control to be found to exist, it makes no difference whether the acquired shareholding is 50% of the share capital plus one share (as in case M.296 *Credit Lyonnais/BFG Bank*) or 100% of the share capital (as in case M.5253 *Sanofi-Aventis/Zentiva*, M.10024 *Blackstone/Winoa* or M.11156 *Cinven/Amara*).

Sole Control by Qualified Minority Shareholding

[110] Where there is no shareholder with an absolute majority, the situation is less predictable. In this event, sole control may be acquired by a *'qualified minority shareholder'* either on a de jure or on a de facto basis.[159] On a de jure basis, sole control may occur where specific rights are attached to the minority shareholding which enables it to determine the strategic commercial behaviour of another undertaking. For example, such rights would include preferential shares leading to a majority of the voting rights, or other rights such as veto rights which enable the minority shareholder to determine the strategic commercial behaviour of the target company, such as the power to appoint more than half of the members of the supervisory board or the administrative board (*see* below paragraph [91] 'Joint Control' for a description of the most important veto rights). For instance, in case M.258 *CCIE/GTE, CCIE* obtained only 19% of the voting rights in EDIL International Lighting B.V. (EDIL), but in addition, it had a permanent seat on the board and the right to appoint the chairman and chief executive officer (CEO). The director appointed by CCIE had a veto over all significant decisions of EDIL, and it was therefore concluded that CCIE was able to exercise sole control. No other shareholder held sufficient rights to counteract CCIE's influence, which would have created a situation of joint control.[160]

[111] A minority shareholder may be deemed to have sole control on a de facto basis if, for example, the minority shareholder is so large in comparison with all other shareholders that it is highly likely to achieve a majority in the shareholders'

158 Fortunately for legal certainty, the Consolidated Notice abandoned the notion in the consultation draft that a notifiable concentration might occur in a move from negative sole control to positive sole control.

159 *See* Consolidated Notice at para. 55.

160 *See also* consecutive cases M.3537 *BBVA/BNL* and M.3768 *BBVA/BNL*, cases M.3198 *VW-Audi/VW-Audi Vertriebszentren*; M.2777 *Cinven Limited/Angel Street Holdings* and M.258 *CCIE/GTE*. In case M.3876 *Diester Industrie/Bunge/JV*, there was the specific situation that a joint venture held a stake in a company by which it had negative sole control over this company. *See also* cases M.5805 *3i/Vedici Groupe* and M.5949 *Deutsche Bank/Actavis*.

meeting. This typically occurs when the remaining shares are widely dispersed since it is unlikely that all the smaller shareholders will be present or represented at the shareholders' meeting. Such an assessment is normally made based on evidence of attendance at shareholders' meetings over the past three years.[161] The Commission's decisions pursuant to the Merger Regulation show that any holding above 30% with other shares dispersed among a number of institutional and individual investors is likely to confer sole control.[162] In June 2009, following the Commission's assessment of de facto control, Belgian electricity producer Electrabel was fined EUR20 m for acquiring control of Compagnie Nationale du Rhône (CNR) without the Commission's prior approval.[163] Although Electrabel formally notified this acquisition in March 2008, the Commission considered that Electrabel enjoyed de facto control over CNR since 2003, when it acquired a shareholding of just under 50% in CNR and took over the function of operational management of power plants and marketing of electricity. In addition, the Commission's investigation found that due to the remaining shares being widely dispersed among other shareholders and past attendance rates at CNR's shareholders' meetings, Electrabel enjoyed a stable majority at such meetings. Another example of how the Commission assesses de facto control can be found in the *Marine Harvest/Morpol* case. On 14 December 2012, Marine Harvest entered into an agreement to purchase shareholdings in Morpol, representing approximately 48.5% of Morpol's share capital. The closing of this acquisition took place on 18 December 2012. On 21 December 2012, Marine Harvest sent a case team allocation request to the Commission to investigate the acquisition of sole control over Morpol. In this request, Marine Harvest informed the Commission that the acquisition of 48.5% of the capital of Morpol had already been closed and that Marine Harvest would not exert its voting rights pending the Commission's approval decision. The Commission examined whether the purchase of 48.5% shareholding granted Marine Harvest sole control over Morpol, and because of the wide dispersion of the remainder of Morpol's capital, the Commission concluded that Marine Harvest would be sure to command a clear majority of votes at Morpol's shareholders' meetings and that Marine Harvest, therefore, had sole de facto control over Morpol.[164] Also, in case M.7538 *Knorr Bremse/Vossloh*, the Commission determined that Knorr Bremse's

161 *See* cases M.3330 *RTL/M6* and M.2404 *Elkem/Sapa*. *See also* case M.1157 *Skanska/Scancem* where the total amount of remaining voting rights held by Skanska and Aker was 89.3% and the remaining 10.7% was dispersed among a large number of institutional and private investors. *See also* cases M.4155 *BNP Paribas/BNL;* M.4956 *STX/Aker Yards;* M.5808 *JSA/Jacquet Metals/IMS* and M.6850 *Marine Harvest/Morpol.*

162 *See* cases M.4730 *Yara/Kemira Growhow*. *See also* case M.5250 *Porsche/Volkswagen* where the Commission considered that based on shareholder attendance at the three most recent annual shareholder's meetings and a forecast of future attendance, Porsche's increased share of Volkswagen's voting capital from 30.9% to 35.56% would be sufficient to confer sole control in circumstances where the remaining shares were widely dispersed.

163 *See* Commission press release at, http://europa.eu/rapid/pressReleasesAction.do?reference=IP/09/895&format=HTML&aged=0&language=EN&guiLanguage=en.

164 The Commission considered it irrelevant that Marine Harvest had not exercised any voting rights in Morpol between acquiring the 48.5% interest and the Commission's clearance of the merger. The purchase of a 48.5% shareholding in Morpol made it possible for Marine Harvest to obtain a clear majority at Morpol's general shareholders' meeting, and allowed it to exercise decisive influence on

acquisition of a 35.8% shareholding in Vossloh conferred sole control even though a shareholding of that size would not have secured a stable majority at one of four recent annual shareholders' meetings because the meeting in question had been unusually well attended compared with prior and subsequent meetings. In addition, the Vossloh family had in the meantime sold its 22% shareholding, making it likely that Knorr Bremse's 35.8% shareholding would confer control going forward.

[112] Generally speaking, a 30% shareholding tends to give the beneficiary the ability to control the company in general meetings, but much will depend upon levels of turnout and voting patterns at the annual and extraordinary general meetings in previous years. However, in certain specific circumstances, the Commission has found the existence of sole control in situations where there is less than a 30% shareholding.

[113] In case M.754 *Anglo American/Lonrho,* the Commission found that Anglo American had sole control of Lonrho with a shareholding of 27.47% (held both directly and indirectly) and required divestment to reduce its share to 9.9%. In case M.343 *Société Générale de Belgique/Générale de Banque,* the Commission took the view that the increase from 20.94% to 25.96% in the stake which Société Générale de Belgique held in Générale de Banque gave the former sole control over the latter based upon the previous participation of all shareholders holding more than 0.06% of the capital. The Commission took an opposite view in case M.159 *Mediobanca/Generali,* where it decided that the increase of Mediobanca's stake in Assicurazioni Generali from 5.98% to 12.84% would not enable Mediobanca to exercise solely or jointly a decisive influence on Generali based on a history of presence of shareholders at annual general meetings (AGMs) for the previous five years. In case M.197 *Solvay/Laporte,* the Commission also held that Solvay's 24.96% shareholding in Laporte was not sufficient to enable Solvay to exercise decisive influence over Laporte, even though the next largest shareholder in Laporte had only 6% of the equity. Finally, in case M.5121 *NewsCorp/Première,* the Commission determined that NewsCorp's acquisition of a 24% shareholding was sufficient to confer de facto control based on attendance at past shareholders' meetings.

[114] There may be situations where, even in the presence of a large number of shareholders, a minority shareholding above 30% does not confer sole control. This was the situation in case M.486 *Holdercim/Origny-Desvroises* where, despite its 42% shareholding, Holderbank Cement und Beton (HCB) did not enjoy a majority of the voting rights present in the last three AGMs of Origny-Desvroises and could only appoint a minority of the members of the board of directors. Consequently, HCB did not have the possibility to exercise, solely or jointly, decisive influence over Origny.[165] Similarly, in case M.5932 *NewsCorp/BskyB,* the Commission determined that NewsCorp's shareholding of 19.14% with voting rights restricted to

Morpol. This possibility is sufficient to establish control within the meaning of Art. 3(2) of the Merger Regulation. *See* case M. 6850 *Marine Harvest/Morpol.*

[165] *See also* cases M.4336 *MAN/Scania* as regards the question of whether Volkswagen had acquired control of MAN; M.2574 *Pirelli/Edizione/Olivetti/Telecom Italia* and M.1519 *Renault/Nissan.* In addition, case T-2/93 *Air France v. Commission* [1994] ECR II-323 where the General Court considered that even

37.19% were not sufficient to confer de facto control. This was primarily due to the fact that: (i) NewsCorp had not accounted for a majority of votes cast at recent shareholders' meetings; (ii) only four out of BskyB's fourteen directors had any connection with NewsCorp, and the board took decisions by simple majority; and (iii) BskyB was not dependent on NewsCorp as a customer or a supplier (and all transaction between BskyB and NewsCorp were conducted on arm's-length basis).

Control by Contractual Rights or Dependence

[115] Contractual arrangements may also confer control over another company. The most common type of agreement is a shareholders' agreement. If such agreement provides one shareholder with the ability to manage or determine the strategic behaviour of the target, or to appoint the majority of the managing body of the target, that shareholder will be considered to have sole control over the company.[166] Any other legally binding agreement conferring on a given party the rights indicated above could also in principle form the basis for an acquisition of sole control.[167]

[116] The Consolidated Notice also notes that '[i]n exceptional circumstances, a situation of economic dependence may lead to control on a de facto basis where, for example, very important long-term supply agreements or credits provided by suppliers or customers coupled with structural links confer decisive influence'.[168] The two core elements underpinning such a finding are (i) a situation of economic dependence and (ii) the existence of structural links in the form of management rights or ownership interests. This can be illustrated by the Commission's *Blokker/Toys 'R' Us* decision, where Blokker, the leading toy retailer in the Netherlands, acquired the rights to the Toys 'R' Us operation in that Member State through a franchise agreement. In the opinion of the merger parties, this arrangement did not amount to a concentration within the meaning of the Merger Regulation.[169] Nevertheless, the Commission, to which the transaction was referred by the Dutch government pursuant to Article 22 of the Merger Regulation, rejected this contention. It was instead determined by the Commission that the acquisition of leases,

---

though an option does normally not in itself lead to a concentration, it can be taken into account for the substantive assessment in a related concentration. Also *see* case M.3696 *E.ON/MOL*.

166 A minority shareholding and board representation may confer some influence, but control will not be conferred in the absence of (i) the right to express an opinion on the definition of the company's strategy, and (ii) decisive influence on the management. For an illustration, *see* cases M.197 *Solvay-Laporte/Interow* and M.3411 *UGC/NOOS* where the Commission determined that a board seat and a minority shareholding were insufficient to confer control in the absence of any veto rights over matters of strategic importance.

167 *See* cases M.3858 *Lehman Brothers/SCG/Starwood/Le Meridien* where the management agreements had a duration of ten to fifteen years; M.2632 *Deutsche Bahn/ECT International/United Depots/JV* where the contract had a duration of eight years; M.2060 *Bosch/Rexroth* concerning a control contract (*Beherrschungsvertrag*) in combination with a business lease; M.3136 *GE/Agfa NDT* concerning a specific contract to transfer control over entrepreneurial resources, management and risks and M.2632 *Deutsche Bahn/ECT International/United Depots/JV* concerning a business lease.

168 Consolidated Notice at para. 20.

169 Case M.890 *Blokker/Toys 'R' Us*. *See also* case M.2060 *Bosch/Rexroth* were the Commission found that Bosch has acquired control over Rexroth after entering into a lease and control agreement with one another.

fixtures and inventory, personnel and trademarks, together with rights afforded by a franchise agreement, conferred control since the transfer of these assets led to a lasting change in the structure of the undertakings concerned.

Options

[117] An option to purchase or convert shares is not considered to be relevant for the control of a company prior to its exercise and therefore does not typically trigger an application of the Merger Regulation.[170] However, where it is clear that the option will be exercised in the near future, in accordance with legally binding arrangements, the option agreements are taken into consideration along with other elements, such as contractual arrangements or minority acquisitions. For example, in case M.967 *KLM/Air UK*, the Commission found that KLM had acquired de facto joint control of Air UK through a minority holding (14.9%) and option agreements coupled with a complex package of financial arrangements. KLM was able to demonstrate that, partly due to the option agreements, in practice, it had the possibility of exercising a joint decisive influence over the target company.

4.3.3 Joint Control

Definition of Joint Control

[118] Article 3(1)(b) of the Merger Regulation refers to a concentration brought about where *'one or more'* undertakings acquire direct or indirect control of one or more other undertakings. The Consolidated Notice deals quite extensively with situations of joint control, identifying the undertakings concerned in different types of transactions and dealing with changes in the nature of joint control, whether the acquisition of control is of a newly created company or of a pre-existing company.[171]

[119] Joint control arises where the parents must agree on decisions concerning the company's commercial strategy and activities.[172] Unlike sole control, which requires a shareholder to have the power to determine strategic decisions, decisive influence in this sense therefore means the power to block actions which determine the strategic commercial behaviour of an undertaking. As is the case for sole control, joint control can occur on a de jure or de facto basis. For example, common decision-making may stem from the distribution of the rights within a joint venture, for example, a 50/50 division of voting shares, or it may be because of contractual or other interests of the parties or because of the joint venture's constitution.

Equality in Voting Rights

[120] The most common situation of joint control is where two undertakings each hold half of the share capital of a joint venture, and there is no shareholders'

[170] Case T-2/93 *Air France v. Commission* [1996] ECR II-235.

[171] *See* Consolidated Notice at para. 62.

[172] *See* Judgment in case T-282/02 *Cementbouw v. Commission*, paras 42, 52, 67 [2006] ECR II-319.

agreement which confers sole control to either undertaking. In this situation, both parent companies will normally be obliged to cooperate so as to avoid reciprocal blocking votes on decisions affecting the joint venture's business strategy. If there are any shareholders' agreements, they must confirm that each partner cannot act independently from the other partner(s) within the joint venture because, for example, each has the same number of representatives in management bodies and that none of the representatives has a casting vote.[173] In case M.4912 *Calyon/Société Générale/ Newedge*, several factors were taken into consideration by the Commission in order to determine whether control over the new joint venture was exercised jointly. These included the 50/50 division of share capital and voting rights, the right to appoint an equal number of directors to the board of the joint venture (four by Calyon and four by Société Générale) and the majority rule (six/seven) that governed the adoption of resolutions dealing with the adoption of any strategic plan or annual budget, major investments and the appointment of senior management. In case M.6150 *Veolia Transport/Trenitalia/JV*, the parties held equal shareholdings and voting rights, the power to appoint top management alternated between the parents, both parents jointly approved the appointment of key managers, and unanimity was required for decisions concerning the joint venture's business plan and budget. In case M.8858 *Boeing/Safran/JV*, each parent had equal interests, board representation, and governance rights in a joint venture which would manufacture auxiliary power units. And in case M.8744 *Daimler/BMW/Car Sharing JV*, Daimler and BMW would each hold 50% of the share capital and voting rights of six joint ventures in which the strategic decisions would be taken by a majority vote. The same constellation prevailed and gave rise to joint control in case M.9587 *ENGIE/EDP Renováveis/EDPR Offshore España* where each parent held 50% of the share capital of the joint venture and appointed an equal number of board directors, giving each of them veto rights over the joint venture's decisions.

Veto Rights

[121] Where the capital participations of the parents are not equal, a situation of joint control can be created by rights, contracts or other means. The acquisition of joint control does not require that the acquirer has the power to exercise decisive influence on the day-to-day running of an undertaking. It is sufficient for the finding of control that there are veto rights relating to strategic decisions on the business policy of the joint venture. Accordingly, a veto right that prevents the sale of a joint venture will not in itself confer joint control. Likewise, minority shareholder protection rights will also be insufficient to confer control, absent the possibility of vetoing decisions on strategic matters.[174]

[173] *See* case M.3097 *Maersk Data/Eurogate IT/Global Transport Solutions JV* where joint control was established by the fact that each of the two parent companies held a 50% shareholding with two seats on a full member board and the ability to block the adoption of the business plan. *See also* case M.5650 *T-Mobile*/Orange.

[174] Case M.6921 *IBM Italia/UBIS*. *See also* case M.9274 *GlaxoSmithKline/Pfizer Consumer Healthcare Business* where the Commission considered that Pfizer's 32% interest in the combined consumer healthcare business did not confer joint control because Pfizer had no veto rights over strategic decisions and would not make any 'vital contribution' to the business in the future.

[122] Minority shareholders may be granted veto rights on strategic commercial decisions.[175] In case M.6168 *RBI/EFG Eurobank/JV*, the Commission determined that a 13% shareholding would confer joint control because it awarded the right to appoint members of a joint venture's supervisory board, consultation rights concerning the approval of the chairman of the board and the CEO, and veto rights over the approval of the budget and business plan. In the Articles of Association of the joint venture or shareholders' agreements, veto rights may also arise because of procedural requirements which mean that minority shareholders form part of the quorum needed for a decision.

[123] In this respect, the most important strategic decisions relating to the joint venture's commercial behaviour are those relating to the appointment of its management[176] and approval of its budget and business plan.[177] A veto over only one of these rights may be sufficient to confer control. Veto rights over sufficiently important commercial investment decisions may also confer control. This would depend on the level of investment (if it is very high, it may be viewed as investment protection only) and the extent to which it is a specific feature of the joint venture's market, but is likely to be relevant in most cases.[178] For example, if the budget and business plans provide details of the aims of the joint venture as well as the means

[175] *See* Consolidated Notice at paras 65–68. *See also* cases T 2/93 *Air France v. Commission* [1994] ECR II-323. In case M.3459 *EPSON/SANYO/JV*, although Seiko would hold 55% of the equity in the JV (with SANYO holding the remainder), Seiko and Sanyo were to run the operations of the JV *'in the spirit of equality'*. It was therefore considered that both parents had joint control over the JV. *See also* case M.3205 *SNPE/Saab/Patria/JV* (Eurenco) where although SNPE held a 60.2% shareholding in Eurenco, two minority shareholders, each owning 19.9% shareholding were found to exercise joint control on the basis of important veto rights: *'After the completion of the transaction, SNPE will have 60.2 per cent of Eurenco's shares, and SAAB and Patria will each have 19.9 per cent of the shares. Pursuant to the Shareholder's Agreement, and given that important decisions of the Board of Directors will require consensus, both SAAB and Patria have veto rights, and will therefore have joint control over EURENCO and indirectly over its wholly-owned subsidiaries.'*

[176] *See* case M.3722 *Nutreco/Stolt-Nielsen/Marine Harvest JV* where the Commission found that *'Nutreco would hold 75 per cent and Stolt-Nielsen would hold 25 per cent of the share capital of Marine Harvest. Both Nutreco and Stolt-Nielsen would be able to block decisions which are essential for the strategic commercial behaviour of Marine Harvest, such as the appointment of the management, important investments, the adoption of the business plan and the adoption of the budget. Thus, the parties would have joint control over Marine Harvest.'* *See also* case M.3217 *Carlyle/Finmeccanica/Avio* where the notified concentration consisted of the acquisition of joint control by Carlyle and Finmeccanica of Avio through a newly created acquisition vehicle ('Avio Holding S.p.A.'). Fiat Avio transferred (effective on 1 Jul. 2003) the target business to the newly created company Avio, which was ultimately to be acquired by Avio Holding S.p.A. Carlyle was to hold 70% of Avio's share capital and Finmeccanica was to hold the remaining 30%. However, Finmeccanica and Carlyle were to exercise joint control over Avio. The Shareholders' Agreement between Carlyle and Finmeccanica provided that Finmeccanica, although a minority shareholder, would hold veto rights over major strategic decisions concerning Avio. *See also* case M.6854 *Cameron/Schlumberger/OneSubsea*.

[177] *See* cases M.4912 *Calyon/Société Générale/Newedge*, M.5222 *Sofinco/Banco Popolare/Ducato/Agos*, and M.10163 *United Internet/Morgan Stanley/Tele Columbus*.

[178] *See* Consolidated Jurisdictional Notice para. 71. In case M.295 *SITA RPC/SCORI*, three minority shareholders had a veto over certain aspects of the expansion policy of an undertaking but this was not regarded as part of its commercial policy or competitive strategy. In case M.7851 *USS Nero/Optrust/PGGM/Global Via* the Commission determined that veto rights over investment and disinvestment decisions were sufficient to confer control over a Spanish infrastructure company as such decisions were 'key for determining the commercial strategy of that company'. Also, in case M.8894

of achieving them, a veto over these may confer control over the holder. In addition, joint control may be conferred by veto rights on market-specific issues. For example, veto rights over technology issues in technology-driven markets or product lines in markets where products are highly differentiated would be essential to the strategic behaviour of the joint venture and may be sufficient to confer joint control. In case M.853 *Bell Cablemedia/Cable & Wireless/Videotron*, minority shareholders Nynex and BCI had veto rights over the commercial policy and strategy of the joint venture which the Commission noted included, in particular, power to veto the adoption of the annual budget and company investments. These were considered essential features in the telecommunications markets of the joint venture and therefore sufficient to confer joint control. Also, in case M.5222 *Sofinco/Banco Popolare/Ducato/Agos*, the Commission considered that Banco Popolare's veto right over the adoption of the joint venture's business plan, and any modifications of such business plan, was sufficient to confer joint control even in the absence of any other veto right, since the business plan contained detailed commercial objectives and plan. Ultimately, whether veto rights are sufficient to constitute joint control is assessed on the basis of the total package of rights having regard to the business of the joint venture. However, veto rights which are simply the normal minority protection rights (e.g., changes to the constitutional documents, increases/decreases in capital, sale or winding-up of the business, very high-level investments) are not regarded as indicating joint control. For example, in case M.6921 *IBM Italia/UBIS*, the Commission considered that UBIS would not acquire joint control over a newly established acquisition vehicle in spite of its 49% shareholding in that vehicle because its customary veto rights did not extend beyond those normally accorded to minority shareholders. Similarly, in case M.9274 *GlaxoSmithKline/Pfizer Consumer Healthcare Business*, the Commission considered that Pfizer's 32% interest in the combined consumer healthcare business did not confer joint control because Pfizer had no veto rights over strategic decisions and would not make any vital contribution to the business in the future.

[124] In case M.229 *Thomas Cook/LTU/West LB*, the two shareholders had 90% and 10% of the shares of Thomas Cook, respectively. However, they also entered into a shareholders' agreement which provided that the consent of both parties was required for important strategic decisions relating to the joint venture (approval of a detailed annual business plan, together with a rolling five-year corporate plan, major proposals on financing, acquisition and disposals, etc.). As a result, the two shareholders exercised joint control over Thomas Cook. An exceptional example of where substantial veto rights were granted despite a very limited shareholding in the common equity can be found in M.526 *Sappi/DLJMB/UBS/WARREN*. In this case, joint control was enjoyed by all three shareholders of Warren despite the fact that UBS held only 2.2% and DLJMB held 10.8% of the share capital (with Sappi holding the remaining 87%). A shareholders' agreement provided that important

ACS/Hochtief Atlantia Abertis Infraestructuras the Commission considered ACS jointly controlled Abertis with Atlantia because it had express veto rights over investments exceeding an agreed threshold and indirect veto rights over the financing and re-financing of projects, allowing it to 'decid[e] about the market presence of Albertis' and affect 'the adoption of strategic decisions'.

decisions required the approval of at least one director of each of Sappi, DLJMB and UBS.

[125] Joint control may also arise without any shareholding. In case M.349 *Aegon/ Scottish Equitable*, for example, Aegon initially had 100% of the capital but only 40% of the voting rights, whereas the other partner, Trustco, had 60% of the voting rights. However, the strategic and business decisions and the appointment of directors were carried out by common agreement. Similarly, in case M.304 *Volkswagen/ VAG*, the Commission concluded that Lonrho, despite its 100% shareholding in VAG, shared joint control with Volkswagen, which did not have any shares, through a Coordination Committee which took joint decisions on major issues of commercial policy. A veto right that does not relate to strategic commercial policy, to the appointment of senior management or to the budget or business plan of the joint venture will not generally be regarded as conferring joint control. Only in very exceptional cases has the Commission determined a situation of joint control in the absence of such veto rights. In case M.5533 *Bertelsmann/KKR/JV*, the Commission took the view that Bertelsmann's veto rights regarding the adoption of the business plan and the dismissal of senior employees of a newly created joint venture were insufficient in themselves to confer joint control over the joint venture as these rights could be invoked only in the event of financial underperformance of the newly created entity. However, given that Bertelsmann would appoint the first group of senior management which were to remain in place 'possibly on a long term basis' and that Bertelsmann had the industrial knowledge regarding the joint venture's field of activity, the Commission took the view that Bertelsmann could reasonably be expected to be in a position to block important strategic decisions, thereby conferring joint control.

Voting Arrangements

[126] Even in the absence of veto rights, joint control can be created where two or more companies each hold less than half the share capital but pool their shareholding to acquire a majority of the voting rights and develop a deliberate common policy of acting together in exercising these voting rights. This can result either from a legally binding agreement[179] to this effect or on a de facto basis. In case M.410 *Kirch/Richemont/Telepiù*, Richemont was to hold 25% of the shares of Telepiù, with the other principal shareholders being Kirch (34.7%), Fin. Tel. Srl (23.4%) and Reti Televisive Italiane (10%). However, Kirch and Richemont signed a shareholders' agreement to coordinate their voting in Telepiù shareholders' meetings and board of directors' meetings in all decisions considered to be essential (including the adoption of the annual budget). Also, in case M.1745 *EADS*, Topco (the consolidated French interests in EADS), DaimlerChrysler and SEPI transferred the legal title to all of their shares in EADS to a holding company. This holding company pooled voting rights corresponding to more than 65% of EADS' shares and was therefore in a position to exercise decisive influence over EADS. In accordance with a participation agreement, the holding company exercised its voting rights in such a way that Topco and DaimlerChrysler were able to nominate and remove an equal

[179] *See* cases M.1853 *EDF/EnBW* and M.2791 *Gaz de France/Ruhrgas/Slovensky*.

number of directors. Given that strategic decisions required a majority vote of these directors, the Commission concluded that Topco and DaimlerChrysler exercised joint control over EADS. In case M.7870 *Fondo Strategico Italiano/Eni/Saipem*, Eni and Fondo Strategico Italiano were considered to hold joint control with 30.6% and 12.5%, respectively, of Saipem's share capital, as they committed to reach agreement on directors to be appointed in the company board, as well as certain strategic decisions. Also, in case M.8773 *LetterOne Holdings/BASF/Wintershall DEA*, the Commission determined that an obligation on two shareholders to uniformly exercise voting rights in accordance with decisions reached by a jointly controlled strategy committee amounted to a legally binding 'pooling' arrangement that conferred joint control. In contrast, in case M.10147 *Mitsui & Co/Mitsui Chemicals/ Honshu Chemical Industry*, the Commission determined that despite holding a majority of voting rights in Honshu Chemical pre-transaction, Mitsui & Co and Mitsui Chemicals did not exercise joint control, as there was no formal or informal arrangement to coordinate their votes and Mitsui Chemicals had never exercised its voting rights.

De Facto Joint Control

[127] In exceptional cases, control on a de facto basis can occur where strong common interests exist between the minority shareholders to the effect that they would not act against each other in exercising their rights in relation to the joint venture.[180] These are possibly the most difficult situations to analyse under the Merger Regulation. In such cases, joint control cannot automatically be presumed, and all the factual and legal circumstances must be examined in order to establish whether a common policy exists among those shareholders in relation to the activities of the joint-venture company. In the case of acquisitions of minority shareholdings, the factors to be taken into consideration are the prior existence of links between the minority shareholders[181] or the acquisition of the shareholdings by means of concerted actions. In case M.6151 *PetroChina/Ineos/JV*, the Commission concluded that the two companies would enjoy de facto joint control over three jointly owned entities where one of the companies owned a majority shareholding in two of the joint ventures and the other owned a majority shareholding in the third because the three entities where interlinked and interdependent, PetroChina and Ineos' interests were aligned and they had to agree on all matters of strategic importance for the joint ventures to operate efficiently. In the situation where a new joint venture is established and where each parent provides a vital contribution to the operation of

[180] *See* case M.4085 *Arcelor/Oyak/Erdemir* where the Commission concluded that although Arcelor, with a 41% interest in the joint venture would legally not be entitled to veto any decisions relating to the strategic behaviour of the joint venture, the strong common interests between OYAK and Arcelor led to the conclusion that the Commission expected they were not going to act against each other in exercising their rights in relation to Erdemir. Accordingly the Commission found that Oyak and Arcelor jointly controlled Erdemir on a de facto basis. In contrast, in case M.6471 *Outokumpu/ INOXUM* the Commission concluded that companies owning 29.9% and 21.7% shareholdings in Outokumpu did not exercise de facto joint control because they did not have common interests, were not dependent upon one another, had not acted in concert, and would not provide any 'vital contributions' to Outokumpu.

[181] Consolidated Notice at para. 77.

the joint venture (such as specific technologies, know-how and supply agreements), the probability that the parents carry a deliberate common policy is very high. However, the Commission recognises that the greater the number of parent companies involved in such a joint venture, the more this situation becomes unlikely. In case JV.55 *Hutchison/RCPM/ECT*, the Commission concluded that Hutchison and RCPM had acquired joint control of ECT because they would have a common interest not to vote against each other. This was due to a commonality of understanding between the parties following an earlier attempt to establish a similar joint venture, which had been abandoned following the issuance of a Statement of Objections. Further, the structure of the shareholding and the voting rules appeared to be tailored to allow Hutchison and RCPM to exercise joint control as they required a 60% majority for most decisions, and Hutchison and RCPM had four out of five seats on the board.

Shifting Alliances

[128] Considering that Article 3(1) of the Merger Regulation is concerned with lasting changes to the market structure and because alliances between minority shareholders may shift over time, the mere possibility that shareholders may form coalitions will generally not be considered sufficient to find joint control. For example, in the case of an undertaking where three shareholders each own a third of the share capital and each elect a third of the members of the board of directors, the shareholders do not have joint control where decisions are required to be taken on the basis of a simple majority, since the majority can on each occasion be any two of the minority shareholders. As a result, none of the shareholders will be considered to have a lasting majority.[182]

Control by a Single Shareholder on the Basis of Veto Rights

[129] An exceptional situation exists where only one shareholder is able to veto strategic decisions of a company, but does not have the power to impose these decisions. An example of this is where one shareholder has 50%, but the remainder of the shares is held by two minority shareholders and there are no voting arrangements controlling joint control, or where a quorum for voting arrangements in fact confers a veto power on a single shareholder. In these circumstances, the single shareholder has the same level of influence as several jointly controlling shareholders (the power to block strategic decisions) but not the powers normally associated with sole control (the power to impose strategic decisions). Since the shareholder can produce a deadlock situation equivalent to joint control, this situation is treated as acquiring control within the meaning of the Merger Regulation.[183] For example, in case M.5148 *Deutsche Telekom/OTE*, despite Deutsche Telekom and the Hellenic Republic each holding 25% plus one of the shares of, and voting rights in, OTE, Deutsche Telekom was deemed to exercise sole control over OTE. This was due to the terms of a shareholders' agreement between Deutsche Telekom and the Hellenic Republic that ensured post-transaction the Hellenic Republic's rights would

[182] Consolidated Notice at para. 80. *See also* case M.4249 *Abertis/Autostrade*.

[183] *See* case M.1920 *Nabisco/United Biscuits*.

be insufficient to confer joint control over OTE. In case M.5496 *Vattenfall/Nuon*, the Commission found that the initial acquisition of 49% of the shares in Nuon Energy, together with an agreement to acquire the remaining shares in three tranches over a period of six years, amounted to the acquisition of sole control as of the date of the acquisition of the 49% interest because the share purchase agreement provided that the acquirer would have exclusive operational control over Nuon Energy and a casting vote in the supervisory board.

Changes in the Structure of Control

[130] The Merger Regulation applies not only to acquisitions of control but also to changes in the nature of the control.[184] It is clear from Article 3 that a concentration may occur where an undertaking previously having sole control over another undertaking introduces a partner as joint controller, increasing the number of shareholders.[185] The reverse is equally true: where one of two joint-venture partners is bought out, a concentration will usually occur as a result of the change from joint to sole control.[186]

[131] As can be seen from the Consolidated Notice, the Commission's policy has changed over the years in that it now accepts that the exit of one or more shareholders from a joint venture which does not result in a change from joint to sole control '*will not normally lead to a notifiable concentration*'.[187] However, an increase or change in the identity of shareholders exercising joint control is considered to lead to a change in the quality of control and requires notification. This is because the entry of a new parent company or substitution of a parent company implies a change in the nature of control over the joint venture.[188]

[132] The Commission has also determined that changes from de facto sole control to de jure sole control are not reportable under the Merger Regulation as these transactions do not involve a change in the pre-existing quality and degree of decisive influence.[189] Similarly, changes from negative sole control (based on veto

[184] In case M.23 *ICI/Tioxide*, the Commission stated '*decisive influence exercised solely is substantially different to decisive influence exercised jointly since the latter has to take into account the potentially different interests of the other party or parties concerned...by changing the quality of decisive influence exercised by ICI on Tioxide, the transaction will bring about a durable change of the structure of the concerned parties*'.

[185] *See* case M.5841 *Cathay Pacific Airways/Air China*/ACC for a situation of change from sole to joint control. *See* cases M.5944 *Osaka/UFG/Infrastructure Arzak/Saggas* and M.4502 *Lite-On/PBDS* for the situation of an entry of a new shareholder that exercises joint control in addition to existing controlling shareholders or as a replacement for one of the shareholders. *See also* cases M.6848 *Aegon/Santander/Santander Vida/Santander Generales* and M.7319 *KKR/Allianz/Selecta*.

[186] Consolidated Notice para. 89. *See also* cases M.5724 *Suez Environnement/Agbar* and M.5812 *Société Lyonnaise des Eaux/Sociétés de Distribution et d'Assainissement*.

[187] Consolidated Notice at para. 90.

[188] In case M.2939 *JCI/Bosch/VB Autobatterien JV*, JCI acquired Vartas' 80% shareholding in an automotive components joint venture with Bosch whose shareholding remained unchanged. JCI and Bosch would exercise joint control. *See also* case M.902 *Warner Bros./Lusomundo/Sogecable*. In case M.6974 *Metinvest/Lanebrook/Southern GOK* the Commission determined that Metinvest would replace Trosilia in its role as controlling shareholder in four companies holding shares in, and controlling, Southern GOK jointly with Lanebrook.

[189] Case M.397 *Ford/Hertz*.

rights on strategic matters) to positive sole control (through imposing strategic decisions) are not considered reportable under the Merger Regulation.

Changes in the Scope of Control

[133] A change or expansion in the scope of a pre-existing joint venture may also require notification where changes to the corporate governance provisions or the scope of the joint venture bring it under the Merger Regulation, for example, by changing the nature, quality of control or giving the joint venture a full-function character which it did not have before. In case M.2276 *Coca-Cola Company/Nestle/JV*, the Coca-Cola Company and Nestle expanded the scope of a joint venture to include a broader range of products and to confer greater autonomy, including the possibility of recruiting employees and a dedicated management team. In the light of the commercial and operational independence resulting from these changes, the Commission determined that the joint venture was full-function and therefore notifiable under the Merger Regulation. However, the mere expansion of a joint venture's field of operation without additional asset contributions or changes in corporate governance will not typically modify the joint venture in a manner that would render a concentration notifiable under the Merger Regulation.[190]

[134] Similarly, the creation of a joint venture between two or more companies, using a company which was previously controlled solely by one parent, is not subject to EU merger control where the joint venture itself is not an independent player on the market. In its *Austria Asphalt v. Bundeskartellanwalt* judgment published on 7 September 2017, the ECJ clarified that the creation of a joint venture can only be subject to the Merger Regulation where the JV is a 'full-function' JV. However, until now it has not been clear whether a change in control of a non-'full-function' JV would also be subject to the Merger Regulation.

[135] In *Austria Asphalt*, an asphalt plant in Austria belonged exclusively to one large construction company. The transaction consisted in converting the plant into a joint venture jointly owned by the company and another construction company. The plant was not deemed 'full-function' because its business was limited to supplying goods to its current parent company, and, in future, to its two parent companies. The Austrian Supreme Court had to decide whether the acquisition of joint control over the asphalt plant required notification to the Commission, and it referred the matter to the ECJ for a preliminary ruling on this point.

190 In case M.933 *Bertelsmann/Kirch/Premiere* the Commission concluded that the increase in the shareholdings of Kirch and CLT-UFA in Premiere following the withdrawal of Canal + (which had previously controlled Premiere with the two shareholders), together with the sizeable extension of Premiere's business activities by the transfer to it of Kirch's digital interests, constituted a concentration. In case M.6763 *VWFS/PON Holdings B.V./PON Equipment Rental & Lease* the Commission determined that the transfer to an existing full-function joint venture, from one of its parents, of significant additional assets and contracts in the form of an entity active in leasing and finance solutions for MAN-branded trucks and buses constituted a reportable transaction. Similarly, in case M.9778 *TUI AG/RCCL/Hapag-Lloyd Cruises*, the Commission considered that the transfer of shares in Hapag-Lloyd Cruise, including several cruise vessels and related rights and assets, to an existing full-function joint venture was reportable, as the transfer would allow the joint venture to expand its cruise operations into new markets.

[136] The ECJ clarified that the Merger Regulation only applies if the joint venture resulting from the change in control is full-function. This is because only full-function joint ventures bring about genuine changes in the structure of the market. This is consistent with the meaning of the Merger Regulation. Accordingly, a change in control of a company which creates a non-full-function joint venture will therefore fall outside the Merger Regulation, although it may be caught by Member States' national merger control rules or by EU/national competition laws prohibiting anticompetitive agreements.

4.4 Joint Ventures

[137] Article 3(4) of the Merger Regulation stipulates that the creation of a joint venture performing on a lasting basis all the functions of an autonomous economic entity shall constitute a concentration.[191] This reflects the fact that the Merger Regulation applies to transactions which have a lasting structural effect on the market. The Consolidated Notice provides guidance as to the concept of *'full-functionality'*.[192] In order to be 'full-function', a joint venture must be a fully fledged, independent, self-standing business entity having a long-term presence operating on a market and performing the functions normally carried out by other undertakings on the same market.[193]

[138] The benefit of structuring a transaction so that it creates a full-function joint venture is the legal certainty which can be achieved, as regards EU and national competition laws, by a notification and merger clearance by the Commission. This has become of greater importance since 1 May 2004 as it is no longer possible to notify a joint venture which is not full-function to the Commission and requires the parties to rely on their own 'self-assessment'.

4.4.1 Full-Functionality

[139] The essential test of full-functionality is whether a joint venture is sufficiently independent from its parents. As the General Court pointed out in *Cementbouw,*[194] what is involved in the concept of autonomy is that the joint venture has its own operational and independent presence on a market since, by definition, every joint venture will be under the control of its parent shareholders. This is interpreted by the Commission to mean that a joint venture must operate on a market and perform the functions normally carried out by competing undertakings on the market

[191] Since 1 May 1998, when the distinction between 'concentrative' (falling under merger control) and 'cooperative' (falling under Art. 101 of the TFEU) joint ventures was abolished, all joint ventures constitute concentrations and are subject to the Merger Regulation in accordance with Art. 3(2), provided that they fulfil the requirement of 'full-functionality'.

[192] *See* para. [150].

[193] However, there are certain Member States, such as Germany, Austria or Poland, that consider that all joint ventures fall within the scope of their Merger Control regimes.

[194] Case T-282/02 *Cementbouw v. Commission* [2006] ECR II-319, at para. 62.

on a lasting basis.[195] The test concerns continuing dependence. The fact that the joint venture relies on its parents in its initial start-up phase will generally not prevent it from being full-function.[196]

4.4.2 Ability to Operate on a Market

[140] A joint venture must be fully equipped to be able to operate on a market. This will ultimately depend on the area of activity of the joint venture but will require sufficient resources including finance, staff and assets (tangible and intangible) in order to conduct its business activities on a lasting basis.[197] It is also likely to require the joint venture to have its own trade name, trademark or other designation to distinguish it from its parent companies.

[141] In case M.160 *Elf Atochem/Rohm and Haas*, the Commission concluded that the joint venture constituted an autonomous economic entity. This was on the basis that the physical and human resources necessary for the production and sale of the product were transferred to it, and the construction of a new production facility in the ownership of the joint venture was to start soon thereafter. Also, the parent companies granted it exclusive irrevocable intellectual property (IP) licences needed for manufacturing, and the joint venture was to have its own research and development facilities and distribution network. This gave it the necessary ability to act as an independent supplier and buyer on the market. By contrast, in case M.6910 *Gazprom/Wintershall/Target Companies*, the Commission considered that a joint venture that would own a gas field in Siberia was not fully functional because the gas field in question was not at the time in commercial production and did not therefore have access to the market. As a result, the joint venture would 'neither play an active role on the market post-transaction, nor involve a structural change in the market'.

[142] It is not essential that the joint venture actually owns all these resources, provided they are securely within its control. The licensing of certain IP rights may be considered equivalent to the transfer of these rights[198] as could the use of a parent's

---

[195] Consolidated Notice at para. 94. In case M.3576 *ECT/PONL/Euromax* the parties claimed unsuccessfully that Euromax, a joint venture to operate a container terminal, was not full-function because its capacity would be dedicated to PONL and its partners in the Grand Alliance consortium who should be treated as captive customers of Euromax, meaning it would not play a role on the market. The Commission found that PONL's partners were not obliged to use Euromax and, therefore, Euromax would have to compete for their trade.

[196] *See* case JV.57 *TPS*. Also, in case M.7307 *Electricity Supply Board/Vodafone Ireland/JV* the Commission concluded that a joint venture was full-function, even though it would depend on its parents for funding because: (1) it had a management team dedicated to its day-to-day business and access to sufficient resources in order to conduct its business activities on a lasting basis; (2) the joint venture's activities extended beyond any one specific function within the parent companies' business activities; and (3) the joint venture would actively seek customers.

[197] In case M.686 *Nokia/Autoliv* the joint venture was able to determine its service agreements with the parent company and move from its site retained by the parent company. *See also* case M.4912 *Calyon/Société Générale/Newedge*.

[198] Case M.527 *Thomson/Deutsche Aerospace AG*.

network.[199] The latter would occur where the parent is acting only as an agent, and this is normal within the relevant industry, or this accounts for only a small part of the joint venture's total business.[200] In case M.791 *British Gas Trading/Group 4 Utility Services*, the transfer of certain assets by the parent companies to a financial institution which leased the assets to the joint venture was considered equivalent to the transfer of the assets to the joint venture. Other factors which have led the Commission to find against the existence of a full-function joint venture include: the substantial dependence of the joint venture on one or more of the parent companies for personnel (cases M.1315 *ENW/Eastern* and M.1135 *Elf/Texaco/Anti freeze JV*);[201] the integration of its production facilities with one or more of the parent companies (cases M.1041 *BASF/Shell (II)*, M.994 *Hitachi/Du Pont*, M.1137 *Exxon/Shell*); the use of technology belonging to the parent companies (case M.58 *Baxter/Nestle/Salvia*); and the use of sales services such as marketing and tendering (case M.1315 *ENW/Eastern*).

4.4.3 Operational Autonomy

[143] Although the parent company's control over the joint venture normally includes the appointment of its management, the operational decisions of the joint venture on competitive issues such as pricing, production volumes, sources of supply and demand should normally be taken by the joint venture itself. If the parent companies are directly involved in its day-to-day operations, the joint venture may not be seen as operating on the market itself. Instead, its activities would be attributed to its parent companies. It is important that the joint venture has an independent dedicated management, particularly in cases where the joint venture continues to have a large number of contractual arrangements with its parent companies. This generally precludes the management and other key personnel of the joint venture being employees of the parent companies.[202] However, this factor is to be assessed on a case-by-case basis as some decisions have demonstrated the Commission's openness in dealing with such criteria. An example of this can be seen in the *Sydkraft/HEW/Hansa Energy trading* decision[203] where the parent companies provided the joint venture with a managing director for up to five years and which did not prevent the joint venture from being considered as full-function.

---

[199] Case M.4048 *Sonae Industria/Tarkett/JV*.

[200] Case M.543 *Zurich Insurance CY/Banco di Napoli* and case M.102 *TNT/GD NET*.

[201] In contrast, in case M.5655 *SNCF/LCR/Eurostar*, the Commission considered that staff secondments from the parent companies did not undermine the full-functionality of a joint venture, as all secondment arrangements would be entered into on an arm's-length basis. Also in case M.9360 *Daimler/Geely/JV* the Commission considered that a joint venture's responsibility for the cost of employees seconded from its parents contributed to the determination of full-functionality.

[202] *See*, for example, case M.3035 *Berkshire Hathaway/Converium/Gaum JV* and case M.9360 *Daimler/Geely/JV* where the fact that the joint venture incurred the cost of the employees seconded from its parents contributed to the determination of full-functionality of the joint venture.

[203] Case M.1732 *Sydkraft/HEW/Hansa Energy*.

4.4.4 Commercial Autonomy

[144] The joint venture must act as an independent supplier and buyer on the market: it must not be merely auxiliary to the parent companies' activities. A joint venture that assumes limited functions within the parent companies' business activities, such as R&D, production, distribution or sales, is not considered to be full-function,[204] nor is one which is established to supply products and services exclusively to its parent companies or which is wholly dependent on its parent companies for supplies.

[145] Commercial relationships between a joint venture and its parent companies will not necessarily endanger its full-function status provided that it is free, particularly in the longer term, to serve third parties on a competitive basis and that the joint venture deals with its parent companies on a truly arms-length basis. As a general rule, however, the Commission's view is that such a start-up period should be limited to a three-year period.[205] Such start-up period is sometimes extended. In case M.394 *Mannesmann/RWE/Deutsche Bank*, the joint venture would initially provide telecommunication services exclusively to its parent companies, although its business plan envisaged that after six years, 60%–80% of its turnover would be realised with third parties. The Commission accepted this as sufficient to give the joint venture full-function status.

[146] In the *TPS* case, the Commission concluded that the joint venture was full-function even if after five years it was still dependent on the financial contribution of its parent companies because it otherwise had all necessary personnel, material resources and channels to operate independently on the market.[206]

[147] It must, however, be demonstrated, for example, by reference to a business plan and the market in general, that any dependency on the parent companies will

[204] A joint venture's narrowly defined field of activity may, however, necessarily preclude its classification as full-function. In case M.2439 *Hitachi/STMicroelectronics/Superh JV*, for example, the Commission found full-functionality in a joint venture that was set up to develop and license SH microprocessor core architecture. *See also* case M.5740 *Gazprom/A2A/JV* where in 2008 the Commission initially had informed the parents of a joint venture that it lacked sufficient autonomy to be reportable, and then subsequently in 2009, when the parents adopted a new business plan, increased the joint venture's infrastructure and personnel, and established an independent sales company that would operate on the open market, the Commission found that the joint venture would operate as a full-function entity and was, therefore, reportable.

[205] Consolidated Notice at para. 97. Also *see*, case M.774 *Saint-Gobain/Wacker-Chemie/NOM* where a three-year purchase agreement did not affect the full-functionality of the joint venture because the scope of the agreement was limited and the joint venture would operate its own processing activities from the beginning. Similar reasoning was applied in case M.2299 *BP Chemical/Solvay/HDPE JV*. In JV.48 *Vodafone/Vivendi/Canal+* the Commission stated that the joint venture would be largely funded by independent revenue within three to five years. In case M.2763 *Toray/Murata/Teijin*, the Commission concluded that the joint venture was full-function from its inception despite the fact it had no manufacturing capability because it had marketing, sales and R&D activities and because the parent companies had agreed to transfer manufacturing facilities to the joint venture after one year.

[206] *See also* case M.4912 *Calyon/Société Générale/Newedge* where the Commission accepted that during a start-up period of five years both parent companies would provide up to 80% of their listed futures and options clearing business to the joint venture.

be reduced and end within the start-up period. In case M.904 *RSB/Tenex/Fuel Logistic,* the Commission concluded that a joint venture was not full-function because it did not have the assets and personnel necessary to operate in the nuclear forwarding market, and although these would be transferred to the joint venture when it was 'economically viable', it was not clear when this would happen. In case M.9479 *PSA/SAFT/ACC,* the Commission considered that a joint venture established to manufacture lithium-ion cells was full-function, notwithstanding initial reliance on one of its parents for orders, because: (i) the joint venture's activities went beyond those of its parents; (ii) the aim of the joint venture was to sell most of its production to automotive OEMs; (iii) the joint venture would participate in tenders independently; (iv) the joint venture would sell products for non-automotive applications; and (v) contracts with the joint venture's parents and third parties conducted at arm's length on the basis of normal commercial conditions.

[148] Where a joint venture's dependency on its parent companies is not limited to a start-up period, the essential question is whether, despite its sales or purchasing relationship with its parents, the joint venture is able to play an active role on the market. In this respect, the Commission will assess separately sales to, and purchases from, the parent company.

[149] Where the joint venture is intended to make sales to its parent companies, factors that will be important in deciding whether the joint venture can be considered full-function include the proportion of these sales compared with the joint venture's total production, whether the joint venture assumes any financial risk and whether sales to its parent companies are made on normal commercial terms.[207]

[150] Again, these assessments are made in the light of the characteristics of the market and normal business practice. In *Linde/Sonatrach JV,*[208] the Commission accepted as full-function a joint venture for liquid helium manufacturing and distribution that would supply 50% of its production to one of its parent companies. However, in *Electrabel /Energia Italiana/Interpower,*[209] the Commission concluded that the joint venture would not be full-function because only 5%–15% of electricity produced by the joint venture would be sold into the electricity pool market. As a rule of thumb, the Consolidated Notice recognises *'an indicative threshold'* at 50%:[210] if the joint venture achieves more than 50% of its turnover through sales to third parties, this will typically indicate it is a full-function joint venture, but below that threshold the issue will be more carefully scrutinised by the Commission and a case-by-case approach will be needed.

[207] Consolidated Notice para. 98. *See* cases M.556 *Zeneca/Vanderhave*; M.751 *Bayer/Hüls-Newco* and M.1189 *Teksid/Norsk Hydro Produksjon/Meridian*. *See also* case M.5936 *EADS DS/Atlas/JV* where a joint venture was considered full-function despite operating as subcontractor for one of its parents on arm's-length terms and in respect of only a 'minor' share of the joint venture's total sales. In case M.8960 *Adient/Boeing/JV* the Commission considered the joint venture to be full-function where it would 'only occasionally' sell aircraft seats to its parent, Boeing.

[208] Case M.2868.

[209] Case M.3003.

[210] Consolidated Notice at para. 98.

[151] Whether a joint venture that purchases from its parent companies can be considered full-function will depend on: the relative proportion of its sales that will be made up by products supplied by its parent companies; whether purchases are made on an arm's-length basis; the ability to source from third parties; and whether the joint venture will add significant value to its parent companies' products. In case M.475 *Shell/Chimie/Elf Atochem*, the parent companies guaranteed to supply all the joint venture's raw material requirements. However, the Commission found that the joint venture was more than just a captive sales outlet, as it would have a genuine industrial processing activity by reference to the value added by the production or processing activity of the joint venture.[211] In some cases, it may not be practicable or possible to transfer essential assets to the joint venture because the parent companies may utilise these assets for other purposes, and it would not be economically feasible for the joint venture to develop these assets itself. The fact that the joint venture utilises resources retained by its shareholders will not necessarily undermine its full-functionality, provided these resources are securely within the control of the joint venture.[212]

[152] In particular, where a joint venture is active in a trade market, any provision restricting its supplies to its parent companies (or vice versa) is likely to be incompatible with the finding of full-functionality.[213] A trade market in this regard is characterised by the existence of companies which specialise in the selling and distribution of products without being active at the upstream production level. According to the Commission, *'[i]n order to constitute a full-function joint-venture in a trade market, an undertaking must have the necessary facilities and be likely to obtain a substantial proportion of its supplies not only from its parent companies but also from other competing sources.'*[214]

[153] The Commission tends to apply the full-function concept broadly in the case of a joint venture entering a new market. In case M.1812 *Telefónica/TERRA/Amadeus*, the Commission approved the creation of a joint venture between Amadeus (a company controlled by Air France, Iberia and Lufthansa) and the Spanish internet company TERRA, a subsidiary of Telefónica. Amadeus operated a computerised reservation system (CRS). The new company represented a virtual travel agency offering services to consumers mainly in Spain and Portugal. TERRA and Amadeus thereby provided their services at market conditions and on a non-exclusive basis. Amadeus provided its CRS booking engine which had been adapted for the internet, and TERRA would provide its online search engine.

[211] *See* cases M.8960 *Adient/Boeing/JV* where the joint venture would design and manufacture its own aircraft seats, 'thus adding considerable value to the components purchased from [its parents]'; M.9315 *Chr. Hansen/Lonza/JV* where the joint venture was considered full-function because commercial relations with its parents 'will be entered into on an arm's length basis and at market price' and M.9360 *Daimler/Geely/JV* where the Commission considered the joint venture to be full-function in part because it would procure services from its parents on a cost-plus and arm's-length basis and remain responsible for its commercial negotiations.

[212] Case M.3349 *Toshiba/Samsung/JV.*

[213] Cases M.788 *Agrevo/Marubeni* and M.511 *Texaco/Norsk Hydro*.

[214] *See* Consolidated Notice at para. 102 and cases M.788 *AgrEVO/Marubeni* and M.511 *Texaco/Norsk Hydro*.

[154] In case JV.19 *KLM/Alitalia*, the Commission found for the first time that a long-term alliance fell within the scope of the Merger Regulation, despite the fact KLM and Alitalia neither merged nor established a joint venture as a separate legal entity.[215] The Commission found that the alliance should be regarded as a contractual full-function joint venture within the scope of the Merger Regulation for, *inter alia*, the following reasons: (i) the operations of KLM and Alitalia would be run jointly by a joined management (as a result of which all main strategic and commercial decisions relating to KLM and Alitalia would be adopted jointly through the alliance); (ii) the alliance would bring about a lasting change in the structure of KLM and Alitalia as the two airlines would withdraw from the air transport market and cease to operate independently; (iii) the alliance would have unconditional access to the aircraft provided by the parent companies and to all the necessary resources to carry out the business plan and operate on the market; and (iv) given the withdrawal of the parent companies from the scheduled air transport markets, the alliance would clearly be run by a dedicated management so as to maximise profits.

4.4.5 Lasting Basis

[155] A full-function joint venture must also be a relatively long-term undertaking: according to Article 3(4) of the Merger Regulation, it should be established with the intention to operate on a *'lasting basis'*. This is likely to be the case where the parent companies invest substantial financial resources in the joint venture or transfer substantial technical or commercial know-how to it.[216] The Commission considers that a joint venture may be operating on a lasting basis where the agreement specifies a period for the duration of the joint venture which is sufficient to bring about a lasting change in the structure of the undertaking concerned or where the agreement provides for the possible continuation of the joint venture beyond this period. In this view, the Commission considers that the duration of a maximum of three years is too short to constitute a full-function joint venture.[217] As a general rule, an agreement established for five years or more is likely to have a significant effect on the market which is not easily reversed.[218] This was the case in the Commission's *F2i/AXA Funds/G6 Rete Gas* decision where veto rights over a five-year period were considered sufficient to satisfy the long-lasting criterion.[219] This is likely, however, to depend on both the maturity of the market and the technology involved in the market in terms of the life cycle of products. For example, in case M.2982 *Lazard/*

[215] One factor in this decision was the specific rules in the airline sector concerning nationality requirements in bilateral air service agreements with third countries. These rules usually require that airlines must remain under the control of nationals of their home country in order to exercise air traffic rights to the third country.

[216] Consolidated Notice at para. 103.

[217] In case M.722 *Teneo/Merrill Lynch/Bankers Trust*, the Commission stated that the parties intended to dispose of the assets of the joint venture within three years and confirmed it was therefore not long lasting.

[218] Mechanisms for dissolution are recognised as necessary to protect shareholders and will not negate the enduring character of the joint venture. *See* the Consolidated Notice at paras 28 and 103.

[219] Case M.6302 *F2i/AXA Funds/G6 Rete Gas*.

Intesa BCI/JV, the Commission considered that a four-year agreement was concluded on a lasting basis where it could be extended by successive five-year periods unless terminated by one of the parties. In contrast, if a joint venture is established for a short duration or to construct a specific project (e.g., a bridge or a power plant), the long-lasting criterion will generally not be met because of the absence of any permanent change in control. Similarly, in situations where joint control may exist for a start-up period only, prior to being converted to sole control, the entire operation will usually be considered as the acquisition of sole control from the outset. The Consolidated Notice acknowledges that the Commission has in the past found that such a start-up period could last up to three years.[220]

[156] An interesting case arises where a business is 'parked' with an interim buyer, often a bank, on the basis of an agreement providing for the future onward sale of that business to an ultimate acquirer. In such circumstances, the first transaction is undertaken only to facilitate the second transaction, as the first buyer is 'directly linked to the ultimate acquirer'. Accordingly, the Consolidated Notice provides that, in such circumstances, the Commission will examine the acquisition of control by the ultimate acquirer, as provided for in the agreements entered into by the parties, and will consider the transaction by which the interim buyer acquires control as the first step of a single concentration comprising the lasting acquisition of control by the ultimate buyer.[221] This interpretation of the Merger Regulation is designed to end the possibility for companies to implement warehousing agreements which involve the temporary transfer of a business to an interim buyer as a means to enable the seller of that business to receive without undue delay the purchase payment from the interim buyer. The Commission implemented this reading of the Merger Regulation by fining Canon in June 2019 EUR29 m for 'gun-jumping' by acquiring control of Toshiba Medical Systems Corporation (TMSC) before it had secured approval under the Merger Regulation.[222] In an effort to meet Toshiba's financing needs at the time and allow it to receive the full purchase price for TMSC prior to receiving the Commission's approval for the acquisition, Canon paid EUR5.3 bn for a 5% shareholding in TMSC and 'parked' the remaining 95% shareholding with an interim buyer that paid EUR800 for its shares, which Canon had an option to acquire following receipt of the Commission's approval. Rejecting Canon's argument that the two transactions were not inter-conditional, the Commission determined that the interim 'warehousing' transaction was: (i) closely connected to Canon's ultimate acquisition of control, (ii) was a necessary step to achieve that change in control, and (iii) had been undertaken solely for that purpose. Accordingly, the interim and ultimate transactions constituted parts of a single reportable concentration, and, by implementing the interim transaction prior to the Commission's approval decision, Canon acted at least negligently in infringing the Merger Regulation's prohibition of 'gun-jumping'. This view of the Merger Regulation was confirmed by the General Court on 18 May 2022 which

220 Consolidated Notice at para. 34.

221 Consolidated Notice at para. 35.

222 Case M.8179 *Canon/Toshiba Medical Systems Corporation*.

ruled that the Commission was entitled to rely on the argument that Canon partially implemented the acquisition when it acquired a 5% stake in TMSC in 2016 plus a share option to buy the remaining 95%.[223]

4.5 Transactions Not Regarded as Concentrations

[157] Article 3(5) of the Merger Regulation identifies three situations where the acquisition of control will not constitute a concentration within the meaning of Article 3(1). These exceptions are interpreted restrictively and are designed to exclude transactions which have neither the object nor effect of exercising control over the target company:

(a) temporary acquisitions of less than one year by insurance companies, credit institutions or other financial institutions, where the securities have been acquired with a view to reselling (so-called warehousing agreements).[224] Voting rights may not be exercised other than as preparation for the sale of all or part of that undertaking or of its assets and securities. The period of sale may be extended by the Commission if the sale could not be reasonably carried out within a year (Article 3(5)(a)). Rescue operations by financial institutions prior to resale of the company will normally fall within the scope of the Merger Regulation since the process normally exceeds the one-year period permitted under Article 3(5)(a) of the Merger Regulation;
(b) liquidations and similar proceedings (Article 3(5)(b)) – this exception is intended to exclude from the Merger Regulation the situation where a liquidator or administrator acquires control acting in that capacity;[225] and
(c) acquisitions by financial holding companies for the purpose of managing an investment only. For this to apply, voting rights must only be exercised in order to maintain the full value of the investments and not to determine directly or indirectly the competitive conduct of those undertakings (Article 3(5)(c)).[226]

[158] In addition, the following transactions will not be regarded as concentrations:

(a) joint ventures which are not full-function, i.e., which do not perform all the functions of an autonomous economic entity; and

[223] *See* case T-609/19 *Canon v. Commission*.

[224] Consolidated Notice, para. 110.

[225] Consolidated Notice, para. 112. However, the sale of the undertaking by the office-holder to a third party will be subject to the Merger Regulation where applicable. For instance, in case M.573 *ING/Barings*, the acquisition by ING of substantially all the assets of Barings from its administrators was considered a concentration and notified to the Commission.

[226] Consolidated Jurisdictional Notice, para. 113.

(b) short-term joint ventures (e.g., less than three years and in certain circumstances less than five years) which are set up for a specific project without ongoing operational responsibility.

5 SCOPE OF APPLICATION: 'COMMUNITY DIMENSION'

[159] Article 1 of the Merger Regulation provides that it will apply to mergers, acquisitions and other forms of concentrations which have a *'Community dimension'*. Community dimension is defined by reference to: (i) the levels of turnover of the undertakings concerned in a concentration; and (ii) the origin of that turnover, i.e., where it is generated. The jurisdictional test therefore relates only to the economic size of the parties and not to their market power or whether the effects of the concentration will be felt mainly within the Community. Concentrations with a Community dimension are subject to scrutiny by the Commission under the Merger Regulation, and not by NCAs under Member States' national merger control regimes. On the other hand, concentrations which have no Community dimension should be subject only to national controls.[227]

[160] Reappointed as the EU's Competition Commissioner for a second term in December 2019, Commissioner Vestager identified as one of her priorities to explore the ways in which competition policy should evolve to promote innovation in the digital sector. In particular, the 'Competition policy for the digital era' report prepared by three special advisers, appointed by Commissioner Vestager, advocated significant changes to EU merger control.[228] However, rather than suggesting a change of the notification thresholds or obligation, the advisers considered that the Commission should focus on new theories of harm and anticompetitive strategies. The report focuses on instances where a dominant platform, which benefits from strong positive network effects and data access, acquires a target with a currently low or inexistent turnover but a large user base and a high future market potential (so-called killer acquisitions).

[161] The question of 'killer acquisitions' has been in the centre of some of the EU Member States' concerns. The competition authorities of Belgium, the Netherlands and Luxembourg hinted at the fact that this sort of transaction might be escaping regulatory scrutiny altogether since start-ups do not generate revenues that would meet the current jurisdictional thresholds. However, echoing the 'Competition policy for the digital era', Commissioner Vestager highlighted that it was not the moment to change the existing Merger Regulation's thresholds (presumably because

[227] Pursuant to Art. 4(5) of the Merger Regulation, a concentration may be notified to the Commission if it would otherwise be subject to the merger control regimes of at least three Member States. However, there is no automatic extension of the Commission's jurisdiction in those circumstances. The notifying parties must take the initiative and make a reasoned submission using Form RS to the Commission that it should examine the concentration. This mechanism will be explained in more detail below at section 'Referrals to the Commission'.

[228] *See* https://ec.europa.eu/competition/publications/reports/kd0419345enn.pdf.

the required unanimity among Member States was unattainable) and that the experience of Germany and Austria, who introduced transaction value-based thresholds, should be monitored.[229]

[162] Nonetheless, in an effort to close what is perceived to be an enforcement gap around such killer acquisitions, in March 2021, the Commission adopted a radically new approach towards the use of the referral mechanism set out in Article 22 of the EU Merger Regulation. Without making any changes to the EU Merger Regulation (which would require the unanimity of Member States), the Commission now interprets Article 22 as allowing it to call in for approval transactions which do not qualify for review under national merger control regimes in Member States. In its Guidance Paper, the Commission indicated that it is targeting deals where turnover values do not reflect accurately the actual or future competitive potential of a business, and where the deal consideration is high compared to the current turnover of a target business.[230] The Article 22 Guidance also explains that referrals may be made in relation to both proposed and completed transactions.[231] The Commission supplemented its Article 22 Guidance in December 2022 by publishing a Q&A guidance note. The Q&A note provides guidance on which cases are typically suitable for referral as well as the Commission's process for reviewing requests by merging parties or third parties to determine whether cases are suitable for referral under Article 22. The Q&A note puts flesh on the bones of the Commission's new review system.

[163] While the additional guidance provides numerous hypothetical examples of cases suitable for referral under Article 22, the added value is very much on how the Commission has sketched out the notification process and in particular the voluntary consultation process including the fact that:

- the process starts with a submission of a case team allocation request and, consistent with formal filings under the merger regulation, can be started on the basis of a good faith intention to conclude an agreement (e.g., based on an MoU). This means the process cannot be run anonymously or hypothetically;
- the briefing paper used for this purpose should include information on: (i) the parties' activities and turnover; (ii) the transaction status (i.e., whether it has closed already), value, structure, rationale and associated documents; (iii) the relevant markets and the competition situation on these markets; and (iv) interactions with NCA (e.g., whether the merging parties have been in contact with NCA and whether the parties are willing to allow the Commission to speak to national authorities);

[229] It should be noted that, as part of the Digital Services Act and Digital Markets Act, the largest tech companies that are designated by the Commission as gatekeepers are required to inform the Commission of the acquisitions they make, regardless of whether those transactions meet the merger control thresholds – as long as "*the merging entities or the target of concentration provide core platform services or any other services in the digital sector or enable the collection of data*" (Art. 14(1) DMA).

[230] *See,* https://ec.europa.eu/competition/consultations/2021_merger_control/guidance_article_22_referrals.pdf.

[231] On 20 Apr. 2021, the first referral under this revised system was accepted by the Commission in relation to the proposed acquisition of the US-based healthcare company GRAIL by Illumina, Inc.

- while there is no legal deadline for the Commission to revert, the Commission commits that it will normally conduct a review of the briefing paper within five working days from receipt to confirm whether it has further questions or not;
- at the request of the merging parties, the Commission 'may' provide an 'early indication' that the relevant transaction does not appear to be a suitable candidate for referral under Article 22. The upshot of the process should be an informal nod with regard to the likelihood of a 'call in'.

[164] The Q&A guidance also sets out how third parties can complain about transactions that are potentially eligible for referral for Article 22.

5.1 Turnover Thresholds

[165] The Merger Regulation establishes the Commission's jurisdiction on the basis of two sets of thresholds, each of which is based on the turnover generated by the parties to a concentration. Hence, Community dimension will exist only if the concentration satisfies one of the two following sets of turnover-related criteria:

First set:

(i) the combined aggregate worldwide turnover of all the undertakings concerned is more than EUR5 000 m (Article 1(2)(a));
(ii) the aggregate Community-wide turnover of each of at least two of the undertakings concerned is more than EUR250 m (Article 1(2)(b));
(iii) each of the undertakings concerned does *not* achieve more than two-thirds of its aggregate Community-wide turnover within one and the same Member State (Article 1(2), last paragraph) (the so-called two-thirds rule).

Second set (Article 1(3)):[232]

(i) the combined aggregate worldwide turnover of the undertakings concerned is more than EUR2 500 m;
(ii) in each of at least three Member States, the combined aggregate turnover of all the undertakings concerned is more than EUR100 m;
(iii) in each of at least three Member States included for the purpose of point (ii), the aggregate turnover of each of at least two of the undertakings concerned is more than EUR25 m;
(iv) the aggregate Community-wide turnover of each of at least two of the undertakings concerned is more than EUR100 m; and
(v) each of the undertakings concerned does *not* achieve more than two-thirds of its Community-wide turnover within one and the same Member State.

[232] This second set of turnover thresholds was introduced by Council Regulation 1310/97 OJ 1997 L180/1 of 30 Jun. 1997 to include concentrations that otherwise would have to be notified in several Member States.

[**166**] The turnover test is of particular importance because it is the absolute arbiter of jurisdiction. It provides a straightforward, practical means to assess whether a planned acquisition falls within the Commission's competence under the Merger Regulation, or national authorities' competence under domestic merger control laws. Generally speaking, the interpretation and application of the turnover criteria is now well established and understood which is reflected in the virtual absence of Article 6(1)(a) decisions (i.e., only four cases) over the last two decades. In March 1998, the Commission introduced the Turnover Notice aimed at clarifying certain procedural and technical questions that often arise when applying the turnover tests. This notice has been updated and incorporated in the Consolidated Notice.

[**167**] The application of these provisions is illustrated by Tables 1 to 3.

Table 1 Acquisition of B's Entire Share Capital by A

EUR (m)	*France*	*Germany*	*Italy*	*EU*	*World*
A	400	300	300	1 000	4 000
B	300	450	250	1 000	2 500
Total	700	750	550	2 000	6 500

This transaction would have a Community dimension because:

(1) the combined aggregate worldwide turnover of the undertakings concerned exceeds EUR5 000 m;
(2) the aggregate Community-wide turnover of each of the two undertakings concerned exceeds EUR250 m; and
(3) neither of the undertakings concerned achieves more than two-thirds of its aggregate Community-wide turnover within one and the same Member State.

Table 2 Acquisition of B's Entire Share Capital by A

EUR (m)	*France*	*Germany*	*Italy*	*EU*	*World*
A	80	50	65	195	2 000
B	35	60	40	135	1 300
Total	115	110	105	330	3 300

This transaction would have a Community dimension because:

(1) the combined aggregate worldwide turnover of the undertakings concerned exceeds EUR2 500 m;
(2) the aggregate Community-wide turnover of each of the two undertakings concerned exceeds EUR100 m;
(3) the combined aggregate turnover of the undertakings concerned in each of at least three Member States (France, Germany and Italy) exceeds EUR100 m;
(4) in the same three Member States, each of the two undertakings concerned has a turnover of more than EUR25 m; and
(5) neither of the undertakings concerned achieves more than two-thirds of its Community-wide turnover within one and the same Member State.

Table 3 Acquisition of B's Entire Share Capital by A

EUR (m)	*France*	*Germany*	*Italy*	*EU*	*World*
A	100	800	100	1 000	4 000
B	150	750	100	1 000	2 500
Total	250	1 550	200	2 000	6 500

[168] This transaction would not have a Community dimension as all the undertakings concerned achieve more than two-thirds of their Community-wide turnover within one and the same Member State, i.e., Germany. However, it must be remembered that even if the Article 1(3) thresholds are not met, the merging parties may be able to employ the Article 4(5) mechanism so that their concentration is deemed to have a Community dimension and reviewed by the Commission.

5.1.1 Definition of Turnover

[169] Article 5 of the Merger Regulation contains complex provisions in relation to the manner in which turnover should be calculated.[233] Generally, turnover is the total sum derived by each of the *'undertakings concerned'* in the preceding financial year. This comprises the sale of products and the provision of services falling within the undertakings' ordinary activities, after the deduction of sales rebates, value-added tax and other taxes directly related to turnover. This is considered to be a fair reflection of the economic strength of the undertakings concerned. The Commission normally bases its assessment on the audited accounts from the last

[233] *See also* Consolidated Notice at para. 157 onwards.

financial year. However, it may take more recent figures into account if they are in final form and would affect the jurisdictional question.[234]

[170] The turnover thresholds are also designed to take account of the economic strength of the undertakings concerned at the time of the operation that triggered notification under the Merger Regulation. As a result, the turnover of the acquirer(s) and the target must be adjusted to take account of acquisitions, disposals and entry into joint ventures that have taken place between the last audited accounts and the triggering date. Furthermore, where a divestiture or closure of an existing operation is an irrevocable pre-condition for the notified transaction, adjustments should also be made to exclude this turnover from the operation.[235] Relevant turnover does not include turnover resulting from transactions with other members of the group as defined in Article 5(4) (intra-group transactions) or turnover that does not relate to the part of the business to be acquired.[236] The turnover to be taken into account is the total turnover generated by the group to which the undertaking concerned belongs, and it is not limited to the turnover of the company making the acquisition. However, when calculating the turnover of the target company, the turnover of the vendor will not be taken into account.

[171] The calculation of turnover for the purpose of evaluating whether a concentration has the necessary Community dimension will require detailed accountancy work, as companies generally do not have turnover data readily available. Acquiring companies may find it useful to maintain up-to-date accounts for the group as a whole (as defined in Article 5(4)) which provide the necessary information regarding aggregate worldwide turnover, Community-wide turnover, and turnover in each of the Member States.

5.1.2 Rules for Specific Sectors

[172] Where credit institutions, other financial institutions or insurance undertakings are involved in a concentration, their actual turnover is considered to be an inappropriate method of evaluating whether the transaction has the necessary Community dimension. The Merger Regulation sets out special rules for the calculation of turnover in these cases. Article 5(3)(a) provides that for credit and other financial institutions, in place of turnover, the Commission will calculate banking

---

[234] Case M.3986 *Gas Natural/Endesa* which was confirmed by the General Court judgment in case T-417/05 *Endesa v. Commission* [2006] ECR II-2533.

[235] In case M.1741 *MCI WorldCom/Sprint* the parties argued that the turnover of Sprint's share of joint venture Global One should be excluded as it was about to withdraw from Global One. However, at the date of signing of the merger (or the mandatory notification date) the withdrawal from Global One was not completed, nor was it an irrevocable condition precedent of the transaction.

[236] In case M.156 *Cereol/Continentale Italiana*, Cereol, a subsidiary of Ferruzzi, acquired parts of the business of Continentale Italiana (in particular the business related to the grinding of oil seeds, the refining and marketing of vegetable oil and the stocking of grain). The Commission found that the operation did not have a Community dimension because financial aid granted by the EU, which the parties included in calculating the turnover of Continentale, could not be taken into account as this aid was not granted for the benefit of oil crushers (such as Continentale) but for the benefit of seed producers and was linked to the latter's sales.

income taking the following into account: interest (and similar income); income from securities; commissions receivable; net profit on financial operations; and other operating income.[237] This is based on the format of banks' profit and loss accounts under the Directive on Annual Accounts of Banks and other Credit Institutions.[238]

[173] In the case of insurance undertakings, the value of gross premiums underwritten is used rather than turnover. This figure will comprise all amounts received and receivable in respect of insurance contracts issued by or on behalf of the insurance undertakings. This includes outgoing reinsurance premiums but not taxes and parafiscal contributions or levies charged by reference to the amounts of individual premiums or the total value of premiums. As regards the assessment of whether the turnover thresholds under Article 1(2)(b), 1(3)(b), (c) and (d) are exceeded (and for calculating total Community-wide turnover for the purposes of the two-thirds rule) the value of the gross premiums received from Community residents is to be used rather than turnover. Similarly, in assessing whether the two-thirds rule is satisfied, the value of the gross premiums received from the residents of the particular Member State will constitute the turnover derived from that Member State, as stated by the Commission in cases M.5384 *BNP Paribas/Fortis* and M.5083 *Groupama/OTP Garancia*. In cases of financial institutions which have businesses across the banking, insurance and industrial sectors, different criteria will be applied for the calculation of the turnover derived from each different business.

[174] Specific issues may arise in the case of acquisitions of control by investment funds and private equity funds as these funds are often set up in the legal form of limited partnerships. In this type of entity, investors participate as limited partners and normally do not exercise control, either individually or collectively. Investment funds usually acquire the shares and voting rights which confer control over their portfolio companies. Depending on the circumstances, control is normally exercised by the investment company which has set up the fund as the fund itself is typically a mere investment vehicle. In such cases, only the turnover of the investment company which exercises control over the fund will be taken into account.[239] The turnover attributed to the limited partners will be excluded from the turnover calculation. Likewise, if an investment company sets up several investment funds (possibly with different investors), the investment company will indirectly have the power to exercise the voting rights held by the investment funds in their respective portfolio companies. Consequently, the turnover of all portfolio companies held by different funds is taken into account for the purpose of assessing whether the turnover thresholds in Article 1 of the Merger Regulation are met in the case that the investment company acquires indirect control of a portfolio company via one of its funds.

---

237 Case M.5363 *Santander/Bradford & Bingley Assets*.

238 Council Directive 86/635, OJ 1986 L372/1.

239 Consolidated Notice at paras 189–191.

5.1.3 Successive Transactions

[175] Sometimes, certain successive transactions are only individual parts of a wider strategy between the same parties. Considering each transaction alone, even if only to determine jurisdiction, would be to ignore economic reality and would eventually circumvent the application of the Merger Regulation. As a result, Article 5(2), second paragraph, provides that '*two or more transactions within the meaning of the first subparagraph which take place within a two-year period between the same persons or undertakings shall be treated as one and the same concentration arising on the date of the last transaction*'. The Commission has applied this provision mainly in three situations:

(1) where a first transaction is not notifiable but the second meets the Merger Regulation's thresholds (either alone or with the turnover derived from the first transaction), the Commission requires a notification on the occasion of the second transaction;[240]
(2) where a first transaction is notifiable under the Merger Regulation but not a subsequent transaction, the Commission requires a second notification even if it falls below the turnover thresholds and relates to a different business from the first transaction;[241] or
(3) where parts of a company have been simultaneously acquired by the same purchaser from the same seller, the Commission considers those acquisitions to constitute a single concentration and aggregates the turnovers of the various acquired parts to assess whether the transaction has a community dimension.[242]

5.1.4 Geographic Allocation of Turnover

[176] In an evaluation of turnover in either the Community as a whole or in any particular Member State, Article 5(1) of the Merger regulation provides that such turnover '*shall comprise products sold and services provided to undertakings or consumers, in the Community or in that Member State, as the case may be*'. Through various decisions, the Commission has affirmed that Article 5 of the Merger Regulation sets out the rules governing the calculation of turnover with a view to determining whether or not the transaction under scrutiny has a Community dimension within the

240 *See* case M.2639 *Compass/Restorama/Rail Gourmet/Gourmet Nova* where Compass acquired sole control through three separate acquisitions, first of Gourmet Nova Finland OY, then part of the business of Gourmet Nova UK Limited and lastly of Restorama and Rail Gourmet. The latter acquisition brought the three transactions within the Community dimension thresholds and was deemed to constitute a single concentration within the meaning of Art. 3(1)(b) of the Merger Regulation. Also cases M.1630 *Air Liquide/BOC* and M.4082 *Cargill/Pagnan II*.

241 *See* case M.4094 *Ineos/BP Dormagen* where Ineos' acquisition of BP's olefins and refining business was reportable under the Merger Regulation in Nov. 2005. When Ineos agreed to buy BP's ethylene business in December 2005, the Commission aggregated the revenues of that business to BP's olefins and refining business and consequently required a second notification. *See also* cases M.6537 *Faurecia/Plastal*; M.224 *Volvo/Lex* and M.261 *Volvo/Lex II*.

242 *See* cases M.1283 *Volkswagen/Rolls-Royce/Cosworth* and M.289 *PepsiCo/KAS*.

meaning of Article 1. The rule contained in Article 1(2) and 1(3) aims in particular at measuring the impact of the concentration in the Community in order to exclude from the scope of the Merger Regulation those concentrations between companies which do not have an appreciable commercial activity in more than one Member State.

[177] As a general principle, the Merger Regulation requires that turnover is allocated not by the location of the seller of the product or the provider of the service but by the *location of the consumer* of the product or service. This location is normally also the place where the service is actually provided and the product delivered. This is deemed to provide the best indication of where competition to achieve the actual sale takes place and where competition with alternative suppliers takes place.[243] In the sale of mobile goods such as cars, the location where the car is actually delivered to the customer is decisive, even if such sale is concluded over the phone or by internet. For example, if a Belgian consumer travels to a car showroom based in France and purchases a car there, the turnover of that sale is allocated to France, whereas if the purchase is made by phone from Belgium and the car is delivered there, the turnover will be allocated to Belgium.

[178] The Consolidated Notice also provides an example in relation to advertising and package holidays where the service may be sold through intermediaries[244] and states that competition for the sale of holidays through travel agents takes place locally, even though the service may be provided in a number of distant locations. As a result, turnover is treated as being earned locally. In case of any doubt, an approach can be made to DG Comp for advice on the correct method of calculation.

[179] It is not always easy for parties to obtain figures on the geographical breakdown of their turnover. The notes to company accounts may give some geographical breakdown, but commonly they are insufficient for the purposes of applying the thresholds of the Merger Regulation.[245] The Consolidated Notice states that, in the absence of figures in the audited accounts, the Commission *'will rely on the best figures available provided by the companies in accordance with the rule laid down in Article 5(1)'*.[246]

[180] Special difficulties have arisen in the geographical allocation of airlines' turnover. In its review of Ryanair's three attempts to acquire Aer Lingus,[247] the Commission followed its traditional approach used in several of its early decisions (cases M.130 *Delta/Pan Am*, M.157 *Air France/Sabena* and M.259 *British Airways/TAT*)

---

[243] Consolidated Notice at para. 196.

[244] *See* Judgment T-417/05, *Endesa v. Commission* [2006] ECR II-2533 which indicates that an undertaking will normally not act as an intermediary if it sells products via a commercial act which involves a transfer of ownership.

[245] Article 49 of the Fourth Company Law Directive requires the following information: *'the net turnover within the meaning of Article 28, broken down by categories of activity and into geographical markets in so far as, taking account of the manner in which the sale of products and the provision of services falling within the company's ordinary activities are organised, these categories and markets differ substantially from one another'*.

[246] Consolidated Notice at para. 195.

[247] Cases M.4439 *Ryanair/Aer Lingus I;* M.5434 *Ryanair/Aer Lingus II* and M.6663 *Ryanair/Aer Lingus III*.

by outlining the three methods of calculating the turnover generated by an airline. Hence, the turnover generated by an airline can be attributed:

(i) to the final destination point of the flight. In the event of a return flight, the country of destination is the one outside the home country of the airline (e.g., in the case of a route New York/Paris/New York served by a US carrier, the revenue is attributed to France);
(ii) on a 50/50 basis between the country of origin and the country of final destination; or
(iii) to the country where the ticket sale took place.

[181] The Commission has shown a preference for the point-of-sale method and the 50/50 method,[248] although in most cases, both tests lead to the same conclusions.

[182] In the three *Ryanair/Aer Lingus* cases, the method of calculating the turnover was determinative of whether the Commission had jurisdiction over the concentration concerned rather than the Irish authority. In that case, the Commission departed from option (iii), the point of sale of the ticket, since, with tickets on point-to-point or low-cost carriers being purchased predominantly via the internet, it was impractical to retain the point-of-sale approach. This would also have led to the Commission being deprived of its jurisdiction, given that both carriers generated more than two-thirds of their turnover in Ireland. Instead, the Commission considered both the place of departure approach and the 50/50 allocation. Given that both methodologies gave the Commission jurisdiction, it was not found necessary to decide between them. However, the Commission still required the turnover information to be provided in both formats. Nevertheless, it is worthy to note that the 50/50 allocation is still the preferred approach for mergers between network carriers involving international flights where return tickets are usually involved.[249]

[183] Similar issues have been considered in relation to telecom services. In case M.856 *British Telecom/MCI (II)*, the Commission stated that there were various possible approaches to the question of geographical allocation of turnover earned by telephone companies on international calls. In this case, the revenues of a US-based company, MCI, were treated for accounting purposes as being earned in

[248] For example, in case M.616 *Swissair/Sabena (II)*, the European Commission allocated the turnover on the basis of the point-of-sale method although it also found that the merger would have a Community dimension on the basis of the 50/50 method. In case M.857 *British Airways/Air Liberté*, the European Commission stated in a footnote to the decision that the geographic allocation of turnover was made on the basis of the point-of-sale method as well as the 50/50 method. A similar approach was taken in case M.2041 *United Airlines/US Airways*. In case M.1626 *SAIR Group/SAA*, the geographic allocation for the turnover achieved by air transport activities was stated as being made according to the *'point of sales method'* only. More recently, in case M. 10149 *Korean Air Lines/Asiana Airlines*, the parties' revenue was assessed pursuant to the 50/50 split methodology (as under the 'point of sale' and 'the point of departure' methodologies the proposed transaction did not meet the thresholds of the Merger Regulation).

[249] *See*, for more recent example, cases M.5181 *Delta Air Lines/Northwest Airlines*; M.5830 *Olympic/Aegean Airlines;* M.5889 *United Air Lines/Continental Airlines*; M.6447 *IAG/BMI*; M.8361 *Qatar Airways/Alisarda/Meridiana*; M.8672 *Easyjet/Certain Air Berlin Assets*; M.8964 *Delta/Air France-KLM/Virgin Group/Virgin Atlantic* and M.9287 *Connect Airways/Flybe*.

the US. However, the parties provided figures to the Commission based on different calculation methodologies, in all of which MCI's Community-wide turnover exceeded EUR250 m. In case M.366 *Alcatel/STC*, the parties included all turnover earned from any submarine telecommunication system which had at least one direct physical link in the Community. However, the Commission rejected this approach and instead apportioned turnover based on the place of establishment of the undertaking owning an individual share of a submarine cable. The market for which turnover had to be judged was not the service of conveying messages via undersea cables but the supply of capacity on such cables by the owners and operators.

[184] The Consolidated Notice indicates that in relation to telecom cases 'the qualification of call termination services may raise problems. Although call termination would appear to fall into the third category, there are reasons to treat it differently. Call termination services are provided, e.g., in situations where a call, originating from a European operator, is being terminated in the United States. Although neither the European nor the US operator travels, the signal travels and the service is provided by the US network to the European operator in the United States. This is also the place where competition takes place (if any). The turnover is therefore to be considered as non-Community turnover'.[250]

[185] In the case of credit or financial institutions, the Consolidated Notice states that the location of the branch of the credit or financial institution receiving the income will determine the geographical allocation of turnover (and not the residence of the credit or financial institution's customers) (Article 5(3)(a)).

5.2 Identifying the Undertakings Concerned

[186] The concept of *'undertaking concerned'* is central to determining whether a concentration is notifiable under the Merger Regulation. The undertakings concerned are those entities whose turnovers are combined or merged by the concentration.[251] Given that control can be exercised jointly, there may be more than one undertaking concerned on the acquiring side. On the other side of the transaction, the seller of a business will not constitute an undertaking concerned unless it retains control jointly with another undertaking. The acquired business alone will be the undertaking concerned.[252]

[187] Take, for example, a transaction where AB, a joint venture between undertaking A and undertaking B, acquires control of undertaking C. Undertaking A and B are major industrial companies with significant turnover earned in operations throughout the Community. Their turnover figures are mentioned in Table 4.

[250] *See* para. 183.
[251] Consolidated Notice at para. 131.
[252] Consolidated Notice at para. 177.

Table 4 AB, a Joint Venture of A and B, Acquires Control of C

Undertaking	*Worldwide Turnover (EUR)*	*Community-Wide Turnover (EUR)*
A	2 500 m	325 m
B	3 000 m	300 m
AB	60 m	60 m
C	50 m	40 m

[188] If undertakings A and B are themselves identified as *'undertakings concerned'*, the acquisition will have a Community dimension: their combined aggregate worldwide turnover exceeds EUR5 000 m (Article 1(2)(a)); and each of at least two of the undertakings concerned has a Community-wide turnover of more than EUR250 m (Article 1(2)(b)). However, if AB is the undertaking concerned, and the turnover of undertakings A and B is brought into account only by virtue of the operation of Article 5(4), the acquisition of C will not have a Community dimension: in fact, there will only be two undertakings concerned, AB and C, and only one of these, AB, has (by virtue of aggregation under Article 5(4)) a Community-wide turnover of more than EUR100 m under the threshold laid down under Article 1(3)(d). This example shows how crucial it is, in applying the Merger Regulation, to identify correctly the undertakings concerned.

[189] The Consolidated Notice provides guidance in order to identify the undertakings concerned in the most frequent types of operations that the Commission has dealt with so far. The concept of an undertaking is a familiar one in EU jurisprudence, and has been considered by the ECJ on several occasions.[253] Broadly speaking, it means an autonomous economic entity, which entails that an undertaking might be a single company, a group of companies, a joint venture, a partnership or an individual, depending, in each case, on whether the entity has economic autonomy.

[190] In the case of a merger, the undertakings concerned will be each of the undertakings that are merging. The position is more difficult to assess in the remaining cases where the concept of acquisition of control, under Article 3(1), determines which are the undertakings concerned. For example:

253 *See* the General Court Judgment in case T-102/92 *Viho v. Commission* [1995] ECR II-17, which considered whether the Parker Pen group in the EU constituted one or more economic units capable of operating intra-group arrangements falling within Art. 101 of the TFEU. This case has important implications for international groups. For more recent applications of the Viho principle *see* case T-41/96 *Bayer AG v. Commission* [2000] ECR II-3383, para. 175 and case T-203/01 *Michelin v. Commission* [2003] ECR II-4071, para. 290. On the separate question of offering goods or services on the market *see* case C-205/03 *FENIN v. Commission* [2006] ECR I-6295.

- in the case of an acquisition of sole control of a company, the undertakings concerned will be the acquiring company (including its entire corporate group) and the acquired or target company;
- in the case of an acquisition of sole control of part of a company, the undertakings concerned will be the acquirer (including its entire corporate group) and the acquired part(s) of the target company;
- where two companies exchange assets (regardless of whether the assets constitute legal entities or not), the acquisitions of control by each company over the other's assets are regarded as separate concentrations. In each case, the undertakings concerned are the acquiring company and the assets acquired.[254] One side of the swap may be a concentration with Community dimension while the other is not, even though the two halves of the transaction are interdependent and each conditional upon the other.[255] Similarly, in the case of a demerger or break-up of a joint venture, there will usually be more than one concentration due to the acquisition of control by each demerging party;[256]
- in the case of concentrations between the same undertakings that take place within a period of two years, the undertakings concerned are the acquirer and the different acquired parts of the target company taken as a whole;[257]
- in the case of acquisition of sole control over a previously jointly controlled entity, the undertakings concerned are the acquiring/remaining shareholder and the entity that was previously jointly controlled (in order to avoid double counting the turnover of the jointly controlled entity is excluded from that of the acquiring shareholder);[258]
- in the case of acquisition of joint control of a newly created company, the undertakings concerned are each of the companies acquiring control of the newly set up joint venture (which, as it does not yet exist, cannot yet be considered to be an undertaking concerned and furthermore it has no turnover of its own at this time);
- in the case of the acquisition of joint control of a pre-existing company, the undertakings concerned are each of the companies acquiring joint control on the one hand and the pre-existing acquired company on the other;[259]
- in the case of the acquisition of joint control of a company currently solely controlled, the undertakings concerned are each of the companies acquiring

[254] Consolidated Notice at paras 41, 148–150.

[255] For an actual example which led to a second stage examination, *see* case M.984 *DuPont/ICI*.

[256] In cases M.1820 *BP/JV Dissolution* and M.1822 *Mobil/JV Dissolution*, the Commission established that Exxon Mobil Corporation and BP Amoco plc had acquired, within the meaning of Art. 3(1)(b) of the Merger Regulation, control of parts of the BP/Mobil joint venture.

[257] In case M.5605 *Crédit Mutuel/Monabanq* Crédit Mutuel agreed to acquire Monabanq from the STET 3 Suisses International group six months after the Commission cleared Crédit Mutuel's acquisition of Cofidis from the same group (case M.5432 *Crédit Mutuel/Cofidis*). The Commission was competent to review the second transaction in light of the Community dimension of the original concentration. *See also* cases M.6537 *Faurecia/Plastal* and M.7473 *Zentraleuropa Lpg Holding/Total Hungaria*.

[258] Consolidated Notice at para. 188.

[259] Consolidated Notice at para. 140.

joint control. The pre-existing company is not an undertaking concerned, but its turnover is treated as part of its initial parent;

- in the case of acquisition of joint control by a joint venture, the situation is more complicated. The general rule is that a joint venture, when it is full-function, is the acquiring party and the undertakings concerned are therefore the joint venture (but not its parents individually) and the target company. However, where the joint venture can be regarded as a vehicle for an acquisition by its parents, the Commission will consider each of the parents rather than the joint venture to be the undertakings concerned, together with the target company. In any event, irrespective of the qualification of the undertaking concerned, the turnover of the parent companies of the joint venture carrying out the acquisition will be taken into account for the purpose of calculating the Community dimension; and
- in the case of an acquisition of control by a state-owned company, the turnover of a state enterprise will comprise the turnover of all undertakings *'making up an economic unit with an independent power of decision, irrespective of the way in which their capital is held or of the rules of administrative supervision applicable to them'*.[260] This principle was applied, for example, in case M.216 *CEA Industrie/France Telecom/Finmeccanica/SGS-Thomson*, where the atomic energy company and the telephone company were regarded as separate 'undertakings concerned' despite the fact that both were owned by the French state.[261] The Consolidated Notice now places more emphasis on state-owned companies being under *'the same centre of commercial decision-making'* in judging which companies make up the group for the purposes of Article 5 of the Merger Regulation.[262] In case M.6801 *Rosneft/TNK-BP*, the Commission attached particular importance to the existence of interlocking directorships between Rosneft and other Russian State-owned companies, and in its competitive assessment of the impact of the transaction, the Commission assumed that Rosneft and other Russian State-owned oil and gas companies constituted a single economic entity. Also, in case M.7850 *EDF/CGN/NNB Group of Companies*, the Commission examined to which extent China's State-owned Asset Supervision and Administration Commission (SASAC) exercised decisive influence over the commercial strategies of various other State-owned enterprises. This case concerned a joint venture formed to construct a nuclear power plant in the UK by Electricité de France S.A. (EDF) and China General Nuclear Power Corporation (CGN), a State-owned enterprise majority-owned by SASAC. Rejecting the merging companies' contention that CGN was independent of SASAC, the Commission identified various provisions of the State Asset Law that 'support the fact that Central SASAC has influence on CGN's major decision making' and, on that basis, found that CGN 'does not enjoy autonomy from the State in deciding major matters like strategy,

[260] Recital 22 of the Merger Regulation makes it clear that the control of concentrations will respect the principle of non-discrimination between the public and the private sectors, implying that a state company may constitute an undertaking concerned.

[261] *See also* decision cases M.4180 *Gaz de France/Suez* and M.5549 *EDF/Segebel*.

[262] Consolidated Notice at para. 194.

business plan or budget'. Accordingly, for purposes of assessing whether CGN's revenues satisfied the Merger Regulation's jurisdictional thresholds, the Commission took account of revenues generated by other Chinese State-owned enterprises controlled by SASAC and active in the energy sector.

[191] The vendor is not an undertaking concerned. As the Commission states in the Consolidated Notice, 'its role ends when the transaction is completed since, by definition, from the moment the seller has relinquished all control over the company, its links with it disappear'. However, an important exception to this is where the vendor retains joint control with the acquiring company as it will be considered to constitute one of the undertakings concerned.

5.2.1 Corporate Group Turnover

[192] Once the undertakings concerned have been identified in a given transaction, their turnover should be calculated, for the purposes of determining jurisdiction, in accordance with the rules set out in Article 5 of the Merger Regulation. In calculating the turnover of the *'undertakings concerned'* in the merger, the turnover of all members of the same group will be taken into account in accordance with the provisions of Article 5(4). This will include both the turnover of the bidding and target undertakings, as well as those undertakings over which they exercise control. Control will be deemed to exist where any of the undertakings concerned in the concentration directly or indirectly:

- owns more than half of the capital or business assets;
- has the power to exercise more than half of the voting rights;
- has the power to appoint more than half of the board; or
- has the right to manage the undertaking's affairs.[263]

[193] The turnover will also include that of undertakings which control the undertakings concerned (parents) and other undertakings which the parents also control (sister companies). In addition, in the case of joint ventures between undertakings concerned (or members of their group) and third parties, the practice of the Commission is to allocate to the undertaking concerned the turnover shared equally by all controlling companies in the joint venture.[264] This is based on the principle of Article 5(5)(b) which concerns sales between group joint ventures and third parties.[265] An example of the effect of these provisions is contained in Figure 1. Finally, the rules of Article 5(4) also have to be adapted in situations involving a change from joint to sole control in order to avoid double counting of the turnover of the joint venture. Even if the acquiring undertaking has rights or powers in the joint venture which satisfy the requirements of Article 5(4), the turnover of the acquiring shareholder has to be calculated without the turnover of the joint venture, and the turnover of the joint venture has to be taken without the turnover of the acquiring shareholder.

263 In practice this should include a situation of control solely on the basis of a blocking minority.

264 Consolidated Notice at para. 187.

265 *See* case M.1046 *Ameritech/Tele Danmark*.

Figure 1 Effect of Article 5(5)(b) Concerning Sales Between Group Joint Ventures and Third Parties

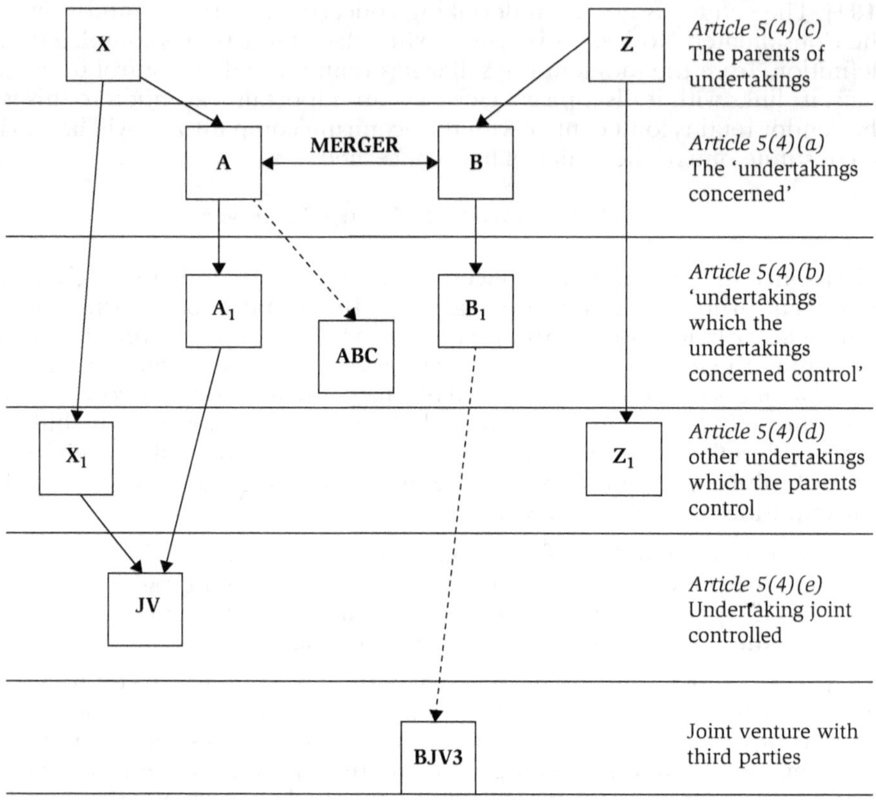

[194] In calculating the aggregate turnover for the purpose of assessing whether the merger of undertaking A with undertaking B (as set out in Figure 1) satisfies the various turnover-related criteria of Article 1 of the Merger Regulation, the turnover taken into account is as follows: the turnover of all the undertakings comprised in A's group (A, A1, X, X1, JV and ABC) together with that of B (B, B1, Z and Z1) and the appropriate proportion of the turnover of its joint venture BJV3 (in this case one-third since there are three shareholders with joint control).

[195] The aim of Article 5(4) is simply to identify the companies belonging to the groups of the undertakings concerned for the purposes of calculation of turnover. As a result, the test of being able to manage the undertaking's affairs in Article 5(4) is different from the test set out in Article 3(3) to establish whether there is an acquisition of control resulting in a concentration. The test under Article 5(4) is likely to take a wider view of what type of control exists in practice. In case M.126 *Accor/Wagon Lits*, the Commission included the turnover achieved by the operations of minority subsidiaries managed by Accor under hotel management contracts in the turnover figures for Accor even though such companies were not included in the consolidated accounts. The management contracts were for a period of ten years. Accor had full control of all policy decisions such as staffing. It operated the hotels under its own name and had pre-emption rights in the event of sale. Thus, the Commission described Accor as a fully fledged manager, and the owner's only contribution was that of providing the capital.[266] In case M.187 *IFINT/EXOR*, the Commission included in the turnover of EXOR a company in which EXOR held a 28.69% interest representing 33.29% of the voting rights. The Commission took account of the fact that at a previous AGM EXOR had held 52% of the votes actually present or represented.[267]

[196] The effect of the above has been to require companies proposing to merge or acquire other companies to look very carefully at which undertakings should be included in the turnover calculations. One cannot assume that a minority interest means that control within the meaning of Article 5(4) does not exist. All links in the corporate chain must be checked carefully, and where minority shareholdings exist, information must be obtained as to what proportion of votes cast at the last general meeting the minority shareholding represented.

[197] Special care must also be taken with regard to activities and businesses which have been acquired or disposed of since the latest audited accounts. If a company has disposed of certain activities, the turnover previously generated by such activities should not be taken into consideration for the purpose of the calculation of whether Community dimension exists. Conversely, where a business has been acquired since the accounts were prepared, the turnover attributable to that business must be added in the turnover calculation required under the Merger Regulation. It is suggested in such a case that the turnover to be taken into account will be that attributable to the acquired business as shown in the accounts of the vendor company for its financial year preceding that in which the concentration being notified occurred.[268]

[198] In circumstances where it is unclear whether or not a concentration satisfies the turnover-related criteria and consequently has a sufficient Community dimension to be required to comply with the onerous mandatory notification and suspensory provisions of the Merger Regulation, it is advisable to consult the Commission on a confidential basis and, if necessary, notify the concentration on a fail-safe basis. The Commission will be obliged to examine the notification and to conclude, within twenty-five working days from the day after receipt of the notification (or the day following receipt of complete information), whether the notified concentration has the necessary Community dimension (Articles 6(1)(a) and 10(1)).

[266] *See also* cases M.25 *Arjomari-Prioux SA/Wiggins Teape Appleton plc* and M.62 *Eridania/ISI*.
[267] *See* case M.147 *Eurocom/RSCG*.
[268] *See* case M.3564 *CVC/ANI Printing Inks* and M.3563 *CVC/BASF Printing Inks*.

6 PROCEDURE: NOTIFICATION

6.1 Prior Notification

[199] As set out in both the Merger Regulation and the Implementing Regulation, concentrations with a Community dimension require notification to the Commission prior to their implementation, following either the conclusion of the agreement, the announcement of the public bid or the acquisition of a controlling interest (Article 4(1)).[269] Article 7(2)(a) of the Merger Regulation states that notification should not be delayed despite there being no specific deadline, and Article 4(1) further encourages the parties to notify as early as possible, permitting notification following a good faith intention to conclude an agreement, or the announcement of a public bid.

[200] The Commission strongly encourages pre-notification contact by the parties of the transaction (such pre-notification contact presupposes that the parties have requested the Commission to designate a case team responsible for reviewing the transaction through the filing of the case allocation request form).[270] This allows the Commission to offer informal views on how the parties should move forward. Pre-notification contact also helps to identify significant issues and timing pressures on the transaction at an early stage, thereby enabling the possibility of a quicker turn-around for the case once notified. It also enables the Commission to organise its team and to indicate the type and quantity of data necessary in the notification to speed up the decision process.[271] The Commission is subject to strict confidentiality obligations throughout these pre-notification discussions. In particular, it must first obtain a waiver from the notifying parties before conducting an informal market test during these discussions – especially when the transaction has not yet been publicly announced.

[201] The particular importance of these pre-notification contacts is illustrated by the Commission's Best Practice Guidelines which indicate that the lack of, or limited amount of, pre-notification contacts is one of the main reasons for the Commission to declare a notification incomplete.[272]

[202] The Commission's Best Practice Guidelines provide that:

- It is always useful, even in seemingly non-problematic cases, to make pre-notification contact with the Commission. Pre-notification contact should preferably be initiated at the very least three weeks before the expected date

---

[269] The previously more rigid deadline of notification within one week was abolished as a result of the 2004 modernisation.

[270] http://ec.europa.eu/competition/mergers/case_allocation_request.rtf.

[271] In case M.7265 *Zimmer/Biomet* the transaction was initially notified on 3 Jun. 2014, without any pre-notification contacts. It was declared incomplete by the Commission, as it did not contain all information necessary for its assessment. Zimmer submitted the missing information and the notification was deemed effective only as of 29 Aug. 2014.

[272] DG Competition Best Practices on the conduct of EU merger control proceedings ('Best Practice Guidelines'), para. 7.

of notification. In cases which raise certain issues, a more protracted pre-notification period may well be appropriate and in the interests of the notifying parties such contacts should be initiated at least six weeks before the expected date of notification, with this period being substantially longer in more complex cases.[273] In all cases, it is advisable to make contact with the case team as soon as possible since this will facilitate the planning of the merger review process.

- Pre-notification contact should be initiated as soon as possible with a draft Form CO or a detailed briefing memorandum providing a brief background to the transaction, a brief description of the relevant sector(s) and market(s) involved, the likely impact of the transaction on competition in general terms and the case language. In 2008, the Commission introduced a standard form, the Case Allocation Request Form which is to be completed at the pre-notification stage and which requests the allocation of a case team. This form requires the provision of basic information concerning the parties to the concentration, the level of confidentiality required, the affected products or service, the complexity of the matter and finally the expected date of notification. This and subsequent submissions should be made in good time before any initial meeting.[274]
- Irrespective of whether pre-notification meetings have taken place or not, it is advisable that the notifying parties systematically provide a substantially complete draft Form CO (or Short Form CO) to the case team. The case team will in general require at least five working days to review the draft before commenting on the adequacy of the draft.
- At pre-notification meetings, a discussion should take place on what should and should not be included in the notification.[275] In some cases, it may be appropriate to request and obtain a waiver covering certain sections of the Form CO.[276] On 20 April 2023, the European Commission adopted a package of measures to simplify its procedures for reviewing concentrations under the Merger Regulation.[277] The package aims to reduce the burden on merging businesses and the Commission through simplification and expansion of the Commission's review of unproblematic mergers and reducing information requirements. The new rules set out to: (i) expand the number of cases that can benefit from the simplified procedure, (ii) streamline the

[273] For example, in case M.6266 *Johnson & Johnson/Synthes* the Form CO was filed five months after the transaction was announced. Similarly in case M.6844 *General Electric/Avio* the Form CO was filed five months after General Electronic announced that it had agreed to acquire Avio's aviation business. In case M.7932 *Dow/DuPont*, the Form CO was filed six months after the deal was announced. In case M.9076 *Novelis/Aleris* the transaction was filed with the Commission seven months after being announced and in case M. 9569 *EssilorLuxottica/GrandVision*, the Form CO was filed five months after announcement of the transaction. In case M.10149 *Korean Air Lines/Asiana Airlines* the transaction was notified to the Commission nearly 26 months after the parties had entered into a binding agreement relating to the contemplated transaction.

[274] Best Practice Guidelines, para. 14.

[275] Article 4(2) of the Implementing Regulation.

[276] Best Practice Guidelines, para. 19.

[277] https://ec.europa.eu/commission/presscorner/detail/en/ip_23_2357.

review of simplified and non-simplified cases, and (iii) establish electronic submissions as the default. In particular, the new rules introduce a new notification form for simplified cases that primarily includes multiple-choice questions on the jurisdictional and substantive assessment of cases. In addition, the Commission identifies a sub-category of 'super-simplified' treatment for: (i) cases involving a joint venture with no current or expected turnover within the EEA and no plans to move assets into the EEA and (ii) cases with no horizontal overlaps or non-horizontal relationships between the merging parties' activities. Transaction parties may also notify directly without pre-notification discussions. Furthermore, the Commission has also streamlined the notification form for non-simplified cases (Form CO), by clarifying waiver possibilities, providing tables for information on affected markets and eliminating certain information requirements, for instance, on cooperative agreements and trade associations. The package, which includes: (i) a revised Merger Implementation Regulation, (ii) a Notice on Simplified Procedure and (iii) a Communication on the transmission of documents will come into effect on 1 September 2023.

- Potentially affected markets should be openly discussed with the case team in good faith, even if the notifying parties take a different view from the case team on market definition. Furthermore, wherever there may be uncertainty or differences of view over market definitions, it would be prudent to produce market shares relating to various interpretations, e.g., by national markets as well as EU-wide.[278]
- Completing a Form CO to the case team's satisfaction, even for transactions that evidently raise no concerns, typically involves multiple rounds of questions and increasingly extensive information-gathering exercises, e.g., often including detailed market share estimates on numerous alternative bases and large volumes of the notifying parties' internal documents. In terms of timing, as pre-notification consultation is not a statutorily prescribed process, there is no time limit for its completion. Depending on the complexity of the case, pre-notification consultations can last as little as a few weeks or as long as several months (in exceptional cases, approaching a year or more).[279]
- A discussion on the other jurisdictions competent to review the proposed concentration should also take place. In this respect, the Commission encourages parties to supply in section 3 of the Form CO a list of the other jurisdictions where the concentration is subject to merger approval.[280] In cases which raise certain substantive issues, the Commission will usually request a waiver from the parties allowing the Commission to share certain

[278] *See* case M.4381 *JCI/FIAMM* where the market share information for the aftermarket battery market was provided both on a national and on a European basis. *See also* case M.8713 *Tata Steel/ThyssenKrupp/JV* where information on the markets for tinplate and ECCS was provided on a European, regional, national and local (i.e., smaller than a country) basis.

[279] *See*, for example, case M.8713 *Tata/ThyssenKrupp/JV* in which the pre-notification discussions lasted over a year. In case M.10149 *Korean Air Lines/Asiana Airlines*, the pre-notification period lasted close to two years.

[280] *See* para. 1.9 of the introduction of the Form CO.

information regarding the transaction with other competition agencies in order to facilitate international cooperation.

- Notifying parties and their advisers should take care to ensure that the information in their notification has been carefully prepared and verified. Contact details for customers and competitors should be carefully checked to ensure that the case team's investigation is not delayed, and the notification is not subsequently declared incomplete.[281]

[203] Following the submission of the notification, the Best Practice Guidelines advise regular State of Play meetings between the Commission and the notifying parties, which are voluntary in nature. The Commission regards that the objective of State of Play meetings is to contribute to the quality and efficiency of the decision-making process and to ensure transparency and communication between the case team and the notifying parties. The Commission uses State of Play meetings to raise concerns about the proposed merger and to request clarification on certain issues from the notifying parties. State of Play meetings held after the Statement of Objections is issued allow the notifying parties to seek clarification from the Commission with regard to the position it has adopted. The meetings are designed to encourage dialogue and establish frameworks for proceedings. Competitive analysis is employed to determine any effects the proposed merger may have on the Community and should any *'serious doubts'* arise, the Commission and the notifying parties are better placed to work together to ascertain the effectiveness and timing of possible remedies.

[204] At meetings in general (both at the pre-notification stage and during notification), the Commission prefers that cases are discussed with both legal advisers and business representatives who have a good technical understanding of the relevant markets. In more complex cases, the presence of an economist may also be warranted.[282]

6.1.1 Form CO and Short Form CO

[205] The Implementing Regulation sets out the requirements for notifications. The Implementing Regulation provides that notifications must be submitted in the manner prescribed by Form CO or Short Form CO, which are both annexed to the Implementing Regulation. Form CO and Short Form CO are not forms as such: instead, they set out what information must be supplied in order to constitute a *'notification'* for the purposes of the Merger Regulation. They also lay down the format in which such information should be provided.

[206] Article 4 of the Implementing Regulation provides that notifications must contain the information requested by the forms and that this information must be correct and complete. An obligation is imposed on the notifying parties to inform

[281] As mentioned above, the Commission may already conduct an informal market test during the pre-notification discussions. This informal market test may only be conducted after the Commission has obtained a waiver from the notifying parties – especially when the transaction has not yet been publicly announced.

[282] Best Practice Guidelines, para. 9.

the Commission without delay of any material changes which come to light following the notification which the parties know or ought to know and which would have had to be notified if known at the time of notification. Where information contained in the notification is incomplete in any material respect, the Commission is obliged to inform the notifying parties in writing without delay. In such cases, the notification only becomes effective (and the time limits only begin to run) from the date on which the complete information is received by the Commission.

[207] The forms require a comprehensive, if not exhaustive, statement of the facts, circumstances and potential consequences and effects of the concentration. The quantity of information needed can therefore impose a severe burden on notifying undertakings, and it is recommended that the preparation of the notification is commenced at the earliest possible stage of the deal. The Commission has the power under Article 4(2) of the Implementing Regulation to dispense with the obligation to provide any particular information requested by Form CO or Short Form CO where it considers that such information is not necessary for the examination of the case. The Commission has shown itself willing to use this provision to reduce the burden of information required, particularly in cases where there is no doubt that the Commission will decide after the preliminary twenty-five working days examination period that the concentration is compatible with the Internal Market and that there is therefore no need to initiate the Phase II proceedings.

[208] The scope of the Short Form CO notification is referred to in Article 3(1) of the Implementing regulation and set out in Annex 2 of the Implementing Regulation. It covers the following circumstances:[283]

(a) joint ventures of limited impact in the EU, specifically where the turnover of the joint venture and the total value of assets of the joint venture is less than EUR100 m within the EEA territory;
(b) where none of the parties to the concentration are active in horizontally or vertically related markets;
(c) where two or more parties are active in horizontally related markets have a combined market share of less than 20% or the increment of the Herfindahl – Hirschman Index is below 150 and the parties combined market share is below 50%;
(d) where two or more parties are active in vertically related markets but there is no individual or combined market share of 30% or above;
(e) where a party acquires sole control of an undertaking over which it already has joint control.

[209] If a transaction qualifies for treatment under the short-form procedure, the amount of information required from the parties under the full Form CO is limited significantly. In particular, the parties are exempt from providing information under sections 7, 8 and 9 of the full Form CO (*see* below). After two rounds of consultation in 2021 and 2022, the Commission, on 20 April 2023, published a package of reforms that, it claims, '*is expected to bring significant benefits for businesses and*

[283] In 2013, the Short Form procedure was significantly revised and expanded.

advisers in terms of preparatory work and related costs'. The reforms expand the scope of transactions that can benefit from a simplified 'Short Form CO' filing form, as well as streamlining the various filing forms and eliminating the need for filings to be submitted in paper format. The new simplified procedure will restrict the existing category relating to joint ventures, by introducing a requirement that the expected turnover of the JV in the next three years must also be less than EUR100 m, and that the assets to be taken into account when assessing the threshold include those that the parties plan to contribute to the JV in the future. It will also expand the definition of 'vertically-related' markets to include those where the upstream product is 'used directly' in the downstream firm's own production or is re-sold by the downstream firm, in contrast to the current simplified procedure which requires that such inputs must be 'important'. The most important change to the simplified procedure is the introduction of two new categories of transactions that qualify, in principle, for the simplified procedure. These are transactions where under all plausible market definitions:

- individual or combined upstream and downstream market shares of the merging parties are below 50%, the increment (delta) of the Herfindahl-Hirschman Index (HHI) resulting from the concentration on this market is below 150, and the company with the smallest market share is the same in the upstream and downstream markets; or
- the individual or combined upstream market share of the merging parties is below 30%, and their combined purchasing share is below 30%.

[210] The new simplified procedure also introduces a 'flexibility clause' which will allow notifying parties to ask for their transaction to be subject to the simplified procedure in cases where the thresholds for simplified treatment are only marginally exceeded (e.g., where they compete and have a market share of between 20 and 25%).

[211] At the same time, it expands the list of circumstances in which the Commission may exercise its discretion not to apply the simplified procedure (or to refuse to apply the flexibility clause), even though the relevant criteria are met, such as those in which there are non-controlling shareholding links between the parties and third-party competitors. Finally, the revised Notice foresees a 'super-simplified' procedure for transactions involving parties with no competitively related activities and extraterritorial JVs, which can be notified without any pre-notification discussions with the Commission.

[212] The new rules also introduce an entirely digital system for the submission of filings and other documents via the Commission's eTrustEx platform, with specifications for electronic signing of the relevant documents, abolishing the requirement for paper copies of filings to be delivered.

[213] The full Form CO is divided into 13 sections:

(a) Sections 1–4 require formal factual details of the undertakings and of the nature of the transaction being notified. The Commission always requires this information in order to determine whether the transaction is a concentration and whether that concentration has a Community dimension.

(b) Section 5 indicates the supporting documents (including internal confidential documents) to be provided by the notifying parties, to enable verification of the information provided in the other sections of the notification. The version of Form CO adopted in 2013 significantly increases the type of internal documents that must be provided to the Commission.

(c) Sections 6, 7 and 8 require information key to any analysis of the competitive effects of the concentration on markets in the EU. The level of detail required is extensive and should enable the Commission to decide whether or not to open proceedings without further data being required from the notifying parties. In straightforward cases, it is possible to obtain a waiver from the Commission for the provision of some of this information. In more complicated cases, however, the Commission may require additional information necessary to enable it to carry out its initial assessment. Section 6 requires a description of the relevant product and geographic markets, and of the markets affected by the notified concentration (i.e., where two or more parties are active in the same product market and the concentration will lead to a combined market of 20% or more (horizontal relationships), where one or more party is active in a product market upstream or downstream of a product market in which another party is active and any of their individual or combined market shares is 30% or more (vertical relationships), and where conglomerate effects may arise).[284] Parties must also provide information on the markets where: (i) either party has a share above 30% and the other party is a potential competitor, (ii) markets in which either party has a share above 30% and the other party holds substantial IP, and (iii) markets neighbouring those on which one party is active and on which the other party has a share above 30%. Sections 7 and 8 request market data (e.g., market size, description of competition, and market shares) in relation to the affected markets.

(d) Section 9 requests information pertaining to the structure of supply and demand in each of the affected markets. This includes, for example, explanations of how the parties and their main competitors produce and sell their respective products or services, the degree to which market actors are vertically integrated along the value chain, and the level of demand-side concentration.

(e) Section 10 covers information on product differentiation and closeness competition. To this end, notifying parties are required to provide, for example, information on how customer groups can be segmented and whether the parties' products are close substitutes. Section 10 also requests information on distribution systems prevailing in the relevant markets, recent examples

[284] A relevant product market comprises all goods and/or services which are regarded as interchangeable or substitutable by the consumer by reason of the product characteristics, prices and intended use. A relevant geographic market comprises the area in which the parties are involved in the supply of products and services, in which the conditions of competition are sufficiently homogeneous and which can be distinguished from neighbouring areas because, in particular, conditions of competition are appreciably different in those areas.

of market entry or exit, the importance of R&D, as well as contact details for the parties' main customers and competitors as well as recent and potential market entrants.

(f) Section 11 involves overall market context and efficiencies. In particular, it requires the parties to describe how the proposed concentration is likely to affect the interests of intermediate and ultimate customers, and the development of technical and economic progress. The option is also provided to detail any efficiency gains which will result from the transaction, and any resulting consumer benefits.[285]

(g) Section 12 requests information relating to the cooperative effects of a joint venture, and is directed at enabling the case team to apply Article 101 of the TFEU in accordance with Article 2(4) of the Merger Regulation.[286]

(h) Section 13 provides for a declaration by the parties that the information given in the notification is true, correct and complete.[287] Upon filing, such a declaration must be signed by the representatives of the notifying parties.

[214] The language of the notification must be one of the official languages of the Community, and this will be the language of the proceedings for the notifying parties. If the notification is made pursuant to the EEA Agreement, it may be submitted in one of the official languages of the EFTA States. On receipt of the notification, the Commission sends a copy of it to each of the twenty-eight Member States and ESA in order to obtain their views, with the other copies being required for the Commission services.

[215] The basic rule is that a notification must be made by the undertaking concerned who is acquiring the controlling interest for the purposes of Article 3(1)(b) of the Merger Regulation (or the bidder in the case of a public bid). In the case of a merger within the meaning of Article 3(1)(a), or where control is being acquired jointly (or a joint venture is established), the notification must be made jointly by the parties to the merger, or those acquiring joint control as the case may be. Where a situation of de facto joint control arises from the acquisition of a significant minority shareholding in another undertaking by a new investor, a joint notification is also required.

[216] Notifications are generally declared incomplete in three main situations: (i) where formal requirements have not been met (e.g., the relevant markets were not

[285] This differs from the section of the Form CO annexed to the 1998 Implementing Regulation which dealt specifically with conglomerate aspects. Although Form CO no longer explicitly refers to conglomerate aspects, where conglomerate issues arise they must be appropriately detailed at s. 6 of the Form CO.

[286] Note that following Regulation 1/2003 and the abolition of the Form A/B Notification procedure, there is no longer the possibility of converting a notification from the Regulation to one in respect of Art. 101 of the TFEU.

[287] Form CO no longer contains any reference to ancillary restraints, for which the merging parties must carry out their own self-assessment regarding the validity of any restrictions contained in their transaction following the abolition of the system of notification for clearance and exemption, as discussed in detail from para. 368.

identified); (ii) where inadequate or insufficiently clear information has been provided (e.g., contact details of customers were not provided or were inaccurate); and (iii) where affected markets have not been identified in the notification. In an increasing number of cases, the Commission has declared notifications incomplete towards the end of the Phase I investigative period, sometimes as a means to obtain more time in which to complete Phase I without having to open a Phase II investigation.[288]

[217] A notification must be complete in order to enable the time period for the assessment of the notification to begin to run. Article 5(2) of the Implementing Regulation allows the Commission to declare a notification as being incomplete where it is incomplete *'in a material respect'* and thereby postponing the start of the period for assessment.[289] Prior contact with the Commission is likely to assist with the avoidance of a declaration of incompleteness, and the Commission's Best Practice Guidelines strongly recommend this. In practice, however, the Commission often allows the notifying party several days to submit the required data in cases where the notification is not considered to be *'materially incomplete'*, without extending the Commission's own deadline for assessment of the transaction.

[218] Misleading or incorrect information will be considered to be incomplete information (Article 5(4) of the Implementing Regulation). However, now that the Commission has the power to suspend the running of the appraisal period, this option tends to be used in preference to a declaration of incompleteness where the notifying parties have exercised their best efforts to fully answer all questions contained in the relevant form, and the information submitted ultimately appears to be less than adequate following third-party comments or a more detailed consideration of the case by the Commission.[290] In several cases, a declaration of incompleteness has been used as a means of delaying a decision under Article 6(1)(c) or Article 8(3) in order to enable the parties to agree to amendments to the transaction[291] or to allow the case team extra time in order to digest and assess all the information provided by the parties following a request for information (RFI).[292] However, in the situation where new information comes to light or a material change in the facts contained in the notification occurs which could have a significant impact on the appraisal of the concentration, the Commission will consider that a notification is incomplete 'in a material respect'. The notification will be considered effective as of the date on which the relevant information is received by the Commission. In the case M.5253 *Sanofi/Zentiva,* the initial notification was filed on 5 September 2008, but the Commission wrote to the parties on 2 October 2008 declaring the notification incomplete in light of the lack of certain material information on certain markets. Two months later, on 5 December 2008, Sanofi-Aventis

[288] *See* case M.10860 *NielsenIQ/GfK*, M.10859 *Trafigura/Ecobat* or M.10560 *Sika/MBCC Group.*

[289] *See* cases M.9406 *Lone Star – Stark Group/Saint-Gobain BDD;* M.7477 *Halliburton/Baker Hughes*; M.7265 *Zimmer/Biomet* and M.6059 *Norbert Dentressangle/Laxey Logistics.*

[290] Case M.3796 *OMYA/J.M. Huber PCC.*

[291] *See* cases M.2041 *United Airlines/US Airways* and M.1795 *Vodafone Airtouch/Mannesmann.*

[292] Case M.5181 *Delta Air Lines/Northwest Airlines.*

made a further submission and in accordance with Article 5(2) of the Implementing Regulation, the notification became effective as of that date.[293]

[219] According to Article 10(4) of the Merger Regulation and Article 9 of the Implementing Regulation, where the Commission has had to request information by a decision pursuant to Article 11 *'owing to circumstances for which one of the undertakings involved in the concentration is responsible'*, it may suspend the period of assessment for the transaction in Phase I or Phase II until receipt of the information. Article 9 of the Implementing Regulation also provides that a suspension of the time limit may also occur where the parties fail to inform the Commission of material changes in the facts contained in the notification, new information coming to light subsequent to notification, or when one of the parties has refused to submit to an investigation deemed necessary by the Commission on the basis of Article 13(1) of the Merger Regulation.

[220] If incorrect or misleading information is supplied, either negligently or intentionally, fines may be imposed on the responsible party and the Commission may revoke its approval decision. While historically, these provisions have been used sparely,[294] there has been a notable increase in more aggressive enforcement by the Commission. In 2017, Facebook was fined EUR110 m for providing incorrect or misleading information during the Commission's 2014 review of Facebook's acquisition of WhatsApp. In April 2019, the Commission fined General Electric EUR52 m for providing incorrect information in connection with its acquisition of LM Wind.[295] The Commission found that General Electric's initial notification contained incorrect information concerning its research and development activities and the development of a specific project. Indeed, in its notification filed on 11 January 2017, GE apparently stated that it did not have any higher power output wind turbine for offshore applications in development, beyond its existing 6 megawatt turbine. However, through information collected from a third party, the Commission discovered that GE was in fact also offering a 12 megawatt offshore wind turbine to potential customers. As a result, on 2 February 2017, GE withdrew its notification of the acquisition of LM Wind and re-notified it on 13 February 2017, this time including information on its 12 megawatt offshore wind turbine capabilities. While the Commission approved the transaction unconditionally, it considered that the omission of that information in the initial notification had affected its analysis of both General Electric's acquisition of LM Wind and Siemens' acquisition of Gamesa that was being reviewed in parallel by the Commission.[296]

---

[293] *See* cases M.7477 *Halliburton/Baker Hughes*; M.7265 *Zimmer/Biomet* and M.6059 *Norbert Dentressangle/Laxey Logistics.*

[294] In case M.3255 *Tetra Laval/Sidel* the Commission stated that *'The obligation of notifying parties to provide correct information applies equally to both replies to requests for information and Form CO ... both points (b) and (c) of Article 14 sanction the supply of incorrect information and in this respect require observation of the same standard.'* Accordingly Tetra Laval was fined EUR45 000 for the failure to provide information about certain new technology in Form CO and a further EUR45 000 for failing to respond to the Commission's request for information on the subject.

[295] Case M.8436 *General Electric Company/LM Wind Power Holding.*

[296] Case M.8134 *Siemens/Gamesa.*

[221] On 3 May 2021, the Commission fined Sigma-Aldrich EUR7.5 m for the provision of incorrect or misleading information to the Commission in relation to its review of Merck's acquisition of Sigma-Aldrich.[297] This case relates to Merck's acquisition of Sigma-Aldrich that was conditionally cleared by the Commission in 2015 subject to Sigma-Aldrich divesting certain assets to remedy the Commission's concerns.[298] However, at the time, Sigma-Aldrich was engaged in an innovation project (iCap), which was closely associated with the business to be divested. However, no information concerning iCap was provided to the Commission – neither during the remedy submissions nor in response to two specific requests for information from the Commission. For this reason, the Commission concluded that Sigma-Aldrich committed three distinct infringements by providing incorrect or misleading information with respect to the iCap project. Although initially the Commission began proceedings against both parties, only Sigma-Aldrich has ultimately been fined (following hearings in 2020, the allegations against Merck were dropped).

[222] The Commission has a solid record for maintaining confidentiality of pre-notification contacts and information provided in the course of the notification procedure. Article 287 of the TFEU, Article 17(2) of the Merger Regulation and the corresponding provisions of the EEA Agreement provide for the non-disclosure of information covered by the obligation of professional secrecy. As a result, officials are required not to reveal business secrets and information acquired through the application of the Merger Regulation. Nevertheless, the principal burden of ensuring confidentiality is on the owner of the business secret. As a matter of practice, where a notifying party has to notify material and the publication or disclosure of which might harm it, it may submit such information separately and clearly marked 'Business Secrets'. In all cases where confidentiality is claimed over notified material, the claimant must give reasons as to why the information must be kept confidential, and be prepared to supply non-confidential versions where needed.

6.1.2 Suspensory Provisions

[223] In accordance with Article 7(1) of the Merger Regulation, a concentration with a Community dimension must not be implemented until it has been declared compatible with the internal market pursuant to a Commission decision or the administrative deadlines prescribed for completion of the Commission's investigation have expired (Article 10(6) of the Merger Regulation). However, two exceptions to the general rule of suspension exist.

[224] Article 7(2) expressly provides that the suspensory provisions shall not impede the implementation of a public bid which has been notified to the Commission prior to, or on the date of, its public announcement.[299] This is on the condition, however, that the acquirer does not exercise the voting rights attached to the shares in question, or does so only to maintain the full value of the investment in

[297] Case M.8181 *Merck/Sigma-Aldrich.*

[298] Case M.7435 *Merck/Sigma-Aldrich.*

[299] *See* cases M.2283 *Schneider/Legrand*; M.3280 *Air France/KLM* and M.2416 *Tetra Laval/Sidel.*

question and on the basis of a derogation granted by the Commission under Article 7(3), on request, as discussed below. It has been extended to cover a series of transactions in securities including those convertible into other securities admitted to trading on a market such as the stock exchange by which control is acquired from various sellers. Such a provision thereby covers commitments to sell shares obtained by a bidder.

[225] The M.2283 *Schneider/Legrand* case illustrates the risk to buyers of acquiring shares and completing transactions that are subsequently prohibited by the Commission. In this case, the exception for public bids applied and Schneider acquired virtually 100% of Legrand's shares following a public offer which closed in July 2001. When the Commission prohibited the deal in October of that year, Schneider was required to reduce its shareholding to 5%. Despite the fact that the Commission's decision was overturned on appeal,[300] Legrand was purchased by another party, KKR. However, the value of Legrand's shares was reduced considerably as a result of the Commission's prohibition decision and the urgency with which Schneider had to divest its shares in Legrand in order to comply with the divestiture decision.

[226] The Commission has power under Article 7(3), upon request, to grant a derogation allowing a concentration to be put into effect notwithstanding the application of the suspensory period. This power has been used very rarely by the Commission which has granted derogations in more than 120 cases, representing about 1.5% of all transactions notified since 1990. In granting such a derogation, the Commission must take into account, *inter alia*, the effects of the suspension on one or more undertakings concerned by a concentration or on a third party and the threat to competition posed by the concentration.[301] Commonly, derogations have been granted in the context of rescue operations such as in cases M.573 *ING/Barings*; M.116 *Kelt/American Express* and M.497 *Matra Marconi/Satcomms*. In case M.2621 *Seb/Moulinex*, a derogation was granted to enable Seb to complete the acquisition of a division of Moulinex which was in administrative receivership.[302] In some cases, a derogation has also been granted where it was considered necessary to meet commitments offered by the parties in order to secure approval, or to ensure the new entity was able to compete effectively on the market.[303] In case M.2777 *Cinven Limited/Angel Street Holdings*, the Commission granted a derogation to close the transaction prior to the Commission decision because the parties would have otherwise been excluded from participating in an auction to acquire the business. The derogation may be made subject to conditions and obligations in order to ensure that conditions of effective competition are maintained. While the Commission remains generally reluctant to grant derogations and a strong case needs to be

[300] Cases T-310/01 and T-77/02 *Schneider Electric v. Commission* [2002] ECR II-4071.

[301] *See* Recital 34 of the Merger Regulation.

[302] *See also* cases M.3209 *WPP/Cordiant* and M.4151 *Orica/Dyno*.

[303] In cases M.1820 *BP/JV Dissolution* and M.1822 *Mobil/JV Dissolution*, a derogation was granted under Art. 7(4) to allow for the speedy transfer of control of the joint venture to BP Amoco. In case M.1667 *BBL/BT/ISP Belgium* a derogation was granted to facilitate the establishment the new joint venture on the market in advance of its main competitor.

made, it is interesting to note that the EC granted the vast majority of these derogations in the wake of past economic recessions, including during the economic downturn linked to the COVID-19 pandemic.

[227] Most recently, in two cases linked to the insolvency of Air Berlin, the Commission granted various derogations from the suspension obligation. In *Lufthansa/Certain Air Berlin Assets*,[304] the Commission allowed Lufthansa to replace Air Berlin as lessee for parts of its fleet before clearance, in order to save the aircraft in question from repossession, avoid disruption to scheduled flights, and ensure that Air Berlin's subsidiary airline NIKI (which Lufthansa was not permitted to acquire) would remain a going concern should another company seek to acquire it. In *Ryanair/LaudaMotion*,[305] the EC granted two derogations – the first permitting Ryanair to lease six aircraft to LaudaMotion, offer LaudaMotion's seats for sale through its own Ryanair system, and provide LaudaMotion with financial support. Without the derogation LaudaMotion would have been forced to reduce scheduled flights, forgoing access to airport slots and jeopardising its ability to operate independently. The second derogation permitted Ryanair to lease further aircraft to LaudaMotion and provide the company with operational support. Finally, in July 2020, the Commission also granted a derogation to the suspension obligation in the *Liberty/Ascoval/Hayange* case where absent this derogation, the Commission found that both targets (Ascoval and Hayange) would not have been able to secure long-term financing from banks and would have been forced into liquidation.[306]

[228] The validity of any transaction carried out in contravention of the suspensory provisions will be dependent upon whether the Commission decides that the concentration is compatible with the Internal Market. An ultimate finding of compatibility will legitimise retroactively, a transaction carried out in breach of the automatic prohibition in Article 7(1). In the meantime, the agreement is unenforceable but not, however, void. It is submitted that Article 7(1) does not operate to prohibit the making of agreements but only their performance to the extent that this amounts to putting the concentration 'into effect'.

[229] Article 7(4) contains certain provisions relating to the validity of transactions in securities traded, and has been broadened beyond recognised stock exchanges. It provides that the validity of the transaction is not affected unless both buyer and seller knew or ought to have known that the transaction was carried out in contravention of Article 7(1).

[230] The Commission may impose fines on the undertakings concerned if they put into effect, intentionally or negligently, a concentration in any of the following circumstances: (i) before its notification; (ii) before a decision has been taken clearing it; (iii) prior to the time periods within which such a decision has to be taken having lapsed; or (iv) in breach of a decision by the Commission to extend the

[304] *See* case M.8633 *Lufthansa/Certain Air Berlin Assets.*

[305] *See* case M.8869 *Ryanair/LaudaMotion.*

[306] *See* case M.9917 *Liberty/Ascoval/Hayange.*

suspension period (Article 14(2)). Fines may be levied up to a maximum of 10% of the aggregate turnover of the undertakings concerned, as defined by Article 5 of the Merger Regulation (i.e., the worldwide turnover of the corporate groups involved in the merger). Such fines may also be levied if the conditions or obligations attached to the Commission's consent to the exercise of voting rights in the suspensory period are not complied with. In addition, periodic penalty payments may be imposed of up to 5% of the average daily aggregate turnover of the undertakings concerned for each working day of delay, in respect of all ongoing infringements (*see* below). Historically, the Commission has rarely taken procedural steps to enforce Article 7. In 2007, however, it demonstrated that it considers any infringement of Article 7 as serious, by conducting a surprise inspection at the premises of merging parties based on allegations of premature implementation of the merger prior to clearance which, however, proved to be unfounded.[307]

[231] At the time of writing, the Commission has imposed fines on seven occasions, in cases M.920 *Samsung/AST*,[308] M.969 *A.P. Moller*,[309] M.4994 *Electrabel/CNR*,[310] M.7184 *Marine Harvest/Morpol*,[311] M.7993 *Altice/PT Portugal*,[312] M.8179 *Canon/Toshiba Medical Systems*, and M.10483 *Illumina/Grail*[313] when the companies had implemented their respective transactions prior to obtaining clearance.[314] In *Marine Harvest/Morpol*, the Commission determined that Marine Harvest's acquisition of a 48.5% shareholding in Morpol granted it de facto control and the Commission a combined fine of EUR20 m – EUR10 m for breaching the standstill obligation and EUR10 m for failure to notify. Both the General Court and the Court of Justice upheld the Commission's imposition of separate fines for breaching the standstill obligation and failing to notify a reportable concentration, and therefore rejected Marine Harvest's argument that the two fines penalised the same conduct in contravention of the '*ne bis in idem*' principle. The Court of Justice concluded that both these obligations of the Merger Regulation pursued separate objectives and that the Commission was therefore entitled to impose separate fines for violation of Article 4(1) and Article 7(1) of the Merger Regulation.

---

307 Cases M.4734 *Ineos/Kerling* and M.6106 *Caterpillar/MVM*.

308 Imposing a fine of EUR33 000 for late filing of fourteen months.

309 Imposing a fine of EUR219 000 for failure to notify three concentrations.

310 Imposing a fine of EUR20 m for late filing. This fine was confirmed by the General Court in case T-332/09 *Electrabel v. Commission*, C 267/129 and subsequently by the Court of Justice on 3 Jul. 2014 in case C-84/13P.

311 Imposing a fine of EUR20 m for late filing (Marine Harvest acquired a 48.5% stake in Morpol which provided de facto sole control over Morpol, and Marine Harvest implemented this acquisition eight months before the formal notification to the Commission).

312 Imposing a fine of EUR124.5 m.

313 https://ec.europa.eu/commission/presscorner/detail/en/ip_23_3773.

314 In case JV.55 *Hutchison/RCPM/ECT* the Commission issued a Statement of Objections against the undertakings which had failed to notify their acquisition of joint control, but ultimately decided not to impose a fine for gun jumping in light of the fact that the parties did not attempt to conceal the operation, notified it to the Commission and demonstrated a cooperative attitude throughout the Commission's investigation. *See* IP/01/940.

[232] In the *Altice/PT Portugal* decision, Altice had notified the transaction in February 2015 and the Commission granted conditional clearance in April 2015. However, two years later, in May 2017, the Commission issued a Statement of Objections, in which it claimed that Altice had implemented certain aspects of the acquisition of PT Portugal without waiting for final clearance, and in relation to certain elements, before it had filed its notification. In its April 2018 decision, the Commission concluded that Altice breached the 'hold-separate' obligation in the Merger Regulation. In particular, the Commission concluded that:

(a) In the purchase agreement, Altice had been given the right to exercise 'decisive influence' (the relevant EU standard) over PT Portugal by acquiring pre-closing veto rights over certain of the company's ordinary business decisions. While it is not unusual to contractually ensure the preservation of the value of a target between signing and closing, under relevant EU regulations such arrangements may not grant rights which exceed those enjoyed by minority shareholders for the preservation of their financial interests.
(b) Altice had exercised decisive influence over aspects of PT Portugal's business by giving PT Portugal instructions on how to carry out a marketing campaign.
(c) Altice had sought and received detailed commercially sensitive information about PT Portugal outside the framework of any confidentiality agreement.

[233] The Commission expressly emphasised that its 2018 enforcement decision did not impact its 2015 clearance decision. The facts giving rise to the infringement of the Article 7 suspensory provision (also called 'gun-jumping' rule) did not affect the Commission's assessment of the substance of the transaction made in 2015. In its *Altice* decision, the Commission justified the significant EUR124.5 m fine for breach of the 'hold-separate' obligation by reference to (i) 'serious infringements' which it concluded had undermined the effective functioning of the EU merger control system; and (ii) the need to send a strong message to deter other companies from gun-jumping. In practice, therefore, merging undertakings must be vigilant not to fall foul, even inadvertently, of the gun-jumping prohibition – and should ensure that they adhere closely to the permitted rules of engagement while final clearance remains outstanding.

[234] It should be noted that the Commission's *Altice* decision pre-dates (and therefore does not take into account) the judgment of the ECJ in the *Ernst & Young/KPMG* case, in which the court established a narrower test for gun-jumping as previously assumed by the Commission in its administrative practice.[315] The request for a preliminary ruling made by the Danish Maritime and Commercial Court related to assess whether the EU suspension obligation had been violated when KPMG's Danish unit terminated a material contract prior to receiving competition clearance for its merger with Ernst & Young.

[235] The ECJ concluded that this measure did not constitute a partial implementation of the transaction and therefore did not infringe gun-jumping rules. The

[315] Case C-633/16 *Ernst & Young P/S v. Konkurrencerådet*, 31 May 2018.

ECJ clarified that the suspension obligation only applies to actions of the merging parties which '*in whole or in part, in fact or in law, contribute to the change in control of the target undertaking*'. The ECJ therefore cut back the much wider understanding of the suspension obligation advocated by the Commission which acted as an intervener in the case. Where the Commission supported a broad and general 'standstill obligation' in the pre-clearance phase, the ECJ limited the suspension obligation to actions directly related to bringing about a change of control over the target company. The ECJ however highlighted that pre-merger coordination outside the scope of the suspension obligation may be prohibited by the EU rules against restrictive agreements in Article 101 TFEU.

[236] The Commission's Altice decision was upheld by the General Court in 2021. However, in the exercise of its unlimited jurisdiction, the GC reduced the fine for the infringement of the notification obligation by 10%. This reduction aimed to reflect that, before signing the sales and purchase agreement, Altice had informed the Commission of the transaction, and after signing the sales and purchase agreement, Altice had submitted a case team allocation request and engaged in pre-notification discussions with the Commission (including sending it a copy of the sales and purchase agreement with a draft of its notification).[316] While Altice appealed the General Court's judgment before the ECJ (at the time of writing, the appeal is still pending), in its opinion of April 2023, Advocate General Collins recommended that Altice's appeal be dismissed in its entirety and sided with the Commission's approach to setting fines for gun-jumping.[317] In particular, Advocate General Collins disagreed with Altice's argument that Article 4(1) is redundant and therefore illegal in light of Article 7(1) of the Merger Regulation. By reference to the judgment adopted in the *Marine Harvest* case,[318] Advocate General Collins considered that the two provisions impose different obligations and pursue autonomous objectives. Article 4(1) 'mandates timely notification', while Article 7(1) 'prohibits early implementation'.

[237] In the *Canon/Toshiba* case, the gun-jumping was based on the so-called warehousing two-step transaction structure used by Canon. Warehousing agreements involve the purchase of the target company by an interim buyer and the parallel transfer of a purchase option to the ultimate buyer. In this case, as a first step, in 2016, an interim buyer acquired 95% of the share capital of Toshiba Medical for EUR800, and Canon directly acquired the outstanding 5% and share options over the interim buyer's stake for EUR5.2 bn. Subsequently, Canon filed its contemplated purchase of Toshiba Medical to a number of competition authorities worldwide, including the Commission. The Commission unconditionally cleared the transaction in September 2016, and Canon then proceeded to acquire 100% of Toshiba Medical after exercising its share option (i.e., the second step of the warehousing structure). However, in June 2019, the Commission fined Canon EUR28 m for

[316] *Altice Europe v. Commission*, Case T-425/18, judgment of 22 Sep. 2021.

[317] *Altice Group Lux v. Commission*, Case C-746/21 P, Opinion of Advocate General Collins, 27 Apr. 2023.

[318] *Marine Harvest v. Commission*, Case C-10/18 P, judgment of 4 Mar. 2020.

gun-jumping as it considered that the initial acquisition of a 95% shareholding constituted part of a single reportable concentration which was implemented prior to notification and prior to receiving the Commission's approval. In September 2019, Canon lodged its appeal against the Commission's decision alleging that the Commission committed a manifest error of law by misapplying the legal test for the assessment of Article 4(1) and Article 7(1) of the Merger Regulation. On 18 May 2022, the General Court upheld the Commission's EUR28 m gun-jumping fine to Canon, ruling that the Commission was entitled to rely on the argument that Canon partially implemented the acquisition when it acquired a 5% stake in Toshiba Medical in 2016 plus a share option to buy the remaining 95%.[319]

[238] More recently, in the Illumina/Grail transaction, the Commission imposed a fine of EUR432 m on Illumina (and EUR1 000 on Grail) for having implemented their merger before approval by the Commission in breach of the standstill obligation contained in the Merger Regulation. This represents the highest fine that the Commission has imposed for gun-jumping to date, and it is the first case in which:

- a fine is imposed in relation to a transaction that did not meet the jurisdictional thresholds of the Merger Regulation or of any EU Member State, but over which the Commission claimed jurisdiction based on an expansive interpretation of the upwards referral clause contained in Article 22 of the Merger Regulation;
- the maximum possible fine for gun-jumping has been imposed (i.e., approx. 10% of Illumina's global turnover; previous fines were much below this, like approx. 1% in the case of Altice); and
- a fine (albeit symbolic, of EUR1 000) has been imposed on the target of a concentration (to date, only acquiring companies had been fined for gun-jumping infringements).

[239] As indicated above, the violation of the Merger Regulation's standstill obligation took place in very specific circumstances. Indeed, in April 2021, the European Commission accepted the referral of the matter by a number of EU competition authorities (none of which had jurisdiction), and opened an in-depth investigation in July 2021. Nevertheless, Illumina and Grail publicly announced the closing of the transaction in August 2021. In reaction, the Commission imposed interim measures to ensure Illumina and Grail remained separate during the Commission's merger control investigation. Ultimately, Illumina complied with the interim order to hold itself separate from Grail, and the enforcement of this standstill obligation via interim measures would be all the more relevant as the concentration was prohibited by the Commission in September 2022. Illumina has challenged this fine before the General Court (Illumina's appeal of the prohibition decision is pending, as is its appeal of the interim measures decision and the ECJ's ruling on the Commission's revised Article 22 policy).

[319] *See*, https://curia.europa.eu/juris/document/document.jsf?text=&docid=259546&pageIndex=0&doclang=EN&mode=lst&dir=&occ=first&part=1&cid=8264355.

7 PROCEDURE: EXAMINATION OF NOTIFICATION

7.1 Two-Stage Procedure

[240] In terms of Commission procedure, there is a clear distinction between the preliminary Phase I examination of a notification and the more detailed Phase II examination. The latter will be carried out if the Commission considers that the notified concentration raises serious doubts as to its compatibility with the Internal Market. The Phase I proceedings must be completed within twenty-five working days following the receipt of a complete notification or within thirty-five working days where the parties have proposed commitments which are intended to form the basis of a decision rendering the concentration compatible with the Internal Market. The timeline starts to run on the day following the actual notification to the Commission, and the case team will send an acknowledgement of receipt certifying that the notification was deemed complete upon filing a few days later. The Phase II proceedings must be completed within ninety working days from the date on which they were initiated. This period may first be extended to one hundred and five working days in cases where commitments are offered if commitments are offered after more than fifty-five working days after the Phase II proceedings have begun. An additional extension to up to twenty working days also applies when the Commission or the parties have requested such an extension during the procedure (*see* paragraph [201] below). At the end of the relevant time period, the concentration will be deemed to have been declared compatible with the Internal Market (Article 10(6)).

7.2 Role of Member States

[241] The Commission is required by Article 19(2) of the Merger Regulation to carry out the procedures contained in the Merger Regulation in *'close and constant liaison'* with the competent authorities of the Member States, who are entitled to express their views on those procedures. This liaison is more pronounced during Phase II procedures.

[242] Article 19(1) provides that the Commission must transmit copies of notifications and other important documents submitted to the Commission or issued by the Commission (which would include commitments offered by the parties pursuant to Article 6(2) or 8(2) second paragraph) to the Member States within three working days of receipt. Article 19(3) requires the Commission to consult the Advisory Committee prior to: adopting a decision on the basis of Article 8 (Phase II procedure); issuing fines or periodic penalty payments under Articles 14 and 15; or adopting implementing rules in respect of the Merger Regulation. The Advisory Committee comprises one or two representatives from each of the Member States' NCAs, at least one of whom is competent in the analysis of restrictive practices and dominant positions. The Advisory Committee is required to deliver an opinion (by majority vote if necessary) on the Commission's draft decision on the merger in the context of a Phase II procedure (Article 8). Such an opinion is then appended to the draft decision considered by the college of Commissioners. While not binding, Article 19(6) of the Merger Regulation requires the Commission to take the utmost account of the Committee's opinion in finalising its decision. The Merger Regulation requires the publication of the Advisory Committee's opinion with the publication of the Commission's Article 8 Decision and the Hearing Officer's report on the conduct of the proceedings (subject to the legitimate interest of undertakings in the protection of their business secrets).

[243] Unless Member States actively raise concerns, they effectively play a very limited role in a Phase I procedure, even when commitments are offered. In a Phase II procedure, delegates from the representatives of the competent authorities of the Member States attend the Oral Hearing and give their views on the draft Commission decision in the Advisory Committee. On occasion, the Advisory Committee has clearly disagreed with a Commission Decision.[320] In other cases, the opinion of the Advisory Committee (and sometimes the minority viewpoint) has otherwise had an influential role on the Commission's decision. For example, in case M.477 *Mercedes Benz-Kässbohrer*, the Advisory Committee criticised the reasoning in the draft decision which had not been preceded by a Statement of Objections or formal hearing for the parties, contrary to what was then the usual practice in Phase II cases. As a result, the Commission went back to the parties with a Statement of Objections and held a hearing before presenting a revised draft clearance to the Advisory Committee.

7.3 Phase I Proceedings

[244] According to Article 6(1) of the Merger Regulation, the Commission is obliged to examine a notification as soon as it has received it. Figure 2 sets out the steps undertaken during a Phase I review period. The Commission has a period of twenty-five working days for a standard Phase I appraisal, beginning on the day after receipt of a complete notification, to come to one of five possible conclusions[321] as follows:

(a) the concentration does not fall within the scope of the Regulation (Article 6(1)(a) decision);
(b) the concentration falls within the scope of the Regulation but does not raise serious doubts as to its compatibility with the Internal Market and is therefore cleared unconditionally (an Article 6(1)(b) decision);
(c) the concentration falls within the scope of the Regulation and raises serious doubts as to its compatibility with the Internal Market but is conditionally cleared following the submission of remedies (pursuant to Article 6(1)(b) in conjunction with Article 6(2));

[320] Case M.906 *Mannesmann/Vallourec*, where the majority opinion of the Advisory Committee considered that the creation of the new entity would give rise to a collectively dominant position on the Western European market for seamless stainless steel tubes.

[321] In some cases, the Commission has taken more than one decision in respect of a notified transaction. *See* case M.4 *Renault/Volvo*.

(d) the concentration falls within the scope of the Regulation and raises serious doubts about its compatibility with the Internal Market which therefore leads to the initiation of Phase II proceedings (an Article 6(1)(c) decision); or

(e) the concentration should be referred in whole or in part to a Member State NCA (pursuant to Article 9(3)).

[245] The Commission rarely renders decisions before the end of the Phase I review period, although it has on occasion been willing to expedite its review of concentrations involving companies in financial distress.[322] Where the Commission does not take one of the above possible conclusions within the twenty-five-day deadline (or thirty-five-day deadline where applicable), the notified transaction is automatically deemed to have been cleared in accordance with Article 10(6). The applicable period of review may also be suspended where, owing to circumstances for which the notifying parties are responsible, the parties do not furnish information as requested by the Commission on a timely basis or the Commission conducts an investigation of an undertaking.[323]

[246] There are few formal rules governing the procedure at this stage in the proceedings. Three to five working days after a transaction is notified to the Commission, a notice is published in the 'C' series of the EU's Official Journal.[324] This rather brief notice indicates the names of the parties, the nature of the concentration, the economic sectors involved, and whether it falls under the simplified procedure. A time limit of ten days from the date of publication is normally set for the receipt of third-party comments.

[247] The Commission can obtain more information, whether from the parties themselves, Member State governments or third parties, by means of requests under Article 11 of the Merger Regulation (*see* below). One or more written requests for information are generally sent to both parties and their customers, competitors and suppliers following notification. Undertakings are required to respond within the fixed response date, which must be set out in the information request. The information request also sets out the penalties for non-compliance. It is also more and more the case that the Commission's investigation, similarly to what already takes place in the US, involves a number of telephone interviews with third parties.[325] What competitors, and particularly customers, say about the operation is very important as they are generally perceived to have a better understanding of the industry and markets concerned than the Commission, especially given the limited time available in Phase I proceedings.[326] The Commission will commonly seek information from third parties on matters such as market

322 Case M. 5384 *BNP Paribas/Fortis* where the Commission approved the transaction two weeks before the formal expiry of the Phase I review period.

323 *See* cases M.3796 *OMYA/J.M. Huber PCC* and M.4799 *OMV/MOL*.

324 Article 4(3).

325 *See* cases M.7265 *Zimmer/Biomet*; M.7342 *Alcoa/Firth Rixson* and M.7593 *Alcoa/RTI International Metals*.

326 For example, in case M.1693 *Alcoa/Reynolds*, a complainant alleged that the merged company would have the availability to restrict output and increase prices, thereby foreclosing the complainant's ability to compete in the downstream market for production of aluminium alloys. These concerns were specifically addressed in the commitments provided by the parties in order to obtain clearance.

definition, market shares and, importantly, on the commitments offered by the notifying parties.[327] Where the notifying parties or third parties fail to respond to an Article 11 request and further to an Article 11 decision, they are liable to a fine and may also be subject to a periodic penalty payment.[328] Such fines are, however, rare in practice.

[248] In its merger review process, the Commission today tends to rely heavily on the parties' internal company documents, such as business strategy, market analysis papers or internal communications between business people concerning such topics. To this end, the Commission often requests transaction parties to provide large numbers of internal documents from a number of identified custodians, even during Phase I proceedings (such requests can even be made during the pre-notification period). Not long ago, the Commission would only make such requests in Phase II proceedings, and they would 'only' ask for several hundred documents in such cases. Now, it has become standard for the Commission to request several hundred thousands of documents from each of the parties to the transaction, often within a short time period. In practice, this means that we are moving to US Second Request types of investigation, in addition to the burdensome requirement of submitting a Form CO notification necessary to start the formal review process. In such extensive requests, the identified custodians are normally senior management persons of the company, including CEOs, chief financial officers and the heads of the business units dealing with the relevant product areas. It is also now increasingly common to see the custodian list include persons from the company's legal department (whose documents are often privileged given their interactions with external legal counsel, which increases the privilege review burden for the parties and advisors).

[249] The Commission regularly includes expansive search term lists in its request for internal documents although there have been instances where the Commission did not provide search terms which meant that the Commission requested all documents (including personal files) from the named custodians. When search terms are provided, they will not be limited to the relevant product markets of concern, but go beyond that. The search term strings can be very lengthy (combinations of approx. 500 terms are not unusual), and often the Commission will also request that search terms are applied not only in English, but additionally in the language of the country where the company is headquartered. The search term list may also include 'legal' search terms, such as 'merger control', 'divestment' or 'remedies'. Finally, the Commission normally requests documents from the relevant custodians for a time period of three years, and in some cases even five years. It is also

[327] In case M.1524 *Airtours/First Choice*, the proposed acquisition of First Choice Holidays by Airtours, the Commission is reported to have received an unusually high number of responses from customers and competitors. In case JV.52 *ECT-Port of Rotterdam*, the proposed acquisition of the Rotterdam container terminal operator European Combined Terminals by Hutchison Port Holding and Rotterdam Port Authority, P&O Nedlloyd submitted a formal complaint to the Commission against the proposed merger.

[328] *See* case M.1634 *Mitsubishi Heavy Industries* where Mitsubishi, a third party, had failed to reply to an Art. 11 request and an Art. 11(5) decision requesting information on pricing and turnover of certain types of boilers despite numerous reminders, saying that it would entail an excessive and disproportionate amount of work. Mitsubishi was fined a total of EUR950 000.

important to note that once the internal documents are provided, the company has to confirm that the response to the RFI has been prepared and assembled in accordance with the instructions set out in the RFI and that it comprises all documents responsive to the RFI. The company also has to confirm that the documents submitted are true, correct and complete. Given the very large volumes of documents it seems very demanding – and in practice often not possible – for the company to confirm completeness. It may thus be sensible to require only a 'substantial compliance' with the RFI (as is the case for US Second Requests).

[250] The Commission's current policy of requesting internal documents is exemplified by a number of complex merger cases. As part of its probe into the USD130 bn merger between Dow Chemical and DuPont announced at the end of 2015, it requested more than 400 000 documents. Meanwhile, the CEO of Bayer described EU merger proceedings in *Bayer/Monsanto* last year as going to '*unimaginable depths*' after having to provide 2.7 m documents to the Commission. In light of this new trend, the Commission announced in January 2018 that it was preparing a set of best practices on requests for internal documents in merger cases,[329] but at the time of writing, these best practices were still not published.

[251] Article 13 of the Merger Regulation also gives the Commission (and NCAs) the power to carry out inspections ('dawn raids') equivalent to those under Regulation 1/2003, implementing Articles 101 and 102 of the TFEU (*see* below). Investigations by the Commission can only be carried out following a Commission decision and the necessary authorisation from the judicial authorities of Member States. Nevertheless, in practice these are rarely used, particularly in Phase I proceedings, because of time constraints.

[252] During the initial notification period the Member State NCAs will also examine the notification. Member States may comment on the case and seek information from, or supply information to, the Commission. If a distinct market problem is identified for which a Member State may seek to take jurisdiction, it must notify the Commission within fifteen working days of receiving its copy of the notification (Article 9(2)) (*see* below). Any such identification causes the initial period to be extended automatically to thirty-five working days and the Commission will notify the parties of this.[330] The Commission can request additional information from the Member State concerned under Article 19(2) on the question of whether the case should be referred to the Member State pursuant to Article 9.

[253] Before reaching its decision on the applicability of the Merger Regulation and the initiation of the Phase I proceedings, there is no requirement for the Commission to put forward formal objections to the parties. However, during this period there will be close contact with the parties so that, wherever possible, both practical and legal problems may be resolved. In theory, this should be mainly done prior to notification so that the notified concentration is already largely in an acceptable form.

[329] Speech of Commissioner for Competition, Margrethe Vestager, Fairness and competition, GCLC Annual Conference, Brussels, 25 Jan. 2018.

[330] Articles 9(2) and 10(1) of the Merger Regulation.

[254] Where it is clear that the transaction raises substantive issues, the parties may submit commitments to the Commission in order to avoid Phase II proceedings. Article 19(1) of the Implementing Regulation provides that commitments intended by the parties to form the basis for a Phase I clearance shall be submitted to the Commission within not more than twenty working days from the date of notification. The Remedies Notice provides that the Commission informs the parties about its serious doubts in 'due time' before this deadline.[331] In such circumstances, the notifying parties will be offered the opportunity of attending a State of Play meeting which will necessarily take place before the expiry of three weeks into Phase I.[332] In this event the twenty-five working day time limit during which the Article 6(1) decision must be taken is increased to thirty-five working days. In practice, the parties are recommended to initiate discussions with the Commission on commitments at an early stage in the procedure during the pre-notification stage. In most cases the commitments would have been largely agreed with the Commission before their formal submission under Article 19(1). It is recommended that commitments are submitted in draft and on an informal basis for discussion with the Commission, as is emphasised in its Best Practice Guidelines. A copy of the definitive commitments is sent to the Member States and will be 'market tested' with third parties. Where the Commission finds that, following modification by the remedies offered, a notified concentration no longer raises serious doubts as to its compatibility with the Internal Market, it may decide to declare the concentration compatible with the Internal Market. Furthermore, the Commission may attach conditions and obligations to its decision which are intended to ensure that the undertakings concerned comply with the commitments they have entered into vis-à-vis the Commission with a view to rendering the concentration compatible with the Internal Market (Article 6(2)).

[255] The Commission must notify its decision to the undertakings concerned and to the Member State NCAs without delay, which normally takes the form of a reasoned letter. The Commission is not obliged under the Merger Regulation to publish its Article 6(1) decisions in the Official Journal but it has adopted the practice of publishing a short notice in the 'C' series of the Official Journal stating the fact that the Commission has adopted an Article 6(1)(a), (b) or (c) decision. The Commission will also issue a press release for the cases which are of a particular interest. Non-confidential versions of Article 6(1)(a), 6(1)(b) and 6(2) decisions, including commitments, are published on the Commission website. Decisions under Article 6(1)(c) are not made public due to their provisional nature but the Commission still publishes a press release that summarises the reasons that have led it to initiate Phase II proceedings.

[256] The majority of notified concentrations are cleared by the Commission by the end of the first twenty-five working day review period on the basis that they are compatible with the Internal Market.

[331] Remedies Notice at para. 77.

[332] Best Practices Guidelines at paras 33(a) and 41. This State of Play meeting normally takes place on the 15th Working Day of the Phase I review period.

7.4 Simplified Procedure

[257] The simplified procedure was first introduced in 2000 and revised in 2023 for the assessment of certain categories of concentrations which do not normally raise competition concerns. The simplified procedure, as is set out in the Commission's Simplified Procedure Notice is intended to reduce the administrative burden on notifying parties and the Commission, while still giving Member States and third parties the opportunity to comment or intervene, as is possible under the ordinary procedure. The Commission may, if necessary, revert to the ordinary investigative procedures at any time with the effect of starting the formal deadlines of investigation.

[258] The Commission's Simplified Procedure Notice identifies the following categories of cases which would qualify for a short-form decision:

- two or more undertakings acquiring joint control over a joint venture, provided that the joint venture has no, or negligible, actual or foreseen activities within the EEA (turnover of less than EUR100 m and assets less than EUR100 m in the EEA);
- none of the parties are engaged in business activities in the same product and geographical market (horizontal relationships), or in a product market which is upstream or downstream of a product market in which any other party to the concentration is engaged (vertical relationships);
- two or more parties are active in horizontally related markets have a combined market share of less than 20% or the increment of the Herfindahl – Hirschman Index is below 150 and the parties combined market share is below 50%;
- two or more parties are active in vertically related markets but there is no individual or combined market share of 30% or above; and
- a party is to acquire sole control of an undertaking over which it already has joint control.

[259] Pursuant to the expansions introduced in 2023, a transaction can benefit from simplified treatment also where under all plausible market definitions:

- the individual or combined upstream and downstream market shares of the merging parties are below 50%, the increment (delta) of the Herfindahl-Hirschman Index (HHI) resulting from the concentration on this market is below 150, and the company with the smallest market share is the same in the upstream and downstream markets; and
- in a vertical relationship, the individual or combined upstream market share of the merging parties is below 30%, and their combined purchasing share in the downstream market is below 30% of upstream inputs.

[260] Certain cases could even qualify for a 'super-simplified' procedure, for which parties can notify directly without pre-notification contacts. Referring to its own experience, the Commission considers that the following concentrations may be reviewed under this super-simplified procedure, in less than twenty-five working days:

- two or more parties acquire joint control of a joint venture, provided that the joint venture has no current or expected turnover within the territory of the European Economic Area (EEA), and the parties concerned have not planned to transfer any assets within the EEA to the joint venture at the time of notification; or
- two or more parties merge, or one or more undertakings acquire sole or joint control of another party, provided that none of the parties to the transaction are engaged in business activities in the same product and geographic market or in a relevant product market that is upstream or downstream from a product market in which any other party to the transaction is engaged.

[261] The new simplified procedure also introduces a 'flexibility clause' which will allow notifying parties to ask for their transaction to be subject to the simplified procedure even if they do not satisfy the related conditions, with four specific situations provided for the 'flexibility clause':

(1) for horizontal overlaps, where the combined market shares of the parties are between 20% and 25%;
(2) for vertical relationships where the individual or combined upstream and downstream market shares of the parties remain below 35%;
(3) for vertical relationships where the individual or combined market shares of the merging parties do not exceed 50% in one market and 10% in the other vertically related market; and
(4) for joint ventures with turnover and assets between EUR100 m and EUR150 m in the European Economic Area (EEA).

[262] The categories above apply alternatively, but not cumulatively. However, and except for the joint venture clause, the notifying party may combine the application of the flexibility clause with the classical simplified treatment cases, when the concentration involves several markets. In other words, if for certain markets the simplified treatment applies and for other markets the Commission agrees to apply the flexibility clause, then the entire transaction would benefit from the simplified procedure.

[263] Finally, the updated Notice also extends and clarifies the circumstances through which the Commission may investigate a case under the normal procedure. The updated Notice includes a non-exhaustive list of examples of types of concentrations that may be excluded from the simplified procedure. It also clarifies that the instance of one or more of the circumstances may be a reason for the Commission to inform the notifying parties that the simplified treatment is not suitable. In particular, three situations are relevant to mention:

(1) joint ventures with negligible activities in the EEA (as falling under the simplified procedure cases and the flexibility clause), where horizontal overlaps or vertical relationships exist between the parties to the concentration;
(2) where one party to the concentration may have significant non-controlling shareholdings in companies active in the market(s) where another party to the transaction is active; and

(3) where at least two parties to the transaction are present in closely related neighbouring markets (i.e., when the products are complementary to each other or when they belong to a range of products that is generally purchased by the same set of customers for the same end-use). This can occur where one or more of the parties holds an individual or combined market share of 30% or more in any product market in which there is no horizontal overlap or vertical relationship.

[264] While the Short Form CO (which is now largely co-extensive in practice with the simplified procedure) reduces the burden on the parties, the simplified procedure also reduces the burden on the Commission in its investigation and in producing its Phase I decision. In practice, the amount of detail that parties will have to provide in the Short Form CO will be limited due to there being no affected markets as defined in the Form CO. On receipt of the notification, the Commission normally makes an assessment of whether or not it qualifies for the simplified procedure. If this is the case, then the Commission does not proceed with its normal market investigation (it does not send out an Article 11 request to competitors, customers or the notifying parties). However, if a third party or a Member State raises substantiated concerns, the Commission will need to revert to its normal decision-making process. In such a case, the parties must re-notify a full Form CO which restarts the twenty-five working days timetable.[333] The Commission is obliged to wait for a period of fifteen working days from notification for the expiry of the period within which Member States can submit comments on the transaction (and effectively to make an Article 9 referral request). However, if during this period there are no objections raised for the transaction or no further information comes to light which leads the Commission to believe that the transaction raises serious doubts, it can in theory approve the transaction from a period of fifteen days after the date of notification.

[265] An Article 6(1)(b) decision under this procedure provides very limited information and are usually no longer than two pages. It identifies the parties, the nature of the concentration and the economic sectors concerned, as well as a statement that the concentration is declared compatible with the Internal Market because it falls within one or more of the categories contained in the Notice. It does not contain any detailed market analysis. The decision is also published on the Commission website and a notice is published in the OJ.

[266] In recent years, the vast majority of notifications have been dealt with under the simplified procedure. Indeed, in 2022 out of the 371 cases filed to the Commission, 291 were approved following a simplified procedure review which represents over 78% of the cases. This proportion was similar to the number of decisions adopted by the Commission using the simplified procedure in 2021, where the Commission approved 309 transactions under this procedure out of a total of 405 notifications made to the Commission.

[333] *See*, for example, cases M.5074 and M.5142 *Bosch/Mahle/JV* where the Commission moved away from the simplified procedure following concerns raised by third parties.

Figure 2 EUMR: Phase I (25–35 Working Days)

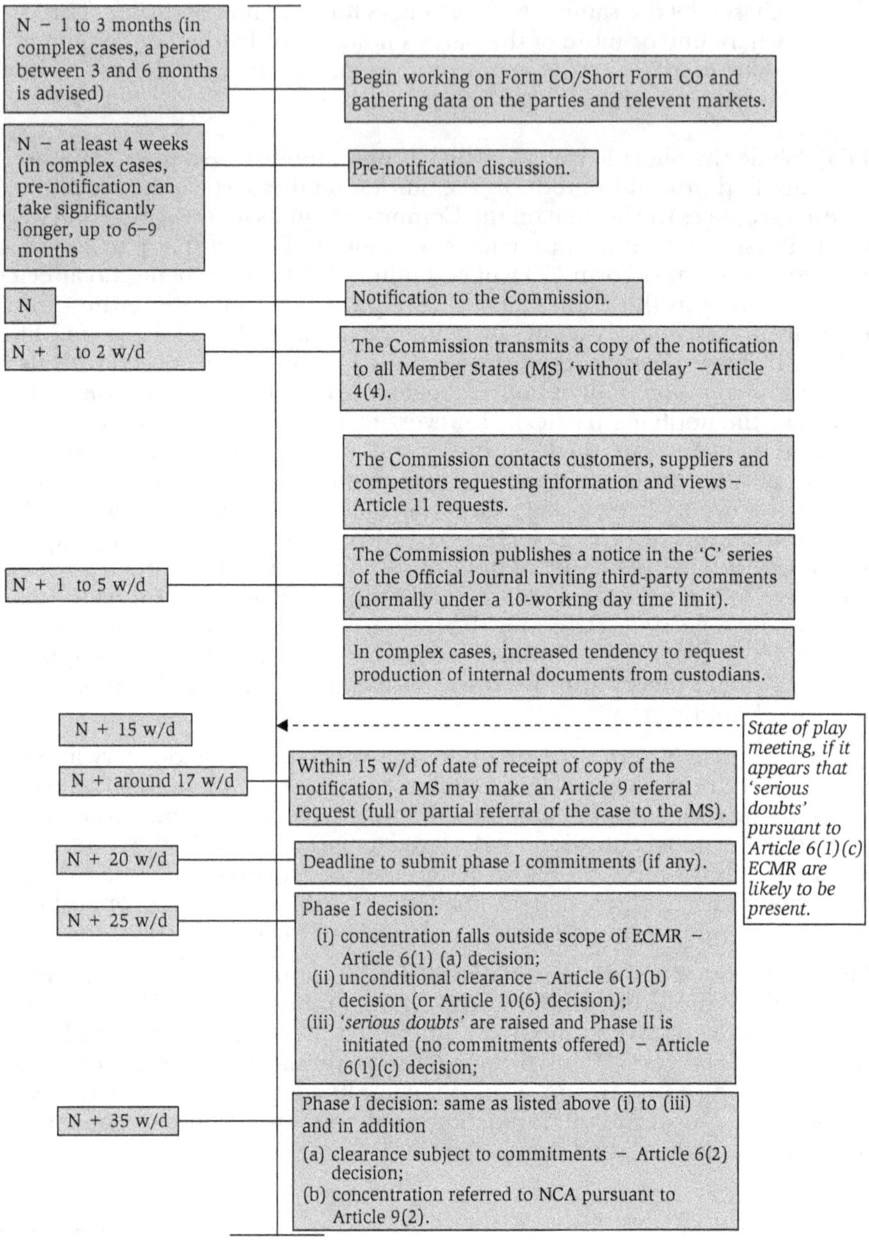

7.5 Phase II Proceedings

[267] Phase II procedure involves a comprehensive examination of the transaction where the Commission has serious doubts as to its compatibility with the Internal Market.

[268] According to Article 10(3) of the Merger Regulation, where the Commission opens Phase II proceedings, it must take a decision within ninety working days from the date of initiation of proceedings (which can be extended if commitments are offered after day fifty-five of the Phase II proceedings if an extension up to twenty working days are requested pursuant to Article 10(3), or if the Commission simply suspends the Phase II review period (a practice increasingly used by the Commission in recent years)) either by:

(a) declaring the concentration to be incompatible with the Internal Market (Article 8(3)).[334] Where the concentration has already been implemented, the Commission may require the undertakings concerned to unwind the concentration, or any other action that may be appropriate in order to restore the situation prevailing prior to the implementation of the concentration (Article 8(4)); or
(b) declaring the concentration compatible with the Internal Market under Article 8(1) of the Merger Regulation.[335] A decision declaring a concentration to be compatible may be conditional on the undertakings concerned complying with commitments they have given the Commission modifying the original merger proposals (Article 8(2)).[336] Failure to comply with commitments taking the form of *'conditions'* (a requirement for achievement of the structural change of the market, i.e., a business is to be divested) made to the Commission renders the decision invalid since it is not deemed to be effective until the commitments or the conditions are fulfilled. Failure to comply with commitments taking the form of *'obligations'* (implementing steps which are necessary to achieve a structural change, i.e., the appointment of a trustee) made to the Commission allows the Commission to revoke its authorisation decision.

[269] Where the Commission fails to take a decision on compatibility or incompatibility under Article 8(1), 8(2) and (3) within the Phase II deadline, the concentration will automatically be deemed compatible with the Internal Market (Article 10(6)).

---

[334] As of June 2023, there have been 32 outright prohibitions, with the latest being case M.10188 *Illumina/*Grail, M.9343 *Hyundai Heavy Industries Holdings/Daewoo Shipbuilding & Marine Engineering*, and M.8713 *Tata Steel/ThyssenKrupp/JV*.

[335] For recent examples *see* cases M.10807 *Viasat/Inmarsat*, M.10658 *Norsk Hydro/Alumetal*, and M.9409 *Aurubis/Metallo Group Holding*.

[336] Conditional clearances at the end of the Phase II proceeding, occur more often than not. As of June 2023 only 65 cases out of 211 cases which were cleared were given unconditional clearance.

[270] The Phase II procedure may be broken down as follows (and as set out in Figure 3):

- Phase II proceedings commence with the adoption by the Commission of a decision indicating that the notified concentration raises serious doubts as to its compatibility with the Internal Market (Article 6.1(c) of the Merger Regulation).
- Within two weeks, the parties have the possibility of providing comments with respect to the Article 6.1(c) decision to the Commission. The parties may choose not to present such comments which must be provided in the form of a written memorandum. In order to prepare such comments, the parties can ask the Commission to grant them access to 'key documents' from its file, and in recent years the Commission has become increasingly ready to share such 'key documents' shortly after the opening of the Phase II investigation (these key documents are generally made available the day following the initiation of the Phase II proceedings).
- Within two weeks after the adoption of an Article 6(1)(c) decision, a State of Play meeting is recommended by the Commission's Best Practice Guidelines in order to map out the procedures and timetable for Phase II in addition to discussing the comments provided by the parties on the Article 6(1)(c) decision and any document in the Commission's file which the parties may have had the opportunity to review.
- Following the initiation of the Phase II procedure, the Commission will raise further questions under Article 11 (with the parties, their suppliers, customers and competitors) and analyse their responses. The Commission may also carry out on-the-spot investigations at the parties' or third parties' premises although this is rare (*see* below). At that time, the Commission will also request a large number of internal documents from the undertakings concerned. It is worthwhile to note that in the recent years such requests have significantly increased in volume and have started to resemble US reviews, as case files bulge to hundreds of thousands of e-mails, letters and other documents. For example, in its conditional clearance of the *ArcelorMittal/Ilva* transaction, the Commission indicated having reviewed more than 800 000 internal documents from the merging parties,[337] while the Commission indicated having reviewed a whopping 2.7 m internal documents from the parties in its assessment of the *Bayer/Monsanto* transaction.[338]
- Within fifteen days of the initiation of the Phase II proceedings, the parties may request an extension of the timetable to allow for a more thorough investigation. The Commission enjoys a similar power and can agree to an extension with the parties subsequently at any stage. In either case, the maximum extension permitted is twenty working days.[339]
- The Phase II investigation period may be suspended while the Commission awaits the response from one or more undertakings concerned involved in

[337] *See* Commission press release IP/18/3721.
[338] *See* Commission press release IP/18/2282.
[339] Article 10(3) of the Merger Regulation.

the concentration to requests for information taken by decision under Article 11,[340] investigations ordered by decision under Article 13 or when the notifying parties have failed to inform the Commission of any material changes. As indicated above, the Commission has increasingly used this tool in recent years, particularly when investigating transactions in economic sectors severely hit by the COVID-19 pandemic. This can be best illustrated by the *Fincantieri/Chantiers de l'Atlantique* case where, before the parties abandoned their deal, the Commission had been investigating the transaction for over sixteen months including a ten-month period where the Commission had stopped the clock awaiting the parties' reply to an RFI.[341] Similarly, in case M.9343 *Hyundai Heavy Industries Holdings/Daewoo Shipbuilding & Marine Engineering*, the Commission stopped the clock for nearly 21 months due to the parties' non-compliance with information requests sent by the Commission.

- Another State of Play meeting is recommended prior to the issue of the Statement of Objections, to allow parties to understand the types of objections that may be raised and to iron out any issues prior to its delivery to the parties.
- The Statement of Objections is finalised and sent to the parties between six and eight weeks into the Phase II proceedings (although neither the Merger Regulation nor the Implementing Regulation provide guidance as to when a Statement of Objections should be sent). However, the Commission does not always issue a Statement of Objections in Phase II cases where the parties are able to convince the Commission to set aside their 'serious doubts', or they offer remedies sufficiently early in Phase II to allow the Commission to approve the transaction[342]. In the preparation of the Statement of Objections, the Commission enters into discussions with other Commission services (e.g., the Legal Service or relevant industry groups in DG Comp).[343] The Statement of Objections will set out in detail the Commission's preliminary findings (both on the facts and on their legal and economic significance) and must fix a time limit for the parties' response. This is generally two weeks, but is often extended by a week. Under Article 18(3) of the Merger

[340] In the case M.3796 *OMYA/Huber*, after a series of suspensions, the Commission decided to wind the clock back three months taking the view that an earlier submission made by OMYA in response to an Art. 11 request was incomplete. Likewise, in case M.4799 *OMV/MOL* transaction, the Commission suspended its investigation for two months when a request for additional information went unanswered by the parties. Also, in the case M.9097 *Boeing/Embraer*, the Commission had to suspend its investigation six times, each time due to the parties' failure to respond to Art. 11 requests. In case M.10078 *Cargotec/Konecranes*, the Commission suspended its investigation for over seven weeks pending the production of internal documents.

[341] *See* case M.9162 *Fincantieri/Chantiers de l'Atlantique*.

[342] *See* cases M.5440 *Lufthansa/Austrian Airlines*; M.6214 *Seagate/HDD Business of Samsung Electronics*; M.6410 *UTC/Goodrich*, M.6314 *Telefónica UK/Vodafone UK/Everything Everywhere/JV*, M.8909 *KME/MKM*, M.10658 *Norsk Hydro/Alumetal*, or M.10807 *Viasat/Inmarsat*.

[343] In addition to the parties to the transaction, third parties that have a sufficient interest in the case (e.g., competitors and customers) will also be provided with a summary (and in many cases a non-confidential version) of the Statement of Objections and are entitled to submit comments to the Commission. *See* in particular cases M.9014 *PKN Orlen/Grupa Lotos* or M.10078 *Cargotec/Konecranes*.

Regulation, the Commission can base its decision only on objections on which the parties have been able to submit their observations.[344] In the past year, in an effort of increased transparency, the Commission has adopted the practice of issuing a public press release informing third parties that such a statement of objections had been issued to the notifying party.

- Once the undertakings concerned have received the Statement of Objections, they will have access to the documents on the Commission file. Such documents include non-confidential versions of replies to requests for information from third parties as well as any complaint from a third party. In light of the Commission's increased reliance on economic data and in order to guarantee the notifying parties' access to such data, the Commission adopted the Economics Best Practice Guidelines in 2011.[345] These guidelines guarantee that the parties' external legal and economic advisors can have access to the data used by the Commission to carry out its econometric analysis. This data will be contained in a so-called data room at the Commission's premises. The advisers can make use of the information contained in the data room for the purpose of defending their client but may not disclose any confidential information to their client. The advisers are also strictly prohibited from taking copies, notes or summaries of the documents and may only remove a final report from the data room, which is to be verified by the case team in order to ensure that it does not contain any confidential information. In case M.9409 *Aurubis/Metallo Group Holding*, the notifying party's external advisors were granted access to a data room to verify the Commission's economic analysis. Access to the file is subject to the supervision of the Hearing Officer, who adjudicates disputes between the Commission and notifying parties.[346]
- The response to the Statement of Objections is to be made in writing, and the original and three hard copies of the response, as well as two electronic copies of the submission in CD- or DVD-ROM format should be supplied. Such a response will be forwarded by the Commission to the NCAs of Member States without delay.
- Further to the receipt of the reply to the Statement of Objections, the Commission will generally request additional information from the undertakings concerned and third parties to test the arguments put forward in the reply to the Statement of Objections.
- The parties can request an oral hearing by the Commission. Such a request must be made in the reply to the Statement of Objections. An oral hearing will typically take place within one week after the Commission receives the parties' response to the Statement of Objections. The purpose of the oral hearing is to give the notifying parties the right to respond orally and to set out their counter-arguments to the Commission's objections. In addition, it

[344] For the consequence of failing to comply with this rule, *see* case T-310/01 *Schneider Electric v. Commission* [2002] ECR II-4071 where Schneider succeeded not only in having the Commission's decision annulled but also on its claim for damages against the Commission for maladministration.

[345] DG Competition Best Practices for the Submission of Economic Evidence and Data Collection in Cases concerning the Application of Arts 101 and 102 TFEU and in Merger Cases – 17 Oct. 2011.

[346] *See* Art. 7(1) of the Hearing Officer Mandate.

provides the forum for other involved parties and interested third parties, where applicable, to comment on the positions of both the Commission and the notifying parties. Importantly, the oral hearing is also attended by the Commission's Legal Service (which will review the decision before adoption) and representatives of NCAs of Member States (which give a non-binding but influential opinion on the merits of the case through the Advisory Committee).[347] There is an increasing tendency for parties not to request such a hearing particularly in view of the insufficient time available to prepare for it and due to the fact that it offers an additional means for certain third parties to challenge the case. In an effort to improve the attractiveness and effectiveness of hearings for the notifying parties, the Hearings Officers have in recent years taken various steps to change the organisation of Oral Hearings. In case M.6101 *UPM/Myllykoski and Rhein Papier*, the Commission decided not to pursue the concerns raised in their Statement of Objections in light of '*the written comments of the notifying party, the contribution of all participants in the oral hearing, and further investigation carried out post-SO*'.[348] Due to the travel and remote working constraints imposed by the COVID-19 pandemic making face-to-face hearings impossible to organise, the Commission also organised 'virtual' oral hearings in at least three cases.[349]

- The oral hearing is conducted by a Hearing Officer. The Hearing Officer's role has been enhanced by the Commission to increase transparency and accountability.[350] The Hearing Officer's report, which must be published along with the Commission's decision, provides an insight into procedural steps taken in the investigation including the proper conduct of the oral hearing, access to the file, disclosure of documents and observance of time limits. The Hearing Officer also decides whether certain third parties may participate in the oral hearing.
- Following the parties' reply to the statement of objections and the oral hearing, a State of Play meeting is recommended to provide the notifying parties with the opportunity to understand the Commission's position after it has considered their reply and heard them during the hearing. If the Commission indicates that it maintains its objections this meeting can also serve as a basis to discuss possible remedy proposals.

---

347 The procedure at the hearing normally takes place as follows: first the Commission's Services present their case summarising their objections against the concentration; the notifying parties are then given the opportunity to respond; NCAs of Member States' representatives and third parties are then encouraged to ask questions of both the Commission and the notifying parties; involved parties and third parties make presentations and are open to questioning by the NCAs of Member States, the parties and the Commission's Services; and finally the notifying parties make their closing statements.

348 Case M.6101 *UPM/Myllykoski and Rhein Papier*, Final Report of the Hearing Officer (2012 OJ C 107/4).

349 *See* cases M.9014 *PKN Orlen/Lotos*, M.9569 *EssilorLuxottica/GrandVision* and M.9343 *Hyundai Heavy Industries Holdings/Daewoo Shipbuilding & Marine Engineering*.

350 This has been occurred predominantly through the Hearing Officers Terms of Reference, *see* Commission Decision of 23 May 2001 on the terms of reference of hearing officers in certain competition proceedings (2001/462/EC) (Hearing Officer Terms of Reference).

- Following the oral hearing, the Commission generally takes one or two weeks to prepare a draft decision. This draft decision is circulated among various services of the Commission and reviewed by the Peer Panel. It is then sent to Member State representatives appointed to sit on the Advisory Committee for consideration at least ten working days before the meeting of the Advisory Committee.[351]
- Simultaneously, and within sixty-five working days of the initiation of the Phase II procedure,[352] the parties may propose commitments to the Commission which deal with the competition problems identified. These are typically discussed with the Commission and revised before a definitive draft set of commitments is 'market tested' with third parties and sent to Member States via the Advisory Committee for their comments. Because of the timing of the issuance of the Statement of Objections and the Oral Hearing, the amount of time remaining for the negotiation of commitments within the ninety working day period (where the remedies are submitted before the end of the fifty-fifth working day of the procedure) can be extremely short.
- The Advisory Committee meets in private after the oral hearing to discuss and give comments on the Commission's draft decision and any commitments that may have been offered by the parties. It is provided with a copy of the Commission's proposed decision, together with an 'indication of the most important documents' relevant for an appreciation of the case. The committee members indicate their agreement or otherwise with the decision by a vote. Notifying parties may not attend and the way in which each Member State has voted is not disclosed at any stage. The Advisory Committee will then issue an opinion either in favour of the proposal, or against it, of specific parts of it, which will thereafter be disclosed to the parties and published in the Official Journal.[353]
- Before the Advisory Committee meeting takes place a further State of Play meeting is recommended to enable the notifying parties to discuss the Commission's views and the impact of any remedies submitted by the parties (if relevant the results of the market testing of the remedies will also be discussed). This meeting also provides the parties with the opportunity to improve any remedy proposal.
- The Commission is bound by Article 19(6) of the Merger Regulation to take the utmost account of the committee's opinion and must inform the committee as to the way in which its opinion has been taken into account. In a number of cases, more than one Advisory Committee meeting has been held.[354]
- Over the following two weeks, the Commission will make appropriate changes to the draft decision and consult associated services within the

[351] Article 19(5).

[352] If the Phase II period is extended following the extension procedure set out in Art. 10(3) of the Merger Regulation, the sixty-five day deadline is automatically extended by a corresponding period.

[353] Article 19(7) of the Merger Regulation.

[354] *See*, for example, in case M.877 *Boeing/McDonnell Douglas* three meetings were held and cases M.993 *Bertelsmann/Kirsch/Premiere* and M.1027 *Deutsche Telekom/BetaResearch*, where more than one meeting was held.

Commission before submitting a final draft to the Commission's Secretariat General. Since this is a decision for the full College of Commissioners, it will also be considered by each Commissioner's head of cabinet at a meeting. They will then make recommendations to their Commissioners as to voting on the decision.

- A further gap of approximately ten working days is necessary between the submission of the draft decision to the Secretariat General and its adoption by the Commission. All decisions adopted after a Phase II investigation, as well as the final report of the Hearing Officer, must be published in the Official Journal.[355]

[271] Where the competition problems identified in Phase I are confirmed by the more extensive analysis undertaken in Phase II proceedings, there are generally only two outcomes available. Either the concentration is declared incompatible with the Internal Market (this is the only remedy to maintain effective competition), or the parties modify the original concentration plan in such a way as to remove the competition problem. Conversely, when the competition concerns have not been confirmed in Phase II, the Commission must grant unconditional clearance[356] as quickly as possible and in certain cases without the issuance of a statement of objections (e.g., in 2019, in nearly 50% of its Phase II investigations the Commission did not issue a statement of objections).[357] Recent years have also seen a significant increase in abandoned transactions late in the Phase II proceedings due to the apparent impossibility to convince the Commission that the proposed remedies offered alleviated the concerns identified in the Statement of Objections. *See* in particular cases M.10325 *Kronospan/Pfleiderer Polska*, M.9987 *Nvidia/Arm*, M.9938 *Kingspan/Trimo*, M.9637 *IAG/Air Europa*, M.9489 *Air Canada/Transat* or M.9162 *Fincantieri/Chantiers de l'Atlantique* where the transactions were reportedly abandoned due to persisting Commission concerns and looming prohibitions.

[355] Merger Regulation, Art. 20(2).

[356] Case M.5141 *KLM/Martinair.*

[357] Cases M.4737 *Ineos Kerling*, M. 4942 *Nokia/Navteq*; M.4956 *STX/Aker Yards*; M.5141 *KLM/Martinair;* M.6214 *Seagate/HDD Business of Samsung Electronics*; M.8394 *Essilor/Luxottica*; M.8788 *Apple/Shazam* and M.8909 *KME/MKM*. *See also* para. 270 above.

Figure 3 EUMR: Phase II (90–105 Working Days)[358]

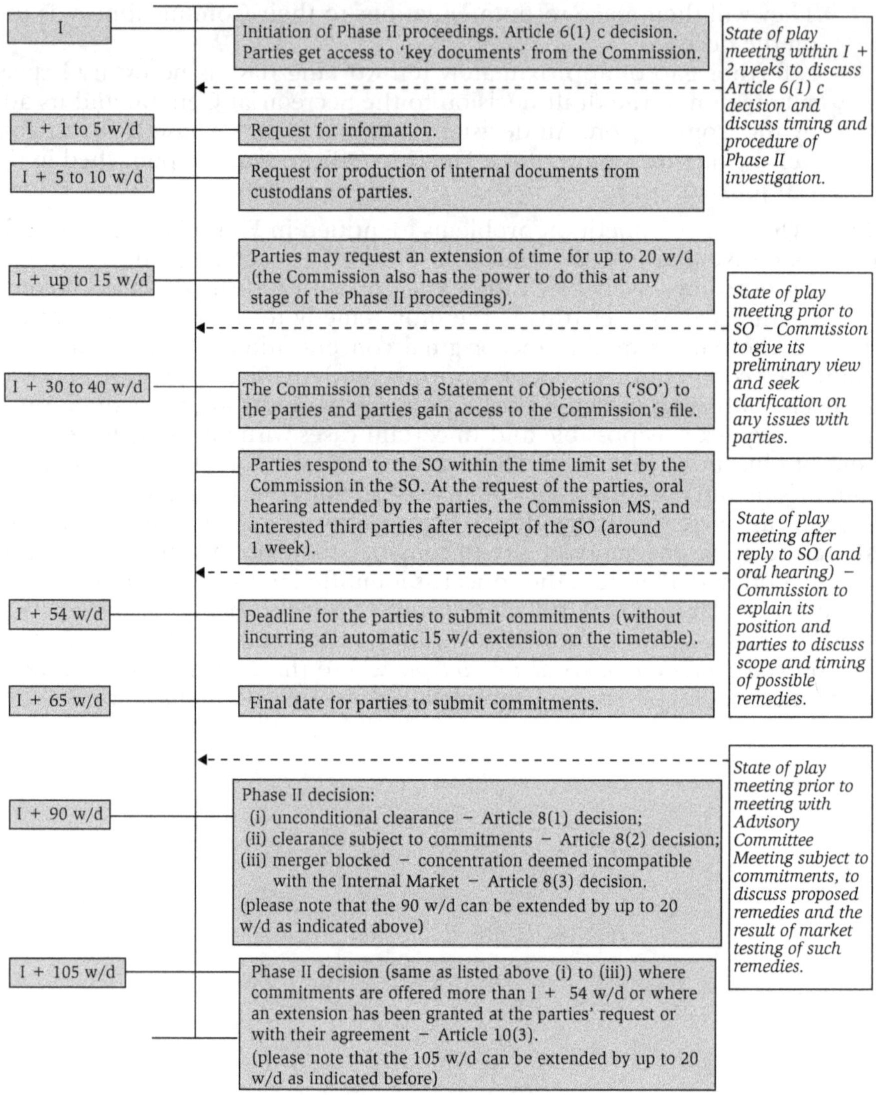

358 Please note that this timeline does not take into account the possibility for the Commission to suspend the timing of its review process – 'stop the clock' – in the event, for example, that the parties fail to reply to a request for information. The timing of the review process which is stopped will be resumed by the Commission once the parties comply with the Commission's request.

7.6 Statement of Objections and Access to the File

[272] As discussed above, the Commission is obliged to address its objections in writing (in the form of Statement of Objections) to the notifying parties and to inform in writing other involved parties and third parties showing sufficient interest in accordance with Article 18(4) of the Merger Regulation (Articles 13(2) and 16 of the Implementing Regulation).

[273] As confirmed by the ECJ, the Statement of Objections is a procedural and preparatory document which delimits the scope of the Commission's administrative procedure preventing the Commission from relying on other objections in its final decision.[359] The Commission then informs the notifying parties in writing of its objections via the Statement of Objections. However, third parties who are entitled to be heard are not automatically entitled to see the objections concerned or to otherwise learn of the Commission's intentions regarding the proposed concentration. Nevertheless, Article 16(1) of the Implementing Regulation provides that the Commission must inform third parties (who have made a written application to be heard) in writing of *'the nature and subject matter of the procedure'*. In some cases, the third parties receive a complete but non-confidential version of the Statement of Objections.[360] The Commission must fix a time limit within which such third parties may inform the Commission of their views (either in writing or orally). The Implementing Regulation contemplates that there may only be sufficient time for oral comments but allows such statements to be confirmed in writing (Article 16(2)).

[274] Once the notifying parties have received the Statement of Objections from the Commission, the Commission issues a press release to that effect, and the notifying parties can request access to the file. Access to the file is granted for the purpose of enabling the exercise of their rights of defence and is expressly recognised in Article 18(3) of the Merger Regulation, and in further detail in Articles 13(3), 17 and 18 of the Implementing Regulation. Reference should also be made to the Commission's Notice on Access to the File and the Best practices on the submission of economic evidence (in particular paragraph [47]). Access to the file is normally arranged by visiting the Commission on the same day that the Statement of Objections is issued and obtaining a CD-ROM or DVD-ROM from the Commission containing all the documents in the file that the Commission believes the parties should have access to. In addition, a list is normally included of all documents in the file and dictates whether they have been provided to the parties in full, in a non-confidential version, or have not been disclosed at all (such as internal documents). It is customary for the parties to have further discussions with the Commission concerning the reasons for confidentiality and non-disclosure of documents,

[359] Case C-413/06 P *Bertelsmann AG and Sony Corporation of America v. IMPALA and the Commission* [2008] at paras 63–64.

[360] *See* footnote 343 above for cases where "interested third parties" were granted a non-confidential copy of the Statement of Objections and had the ability to provide their comments on this document to the Commission. A non-confidential version of these comments were later also provided to the notifying parties.

which may amount in some cases to breaching their rights of defence. Parties will have further access to the file as documents are submitted to the Commission by third parties during the ongoing investigation. Access to the file is subject to the supervision of the Hearing Officer who deals with the possible disputes between the Commission and the notifying parties. Documents to which access is granted may be used only for the purpose of the proceedings under the Merger Regulation.[361]

[275] Other involved parties may similarly be given access to the file through request but only insofar as this is necessary for the purposes of preparing their comments (Article 17(2), Implementing Regulation). The Commission may be reluctant to grant such requests by third parties, especially because of their implications for resources and timing. In any event, the Commission will not allow access to the business secrets or other confidential information which is not considered necessary by the Commission for the purpose of the procedure, or where internal documents of the authorities (i.e., the Commission and the NCAs) are concerned. Accessible papers therefore comprise the non-confidential data submitted by the parties together with information in the public domain such as press articles, independent statistical data and Commission reports. Partially accessible data will generally comprise parts of third-party responses submitted to the Commission which do not contain business secrets,[362] as well as notes of meetings from which names have been deleted. Non-accessible papers will include internal Commission documents, correspondence with Member States and business secrets data submitted by third parties.

7.7 Conditions Attached to Clearances and Form RM

7.7.1 Legal Basis

[276] Both Article 6(2) and Article 8(2) of the Merger Regulation empower the Commission to attach conditions or obligations to its decision where these are intended to ensure that the undertakings concerned comply with the commitments they have entered into with the Commission to make the concentration compatible with the Internal Market. Between 1990 and June 2023, just below 6% of Commission merger decisions have involved clearances with commitments. In addition, close to 60% of the decisions taken by the Commission clearing a concentration after a Phase II investigation were subject to commitments (*see* below). The Commission issued a new Remedies Notice in October 2008 (replacing the previous 2001 Remedies Notice) setting out guidance on the procedure for submitting commitments and the type of remedies acceptable under the Merger Regulation and

[361] Implementing Regulation Art. 17(4).

[362] It is possible for third parties to secure anonymity in their responses. *See* paras 10–25 of the Commission Notice on access to the file. *See also* case C-310/93 *BPB Industries and British Gypsum v. Commission* [1995] ECR I-865.

Implementing Regulation.[363] In addition to the Remedies Notice, which comprehensively sets out the principles, requirements and procedures for submitting commitments, two other highly relevant Commission documents should also be taken into account when considering the formulation of commitments: (i) the Form RM, which parties must use to describe in detail the precise content of the commitments they intend to offer and to explain why those commitments will eliminate the Commission's competition concerns; and (ii) Best Practice Guidelines for divestiture commitments consisting of model texts to be used in formulating the commitments and in conferring mandates on the monitoring and divestment trustees. Any deviation from the model texts needs to be drawn to the Commission's attention and justified.[364]

[277] Conditions and obligations attached to decisions are the result of an agreement between the parties and the Commission following proposals made by the parties. The Commission may not unilaterally impose commitments. The parties may propose amendments to the notified transaction in order to obtain approval in both stages of the procedure: within twenty working days of notification in a Phase I procedure and within sixty-five working days of the initiating of a Phase II procedure.[365] However, if the Phase II period is extended, the sixty-five-day deadline is automatically extended by a corresponding period. The purpose of these time limits is to enable the Commission to have sufficient time to analyse these undertakings and to 'market test' them with third parties and Member States.[366] As indicated above, when offering commitments to the Commission, the parties must complete the Form RM.[367] One original and three paper copies of the Form RM and supporting documents as well as two copies of the submission in CD- or DVD-ROM format must be submitted to the Commission. These will then be distributed to NCAs (the Advisory Committee in a Phase II procedure) and (non-confidential versions) to interested third parties.

[278] Following the Commission's Remedies Study, in addition to the introduction of Form RM, the roles of the *'hold-separate manager'* and *'monitoring trustee'* were established to protect against any degradation of the business to be divested and to identify any key components or requirements essential in the divestment package. The hold-separate manager is appointed for the duration of the divestiture process and is responsible for the management of the business and the implementation of the hold-separate and ring-fencing obligations. This helps ensure that essential

---

363 Commission Notice on remedies acceptable under Council Regulation (EC) 139/2004 and under Commission Regulation (EC) No. 802/2004, OJ 2008 C 267/1.

364 The case team's practice has been to request an electronic version of the parties' draft commitments comparing them with the model text version but this practice is now formalised by s. 3 of the new Form RM, entitled *'Deviation from Model Texts'*.

365 Article 19(1) and (2) of the Implementing Regulation.

366 In cases involving a geographic market as wide as the EEA, proposed remedies may also be discussed with non-EU competition authorities in the framework of the Commission's bilateral cooperation arrangements for these countries.

367 Use of this form is not only important to meet the procedural requirements of the Commission, but also because it encapsulates many of the essential substantive features which commitments must have if they will be accepted by the Commission.

support and personnel remain available from the parent company and that competitively sensitive information is not passed to the parent which could jeopardise the future viability of the business being divested. The hold-separate manager should act under the supervision of the monitoring trustee. The monitoring trustee is appointed and remunerated by the party offering the divestiture in order to monitor the disposal process generally and report to the Commission on progress, the Commission having approved a short list of candidates for the role. Essentially, the monitoring trustee acts as the Commission's eyes and ears during the disposal process. The monitoring trustee is obliged to submit periodic reports to the Commission and any additional reports requested by the Commission.[368]

[279] In situations where merging parties do not succeed in finding a suitable purchaser within the initial divestiture period, then a divestiture trustee is typically given an irrevocable and exclusive mandate to dispose of the business within a specific deadline at no minimum price to a suitable purchaser.[369] Commitments typically allow a divestiture trustee to include in the sale and purchase agreement such terms and conditions as it considers appropriate for an expedient sale, in particular customary representations, warranties, and indemnities. Merging parties are required to support, inform, and cooperate with divestiture trustees, and to grant them any necessary powers of attorney. In December 2013, the Commission updated its model text for divestiture commitments and the Trustee Mandate to reflect the increased involvement of trustees in the divestment process and the importance of ring-fencing competitively sensitive information while that process is ongoing. The Commission also issued a new set of Best Practice Guidelines concerning the obligation prescribed in these model texts.

[280] The Commission may, in exceptional circumstances, extend the sixty-five working day period for commitments in the Phase II procedure. In case M.1439 *Telia/Telenor*, the Commission accepted commitments one week after the expiry of the legal deadline. This was apparently due to the fact that the notifying companies faced additional and exceptional constraints as the Swedish and Norwegian Parliaments had to be consulted prior to the submission of the proposed remedies. The Commission also took account of the fact that the parties had already indicated what the additional commitments would be in their request for an extension submitted within the legal deadline and that the proposed undertakings were clear-cut. In case M.1524 *Airtours/First Choice*, however, the Commission rejected the submission of undertakings outside the legal deadline on the basis that the parties had not established any exceptional circumstances. In addition, it was observed that the undertakings did not contain anything which could not have been proposed within the sixty-five working day period, and there was insufficient time to analyse the late proposals.

[281] The Commission also allows scope for limited flexibility in the interpretation of commitments in order to alleviate the strict legal deadlines under the Merger Regulation procedure. In its Remedies Notice, the Commission states that it will

[368] *See* Remedies Notice, para. 119.
[369] *See* Remedies Notice, para. 121.

permit only limited modifications to commitments during the Phase I procedure. This is because Phase I remedies are designed to provide a clear-cut answer to a readily identifiable competition concern. With respect to undertakings in the Phase II procedure, the Commission will allow some modifications to commitments after the sixty-five working day period, where the Commission can clearly determine (without further detailed market testing) that the commitments resolve the competition problems identified.[370]

[282] Because of the strict time limits imposed on the offer of commitments, especially during the Phase I procedure, parties must consider the potential commitments they would be prepared to offer (if any) at the outset of the notification in order to avoid the commencement of a Phase II procedure where possible and to obtain approval at the earliest opportunity. In exceptional cases, the Commission has also engaged in remedy discussions with the parties during pre-notification discussions. This was the case in the *Holcim/Lafarge* transaction where in a July 2014 press release, well in advance of the formal filing of the transaction and pursuant to pre-notification discussions with the Commission, Holcim and Lafarge announced a list of assets to be included in the remedies package. The parties presented remedies together with their formal notification at the end of October 2014. The proposed package of divestments contained several changes compared to the parties' earlier statement. The parties made it clear that they had made the changes following preliminary constructive discussions with the Commission during pre-notification contacts.[371]

[283] The basic aim of remedies is to ensure competitive market structures. Remedies proposed by the parties must be proportionate to and entirely eliminate the competition concern. The remedy must also be capable of being implemented effectively within a relatively short period of time, and of being easily monitored. Commitments that are structural in nature are as a rule preferable from the point of view of the Merger Regulation's objective of preventing mergers which threaten to significantly impede effective competition. The Commission's preference for structural remedies is also in part due to the difficulties and resources related to the ongoing monitoring and enforcement of behavioural remedies. Nevertheless, it is recognised in the Remedies Notice that in exceptional circumstances, behavioural remedies may eliminate competition concerns, especially where the concern arises only from the ability and incentive of the merged entity to behave in certain anti-competitive ways.[372] In all cases, it is the responsibility of the parties to provide the necessary information and explanations to demonstrate that the proposed remedy will eliminate the competition concerns identified by the Commission. As of 2008, such information and explanations must be provided in the Form RM which requires:

---

370 *See* cases M.7278 *General Electric/Alstom (Thermal Power – Renewable Power & Grid business)* and M.4180 *Gaz de France/Suez*.

371 Case M.7252 *Holcim/Lafarge*.

372 In case T-102/96 *Gencor v. Commission* [1999] ECR II-753, the General Court specifically stated that the decisive point is not whether a remedy is behavioural or structural in nature but whether it prevents the creation or strengthening of a dominant position.

- a description of the commitment;
- an explanation of the commitment's suitability to remove the competition concerns identified;
- an identification of any deviation from the model texts contained in the Best Practice Guidelines;
- detailed information on the business to be divested; and
- an explanation of the reasons why the merging parties consider that a suitable purchaser will be identified in the proposed time frame.

7.7.2 Standard for Commitments

[284] As indicated in Recital 30 of the Merger Regulation, commitments should be proportionate to the competition problem created by a concentration, and they should entirely eliminate it. This principle of proportionality will be of the utmost importance during the remedy discussion with the Commission as it requires the Commission to accept the least burdensome, complex or intrusive remedy when there is more than one satisfactory method of eliminating the impediment to competition.[373] The Commission has recognised in a number of cases that the scope of divested assets may be broader than what is strictly necessary to remedy the competition concerns that have been identified, but has justified this by the fact that due to the specific characteristics of certain markets, it encountered difficulties in tailoring remedies to address only the specific concerns identified.[374] The Remedies Notice confirms that the remedies must eliminate entirely the competition concerns identified by the Commission. The appropriateness of any commitment is assessed on a case-by-case basis taking into account the structure and the characteristics of the relevant market(s).

[285] The Remedies Notice draws a distinction between commitments offered in Phase I and Phase II procedures. Given the time limits in a Phase I procedure, remedies offered must be designed to provide a straightforward and clear-cut answer to readily identifiable competition concerns. A structural solution removing the entire overlap normally qualifies as a clear-cut solution. The desire of most merging parties to avoid an in-depth Phase II investigation often means that they are prepared to give commitments before the Commission has had the opportunity to fully substantiate its concerns, and in some cases this has led to parties proposing remedies which went well beyond the concerns identified in the first four weeks of the procedure (i.e., selling a subsidiary when effectively the disposal of any one business would have been required). In cases where remedies are accepted during a Phase II procedure, the parties and the Commission have a greater amount of time to assess those competition concerns and the measures necessary to alleviate them.

[373] For a summary of the approach to be taken, *see* the ECJ's judgment in case C-202/06 P *Cementbouw Handel v. Commission* [2006] ECR II-319, at paras 52–54.

[374] *See* cases M.5086 *BAT/Skandinavisk Tobakskompagni* and M.7252 *Holcim/Lafarge*.

[286] Where time is not 'of the essence' for the deal, parties may prefer a Phase II enquiry as it allows more time and opportunity to respond effectively to the Commission's and third parties' complaints (and so avoids the need for remedies).[375] It may also allow more precise, targeted remedies to be agreed with the Commission, or for the Commission to be persuaded of the merits of commitments it rejected in Phase I. In case M.3431 *Sonoco/Ahlstrom/JV*, for example, the Commission cleared a transaction in Phase II on the basis of divestiture commitments it had rejected in Phase I. The Commission explained that its view had changed as a result of the market investigation and the fact there would be an upfront buyer. Similarly, in case M.6106 *Caterpillar/MWM*, the Commission opened a Phase II investigation where Phase I remedies addressed only one of three concerns identified by the Commission. However, the transaction was ultimately approved unconditionally. In view of the increasing number of the Phase II proceedings which are cleared without any commitments, if parties believe that they have solid grounds to alleviate any concern through providing persuasive and informative arguments to the Commission, it may be more advisable to have a longer Phase II which might in the end prove costless in terms of remedies as opposed to an expedited and costly Phase I.[376]

[287] Furthermore, it is worthy to note that the Commission has significant discretion as to whether or not to accept amendments or commitments offered by the parties in Phase I or Phase II proceedings. The Commission is not required by the Merger Regulation to have already established that the concentration would significantly impede effective competition in the Internal Market or a substantial part of it in order to accept commitments.[377] Only if the Commission has erred in law or has manifestly erred in its assessment by rejecting the commitments may the decision be annulled by the General Court.[378] Consequently, the prospect of succeeding in a judicial review action against the Commission resulting from its approach to remedies is regarded as being remote. Third parties are thereby best advised to

---

[375] *See* cases M.4734 *Ineos/Kerling;* M.4523 *Travelport/Worldspan* and M.5141 *KLM/Martinair.*

[376] As of June 2023, 30% of cases cleared under a Phase II procedure have been cleared without commitments. Recent examples are: cases M.10807 *Viasat/*Inmarsat, M.10658 *Norsk Hydro/Alumetal*, M.9409 *Aurubis/Metallo Group Holding*; M.8909 *KME/MKM*; M.8792 *T-Mobile NL/Tele2 NL*; M.8788 *Apple/Shazam*; M.8394 *Essilor/Luxottica;* M.7630 *Fedex/TNT Express*; M.7429 *Siemens/Dresser-Rand*; M.7054 *Cemex/Holcim Assets*; M.7009 *Holcim/Cemex West*; M.6796 *Aegean/Olympic II*; M.6360 *Nynas/Shell/Harburg Refinery*; M.6314 *Telefónica UK/Vodafone UK/Everything Everywhere/JV* and M.6214 *Seagate Technology/the HDD Business of Samsung Electronics.* Cases M.10658 *Norsk Hydro/Alumetal*, M.8909 *KME/MKM*; M.8788 *Apple/Shazam*; M.2495 *Haniel/Fels* and M.1882 *Pirelli/BICC* are examples of cases cleared without the issuance of a statement of objections.

[377] Article 8(2) of the Merger Regulation.

[378] Accordingly, in cases such as case M.619 *Gencor/Lonrho*, case M.774 *Saint-Gobain/Wacker Chemie/NOM*, case M.784 *Kesko/Tuko*, case M.993 *Bertelsmann/Kirch/Premiere*, case M.1672 *Volvo/Scania*, case M.2097 *SCA/Metsä Tissue*, case M.2220 *GE/Honeywell* and case M.4439 *Ryanair/Aer Lingus* the Commission rejected commitments and declared the transaction incompatible with the Internal Market, whereas in cases such as case M.877 *Boeing/McDonnell Douglas*, case JV.48 *Vodafone/Vivendi/Canal+*, case M.986 *Afga-Gevaert/DuPont*, case M.1221 *Rewe/Meinl*, case M.2139 *Bombadier/ADtranz*, case M.1853 *EDF/EnBW*, case M.1673 *Veba/Viag*, case M.1630 *Air Liquide/BOC*, case M.1663 *Alcan/Alusuisse.* In case M.4898 *Compagnie de Saint-Gobain/Maxit* and case M.5190 *Nordic Capital/Convatec*, the Commission accepted the parties' commitments and declared the transaction compatible with the Internal Market.

put their case to the Commission during the market testing of the parties' remedies.

[288] Finally, a clear distinction must be made between the formal commitments offered by the parties to the Commission during its review process and informal statements made by the parties which generally take the form of undertakings to engage or not in certain practices. For example, in certain cases, in order to address potential foreclosure issues raised by the Commission, parties to a concentration have sent letters to their customers or suppliers offering to extend the term of existing contracts. While the General Court has confirmed that these informal statements have no legal effect and that a failure to comply with such statements would not expose the parties to fines or revocation of the clearance decision,[379] in a number of cases the Commission has taken note of these statements intended to provide reassurance as to future market conduct. For example, in case M.6381 *Google/Motorola Mobility* the Commission took note of a letter sent by Google to a number of standard setting organisations in which it indicated to honour Motorola Mobility's previous commitments to license its standard essential patents on fair, reasonable, and non-discriminatory terms. This letter addressed a concern raised by competing producers of smartphones that the merger would deprive them from being able to access these patents. Also, in *Rolls-Royce/ITP*, the Commission accepted that contractual assurances between the parties and a downstream competitor were sufficient to remove the merged entity's ability to engage in input foreclosure, even though these assurances were not reflected in the formal commitments.[380]

7.7.3 Type of Remedies

[289] The Remedies Notice categorises remedies as *'structural'*, *'access'* and *'behavioural'*. Although such categorisation may be deemed to be convenient, in reality the types of remedies actually adopted represent a variety taken across a wide spectrum. Remedies must be carefully designed to resolve the Commission's particular doubts about a merger or to eliminate the competition concerns it identifies. Remedies are therefore highly case specific as recognised by the notice. The Commission has a general preference for structural commitments and in particular divestitures that unlike behavioural remedies do not require medium or long-term monitoring.[381] However, the EU courts have confirmed that non-structural commitments may be capable of addressing competition concerns, and the Commission has lately proven to accept other types of remedies, including commitments to grant access to infrastructure or inputs that 'durably' remove the competitive concerns that have been identified.

[379] Joined cases T-125/97 and T-137/97 *The Coca-Cola Company and Coca-Cola Enterprises v. Commission*, 2000 ECR II-1733.

[380] *See* case M.8242.

[381] *See* Remedies Notice, para. 17.

Structural Divestiture to Create Conditions for the Emergence of a New Competitor or the Strengthening of Existing Competitors

[290] The divested activities must constitute a viable business able to operate on a stand-alone basis to compete effectively with the merged entity and must relate to the most appropriate business regarding the markets where the Commission has raised competition concerns.[382] Divestiture commitments may also be used to remove links between the parties and competitors in cases where these links contribute to competition concerns raised by the merger. The divestiture of a minority shareholding in a joint venture may be necessary in order to sever a structural link with a competitor, or, similarly, the divestiture of a minority shareholding in a competitor.[383]

[291] In most cases, however, the divestment will relate to an overlapping business.[384] In certain circumstances, divestment may mean that the acquirer has to sell off more than it is actually acquiring or divest itself of assets in markets in which the

[382] *See* case M.4439 *Ryanair/Aer Lingus* where the Commission's investigation and market testing of the remedies offered by Ryanair demonstrated that such remedies were inadequate to remove competition concerns. In particular the limited number of airport 'slots' offered was not likely to lead to competition sufficient to replace the competitive pressure currently exercised by each airline on the other. In case M.6166 *Deutsche Börse/NYSE Euronext* the Commission considered that the proposed divestment remedy was not suitable to address the competition concerns it had identified as it would only create a small operator that would have to compete head to head with the merged entity. In case M.7278 *General Electric/Alstom*, the parties offered to divest Alstom's servicing subsidiary and the most technologically advanced parts of its heavy-duty gas turbines (HDGT) business, including its technology for large and very large 50 Hz HDGT, to competitor Ansaldo under a fix-it-first structure. The commitments included the transfer of existing servicing agreements for Alstom's HDGT installed base, with a view to improving the competitiveness and viability of the divestment business. Also, to preserve the purchaser's innovation capabilities, the divestment package also included pipeline technologies for future upgrades, testing facilities, and a large number of Alstom's R&D engineers, who would continue to develop the Alstom technology. In case M.9110 *Amerra/Mubadala/Nireus/Selonda*, the parties offered to divest a package of fish farms, packaging facilities, and hatcheries. The eventual purchaser or purchasers would be entitled to select from several combinations of assets so as to form an efficient cluster with their existing operations, with the aim that the divestment business would be able to replicate a level of competitiveness at least comparable to the retained businesses. Although the divestitures did not eliminate the entire market share increment, they removed a sufficient portion of the overlap to dispel the Commission's concerns and ensured that the merged entity would face a viable competitor. Similarly, in case M.10438 *MOL/OMV Slovenija*, MOL offered to divest a nationwide retail network of 39 fuel stations in Slovenia, currently operating as part of the fuel station networks of both MOL and OMV Slovenija, to the Shell Group. Feedback received from customers and competitors in the market test of the proposed commitments confirmed the Commission's view that the divested assets constitute a viable business that would enable the Shell Group to effectively compete with the merged entity.

[383] Case M.5406 *IPIC/Man Ferrostaal*. In case M.8900 *Wieland/Aurubis Rolled Products/Schwermetall*, the Commission prohibited the transaction, in part because it would have given Wieland full control over an upstream joint venture company, Schwermetall, that supplied important inputs to its parent companies (the merging parties) as well as to third parties. Wieland's proposed remedy did not include the divestment of Aurubis' stake in Schwermetall, and thus did not address the Commission's vertical concern regarding the supply of inputs to smaller downstream competitors.

[384] *See* case M.4898 *Compagnie de Saint-Gobain/Maxit* where the parties agreed to divest two wholly owned Maxit subsidiaries operating the business in which there were competition concerns. In case M.4753 *Antalis/Map* the remedy package consisted of the divestment of an independent and economically viable subsidiary. In specific circumstances, the Commission will accept divestiture of a combination

Commission has not raised competition concerns.[385] However, in the majority of cases, the Commission will be open for discussion with the parties to circumvent the scope of the divestiture to the concern(s) identified and respect the principle of proportionality[386] through the carving out of the divestiture business from the existing business as long as it is deemed to constitute a viable business.[387] In order to ensure that the divested business is viable, the Commission will often prefer a 'reverse carve out' when the parties carve out the limited parts of the business they may keep.[388]

[292] The intended effect of the divestiture will only be achieved if the business is transferred to a suitable purchaser in whose hands it will become an active competitive force in the market. The divested business must be sold to a suitable purchaser within a specific deadline, and the purchaser is required to be a viable existing or potential competitor which is independent of the parties and possesses sufficient financial resources, experience and incentive to develop the divested business as an

---

of assets from both the purchaser and the target company, although in general this is regarded as less likely to result in the creation of a viable company.

385 *See* case M.5190 *Nordic Capital/Convatec* in which Nordic Capital committed to divest the entire wound care business. The commitment also provided for the divestiture of the ophthalmic business (where there was no competition concern) because the entire manufacturing and distribution/sales functions were located on the same site as the wound care business. In case JV.15 *BT/AT&T*, the Commission approved the creation of a joint venture for global telecommunication services to multinational companies and international carrier services subject to commitments that AT&T would divest its UK subsidiary, ACC Long Distance, competing with BT in the UK. In addition, the Commission was concerned about a majority shareholding of AT&T in Telewest which competed with BT for provision of voice telecommunications and internet access. It accepted an undertaking from AT&T to establish and enhance a vertical firewall (structural separation preventing AT&T directors from receiving information or considering issues relating to Telewest) as providing an adequate safeguard against possible coordination. In case M.1578 *Sanitec/Sphinx*, the parties undertook to divest a business in the ceramic bathware market where the Commission had identified concerns. The Commission considered it important for the viability of this business that the parties also divested a taps and mixer business to enable the acquirer to offer a full range of products. Similarly, in case M.9014 *PKN Orlen/Grupa Lotos*, the Commission obtained far-reaching remedies beyond the markets directly impacted by the concentration and considered that the combination of divestitures and other commitments would enable the purchasers of the divested businesses, as well as other competitors, to compete effectively with the merged entity in the relevant markets in the future.

386 Case M.7292 *DEMD/Mondelez/Charger OPCO* where the Commission accepted that the parties offer, as part of their remedy package, a licence to use a brand in Austria rather than requesting a full divestiture of the brand in the EEA which was deemed to be disproportionate by the Commission. Similarly *see* case M.7265 *Zimmer/Biomet* where the Commission found that the granting of a non-exclusive licence to manufacture a product rather than the divestment of a whole business was sufficient to alleviate the competition concern identified.

387 *See* cases M.7975 *Mylan/Meda*; M.7265 *Zimmer/Biomet* and M.5611 *Agilent/Varian*. *See also* case M. 10078 *Cargotec/Konecranes* where Cargotec committed to divest its full cranes and straddle/shuttle carrier business, including a manufacturing plant in Poland and a licence for use of Cargotec's Kalmar brand for the divested product categories. In the mobile equipment markets, including for mobile equipment spreaders, Cargotec committed to divest Konecranes its business for the manufacturing and commercialisation of reach stackers, full container handlers, empty container handlers, as well as forklift trucks. This includes manufacturing plants in Sweden and China, and contracts with distributors.

388 Case M.5181 *Gaz de France/Suez* where the seller retained certain businesses of Distrigaz which was divested as an entity. *See also* cases M.7567 *Ball/Rexam* and M.7435 *Merck/Sigma-Aldrich*.

active competition force.[389] In certain cases, where concerns exist as to the viability and attractiveness of a business to purchasers, the Commission may require an 'upfront' purchaser and an agreement for sale prior to closing of the transaction rather than allowing divestiture during a transitional period after closing.[390] A variant of this is the 'fix-it-first' approach where the notifying party enters into a conditional sale agreement before approaching the Commission with the notification of the transaction.[391]

[293] In situations where the implementation of the parties' preferred divestiture option raises particular uncertainties, the Commission will consider alternative divestment proposals where they each clearly address the Commission's concerns. Where such an alternative commitment is put forward, it should normally be a 'crown jewel' which should not involve any uncertainties as to its implementation and should be capable of being implemented quickly.[392] In addition to the divestiture of businesses or specific assets, the Commission will also consider the divestiture of shareholdings in joint ventures, in order to eliminate structural links with major competitors as well as minority shareholdings, and to increase incentives for competition in the market.[393] The Commission does not always require shareholdings or other links in competitors to be sold outright, provided it is satisfied that influence over the competitor's commercial strategy is eradicated.[394]

---

389 Cases M.5579 *TLP/Ermewa* and M.5611 *Agilent/Varian.*

390 This practice was applied, for example, in case M.6203 *Western Digital/Viviti Technologies* where the parties committed not to implement the transaction until they had divested a hard disk drive business to a suitable purchaser that was committed to maintaining its competitiveness. Also in case M.4513 *Arjowiggins/M-real Zanders Reflex* where given the very limited number of suitable potential purchasers, it was agreed that the parties could not implement the transaction until a binding purchase agreement with a viable purchaser had been signed and that they would abandon the transaction in case the sale to a viable competitor within the prescribed divestiture failed. This fix-it first solution has been widely applied in the US. *See also* cases M.10433 *Vivendi/Lagardere*, M.10438 *PKN Orlen/Grupa Lotos,* M.10078 *Cargotec/Konecranes*, M. 9569 *EssilorLuxottica/Grandvision*, M.9829 *Aon/ Willis Towers* Watson, M.9076 *Novelis/Aleris;* M.8674 *BASF/Solvay's EP and P&I Business*, M. 7278 *General Electric*/Alstom; M.7435 *Merck/Sigma-Aldrich*; M.7252 *Holcim/Lafarge*; M.4835 *Hexion*/Huntsman; M.2060 *Bosch/Rexroth* and M.1915 *Post Office/TNT Post M.V./Singapore Post.*

391 *See* cases M.8864 *Vodafone/Certain Liberty Global Assets*, M.9564 *LSEG/Refinitiv Business* and M.10438 *MOL/OMV Slovenia*.

392 *See* cases M.5865 *Teva/Ratiopharm* and M.6905 *Ineos/Solvay/JV.* In case M.9110 *Amerra/Mubadala/ Nireus/Selonda* the Commission approved commitments that allowed the divestment buyer to choose from various combinations of assets at its discretion. The transaction involved Mediterranean fish farming, which the merging parties each conducted in several different locations. To address horizontal concerns, the Commission approved a remedy that allowed one or more purchasers to select from among several asset combinations, representing in aggregate a specified volume of production, to form an efficient cluster with their existing operations.

393 In case M.1853 *EDF/EnBW*, EDF undertook not to exercise voting rights in a French electricity generator and to remove its representative from the board. *See also* case M.1082 *Allianz/AGF*, case M.1980 *Volvo/Renault V.I.*, case M.1673 *Veba/Viag* and case M.1229 *American Home Products/Monsanto.* In case M.754 *Anglo American/Lonrho*, the Commission required the reduction of Anglo American's shareholding in Lonrho from 27.5% to 9.9%.

394 In case M.2947 *Verbund/Energie Allianz* the Commission accepted a transfer of rights to an independent trustee and in case M.619 *Gencor/Lonrho* it permitted a shareholding to remain provided it was reduced below 10% and was not accompanied by board representation. Also, in case M.6844 *General Electric/Avio*, the Commission was concerned that, following its acquisition of Avio, a participant in

[294] The Remedies Notice sets out the procedural requirements in terms of the mechanism for the sale of businesses. The identity of the purchaser and terms of the purchase agreement are subject to the prior approval of the Commission, usually following the reasoned opinion of the monitoring trustee (except in the case of a 'fix-it-first' solution). Although the Commission does not select the purchaser, an application must be made by the party giving the disposal commitment for approval, and a formal Commission decision is taken as to both the purchaser and the terms of sale (while such a decision is not normally published it can nevertheless be appealed to the courts in Luxembourg[395]). As set out above, vetting the suitability of a proposed purchaser is one of the main tasks of a monitoring trustee and in practice the Commission will rely heavily on the monitoring trustee's opinion. The Commission will need to approve the appointment of the monitoring trustee which the parties will have initially chosen. A high level of information is needed to satisfy the Commission as to the stability of a proposed purchaser, including accounts, other financial statements and evidence of funding to verify the purchaser's financial status.

[295] The Remedies Notice also sets out the requirements which must be fulfilled to ensure that, prior to divestiture, the integrity and viability of the business and its key assets pending sale are protected. As set out above, this obligation is monitored through the use of the hold-separate manager and the monitoring trustee.

Access Remedies

[296] Providing access to certain infrastructure may be necessary when the notifying parties have access to essential infrastructures which enhance their market power or where the notifying parties have a strong hold on the distribution assets needed to access the market. Such commitment is therefore necessary to facilitate market entry by competitors. Often, the Commission will combine such a commitment with other measures such as the divestiture of a business where it is thought that the reduction of entry barriers will not be achieved by individual measures,[396]

---

the Eurojet consortium (a consortium formed with the support of four European Governments to design and manufacture an engine for the Eurofighter military aircraft), General Electric might exercise influence over, and secure access to confidential information of, Eurojet, which competed with engines developed by General Electric. To address this issue to the satisfaction of the Commission, General Electric accepted limits on Avio's post-transactional decisional powers in respect of Eurojet and put in place safeguards to avoid securing access to confidential information.

395 In case M.2978 *Lagardère/Natexis/VUP* Lagardère secured the Commission's approval subject to the divestment of certain assets from VUP. Lagardère approached both Wendel and Odile Jacobs as potential purchasers for the divested business. Lagardère ultimately chose Wendel which was approved by the Commission as a suitable purchaser. Odile Jacob then applied to the General Court for annulment of the decision authorising the concentration and of the decision approving Wendel as purchaser. By judgments of 13 Sep. 2010 (Cases T-279/04 and T-452/04) the General Court confirmed the decision authorising the concentration but annulled the approval decision, on the ground that the latter decision had been adopted on the basis of a report drawn up by a trustee who did not satisfy the required condition of independence set by the Commission. The judgments of the General Court were confirmed by the Court of Justice in 2012 (Cases C-551/10P, C-553/10P and C-554/10P).

396 *See* cases M.6166 *Deutsche Börse/NYSE Euronext*; M.5984 *Intel/McAfee;* M.5655 *SNCF/LCR/*Eurostar; M.3868 *DONG/Elsam/Energi E2*; M.3770 *Lufthansa/Eurowings;* M.3083 *GE/Instrumentarium*; M.6471

although in certain instances, the Commission has accepted clear-cut divestitures of only distribution assets without any divestiture of production capacity.[397] In cases where the relevant market is characterised by overcapacity and therefore production capacity is not a barrier to entry, the Commission has also accepted 'know-how' divestitures, including the transmission of the production process and brands, to enable a competitor to produce a product with specific characteristics or for specific end-use applications.[398]

[297] Pure access remedies were also accepted in the Commission's Phase I clearance of six joint ventures between Daimler and BMW in 2018. This transaction aimed to bring together the parties' respective mobility services in five business areas, including in free-floating car-sharing services where the transaction led to significant overlaps in six German and Austrian cities. The Commission's preliminary investigation found that after the transaction, Daimler and BMW would have the ability and incentive to shut out: (a) rival providers of integrator apps, to the benefit of Daimler's own integrator app 'moovel', and (b) rival car-sharing providers, to the benefit of their own car-sharing services. To address the Commission's concerns, Daimler and BMW offered, in the six relevant cities, a two-fold remedy package, granting:

(1) application programming interface access to third-party aggregator platforms for mobility solutions, so that they can also re-direct users to Daimler and BMW's car-sharing services; and
(2) access to Daimler 'moovel' integrator app to interested car-sharing providers.

[298] The Commission considered that these two access remedies addressed its concerns as they would reduce the barriers to entry for competing free-floating car-sharing providers by ensuring that smaller competitors could enter the market in any of the cities concerned and be immediately visible on 'moovel'. The commitments would also allow integrator apps to also display DriveNow and car2go (BMW and Daimler solutions) to customers seeking a mobility solution.[399]

Behavioural Remedies

[299] The Remedies Notice explicitly states that in exceptional cases behavioural commitments may eliminate competition concerns.[400] This will be the case, for example, when the concern arises only from the ability and incentive of the merged firm to have behaved in certain anticompetitive ways, which may also infringe

Outokumpu/Inoxum; M.7421 *Orange/Jazztel*; M.7612 *Hutchison 3G UK/Telefónica UK*, M.7758 *Hutchison 3G Italy/WIND/JV* and M.10438 *PKN Orlen/Grupa Lotos*.

[397] Case M.7155 *SSAB/Rautaruukki*.

[398] Case M.7061 *Huntsman Corporation/Equity Interests Held by Rockwood Holdings*.

[399] *See* case M.8744 *Daimler/BMW/Car Sharing JV*.

[400] At para. 17.

Article 102 of the TFEU.[401] In the *Tetra Laval* case, the ECJ (upholding the General Court's decision) agreed that the Commission had been wrong not to consider the behavioural commitments proposed by Tetra Laval involving undertakings not to engage in abusive conduct, particularly given the nature of the Commission's conglomerate concerns, which centred on leveraging from the carton market into the polyethylene terephthalate market. The ECJ indicated that: '*With respect to consideration of the behavioural commitments offered by Tetra, the Court of First Instance was right to hold...that the fact that Tetra had...offered commitments relating to its future conduct was a factor which the Commission had to take into account when assessing the likelihood that the merged entity would act in such a way as to make it possible to create a dominant position on one or more of the relevant markets for PET equipment.*'[402]

[300] Nonetheless, despite the observations of the Community Courts in *Tetra Laval*, the Commission retains a strong prejudice against behavioural remedies and will often require such commitments to be bundled with a purely structural remedy.[403]

[301] However, in the *Google/Fitbit* transaction, the Commission has shown its willingness to accept purely behavioural remedies to address its concerns regarding the possible anticompetitive effects of the merger.[404] The Commission had three main concerns. The first related to the business model of companies providing services to Fitbit users and access user data. Services from these companies are provided via the use of an application programming interface (API), and the Commission feared that after the completion of the transaction, Google would have the ability to control the API and restrict its access for other, competing service providers. The second concern related to Fitbit's competitors in the production of wrist-worn wearable devices and the interoperability of competing wearable devices with Android phones. The Commission was concerned that Google might degrade the interoperability with Android phones of competing devices in order to favour Fitbit's products. Finally, the Commission raised a concern relating to Google's market position as a provider of advertising space and related services. In particular, the Commission feared that by acquiring Fitbit's database, Google would increase its already vast data portfolio, thus enabling Google to provide even more personalised advertisements and further improve its position with regard to online search advertising, online display advertising and related technologies.

[302] To address these three concerns, Google submitted the following four behavioural remedies that did not entail any divestiture:

---

[401] *See* case M.5046 *Friesland Foods/Campina*, where the parties committed to ensure the adequate supply of raw milk to all Dutch dairy processors, applying a non-discriminatory pricing formula agreed with the Commission and monitored by an independent foundation.

[402] *See* para. 85 of the ECJ Judgment.

[403] *See* case M.5181 *Gaz de France/Suez* where the divestment of Distrigaz was bundled with the undertaking from the parties to enter into gas supply contracts.

[404] *See* case M.9660.

- First, Google undertook not to use user data collected from Fitbit devices for Google search and display advertising and advertising intermediation products and to technically separate such data from other Google data that is used for advertising purposes (the 'Ads Commitment').
- Second, Google assured that, following the acquisition, users would have an 'effective choice' to grant or deny the use of health and wellness data by other Google Services.
- Third, subject to the users' consent, Google undertook to continue to grant third-party service providers access to users' health and fitness data via the Fitbit API without charging for such access.
- Fourth, Google undertook to continue to license for free those public APIs covering all current functionalities that wrist-worn devices need to interoperate with an Android smartphone as well as future updates, improvements of functionalities and APIs that Google makes available to Android smartphone app developers without any degrading of the user experience or other discriminatory conditions.

Google agreed that all four commitments will remain in place for ten years and that the Ads Commitments may be extended for up to an additional ten years by the Commission.

[303] In May 2023, the Commission adopted a similar approach when it conditionally cleared Microsoft proposed acquisition of Activision Blizzard pursuant to purely behavioural remedies.[405] The Commission's Phase II investigation found that the proposed acquisition would harm competition in the distribution of PC and console games via cloud game streaming services, an innovative market segment that could transform the way many gamers play video games. The Commission found that the popularity of Activision's games could promote its growth. Instead, if Microsoft made Activision's games exclusive to its own cloud game streaming service, Game Pass Ultimate, and withheld them from rival cloud game streaming providers, it would reduce competition in the distribution of games via cloud game streaming. The Commission also found that if Microsoft made Activision's games exclusive to its own cloud game streaming service, Microsoft could also strengthen the position of Windows in the market for PC operating systems. This could be the case should Microsoft hinder or degrade the streaming of Activision's games on PCs using operating systems other than Windows. In order to address these concerns, Microsoft offered the following comprehensive licensing commitments with a 10-year duration:

- a free licence to consumers in the EEA that would allow them to stream, via any cloud game streaming services of their choice, all current and future Activision Blizzard PC and console games for which they have a licence; and
- a corresponding free licence to cloud game streaming service providers to allow EEA-based gamers to stream any Activision Blizzard's PC and console games.

[405] *See* case M.10646.

[304] The Commission's investigation of the effectiveness of these remedies found that cloud game streaming service providers gave positive feedback and showed interest in the licences. Some of these providers had actually already entered into bilateral agreements with Microsoft based on the proposed licences to stream Activision's games, once the transaction is completed.

[305] Normally, the question of varying commitments will simply not arise because a divestiture commitment creates a permanent and irreversible solution through the 'clean break' of a business disposal. Nevertheless, a standard provision in the Model Commitments precludes the disposing party from acquiring control or influence over the divested business or assets for a period of ten years unless the Commission has previously found that the structure of the affected market has changed so much that doing so would not give rise to a significant impediment to effective competition (SIEC). However, it is open to the merged entity to approach the Commission for its approval of a reacquisition. The Commission may also exceptionally agree to the variation of a commitment where a change of circumstances means that the concerns are no longer relevant.[406] Similarly, the Model Commitments contain a standard review clause, which deals with extensions (for the disposal deadline), waiver, modification and substitution in exceptional circumstances, of any of the obligations in the commitments given. The Commission will usually adopt a formal decision in respect of any waiver, modification, or substitution of the commitments as illustrated in the *Nidec/Whirlpool*[407] and *Takeda/Shire*[408] transactions. In the *Nidec/Whirlpool* case, Nidec initially divested its entire global household and light commercial refrigerator compressor business, including plants in Austria, Slovakia, and China. Just a year after the conditional approval decision, in May 2020, the Commission agreed to waive Nidec's commitment not to re-acquire a fixed-speed household compressor manufacturing line that was initially part of the divestiture package. The Commission concluded, after a market investigation, that the structure of the relevant market had changed to such an extent that Nidec's ownership of the asset would no longer have anticompetitive effects. In *Takeda/Shire*, Takeda divested Shire's pipeline product in the field of inflammatory bowel disease to a buyer that would have an incentive to develop the drug. In 2020, less than 18 months after the conditional approval decision, Takeda asked the Commission to waive the commitment, as neither Takeda nor the appointed divestiture trustee had been able to find a suitable buyer, despite engaging with more than sixty potential purchasers over a fourteen-month period. Following an investigation, the Commission found that: (i) new promising drugs had emerged, with a better efficacy and safety profile than both the concerned pipeline

[406] *See* case M.269 *Shell/Montecatini* for an early and rare illustration of a release of commitments. The merger gave the merged entity ownership or influence over the only two manufacturing technologies for polypropylene. To secure clearance, the merging parties committed to transfer one of their interests in one of the polypropylene manufacturers to a new independent technology company. However, the FTC required the same merging party to go as far as divesting itself of all its assets and interests to a third party, and thereby sever all links with the polypropylene manufacturer. The Commission's initial remedy was thereby made redundant.

[407] *See* case M.8947 *Nidec/Whirlpool*.

[408] *See* case M.8955 *Takeda/Shire*.

product and Takeda's existing treatment; (ii) studies on Shire's pipeline product had yielded negative results; and (iii) the divestment business had experienced difficulties in recruiting patients for clinical trials. The Commission concluded that these developments constituted 'exceptional circumstances' that severely impaired the prospects of anyone successfully developing the pipeline product, and accordingly waived the divestiture commitment. Furthermore, in its 2006 *Gaz de France/ Suez* decision,[409] the Commission conditionally approved the merger between France's incumbent gas supplier GDF and one of its main competitors, Suez, but identified concerns regarding the transaction's effect on third parties' ability to supply gas to customers in France, which required access to upstream infrastructures, the bulk of which belonged to GDF. Because GDF controlled extensive underground gas storage sites and had reserved 80–90% of the capacity in one of France's two transmission networks (and Suez a sizeable chunk of the remainder), the transaction risked making access to gas storage more difficult and raising entry barriers as a result. To address this concern, the parties offered to develop new gas storage sites in France (Etrez and Trois Fontaines) and to sell the new storage capacity in the market via transparent and non-discriminatory auctions. The commitments were not limited in time. In 2019, the merged entity (now called Engie) invoked the review clause contained in the 2006 commitments to request that the Commission waive the commitment to auction off the new storage capacities. The Commission's investigation revealed that market circumstances had changed enough to render the commitment unnecessary to ensure access to gas storage and to preserve competition in downstream gas supply markets. The Commission therefore approved the requested waiver, in two stages. On 26 October 2020, the Commission lifted the commitments relating to the new site at Etrez,[410] and on 16 June 2022, following further investigation, the Commission waived the remaining commitments relating to the site at Trois Fontaines.[411]

[306] The Commission specifically states in the Remedies Notice that there are some situations which cannot be resolved by remedies, and the only remedy is prohibition. For example, in several media cases, dominance was created by strong vertical links between the media companies.[412] Any suitable remedies would have deprived the deals of their rationale, and as such the notifying parties may not have been willing to offer them. The same is likely to be the case where the merged entity may be so dominant that there is no prospect of restoring effective competition because of incumbency advantages, such as its economies of scale and scope or established brand and reputation, which would defeat any attempt to restore competition and deter new entry.[413]

[307] Divestitures should not require additional monitoring once they are implemented. However, other types of commitments will require effective monitoring

---

[409] *See* case 4180 *Gaz de France/Suez* (2006).

[410] *See* case 4180 *Gaz de France/Suez* (2020).

[411] *See* case 4180 *Gaz de France/Suez* (2022).

[412] *See*, for example, case M.993 *Bertelsmann/Kirch/Premiere* and case M.1027 *Deutsche Telekom/Beta Research*.

[413] *See*, for example, case M.4439 *Ryanair/Aer Lingus* and M.6166 *Deutsche Börse/NYSE Euronext*.

mechanisms in order to ensure that their remedial effect is not compromised. Some cases have required commitments so extensive and complex that this alone would have rendered monitoring impossible in practice and therefore unacceptable.[414] The Commission has however been prepared to accept ongoing monitoring in some cases.[415]

[308] As set out above, the Commission has no power to authorise a concentration it finds significantly impedes effective competition in the Internal Market or a substantial part thereof. However, it may clear a concentration subject to commitments that will render the concentration compatible with the Internal Market and may attach conditions and obligations to its decision to ensure compliance with those commitments.

[309] Conditions are commitments to implement measures that address competition concerns identified by the Commission, while obligations are undertakings to implement measures necessary to achieve the conditions. A condition attached to the decision must be fulfilled, failing which, the decision will no longer stand.[416] Failure to comply would make the transaction invalid with the civil law consequences to be determined in accordance with national law. Failure to comply would also subject the parties to fines under Article 14(2)(d) insofar as they put into effect a transaction in breach of Article 7(1) which has not effectively been cleared by the Commission. Failure to comply with an obligation attached to a decision does not make the decision ineffective but may lead to withdrawal of the decision at the Commission's discretion under Article 6(3)(b) (Phase I procedure) or Article 8(6)(b) (Phase II procedure).[417] At the time of writing, the Commission has neither revoked a clearance decision nor fined any company for breaching a commitment. Indeed, while the Commission sent in 2019, for the first time, a statement of objections to Telefónica Deutschland alleging that the company failed to comply with and breached its merger commitments offered to secure the approval of its acquisition of E-Plus in 2014, the Commission closed its proceedings in March 2021

[414] *See*, for example, case M.2093 *Airtours/First Choice* where the Commission rejected behavioural commitments because they would be difficult to monitor and enforce. In case M.1741 *MCI WorldCom/Sprint*, the Commission found that monitoring of the proposed commitments would require considerable staff and skills resources which would result in uncertainty. Also one of the reasons why the Commission rejected certain of the behavioural commitments proposed by Ryanair in an effort to secure approval of the Ryanair/Aer Lingus I transaction was that they would have been too difficult to monitor.

[415] *See*, for example, case M.2684 *EnBW/EDP/Cajastur/Hidrocantabrico*, where the Commission accepted undertakings by EDF and RTE to increase commercial interconnection capacity between France and Spain in accordance with a three-stage construction plan which included participation in user groups and studies.

[416] Remedies Notice, paras 19 and 20. *See also* the most recent decisions in the airline industries where in addition to slot divestments, parties usually also offer commitments relating to a frequency freeze, interlining agreements, access to frequent flyer programme, blocked space agreements and conditions on fares.

[417] In several cases the Commission has expressly reserved its rights to impose fines, for example, case M.430 *Procter & Gamble/VP Schickedanz (II)*. In case M.623 *Kimberley-Clark/Scott Paper*, the Commission reserved the right to revoke the decision.

without imposing any fines or correctives measures on the parties.[418] It is also worth noting that in the recent *Novelis/Aleris* transaction which the Commission cleared further to the commitment to divest a plant in Belgian, Novelis found itself in the peculiar position of not having yet implemented the divestment despite being granted several extensions of the divestment period by the Commission. With the Commission rejecting the company's latest extension request, Novelis found itself in breach of the commitments offered to the Commission. In order to solve the legal vacuum resulting from the fact that the Commission's decision clearing the acquisition of Aleris became inapplicable pursuant to paragraph 20 of the Remedies Notice, and the divestment itself also became inapplicable, in a rare move, the Commission adopted provisional interim measures to preserve competition pursuant to Article 8(4) of the Merger Regulation. The decision, adopted in February 2021, ensures that competition is preserved by imposing final measures on Novelis. These include obligations similar to the commitments originally attached to the 2019 clearance decision that also ensure that the divested Duffel plant remains a competitive and autonomous player on the market.[419] This is a rare example of the Commission adopting a decision under the Merger Regulation to replace the commitments infringed by the parties, and force the divestment of a business.

[310] Moreover, if the parties fail to implement a disposal commitment within the period specified, a divestiture trustee may be appointed with an exclusive mandate to effect a sale at no minimum price and on any terms and conditions it considers appropriate to expedite the sale. In accordance with the Commission's Model Commitments, a divestiture trustee must be appointed within one month of the end of the initial period allowed for disposal by the parties. However, the Commission is normally reluctant to resort to a divestiture trustee, and if progress is being made towards a sale, it will not insist on the appointment.

7.8 Withdrawal and Abandonment

[311] Notifications may be withdrawn by the parties at any stage of the proceedings, although most of the withdrawals occur during Phase I when a Phase II procedure is inevitable. In such cases, the parties may choose to withdraw the notification, and subsequently re-notify the proposed transaction to the Commission (without any modification of the proposed transaction as such) or alternatively abandon the transaction (this will generally be the case when the scope of the remedies requested by the Commission significantly impacts the economic rationale and viability of the proposed transaction).[420]

[418] *See* https://ec.europa.eu/competition/elojade/isef/case_details.cfm?proc_code=2_M_9003.

[419] *See* https://ec.europa.eu/commission/presscorner/detail/en/IP_21_687.

[420] For recent examples of notifications withdrawn *see* cases M.9637 *IAG/Air Europa*; M.9938 *Kingspan Group/Trimo*; M.9987 *Nvidia/Arm*; M.10319 *Greiner/Recitcel*; M.10325 *Kronospan/Pfleiderer Polska*; M.9997 *HMM/CMA CGM/DIF/TTIA;* M.9097 *Boeing/Embraer*; M.9162 *Fincantieri/Chantiers de l'Atlantique*; M.6362 *CIN/Tirrenia Business Branch*; M.5969 *SCJ/Sara Lee* and M.5454 *DSV/Vesterhavet/*

[312] Where the parties decide to re-notify the proposed transaction without modifying it (so-called pull and refile), this new notification will bear the same case number as the original notification but will give rise to the publication of a notice in the Official Journal, as provided for in Article 4 of the Merger Regulation. On the other hand, if the structure of the transaction is modified (i.e., change in the structure or quality of control), then the notification will receive a new case number and will also give rise to the publication of a notice in the Official Journal. It should be noted that such 'pull and refile' mechanism cannot take place in Phase II unless the transaction has been formally abandoned as set out in DG COMP's information note on Article 6(1)c 2nd sentence of the Merger Regulation on the abandonment of concentrations, and the parties enter into a new agreement giving rise to a modified concentration and a new notification.

[313] Following case M.1741 *MCI WorldCom/Sprint* (where the Commission refused to let the parties withdraw the notification just prior to the release of its prohibition decision), Article 6(1)(c) of the Merger Regulation was amended to clarify that Phase II proceedings must culminate in a decision of one of the kinds provided for in Article 8(1)–(4) unless the undertakings concerned satisfy the Commission that they have abandoned the concentration. As set out in the Commission's Consolidated Notice, to do so, the Commission requires evidence on par with that which it accepted to establish the existence of the concentration (or proposed concentration) which would trigger a Phase I examination.[421] As such, the mere withdrawal of a notification is not considered as sufficient proof that a concentration has been abandoned. For instance, where the concentration came about through binding legal obligations, the Commission would expect to see an arrangement bringing the obligations to an end.

[314] The most problematic situations are likely to occur where the Commission has accepted a notification on the basis of a good faith intention to enter into arrangements constituting a concentration. In such a case, the most certain approach will be for the parties to execute a document or agreement acknowledging *inter se* that no such intention continues to exist, i.e., providing proof which exceeds '*in terms of form and intensity*' the initial expression of intent so as to put the matter beyond doubt.[422] Similarly, where a concentration has been implemented, the parties would have to demonstrate that the status quo has been re-established.

DFDS. For examples of notifications withdrawn and re-filed to avoid a Phase II, *see* cases M.398 *Procter & Gamble/VP Schikedanz*; M.562 *Swissair/Sabena*; M.608 *Ericsson/Ascom*; M.948 *Watt AG;* M.1388 *Total Petrofina* and M.2117 *Aker Maritime/Kvaerner.*

[421] *See* para. 314, footnote 422.

[422] The Consolidated Jurisdictional Notice deals explicitly with the reversal of a concentration notified on the basis of a good faith intention, stating that '*the abandonment must reverse this good faith intention and correspond in terms of form and intensity to the initial expression of intent*' (para. 120). Note particularly case M.4381 *JCI/FIAMM* where the Commission did not accept the withdrawal of the notification as only JCI no longer wished to implement the agreement bringing about the concentration, whereas FIAMM still considered the agreement to be binding and enforceable.

7.9 Commission's Fact-Finding Powers

[315] The Form CO is the Commission's most important source of information, although the Commission supplements it by asking both the notifying parties and third parties (mainly competitors and customers) for further information. Where appropriate, the Short Form CO and the simplified procedure is an alternative method that the Commission uses in order to reduce the burden both on itself and on the parties on occasions where the thresholds requiring notification are met, but where the activities of the parties do not overlap, or overlap in such a limited way that there is no realistic possibility of competition concerns arising. However, delivery of a Short Form CO does not preclude the Commission from asking for further information for its analysis. In fact, in most cases, the Commission will ask a large number of questions to the notifying parties to ascertain whether the notified transaction qualifies for treatment under the simplified procedure.[423]

7.10 Request for Information

[316] The Commission is empowered to *'obtain all necessary information'* from Member State governments and competent authorities as well as from undertakings, associations of undertakings and other persons. In certain cases, investigations can involve a large number of companies, and as a general matter, considerable importance is attached to information and explanations provided by customers. Such a request from the Commission may be made in a *'simple'* letter, or by means of a *'formal'* decision.[424] Normally, a simple request under Article 11(2) of the Merger Regulation is initially made by written letter. However, the Commission may also make requests by telephone.[425] Where an Article 11 request is sent to a person, an undertaking or an association of undertakings, the Commission is obliged to send a copy of the request to the NCA of the Member State within whose territory it is resident.[426] In terms of process information requests are normally sent after the notification of the proposed transaction. However, it should be noted that in an increasing number of cases where the existence of the transaction is in the public domain, the Commission has contacted third parties and started its market test during the pre-notification period. Before doing so, the notifying parties will have to be consulted by the Commission and will have the opportunity to *'express their views on such measures'*.[427]

[423] *See* above discussion on the Commission's simplified procedure rules.

[424] The main difference being that with a formal request the Commission is able to impose periodic penalty payments (Art. 15 of the Implementing Regulation) in addition to the penalties under Art. 14 of the Merger Regulation.

[425] Case T-221/95 *Endemol* [1999] ECR II-1299.

[426] Article 11(5) of the Merger Regulation.

[427] Best Practice Guidelines at para. 26.

[317] In practice, requests for information by formal decision are typically utilised as a 'last chance' for parties to comply with a request before the imposition of penalties. Consequently, where the information sought after in a simple request is not provided within the specified period or if incomplete information is provided, the Commission will require the information to be provided by means of a formal decision under Article 11(3). However, it is no longer necessary for the Commission to have failed to receive a response to a simple request in order to issue a formal decision, which of itself can be the first request made for information where desired.

[318] The provision of incorrect information in response to an Article 11(2) request or the failure to supply information within the period fixed by a formal Article 11(3) decision will make the persons or undertakings concerned liable to a fine of up to 1% of group aggregate turnover, whether such conduct was intentional or negligent.[428] In addition, where the Commission formally requests information via an Article 11(3) decision, it may additionally levy periodic penalty payments not exceeding 5% of the average daily aggregate turnover for each working day of delay, calculated from the date set out in the decision in order to compel the party to supply complete and correct information as requested pursuant to the Article 11(3) decision (*see* below).[429] Further, it should be recalled (as indicated in paragraph [226] above) that third parties are also liable to a fine and may also be subject to a periodic penalty payment should they not respond to the Commission's requests for information.

[319] In 2017, the Commission imposed a fine of EUR110 m on Facebook for submitting misleading information during the merger control clearance process for its 2014 acquisition of WhatsApp. This was the first time that the Commission's power to impose sanctions for misleading information was used. Facebook's purchase of WhatsApp was announced in 2014 and was subject to merger control clearance, including from the Commission. One of the focuses of the Commission's investigation was the extent to which the transaction would substantially strengthen 'network effects'. Would the merger allow the Facebook Messenger and WhatsApp networks to be integrated to create one substantially larger network? Third parties told the Commission that this would be relatively easy from a technical perspective. However, Facebook countered that there would be significant technical difficulties, including the two apps using different account identifiers, and having fundamentally different architecture. The Commission therefore concluded that technical integration was unlikely to be as simple as third parties claimed and, even if it did occur, it was unlikely to strengthen the existing network effects substantially. The merger was cleared in October 2014.

[320] In August 2016, it became clear not only that the integration of the Facebook Messenger and WhatsApp networks was planned but also that: (a) it had been technically possible in 2014 and (b) contrary to the statements made to the Commission, Facebook staff had been aware that it was technically possible in 2014. The

[428] Article 14(1)(b) and (c) of the Merger Regulation.

[429] Article 15(1)(a) of the Merger Regulation.

Commission started proceedings against Facebook for providing misleading information, sending a Statement of Objections in December 2016, and ultimately imposing a fine of EUR110 m. Facebook acknowledged that it was at fault and waived some of its procedural rights, earning a discount from the fine.[430] The fining decision had no impact on the clearance decision as the latter was based on a number of elements going beyond automated user matching. At the time of the clearance decision, the Commission also carried out an 'even if' assessment that assumed user matching as a possibility.

[321] In April 2019, the Commission imposed a fine of EUR52 m on General Electric for providing incorrect information in its merger notification form relating to the acquisition of LM Wind. In January 2017, GE notified its proposed acquisition of LM Wind to the Commission. In the notification, GE stated that it did not have any higher power output wind turbine for offshore applications in development, beyond its existing 6 megawatt turbine. However, through information collected from a third party, the Commission found that GE was simultaneously offering a 12 megawatt offshore wind turbine to potential customers. As a result, GE withdrew its notification and re-notified the same transaction, this time including complete information on its future project. In March 2017, the Commission approved the proposed acquisition. When setting the EUR52 m fine, the Commission noted that GE committed the infringement by negligence and that the infringement was serious in particular because, from the continuous contacts GE had with the Commission in the merger review process, especially regarding GE's pipeline products in this market, GE should have been aware of the relevance of the information for the Commission's assessment.[431] The fining decision has no impact on the Commission's clearance of the transaction as it was based on rectified information.

[322] On 3 May 2021, the Commission fined Sigma-Aldrich EUR7.5 m for the provision of incorrect or misleading information to the Commission in relation to its review of Merck's acquisition of Sigma-Aldrich.[432] In 2015, the Commission received the notification of the deal and cleared it on condition that the parties divest certain Sigma-Aldrich assets to address concerns in relation to specific laboratory chemicals.[433] However, at the time, Sigma-Aldrich was engaged in an innovation project (iCap), which was closely associated with the business to be divested. However, no information concerning iCap was provided to the Commission – neither during the remedy submissions nor in response to two specific requests for information from the Commission. For this reason, the Commission concluded that Sigma-Aldrich committed three distinct infringements by providing incorrect or misleading information with respect to the iCap project. Although initially the Commission began proceedings against both parties, only Sigma-Aldrich has ultimately been fined (following hearings in 2020, the allegations against Merck were dropped).

430 *See* Commission Press Release IP/17/1369 of 18 May 2017.

431 *See* Commission Press Release IP/19/2049 of 8 Apr. 2019.

432 Case M.8181 *Merck/Sigma-Aldrich*.

433 Case M.7435 *Merck/Sigma-Aldrich*.

7.11 Powers of Investigation

[323] The Commission has the power under Article 12 of the Merger Regulation to request the competent authorities of the Member States to undertake on-the-spot investigations. However, it is likely that the Commission will undertake an investigation itself under Article 13. With the exception of investigatory powers against individuals, Commission officials have broadly similar powers of investigation as those conferred by Regulation 1/2003, namely:

(a) to enter company premises, land or vehicles;
(b) to examine the books and other business records in any form;
(c) to take or demand copies of such records;
(d) to seal premises, books or records as necessary to maintain the integrity of the investigation;
(e) to ask for explanations of facts or records from any individual associated with the parties in question.

[324] In practice, the Commission has rarely used its powers under Article 13, and therefore it is not clear whether the Commission would be likely to always issue a decision. These powers have been used in connection with two particular cases: one where there were indications that a notifiable transaction had not been notified[434] and in another where the Commission had been tipped off that the parties had implemented the transaction before the truncated Phase II enquiry had led to a clearance decision, although such an allegation was found to be unsubstantiated.[435]

[325] If an undertaking fails to submit to an investigation ordered by the Commission by a decision pursuant to Article 13, it will be liable to periodic penalty payments not exceeding 5% of the average daily aggregate turnover for each working day of delay, calculated from the date set in the decision (*see* below).[436]

7.12 Sanctions

[326] Article 14(4) of the Merger Regulation expressly provides that decisions to fine parties in connection with mergers are not of a criminal nature. However, it is useful to note that in contrast to Regulation 1/2003, fines may be imposed on individuals under the Merger Regulation if they are persons named pursuant to Article 3(1)(b) of the Regulation.

[327] Article 14(1) of the Merger Regulation provides that the Commission may impose on undertakings or associations fines not exceeding 1% of the aggregate turnover of the undertaking or the association of undertakings concerned where they intentionally or negligently:

[434] Case M.1157 *Skanska/Scancem*.
[435] Cases M.4734 *Ineos/Kerling* and M.6106 *Caterpillar/MVM*.
[436] Article 15(l)(b) of the Merger Regulation.

(a) supply incorrect or misleading information pursuant to Article 4 (notification of a concentration), Article 10(5) or Article 22(3);
(b) supply incorrect or misleading information in reply to a request under Article 11(2);
(c) supply incorrect, incomplete or misleading information, or failing to supply information within the time limit, requested by decision under Article 11(3);
(d) refuse to submit to an investigation order under Article 13, or supply incomplete documents during an investigation;
(e) in response to a question asked during an investigation, where an incorrect or misleading answer is provided and is not rectified within the time limit provided or where there is a failure or refusal to provide a complete answer on facts; or
(f) cause seals affixed by officials or other accompanying persons authorised by the Commission in accordance with Article 12(2)(d) to be broken.[437]

[328] Article 14(2) of the Merger Regulation provides that fines of up to 10% of the parties' (including group) aggregate turnover may be imposed against any party which, either intentionally or negligently:

(a) fails to notify a concentration in accordance with Article 4 or 22(3) prior to its implementation (unless expressly authorised to do so pursuant to Article 7(2), or by decision taken pursuant to Article 7(3));
(b) implements a concentration in breach of Article 7;
(c) implements a concentration declared incompatible with the Internal Market by a decision pursuant to Article 8(3) (prohibition), or does not comply with any measure ordered by decision pursuant to Article 8(4) or (5); or
(d) fails to comply with a condition or obligation that is imposed by decision for waiving or lifting a suspension under Articles 6(1)(b), 7(3) or under the terms of a clearance decision under Article 8(2).

[329] Article 15 of the Merger Regulation provides that the Commission may, in addition, impose on the persons referred to in Article 3(1)(b), undertakings or associations of undertakings, periodic penalty payments not exceeding 5% of the average daily aggregate turnover of the undertaking concerned for each working day of delay (from the date set within the decision) for failing to:

(a) supply complete and correct information requested by decision pursuant to Article 11(3);
(b) submit to an investigation ordered by decision taken pursuant to Article 13(4);

[437] While this has not yet been applied in practice in relation to merger control at the time of writing, a fine amounting to EUR38 m was imposed on E.ON for the breach of a Commission seal in E.ON's premises during an ongoing inspection in 2006 under Regulation 1/2003. The seal had been fixed by Commission officials during a dawn-raid to protect confiscated documents. The fine imposed by the Commission was upheld by the ECJ in 2012. In 2011 the Commission imposed a fine of EUR8 m on Suez Environnement and Lyonnaise des Eaux for a similar conduct.

(c) comply with obligations imposed by decision pursuant to Articles 6(1)(b), 7(3) or 8(2); or
(d) comply with any measures ordered by decision pursuant to Article 8(4) or (5).

[330] Articles 6(3) and 8(6) of the Merger Regulation provide that the Commission may revoke decisions pursuant to either Article 6(1)(a) or (b) or Article 8(1) or (2) respectively declaring a concentration to be compatible with the market where either:

(a) the decision is based on incorrect information for which one of the undertakings is responsible or where it has been obtained by deceit; or
(b) the undertakings breached an obligation attached to the decision.

[331] Where the Commission finds that a concentration has already been implemented and has been declared incompatible with the Internal Market or has been implemented in contravention of a condition attached to a decision under Article 8(2) of the Merger Regulation, Article 8(4) provides a number of measures that the Commission may impose on the undertakings by decision to dissolve the concentration or otherwise take other restorative measures. Such measures may include a requirement that the undertakings or assets brought together are separated, a joint venture is disbanded, or any other action that may be appropriate in order to restore conditions of effective competition.

[332] A decision of compatibility may be revoked under Article 6(3) where it is based on incorrect information for which one of the undertakings is responsible or where it has been obtained by deceit. This may also occur where the undertakings concerned commit a breach of an obligation. To date, the Commission has used its powers to revoke a clearance decision in only two cases. In 1999, five weeks after its decision under Article 6(1)(b) clearing the merger, the Commission, pursuant to Article 6(3)(a), revoked its decision approving the merger between Sanofi and Synthélabo.[438] The two French chemical and pharmaceutical companies had failed to describe their activities of production and marketing of tranquilisers in their original notification.[439] The deal was later cleared following a complete re-notification subject to a commitment by Synthélabo to divest its tranquiliser interest. Thereafter, in 2000, in two related joint venture cases, the Commission withdrew a decision and issued a second decision in an attempt to reverse the approval it had granted to certain provisions which had been erroneously treated as ancillary restraints.[440] However, the second decision was ultimately annulled by the General Court on appeal on the basis that the general principles of EU law concerning legitimate expectations prevented the withdrawal of any Community measures (including a merger decision) which confer rights or similar benefits on individuals unless the

[438] Case M.1397 *Sanofi/Synthélabo.*

[439] *See* Commission Press Release IP/99/255. The Commission reopened its examination of the case but allowed a partial exemption from the Art. 7(1) suspension because the parties offered undertakings to address competition concerns and because of the significant prejudice that delay would have caused to the parties and their shareholders.

[440] Cases COMP JV.40 *Canal+/file:Lagardère* and COMP JV.47 *Canal+/file:Lagardère/Liberty Media.*

decision was tainted by illegality. It was confirmed that the Commission must show reasons for its actions and respect for the legitimate expectations of any party who might have relied on the legality of the decision.[441]

[333] As explained earlier on, failure to comply with commitments offered to the Commission to secure merger control approval will lead to the clearance decision to be considered invalid and will expose the parties to fines pursuant to Article 14(2) of the Merger Regulation. To date in 2019, the Commission sent for the first time a statement of objections to Telefónica Deutschland alleging that the company failed to comply with and breached its merger commitments offered to secure the approval of its acquisition of E-Plus in 2014. However, the Commission closed its proceedings in March 2021 without imposing any fines or corrective measures on the parties.[442]

[334] Additionally, the Commission has not been reluctant to impose fines for failure to supply the correct information in notifications. The *Sanofi/Synthélabo*[443] case saw the Commission impose the then maximum fine of EUR50 000 on the parties for supplying *'manifestly incorrect'* information on the markets where they held monopoly positions and could not have been ignorant of the market conditions. The Commission also imposed fines of EUR50 000 on Deutsche Post and EUR40 000 on KLM for supplying incorrect information in relation to notifications.[444] Both notifications were subsequently withdrawn. With respect to Deutsche Post, the Commission stated that it had deliberately supplied incorrect and misleading information in respect of its control of the target company in order to deceive the Commission about its jurisdiction. It also fined it an additional EUR50 000 under Article 14(1)(c) for supplying incorrect information in response to an Article 11 request.

[335] These and a number of other cases were decided under or subject to the fining regime of the 1989 Regulation. However, fining levels have since increased significantly, and there is little doubt that the Commission will be more than prepared to use its enhanced powers. While the Commission must still impose a fine that reflects the nature, gravity and duration of any violation under Article 14(3), undertakings must heed the warning that fines are likely to approach the (new) maximum where there appears to have been any hint of deception as to the significance of competition issues. By way of illustration, as mentioned, in 2017, Facebook was fined EUR110 m for providing incorrect or misleading information during the Commission's 2014 review of Facebook's acquisition of WhatsApp.[445]

[336] It should also be noted that the Commission has imposed fines on a number of companies for late notification of transactions and implementation of a transaction without prior authorisation, and its approach was confirmed by EU courts. In

---

[441] Case T-251/00 *file:Lagardère and Canal+ v. Commission* [2002] ECR II-482.

[442] *See* https://ec.europa.eu/competition/elojade/isef/case_details.cfm?proc_code=2_M_9003.

[443] Case M.1397 *Sanofi/Synthélabo.*

[444] *See* Commission press release IP/99/985 of 14 Dec. 1999.

[445] *See also* the cases concerning General Electric and Merck (including Sigma-Aldrich) mentioned in s. 7 above.

2020, the ECJ confirmed that the Commission was right in fining Marine Harvest both for failure to notify its acquisition of Morpol (Article 4(1) infringement) and for carrying out the transaction before the Commission cleared the concentration (Article 7(1) infringement).[446] The ECJ, upholding a General Court's judgment, held that the principle of *ne bis in idem* did not apply in this case as the penalties were imposed by the same authority in a single decision. The ECJ also considered that there was no particular regime on concurrent offences in EU competition law, that EU law does not view one of the two infringements as being more serious than the other, and that even though an infringement of Article 4(1) automatically results in an infringement of Article 7(1), the converse is not true (i.e., a transaction can be notified but implemented prior to the Commission's clearance). Consequently, the Court found that the Commission was entitled to impose separate fines (totalling EUR20 m) for these infringements.

[337] In 2019, the Commission imposed a EUR28 m fine on Canon for implementing its acquisition of Toshiba Medical Systems Corporation before notification to, and approval by, the Commission. In August 2016, Canon notified the transaction to the Commission, which cleared the deal in September 2016. For the acquisition, Canon used a so-called warehousing two-step transaction structure involving an interim buyer. As a first step, the interim buyer acquired 95% in the share capital of TMSC, and Canon acquired the remaining 5% of the shares and share options over the interim buyer's stake. This first step was carried out prior to notification to or approval by the Commission. As a second step, following approval of the merger by the Commission, Canon exercised its share options, acquiring 100% of the shares of TMSC. Only this second step was notified to the Commission, and cleared. In July 2017, the Commission addressed a Statement of Objections to Canon detailing its concerns that, through the two-step transaction structure, Canon had implemented the acquisition before notifying it to the Commission and obtaining approval. The Commission ultimately fined Canon, finding that the two steps formed together a single notifiable merger. The first step contributed to the acquisition of final control over TMSC, which occurred with the second step. And by carrying out the first step, Canon partially implemented its acquisition of TMSC before both the notification and the approval of the Commission. As a result, Canon breached the notification requirement and standstill obligation and was fined EUR28 m.[447] The General Court confirmed the decision of the Commission on 18 May 2022.[448]

[338] In 2018, the Commission fined Altice EUR125 m for breaching EU rules by controlling PT Portugal before obtaining merger approval. Although the transaction was conditionally cleared in April 2015, the Commission later addressed a Statement of Objections to Altice (in May 2017) detailing its concerns that Altice had implemented its acquisition of PT Portugal before obtaining the Commission's clearance, and in some instances, even before its notification of the merger. A fine

[446] Case C10/18 P *Mowi (formerly Marine Harvest) v. European Commission* [2020] ECLI:EU:C2020:149. *See also* para. 231 above.

[447] *See* Press Release IP/19/3429 of 27 Jun. 2019.

[448] Case T-609/19, *Canon Inc. v. European Commission* [2022] ECLI:EU:T:2022:299.

of EUR125 m was ultimately imposed on Altice in April 2018. The General Court dismissed Altice's appeal on 22 September 2021.[449]At the time of writing, Altice's appeal against this judgment is ongoing before the ECJ.[450]

[339] In 2009, the Commission fined Electrabel EUR20 m for acquiring control of CNR without prior Commission approval.[451] Although this acquisition was cleared by the Commission in 2008 following its notification, the Commission left open the precise date when control was acquired by Electrabel in their decision.[452] Following a separate investigation, the Commission concluded that the Belgian energy operator had already acquired de facto sole control of CNR back in December 2003 when it acquired the CNR shares, privately held by EDF, i.e., more than four years before the notification. The Commission imposed a hefty fine on Electrabel which had breached its obligation not to implement its acquisition of control before obtaining the Commission's authorisation. The fact that ultimately Electrabel voluntarily approached the Commission was taken into account as mitigating circumstances. However, even though the merger was cleared unconditionally, this did not change the fact that the Commission considers breach of the standstill condition to constitute a serious infringement (although the fine may have been even higher where the transaction resulted in a negative impact on the market). By a judgment of 12 December 2012, the General Court upheld the fine imposed against Electrabel.

[340] In 1999, the Commission imposed a fine on the Danish company A.P. Møller in relation to three concentrations. The relatively moderate amount of the fine was explained by the fact that the breach had no damaging effect on competition, was not intentional and took place before the Commission had adopted its first decision imposing fines under the Merger Regulation.[453] In 1998, the Commission imposed a fine on Samsung in relation to its acquisition of control over AST Research Inc.[454] The relatively minimal level of the fine was explained by the fact that the operation had no damaging effect on competition, and the breach was not intentional. In contrast, the transaction involving *Hutchison/RCPM/ECT*[455] involved the imposition of a Statement of Objections against the companies which had failed to notify an acquisition of joint control, but the Commission did not impose any fine.

7.13 Right to Be Heard

[341] The Implementing Regulation contains detailed provisions relating to the hearing of the parties and of third persons. These rights are safeguarded by the

[449] Case T-425/18, *Altice Europe NV v. European Commission* [2021] ECLI:EU:T:2021:607.

[450] *See* Official Journal of the European Union, OJ C 119, 14.3.2022, pp. 19–21.

[451] *See* Press Release IP/09/895 of 10 Jun. 2009.

[452] Case M.4994 *Electrabel/Compagnie Nationale du Rhône*.

[453] Commission press release IP/99/100 and Commission Decision of 10/02/99, OJ 1999 L183/29.

[454] Commission press release IP/98/166 and Commission Decision of 18/02/98, OJ 1999 L225/12.

[455] Case M.1412 *Hutchison/RCPM/ECT.*

Hearing Officer, whose primary role is to independently oversee an investigation.[456] This is reinforced by the appointment of the Hearing Officers being independent of DG Competition, and attached directly to the Commissioner in charge of competition policy.

[342] Parties (including third parties who demonstrate a 'sufficient interest' and addressees of a fine or periodic penalty payment as discussed below) may submit a written request to the Hearing Officer if they wish to be heard orally in addition to the written procedure. For the notifying parties, such request must be made in their reply to the Statement of Objections.

[343] It is the Commission's view that where the notifying parties waive their right to an oral hearing, third parties will similarly not have any independent right for an oral hearing. The General Court has also held that the observance of the rights of defence of third parties must be reconciled with the primary aim of the Merger Regulation *'which is to ensure effectiveness of control as well as legal certainty for the undertakings to which the Regulation applies'*.[457]

[344] The hearing, which is not public, is conducted by the Hearing Officer. In 2011, the Commission adopted a revised Hearing Officer Mandate which, among other things, strengthened the Hearing Officer's role in preparing and conducting oral hearings. The Hearing Officer will conduct hearings in full independence and has the power to hold preliminary preparatory meetings with the parties prior to the hearing. The Hearing Officer also has the opportunity to supply in advance a list of questions to the persons attending the hearing and/or indicate the main areas of debate in light of the facts and issues which the notifying parties wish to raise.

[345] The Hearing Officer will also prepare an interim report on the procedural aspects of the case which is submitted to the Competition Commissioner with the draft decision and subsequently published in the Official Journal. This provides an insight into the procedural steps taken, including the proper conduct of the oral hearing as well as access to the file, disclosure of documents and observance of time limits.

[346] Article 18(1) of the Merger Regulation provides that the Commission is obliged to give the persons, undertakings and associations of undertakings concerned the opportunity (at every stage of the procedure up to the consultation of the Advisory Committee) to make their views on any objections known before taking any of the following decisions:

(a) a revocation of a clearance decision which is based on incorrect information or where the undertakings concerned committed a breach of an obligation attached to the decision (Article 6(3));

[456] The terms of reference of Hearing Officers were amended in 2001 and in 2011, when the role of the Hearing Officer was enhanced in terms of transparency and accountability. The terms of reference include all stages of the procedure (Commission Decision of 13 Oct. 2011 on the terms of reference of Hearing Officers in certain competition proceedings (OJ 2011 L 275/29 of 20 Oct. 2011)).

[457] Case T-290/94 *Kaysersberg SAA v. Commission* [1997] ECR II-2137.

(b) the grant of a derogation from obligations imposed pursuant to Article 7(1) or (2) (Article 7(3));[458]
(c) a declaration of compatibility which contains conditions and obligations (Article 8(2));
(d) a declaration of incompatibility (Article 8(3));
(e) a requirement to dissolve the concentration, such as the dissolution of the merger or the disposal of all the shares or assets acquired so as to restore the situation prevailing prior to the implementation of the concentration, or any other appropriate measure (Article 8(4));
(f) to adopt interim measures appropriate to restore or maintain conditions of effective competition where a concentration has been implemented in contravention of Article 7, a condition attached to the decision or where it has already been declared incompatible with the Internal Market (Article 8(5));
(g) a revocation of an earlier compatibility decision (whether or not it was conditional) which was based on incorrect information, where it was obtained by deceit or where the undertakings concerned committed a breach of an obligation attached to the decision (Article 8(6)); and
(h) the imposition of fines (Article 14) or periodic penalty payments (Article 15).

[347] In accordance with Article 346 of the TFEU, decisions must give the reasons on which they are based, and, in accordance with Article 18(3) of the Merger Regulation, the Commission can only base its decision on objections to which the parties have been given the opportunity to submit their observations.

[348] In 2019, the ECJ upheld the General Court's annulment of the Commission's decision prohibiting the acquisition of TNT Express by UPS. The Court confirmed that the Commission had infringed UPS' rights of the defence by not disclosing, during the administrative procedure, the amendments to an econometric model it later relied upon in its decision.[459] The Court confirmed that the decisive factor on which the prohibition was based was an econometric analysis from the Commission. This analysis differed considerably from that disclosed to UPS during the administrative procedure, without the Commission giving UPS the opportunity to submit observations on the amendments made. The Court considered that without that procedural irregularity, UPS would have had the opportunity to better defend itself. The Court rejected the Commission's argument based on the need for speed that characterises merger control proceedings, noting that the Commission sat on the revised econometric model for two months, and that the need for speed must be reconciled with observance of the rights of defence.

[349] The Implementing Regulation contains detailed procedural provisions which supplement those contained in the Merger Regulation. First, it is important

[458] As a derogation from the right to be heard in Art. 18(1), pursuant to Art. 18(2) a decision may be taken provisionally, without giving the persons or undertakings concerned the opportunity of making known their views beforehand, provided an opportunity is provided as soon as possible after the Commission has taken its decision. The Commission must however inform the notifying parties and other involved parties in writing of its objections, fixing a time limit within which they may make known their views before taking a final decision (Art. 12(2) of the Implementing Regulation).

[459] Case C265/17 P *Commission v. United Parcel Service* [2019] ECLI:EU:C:2019:23.

to determine which parties have the rights to be heard. For this purpose, Article 11 of the Implementing Regulation distinguishes between the following parties:

(a) *notifying parties*, that is, persons or undertakings submitting a notification pursuant to Article 4(2) of the Regulation;
(b) other *involved parties*, that is, parties to the proposed concentration other than the notifying parties, such as the seller and the undertaking which is the target of the concentration;
(c) *third parties*, that is, natural or legal persons including customers, suppliers and competitors, provided they demonstrate sufficient interest within the meaning of Article 18(4) of the Regulation (which is automatically the case for members of administration or management bodies of the undertakings concerned or the recognised representatives of their employees, and for consumer associations where the proposed concentration concerns products or services used by final customers);[460]
(d) *parties* regarding whom the Commission intends to take a decision pursuant to Article 14 or 15 of the Regulation *in relation to fines or periodic penalties*.

[350] Where the Commission intends to take a decision pursuant to Article 6(3), Article 7(3), Article 8(2)–(6), and Articles 14 and 15 of the Merger Regulation, it must allow the persons, undertakings and associations of undertakings concerned the opportunity, at every stage of the procedure, to make known their views on the objections levelled against them (Article 18(1) of the Merger Regulation and Articles 12 and 13(2) of the Implementing Regulation).

8 REFERRALS AND POWERS OF MEMBER STATES

[351] While the Commission retains exclusive jurisdiction over mergers with a Community dimension (even if they only involve undertakings based in one Member State, provided that at least one party earns more than a third of its Community turnover in other Member States), the role of the Member States' national merger control law and NCAs in the application of the Merger Regulation cannot be overlooked. Figure 4 provides the Commission's statistics in merger cases.

[352] Article 21(3) of the Merger Regulation provides that Member States are precluded from applying national competition legislation to any concentration that has a Community dimension. However, this much heralded 'one-stop shop' is also subject to a short list of limitations which at the time of passing, Member States agreed should entitle a Member State to intervene. First, concentrations which are caught by the criteria of the Merger Regulation can be referred in whole or in part

[460] The issue of workers' participation was considered in case M.1802 *Unilever/Amora Maille* where the Commission clarified that this is limited to aspects of the transaction governed by competition law. The Commission is given residual discretion to allow *'any other'* third parties the opportunity to express their views (case T-12/93 *Comité Central d'Enterprise de la Société Anonyme Vittel and Comité d'Etablissement de Pierval and Fédération Générale Agroalimentaire v. Commission* [1995] ECR II-1247).

to one or more NCA. Such referral may be made either at the request of an NCA[461] or since the reform of 1 May 2004, following an application by the notifying parties.[462] Second, NCAs may refer concentrations that do not have a Community dimension to the Commission. Such referrals can be initiated either by an NCA[463] or since 1 May 2004, by the notifying parties where the concentration would fall within the jurisdiction of at least three Member States.[464] These referral mechanisms have been classified by the Commission's Case Referral Notice (the 'Referral Notice') which explains the legal criteria to be met in each case and also provides practical guidance on the steps leading to a referral.[465] In November 2011, a working group comprised of representatives of DG Competition and NCAs issued a set of best practices concerning the cooperation between EU competition authorities in merger reviews. These guidelines acknowledge that coordination among NCAs may also facilitate the smooth functioning of the reattribution mechanisms set out in the Merger Regulation.

[353] Finally, an NCA may also retain concurrent jurisdiction for transactions which touch upon public security, plurality of the media and so-called prudential rules of a Member State. Any other interests have to be notified to the Commission and recognised in advance by decision before they can be protected by Member States, in accordance with their obligations under the Merger Regulation.

8.1 Referral to NCAs

8.1.1 Pre-notification Referrals to NCAs: Article 4(4)

[354] Reallocation of cases prior to notification at the request of those responsible for notifying was introduced by the current Merger Regulation. However, the Commission and Member States have not ceded control over the choice of jurisdiction to the notifying parties – the criteria set out in the Referral Notice aims to ensure that the mechanisms in Article 4 of the Merger Regulation are operated consistently with the overall principles of case allocation provided for under the Merger Regulation.

[355] Article 4(4) enables the parties to a concentration with a Community dimension to ask the Commission to refer the transaction (or part of it) back to a Member State. Two legal requirements must be met:

(1) First, there must be an indication that the concentration *'may significantly affect competition'* in a market within a Member State. According to the Referral Notice, the parties are not expected to demonstrate that the effect

[461] *See* Art. 9 of the Merger Regulation.
[462] *See* Art. 4(4) of the Merger Regulation.
[463] *See* Art. 22 of the Merger Regulation.
[464] *See* Art. 4(5) of the Merger Regulation.
[465] Commission Notice on case Referral in respect of concentrations [2005] 05/C-56/2, 5 Mar. 2005.

on competition is likely to be an adverse one. Instead, the parties should point to indicators that are *'generally suggestive of the existence of some competitive effects stemming from the transaction'*. The existence of an affected market (within the meaning of the Form RS) would suffice or, failing that, an overlap in activities or vertical integration.

(2) Second, the market in question must be within a Member State and present all the characteristics of a *'distinct market'*. In other words, the geographic market affected by the transaction must be national or narrower than national in scope. In order to determine whether a market is a *'distinct'* one, it is necessary to consider both the goods and services concerned (the product market) and the market's geographical extent (the geographical market). To meet this requirement, the parties will need to consider factors which are generally indicative of national or local markets, for example, low value of product as compared to significant cost of transport, national consumer habits, different regulatory frameworks and the like.

[356] Procedurally, to make a referral request under Article 4(4), the parties must make a *'reasoned submission'* by supplying the information specified in a Form RS. For a referral to Member States, the parties need to fulfil the following requirements:

(a) specify which Member State(s) should examine the concentration indicating whether or not informal contact has been made with them;
(b) indicate whether a partial or full referral is being requested. For a full referral, it is necessary to confirm that there are no affected markets outside the territory of the Member State to which the parties request the referral be made; and
(c) explain how each of the affected markets constitutes a distinct market and how competition may be significantly affected in them.

[357] The Commission encourages parties to consult with it, in advance, on the adequacy of the information on which the parties intend to base their reasoned submission. This is particularly important as the decision on whether or not to accede to a reasoned submission will normally be taken on the basis of the information contained in the submission, without further investigative efforts being undertaken by the authorities involved.[466]

[358] The Commission will transmit the reasoned submission to all Member States *'without delay'*, and the Member State(s) referred to in the submission has fifteen working days from the date of receiving the submission to accept or refuse the referral. In practice, the Commission will hold a conference call with the Member State(s) concerned about ten days after the submission. Where a Member State fails to take a decision within this period, it is deemed to have consented to the request.

[359] The internal process of transmission is irrelevant to the decision timetable, which is dictated by the deadline imposed on the Commission for adopting its

[466] Form RS, para. B(a).

referral decision. It has twenty-five working days (starting from the receipt of the reasoned submission) to decide whether or not to refer the case (or part of it) to the Member State(s) but can do so only with the consent (actual or deemed) of the relevant Member State(s). If the Commission itself does not adopt a decision within this period, it is deemed to have adopted a decision to refer the case. The default position is therefore that a case moves to the Member State(s) identified in the reasoned submission.

[360] The Commission must inform the other Member State(s) and the parties to the concentration of any decision it takes. They have no power of veto but clearly can make representations as to what the Commission's stance on referral should be.

[361] Where the Commission decides to refer the whole case, no notification needs to be made to the NCA, and national merger control law will apply instead of the Merger Regulation. However, while there is no provision which formally sets out the starting day of the NCA's review of the proposed transaction, Article 9(6) still applies (*see* below) and provides that the NCA must also carry out its review *'without undue delay'*. Moreover, the NCA must inform the parties to the concentration of the result of its *'preliminary competition assessment'* and any *'further action'* it proposes to take within forty-five working days of the Commission's referral. The Referral Notice makes it clear that the merging parties should be provided with sufficient information to enable them to understand the nature of any preliminary competition concerns the authority may have and be informed of the likely extent and duration of the investigation.

[362] Since the procedure was introduced in 2004 and as of 31 May 2023, the Commission received 217 requests for a referral to the NCAs and granted 190 full referrals and 22 partial referrals. For notifying parties, the attraction of Article 4(4) is the ability to short-circuit processes under the Regulation, which may ultimately result in a referral under Article 9 and to confine a notification and assessment to one particular national or regional market. However, this may not always save time or costs since the Form RS is generally regarded as being burdensome, and Member States' national merger regimes may not be as speedy and transparent as the Merger Regulation.

8.1.2 Post-notification Referrals to the NCAs: Article 9

[363] Under Article 9 of the Merger Regulation, there are two possible avenues for a Member State wishing to request a referral, in whole or in part, at the national level of a transaction which has a Community dimension and has been notified to the Commission: Article 9(2)(a) and 9(2)(b).

[364] Two conditions must be satisfied to make use of Article 9(2)(a). First, the transaction must threaten to *'affect significantly competition'* in a market within the requesting Member State.[467] Second, the market in question must present all the

[467] This is a lower hurdle than in the 1989 Regulation, which tracked the Art. 2 compatibility test (as then formulated) and required a threat of dominance.

characteristics of a distinct market. To make use of Article 9(2)(b), two different conditions must also be satisfied. First, the transaction must *'affect competition'* in a market within the requesting Member State. Second, the market in question must present all the characteristics of a distinct market and not constitute a substantial part of the Internal Market. According to the Referral Notice, such cases are generally limited to markets with a narrow geographic scope.[468] However, the Commission has, in the past, defined the notion of 'substantial part of the Internal Market' quite broadly.

[365] The difference between Article 9(2)(a) and 9(2)(b) is namely that where the conditions for Article 9(2)(b) are met, the Commission is obliged to refer the case to the Member State, at least as regards the market or markets concerned, whereas it has a discretion whether to do so when the Article 9(2)(a) criteria for referral are met. In at least one case, the Commission has avoided the need to rule on Article 9(2)(b) by exercising its discretion under Article 9(2)(a) in favour of the national authority.[469] By contrast, under Article 9(2)(a), even if the criteria for referral are met, the Commission may consider that it should itself deal with the whole case in order to maintain competition on the market concerned. An example of this was the Commission's decision to reject Belgium's request for a partial referral in case M.5549 *EDF/Segebel*.[470]

[366] As of 31 May 2023, the Commission received 132 requests to reallocate jurisdiction to one or more national authorities and had referred 100 concentrations, in whole or in part, to the NCAs. The burden is on the NCA to inform the Commission that a concentration has an impact on competition on a distinct market within that Member State within the terms of Article 9(2)(a) or (b). The NCA must do this within fifteen working days from the receipt of its copy of the notification from the Commission. The Commission must consider the application and can ask an NCA for more information under Article 19(2). The parties may also make observations.[471] The Commission then has to decide whether or not to allow the requesting Member State to apply its own national competition law to the concentration or to part of it,[472] although the Commission does not always accede to the NCA's request.[473]

---

[468] Referral Notice at para. 40.

[469] Case M.4999 *Heineken/Scottish and Newcastle Assets*, a partial referral to the Irish Competition Authority.

[470] Although the conditions for a formal referral were met, the Commission did not accede to the referral request as its own preliminary investigation had revealed competition concerns in other Member States. The Commission therefore did not want to fragment the case. *See also* cases M.4721 *AIG Capital Partners/Bulgarian Telecommunications Company* and M.5960 *Crédit Agricole/Cassa di Risparmio della Spezia/AgencesIntesaSanpaolo*.

[471] For example, in case M.3823 *MAG/Ferrovial Aeropuertos/Exeter Airport* the parties sought to argue that the requirements of Art. 9(2)(a) were not met. In other cases, the views of the NCA have gone without challenge by the parties: case M.5112 *REWE/Plus Discount*.

[472] Case M.2621 *Seb/Moulinex*, and further *Babyliss SA v. Commission*, T-119/02 [2003] ECR II-1433 regarding the General Court's judicial review.

[473] *See*, for example, case M.4721 *AIG Capital Partners/Bulgarian Telecommunications Company*, where the Commission rejected the arguments of the Bulgarian Competition authorities that Art. 9(2)(a) and (b) were met and proceeded to deal with, and clear, the takeover of BTSC by the American company.

[367] Where an NCA makes a referral request under Article 9, Phase I is automatically extended from twenty-five to thirty-five working days.[474] The period within which the Commission must adopt a decision on referral varies according to whether or not Phase II proceedings have started. If the relevant Member State's request is sent to the Commission before Phase II has started, the Commission has thirty-five working days from the date of notification within which to adopt a decision. If the request is received once the Commission has initiated the Phase II proceedings, the period is extended to sixty-five working days from the date of notification.[475] However, the Commission is not obliged to refer the case where it has itself taken preparatory steps (these will normally take the form of a notification of objections within the meaning of Article 18(1)).

[368] In the unlikely event that the Commission has not made a decision either to refer the matter to the relevant Member States or to refuse to refer the concentration within sixty-five working days of notification, the Commission will be deemed to have decided to make such a referral.[476]

[369] Once the referral has been made, the relevant NCA must inform the undertakings concerned of the *'result of the preliminary competition assessment and what further action, if any, it proposes to take'* within forty-five working days.[477] The Referral Notice explains that accordingly, within forty-five working days after the referral, the merging parties should be provided with sufficient information to enable them to understand the nature of any preliminary competition concerns that the NCA may have and be informed of the likely extent and duration of the investigation.[478] The Member State must publish its final decision on the case *'without delay'*.[479] The absence of any specific deadline in the Merger Regulation[480] could however result in extra delay and uncertainty.

In case M.7009 *Holcim/Cemex West* the Commission rejected the request from the German federal cartel office to refer a transaction found to affect French, Belgian and German cement markets. Also, in case M.7018 *Telefónica Deutschland/E-Plus* the Commission rejected the request for referral on the grounds that it had significant experience in assessing transactions impacting national mobile telecommunications markets and that it had an interest in ensuring a consistent application of the Merger Regulation.

[474] Article 10(1), para. 2.

[475] Article 9(4).

[476] Article 9(5) of the Merger Regulation.

[477] The forty-five working day period begins on the working day following that of the receipt of a complete notification by the relevant NCA or NCAs where such notification is required or requested under national law. Otherwise, the period begins the day after the Commission's referral. Note that the Member State may exceptionally suspend this time limit where the necessary information has not been provided by the undertakings concerned.

[478] *See* para. 82 of the Referral Notice.

[479] Article 9(6) of the Merger Regulation.

[480] In contrast under the 1989 Regulation Member States had four months (the same period as if the case had remained with the Commission) in which to issue a decision on a concentration once the referral had taken place.

8.2 Referrals to the Commission

8.2.1 Pre-notification Referrals to the Commission: Article 4(5)

[370] Pre-notification referrals to the Commission under Article 4(5) of the Merger Regulation represent a step towards conferring jurisdiction on the Commission as a result of the number of merger filings which would otherwise be required in a number of Member States. This is recognised in describing such cases as having a deemed Community dimension. However, jurisdiction is not conferred automatically on the Commission, and the parties do not have an automatic right to have their case handled by the Commission. Any Member State which has jurisdiction over the concentration may veto a referral to the Commission (although this is rare).[481] As of 31 May 2023, the Commission received 429 requests to take jurisdiction over a transaction which did not have Community dimension. The referral of the case to the Commission was approved in 415 cases and vetoed by the Member States in 7 cases (the 7 referral requests were withdrawn when it became clear that the transaction was not reportable in at least three Member States).

[371] Before any notification is made, the parties to a concentration which does not have a Community dimension according to the turnover thresholds in Article 1, but which is capable of being reviewed under the merger control rules of at least three Member States, may ask the Commission to review it instead of the NCAs of those Member States. Two legal requirements must be met in order for the parties to be able to request the referral of the case to the Commission:

- First, the transaction must be a concentration within the meaning of Article 3 of the Merger Regulation. This is significant since it means that joint ventures which are not structural or certain acquisitions of minority shareholdings (which may be capable of being reviewed under some domestic merger control rules) are not eligible for referral.
- Second, the concentration must be capable of being reviewed under the national competition laws for the control of mergers of three or more Member States. It need not, however, be subject to mandatory filings in any of the Member States concerned.

[372] The referral mechanism in Article 4(5) requires only satisfaction of the above formal jurisdictional requirements. The reasoned request of the parties need not fulfil substantive requirements, unlike in the case of Article 4(4) described above. In relation to the timing of an Article 4(5) request, the Commission applies the same type of approach as that applied in respect of Form CO notifications and accepts an Article 4(5) request when the parties can demonstrate a good faith intention to conclude an agreement or have announced the intention to make a public offer.

[481] *See* case M.3439 *Agfa-Gevaert/Lastra* which was the first case where such type of upward referral took place. However it is understood in this case that the Commission, further to negotiations, bypassed a veto formulated by the NCA in Cyprus which was competent to review the transaction in the first place.

[373] As with Article 4(4), the parties must make a referral request under Article 4(5) by means of a *'reasoned submission'*. This is done by completing Form RS, and the parties need to fulfil the following requirements:

(1) specify the Member States in which the concentration is notifiable, showing in an Annex (section 6.3.1) why this is or is not the case; and
(2) explain why the case should be examined by the Commission – in particular, whether the concentration might affect competition beyond the territory of one Member State.

[374] The Commission must again transmit the submission to all Member States *'without delay'*. Any Member State competent to examine the transaction under its national law may, within fifteen working days of receiving the submission, express its disagreement to referral. There is no scope for partial referrals. If any Member State capable of reviewing the concentration objects to the referral, the concentration remains subject to all the applicable national merger control rules. Conversely, if no Member State capable of reviewing the concentration expresses its disagreement, the case is deemed to acquire a Community dimension, and the Commission has no choice but to accept the referral. It is then for the parties to notify the case to the Commission using a Form CO. In practice, it is recommended that the parties provide additional information in the Form RS to mirror what is required in the Form CO. This will have the additional advantage of alleviating the parties' burden to run through the exercise data twice when they have to prepare the Form CO.

[375] Contact with NCAs and the Commission is recommended before filing a Form RS in order to confirm that the criteria under Article 4(5) are met. However, NCAs cannot decide on an Article 4(5) referral until they have received the Form RS. It may also be useful for NCAs to have informal contact with each other prior to receiving the Form RS, and therefore it is advisable for the parties to provide details of the other NCAs that are likely to be capable of reviewing the concentration. Likewise, further to the filing of the Form RS, it is advisable to contact the key NCAs which would have jurisdiction in order to inform them of the parties' request and ensure that the parties are not trying to circumvent the enforcement of national merger control.

[376] The effect of a successful request under Article 4(5) is that the concentration concerned is deemed to have a Community dimension. Consequently, the Merger Regulation in its entirety will apply, including the waiting period in Article 7, and it will be for the parties to notify the case to the Commission using the Form CO (although much of that work will have been carried out already to make the Article 4(5) submission in accordance with the Form RS).

[377] In practice, most Article 4(5) cases refer to three, four or five Member States (and sometimes EEA States), but on occasion a larger number of merger jurisdictions may be triggered. In one case, the merger laws of sixteen Member States, one EEA State and three other states were affected.[482] Finally, it should be noted that a

[482] *See*, for example, case M.4912 *Calyon/Société Générale/Newedge*.

number of complex cases considered by the Commission in recent years have been subject to notifications made under Article 4(5), including cases M.4731 *Google/Double Click*, M.4747 *IBM/Telelogic*, M.4854 *TomTom/TeleAtlas*, M.6281 *Microsoft/Skype* and M.7217 *Facebook/WhatsApp*.

8.2.2 Post-notification Referrals to the Commission: Article 22

[378] Article 22 of the Merger Regulation allows Member States which have received a notification to request that the Commission should investigate a concentration *without a Community dimension* where it *'affects trade between Member States and threatens to significantly affect competition within the territory of the Member State or States making the request'* (Article 22(1)). The Commission may also invite Member States to request a referral where it considers the relevant criteria to be met. Unlike pre-notification referrals to the Commission, a post-notification referral can be partial. In the case of Article 22, the Commission also has discretion as to whether or not to accept a referral request.

[379] In order for a referral to be made to the Commission under Article 22, two conditions must be met. First, the concentration must affect trade between Member States. The notion of effect on trade is the same as that which applies under Articles 101 and 102 of the TFEU. Second, the concentration must threaten to affect competition significantly within the territory of the Member State making the request. NCAs are, in essence, required to demonstrate on a preliminary analysis that there is a real risk the transaction may have a significant adverse impact on competition. Consequently, NCAs need only show that the transaction affects trade between Member States and threatens to affect competition significantly within the territory of the Member State.

[380] In the interests of legal certainty and the timely handling of notifications, a Member State must act promptly if it wishes to take advantage of the procedure pursuant to Article 22. The request must be made within fifteen working days of the date on which the concentration was notified or, if no notification is required, was otherwise *'made known'* to the Member State concerned.[483] The Case Referral Notice explains that *'made known'* should be interpreted as implying sufficient information to make a preliminary assessment as to the existence of the criteria for the making of a referral request under Article 22. The General Court sets out in its judgment in *Illumina/Grail* that *'made known'* within the meaning of Article 22 must consist of the active transmission of relevant information to the Member State concerned and must contain sufficient information to enable that Member State to carry out a preliminary assessment of the conditions laid down in Article 22.[484] In

[483] Under the 1989 Regulation, the request had to be made to the Commission within one month of the date on which the concentration was *'made known'* to the Member State or to all the Member States making the joint request, or effected, whichever was earlier. This created practical difficulties since it was not entirely clear when the one month period began running where the merger was made known to Member States at different times.

[484] Case T-227/21, *Illumina, Inc. v. European Commission* [2022] ECLI:EU:T:2022:447.

this case, the General Court argues that the Invitation Letter sent by the Commission to the Member States on 19 February 2021 enabled the Member States to carry out a preliminary assessment of whether the conditions of Article 22 were met in the case at hand. In the UK, which has a voluntary merger control regime, '*made known*' means either the date of notification of the transaction or the date on which the UK Office of Fair Trading has received sufficient information to determine whether the relevant criteria for a referral are met. In case M.4465 *Thrane & Thrane/Nera,* the UK Office of Fair Trading made a referral request shortly after it had requested and received from the parties information relating to the transaction. The referral was made after the transaction had already been notified and approved by NCAs in Norway, Spain and Greece.

[381] The request for this procedure must be made to the Commission within one month from (i) the date on which the concentration was made known to the Member State or to all Member States making a joint request, or (ii) the date on which the concentration was effected, whichever is the earlier. The suspensive effect of Article 7 of the Merger Regulation will apply to cases assessed in accordance with Article 22, unless the concentration has already been put into effect when the Commission informs the parties about the request.

[382] The Commission then has ten working days to decide whether or not to accept the referral. This period starts from the expiry of the fifteenth working day, within which Member States that were not party to the request have to decide whether or not to join the request.[485] It should be noted that even Member States which do not have jurisdiction to review such transaction can decide to join the referral (there have been instances where a Member State joined the referral process even though the merging parties did not generate any revenue in such countries). The Commission will then inform all Member States of its decision and, if it accepts, can request the submission of a notification pursuant to Article 4 of the Merger Regulation. The Member State(s) that made the request are then not able to apply their national legislation on competition.

[383] To counter the problems of differing national notification requirements, the Merger Regulation suspends all national time limits relating to a concentration which is the subject of an Article 22 referral request until the Commission has decided where the concentration is to be examined.[486] As soon as a Member State has informed the Commission and the undertakings concerned that it does not wish to join the request, the suspension of its national time limits comes to an end, and that Member State can review the proposed transaction under its own national merger control rules in concurrence with the review to be carried out by the Commission after accepting the referral request.

[384] The same decision process applies to Article 22. The procedure has two stages, and the Commission has powers of enquiry and decision (with fines and

[485] If the Commission does not take a decision within this period, it is deemed to have adopted a decision to examine the concentration in accordance with the request.

[486] Article 22(2). The suspension of national time limits begins from when the Commission informs the NCAs of a request received which it must do '*without delay*'.

penalties) and the obligation to act in cooperation with Member States as in the case of a concentration with a Community dimension. Once a Member State has referred the concentration to the Commission, the matter is regarded as being in the hands of the Commission, which may request the submission of a notification pursuant to Article 4 of the Merger Regulation.[487] The Member State has no power to control the conduct or define the scope of the Commission's investigation. From a substantive point of view, Article 22 allows the Commission to investigate the impact of a concentration only in those countries that have made, or joined, a referral.

[385] As of 31 May 2023, there have been 46 requests for referral under Article 22 of which only 4 were refused. A number of the earlier (pre-2004) cases involved single-State referral applications from Member States which, at the time, did not have merger control laws. However, a difference that has become apparent more recently is the joint request by the NCAs of a number of Member States (with developed national merger controls) to refer a transaction to the Commission. Member States have availed themselves of the opportunity provided by Article 22(2) in a number of cases. The purpose of Article 22 has changed to encourage referrals from Member States where the impact of a concentration is significant in more than one Member State or where the Commission has some other investigative or enforcement advantage over requesting Member State(s). Article 22 is now part of the machinery for allocating a concentration to the authority best suited to dealing with it, though it does not confer even a deemed Community dimension. However, a concentration with only local or regional effects, or with a wider impact but limited to one Member State, is unlikely to be a candidate for referral under Article 22.

[386] Basing itself on the guiding principle of the referral system that cases should go to the more appropriate authority, as part of the consultation process initiated on 20 June 2013 and its subsequent White Paper of 2014, the Commission has considered that in cases where it is the better-placed authority, it should obtain EEA-wide jurisdiction and not only competence for the Member States making or joining such referral request. In the Commission's view, this would ensure a coherent treatment of a case displaying cross-border effects, reduce the risk of diverging decisions and increase legal certainty. In this respect, the Commission has proposed the following main changes:

- the Commission may accept a referral of a case where at least one competent Member State requests the referral pursuant to Article 22, and no Member State competent to review the merger under national law opposes the referral. It is no longer required that a Member State joins the request;
- the Commission's decision to accept a referral gives it jurisdiction for the whole of the EEA. However, if at least one competent Member State opposes the referral, the Member States retain their jurisdiction. This would align the scope of the referral under Article 4(5) and Article 22, i.e., EEA-wide jurisdiction for the Commission, and fully implement the one-stop-shop principle.

[487] Article 22(3), para. 2.

[387] The Commission considered these changes and launched an additional public consultation in 2016. As mentioned, this consultation was designed to build upon the results of the above-mentioned 2014 considerations and focused on a number of specific procedural and jurisdictional aspects of EU Merger Control. Four topics – including the Commission's referral system – formed part of this 2016 consultation: (i) possible further simplification of EU merger control; (ii) the functioning of the jurisdictional thresholds; (iii) the functioning of the referral system; and (iv) specific technical aspects.

[388] In March 2021, the Commission published new guidance on the application of the referral mechanism set out in Article 22 of the Merger Regulation (the 'Article 22 Guidance').[488] In December 2022, the Article 22 Guidance was complemented by the Q&A Guidance note published by the Commission in December 2022.[489] The Q&A note offers advice on which cases are typically suitable for referral as well as the Commission's process for reviewing requests by merging parties or third parties to determine whether cases are suitable for referral under Article 22 (please refer to section 5 above for more detailed information in this regard). Importantly, the Article 22 Guidance reverses the Commission's policy of discouraging referral requests under Article 22 from Member States that did not have original jurisdiction over the transaction at stake. This practice was notably based on the experience that such transactions were not generally likely to have a significant impact on the internal market. However, the Commission now believes, based on recent market developments notably in the digital or pharmaceutical sectors, that even transactions that may significantly affect competition in such sectors often escaped merger control because of low turnover. The new guidance aims at addressing this perceived enforcement gap with respect to so-called killer acquisitions falling below all merger thresholds in the EU. Although the new guidance explicitly refers to the digital and pharma/biotech sectors, the Commission's renewed practice is not limited to those specific sectors and leaves the door open for any transaction which falls below the national merger control thresholds and threatens to affect competition in the EU. As set out in the Article 22 Guidance, potential candidates for referral include transactions where the target:

- is a start-up or recent entrant with significant competitive potential and low (or no) revenues. The Commission may also take into account whether the value of the consideration received by the seller is particularly high compared to the current turnover of the target;
- is an important innovator or is conducting potentially important research;
- is an actual or potential important competitive force;
- has access to competitively significant assets (such as raw materials, infrastructure, data, or IP rights);
- provides products or services that are key components for other industries.

[488] *See,* https://ec.europa.eu/competition/consultations/2021_merger_control/guidance_article_22_referrals.pdf.

[489] *See,* https://competition-policy.ec.europa.eu/system/files/2022-12/article22_recalibrated_approach_QandA.pdf.

[389] The Article 22 Guidance states that Member States may request a referral of transactions already closed. As a rule of thumb, the Article 22 Guidance suggests that the EC will generally not consider a referral appropriate if a deal was closed more than six months ago. If the closing is not publicly known, the six-month deadline will be based on the date when material facts about the transaction have been made public in the EU. The six-month timeframe is generous. By way of comparison, the UK Enterprise Act requires the Competition and Markets Authority to complete its Phase I investigation within four months of deal closing. However, the EC considers that it may be appropriate for a Member State to request a referral more than six months after closing based on certain factors, such as the magnitude of the potential competition concerns and the magnitude of the potential detrimental effect on consumers. And while Guillaume Loriot, Deputy Director-General for Mergers, publicly indicated that the Commission will not call in transaction that had closed for more than a period of six months, as it is currently drafted, the guidance technically leaves the door open for referrals potentially indefinitely after a transaction has closed.[490] In practice, the Commission has already started applying this new policy with respect to Illumina's proposed acquisition of Grail. While this transaction between two US-based companies which was announced in September 2020 did not meet the statutory threshold of any EU Member State, in February 2021, the Commission asked the 27 Member States to refer this transaction back to Brussels after having received a complaint. The French competition authority made such a referral request to the Commission who ultimately accepted it in April 2021, hence leaving no option to the parties but to formally engage with the Commission and formally file this transaction for approval (thereby suspending the possible implementation of the transaction).[491] Illumina closed the transaction in August 2021, while the Commission's review was still in progress, leading to the Commission imposing interim measures to keep Grail independent of Illumina.[492] The Commission prohibited the transaction on 6 September 2022 and required Illumina to divest Grail. In addition, the Commission imposed a fine against Illumina of EUR432 m and EUR1 000 against Grail due to the breach of EU merger control rules.[493] On 13 July 2022, the EU's General Court judgment confirmed that the Commission has jurisdiction to review transactions which were referred to it under Article 22 even if the referring Member State does not have jurisdiction to review the proposed transaction itself because it does not meet the thresholds set out in the Merger Regulation or national EU Member State Law.[494] The General Court ruled that because Article 22 refers to 'any transaction' without further mention of the existence or applicability of national merger control rules, the Commission is competent to review transactions that may materially affect competition in one or more Member States, regardless of whether the

490 'Merger assessment below the radar – the Commission's approach to Article 22 of the EUMR', 120th GCLC Virtual Lunch Talk, 10 Jun. 2021.

491 *See,* case M.10188 *Illumina/Grail.*

492 Cases M.10493 Illumina/Grail and M.10938 Illumina/Grail.

493 *See,* case M.10188 *Illumina/Grail* and https://ec.europa.eu/commission/presscorner/detail/en/ip_23_3773.

494 Case T-227/21, *Illumina, Inc. v. European Commission* [2022] ECLI:EU:T:2022:447.

transactions meet the EU or Member States merger control thresholds. Since Article 22 is interpreted by the General Court as supplementing the EU merger control thresholds to enable the Commission to review transactions that do not meet these thresholds, a Member State is therefore permitted to refer any transaction that satisfies the requirements of Article 22 to the Commission in order to permit effective control of all transactions with significant potential effects on the structure of competition in the internal market. Further, the General Court found that the Commission had not infringed the principles of legal certainty and the protection of legitimate expectations as the Commission had not given precise, unconditional and consistent assurances to the parties. At the time of writing, the GC's judgment remains under appeal before the ECJ.

8.3 Legitimate Interest Exception: Article 21(4)

[390] Member States are entitled under Article 21(4) of the Merger Regulation to take appropriate measures to protect certain specified *'legitimate interests'* which are not taken into consideration by the Merger Regulation (i.e., non-competition related matters) and which are compatible with Community law. The Merger Regulation specifically lists the following as types of legitimate interest:

(a) *public security* – covers matters outside the scope of the general derogation contained in Article 346 of the Treaty. It includes, but is not confined to those matters dealt with in Articles 297 and 30 of the Treaty which are very wide ranging. It may therefore apply to ensure the security of the supply of products or services considered essential for the protection of the population's health. Public security may overlap but is not synonymous with national defence and may be more restricted. The ability of Member States to take action under Article 346 of the TFEU is unaffected (*see* below).[495] In its Interpretive Statement on Article 21, the Commission acknowledges that there may be wider concerns of public security, referring to Articles 297 and 30;

(b) *plurality of the media* – recognises Member States' right to intervene in concentrations to maintain diversified sources of information for the sake of plurality of opinion and multiplicity of views.[496] It is notable that both Member States and many countries outside the EU apply specific media ownership regimes which go beyond normal competition laws; and

(c) *prudential rules* – these are of particular relevance to the financial services sector. The application of these rules is normally confined to specific national regulatory authorities and concerns the good reputation of individuals, the integrity of transactions and solvency rules. For example, Member States will be able to apply national rules to concentrations in sectors such as banking,

[495] In case M.336 *IBM France/CGI*, the French authorities notified the Commission that they had taken measures in respect of two subsidiaries working with the French Ministry of Defence. More recently it was invoked in case M.1258 *GEC Marconi/Alenia*, case M.877 *Boeing/McDonnell Douglas* and case M.1858 *Thomson-CSF/Racal (II)*.

[496] Case M.423 *Newspaper Publishing*.

stock broking and insurance where a potential acquirer did not meet acceptable requirements or supervisory standards.[497]

[391] Any *'legitimate interests'* other than those specified above may be invoked only if they are compatible with the general principles and other provisions of EU law. The Member State must notify any other interests to the Commission, and the Commission must make a decision on compatibility in advance, before such interests may be protected in accordance with the obligations of the Member States under the Regulation.[498] To date, this has been relied on in more than a dozen cases and has also been specifically considered by the Courts.[499]

[392] As an exception to the general rule and exclusive competence for the Commission, this provision is generally interpreted narrowly. Article 21(4) of the Merger Regulation prohibits any measures to be taken by the Member State before the legitimate interest is recognised by the Commission. In case M.10494 *VIG/AEGON CEE*, the Commission stated that such measures must be communicated to the Commission before their adoption, and the Member State must establish that the measure is suitable and proportionate to protect the legitimate interest.[500]

[393] On the basis of the text contained within Article 21(4) of the Merger Regulation, namely that Member States may take overriding measures *'to protect legitimate interests other than those taken into consideration in the Regulation and compatible with the general principles and other provisions of Community law'*, there appears to be three restrictions on what may qualify as such a legitimate interest. The first is that the interest must be a *'public'* one. The second that the interest must be *'other than those taken into consideration'* by the Merger Regulation. And the third that the interest must be compatible with the general principles and other provisions of Community law. It is noteworthy that reference is not made to the specific prohibitions contained within the Treaty, but instead to general principles, which are generally understood to encompass such matters as the protection of fundamental rights and freedoms, the prohibition on discrimination, the principle of proportionality and the principle of legal certainty.

[394] In case M.1616 *Champalimaud/BSCH/A.*, the Portuguese government blocked the acquisition of a Portuguese insurance company by the Spanish banking group, Banco Santander, even though it had been cleared by the Commission. The Commission adopted a decision against the Portuguese government under Article 21(4) and subsequently opened formal infringement procedures against Portugal. Their reasoning was that its actions could not be regarded as protecting legitimate interests within the meaning of Article 21(4) of the Merger Regulation, not only because the Portuguese authorities failed to notify them to the Commission but also

[497] In case M.759 *Sun Alliance/Royal Insurance*, the Commission acknowledged that the UK government could apply the UK Insurance Companies Act to a proposed merger of two insurance companies alongside the Commission's application of the Merger Regulation. *See also* case M.1082 *Allianz/AGF*.

[498] For example, in March 1995 the Commission made a decision recognising the legitimate interest of the UK in applying ss 32–34 of the Water Industry Act 1991 (as amended).

[499] Case C-42/01 *Portugal v. Commission*.

[500] Case M.10494 *VIG/AEGON CEE*.

because the alleged prudential interests advanced by the Portuguese authorities could not be considered legitimate.[501] Portugal subsequently withdrew the measures in question, and the Commission closed its procedure.

[395] However, it is important to note that Article 21(4) creates no new rights for Member States. It is effectively restricted to the recognition of existing powers to intervene in certain aspects of concentrations affecting the territory of the particular Member State on grounds other than those covered by the Merger Regulation. The Commission has recognised certain interests as legitimate, for example, in case M.567 *Lyonnaise des Eaux/Northumbrian Water*, where the Commission recognised the legitimate interest of the UK in applying sections of the Water Industry Act 1991, as amended by the Competition and Services Utilities Act 1992. This was subject to the condition that the UK authorities did not examine matters which fell to the Commission to consider under the Merger Regulation and that the UK authorities notified the Commission each time they applied the UK legislation. This enabled the Commission to check that the measures were appropriate, proportional and non-discriminatory.[502]

[396] It is also possible to advance a general rule (i.e., not related to a specific concentration). However, in case M.1346 *EDF/London Electricity*, the Commission rejected the UK's request for recognition of a legitimate interest based on the role of the Director-General of Electricity Supply (DGES). The domestic measure related to the DGES ensuring regulatory transparency and protection of consumers from adverse effects of vertical integration. The Commission considered such measures to be part of the ongoing regulation of the UK electricity industry, not aimed at the merger itself; thus, it was not necessary for the Commission to recognise the ongoing regulatory activity as a legitimate interest under Article 21(3) of the Merger Regulation. Vertical integration is also essentially a competition issue which is not uncommonly considered in applying the test of compatibility.

[397] The practical effect of Article 21(4) is to create a concurrent jurisdiction: this means that a concentration with a Community dimension can be notified both to the Commission under the Merger Regulation and to the relevant NCA in compliance with Article 21(4) of the Merger Regulation. For instance, in case M.423 *Newspaper Publishing*, the acquisition by the Mirror Group of the Independent was subject to the concurrent jurisdiction of both the Commission and the UK authorities.[503] However, this concurrent jurisdiction has a limit: the protection of *'legitimate interests'* by Member States may only be used to prohibit a concentration or to make it subject to additional conditions and requirements. It does not, however, enable Member States to authorise a concentration which the Commission has prohibited under the Merger Regulation on the basis that it is incompatible with the Internal Market. Furthermore, in conducting its assessment, the Member State is precluded

[501] For example, they violated EU Insurance Directives as well as TFEU rules on freedom of measures and free movement of capital.

[502] *See also* case M.423 *Newspaper Publishing* and case M.759 *Sun Alliance/Royal Insurance*.

[503] *See also* case M.759 *Sun Alliance/Royal Insurance* and case M.1413 *Thomson-CSF/Racal*.

from applying considerations which the Commission must take into account in assessing the compatibility of concentrations. The Member State is therefore prevented from using such means to reopen the competitive analysis made by the Commission.

[398] The Merger Regulation lays down a procedure for notifying a *'public interest'* to the Commission and obliges the Commission to take a decision on whether it is a legitimate interest for the purposes of Article 21(4) within a period of twenty-five working days. In the Commission's view, the procedure should be followed *'whenever there are reasonable doubts as to whether national measures...genuinely aim to protect a 'recognised interest' and/or comply with the principles of proportionality and non discrimination'.*[504] Formally, the Commission's decision in such a case will *'recognise'* the interest. There is no time set as to when a Member State should apply, nor any requirement that an application relates to an identifiable concentration proposal.

[399] Where a Member State acts in contravention of Article 21, the Commission may take appropriate action to restrain the Member State and back up such decisions by proceedings in the ECJ under Article 258 of the TFEU. The Commission, however, is neither required to undertake, nor is limited to action under Article 258 of the TFEU.

[400] This situation arose in the *E.ON/Endesa* case, where the Commission had cleared the acquisition by the German company E.ON of the Spanish energy company Endesa,[505] but within a few days of E.ON's bid, the Spanish Council of Ministers increased the powers of the Spanish energy regulator, Comisión Nacional de Energía (CNE). Subsequently, when E.ON requested the CNE to authorise (unconditionally) the merger, CNE made its approval of the merger subject to a substantial number of conditions. The Commission took the position that some of these conditions breached the freedom of capital movement (Article 63 of the TFEU) and the right of establishment (Article 49 of the TFEU) and opened an infringement procedure under Article 258 of the TFEU. The Commission argued that there had been a breach of Article 21 of the Merger Regulation by adopting the measure without prior notification and approval by the Commission. By decision under Article 21, it required Spain to withdraw the conditions imposed by CNE. As a result, some of the conditions were revoked but some remained. These were reconsidered by the Commission in a further decision and also found by the Commission to be contrary to Community law. Spain was ordered to withdraw them. Spain failed to comply, and infringement proceedings were initiated in the ECJ. The Court found that Spain had infringed Community law by not withdrawing the conditions as required by Commission decisions.[506] The fact that E.ON's offer for Endesa ultimately failed did not absolve Spain from the need to comply with the Commission's decisions.

504 Case M.4685 *ENEL/Acciona/Endesa* at para. 25.

505 Case M.4110 *E.ON/Endesa*.

506 Case C-196/07 *Commission v. Spain* judgment of 6 Mar. 2008.

8.4 Defence Interests: Article 346 of the TFEU

[401] A further exception to the basic rule set out in Article 21(3) of the Merger Regulation derives from Article 346(1)(b) of the TFEU itself, which provides that the provisions of the Treaty do not preclude Member States from taking:

> such measures as it considers necessary for the protection of the essential interests of its security which are connected with the production of or trade in arms, munitions and war material; such measures shall not adversely affect the conditions of competition in the Internal Market regarding products which are not intended for specifically military purposes.[507]

[402] Consequently, Member States retain the exclusive power to intervene in respect of concentrations which would be contrary to the essential interests of their security as specified in Article 346(1)(b) of the TFEU. This provision is, however, strictly construed, and Article 348 of the Treaty expressly gives the Commission or any Member State the right to bring the issue before the ECJ if it considered that another Member State was making improper use of the powers under Article 346 of the TFEU. A Member State may therefore take such measures which it considers necessary for the protection of the essential interests of its security which are connected with the production of trade in arms, munitions and war material. Such action must not adversely affect the conditions of competition regarding products which are not specifically intended for military purposes.

[403] Some Member States have been active in using this provision, and there have been a number of cases to date which have involved intervention by governments of the UK,[508] Germany and France[509] to ensure that the Commission limited its considerations to the civilian and excluded the specific military aspects of the concentration in question. Not every case which might have been subject to intervention has prompted action by national governments. Nevertheless, the Commission takes the position that it is entitled to review the civilian applications of military products even in mergers between defence companies.

[404] In practice, the measures have taken the form of requests from the government of the Member State concerned to the parties not to notify the Commission of the merger notwithstanding its Community dimension. Where, for example, the merger has covered both military and non-military activities, the request has been limited to the former aspects.[510] In some cases, the parties have chosen to notify the military part of the transaction only insofar as military secrets are concerned.

[507] The list of products to which Art. 346(1)(b) applies was specified in a Council Decision of 11 Apr. 1958.

[508] *See*, for example, case M.528 *British Aerospace/VSEL*, case M.529 *GEC/VSEL*, case M.724 *GEC/Thomson CSF (II)*, case M.820 *British Aerospace/file:Lagardère*, case M.1258 *GEC Marconi/Alenia* and case M.1438 *British Aerospace/GEC Marconi*.

[509] *See*, for example, case M.1309 *Matra/Aérospatiale*.

[510] Case M.4160 *ThyssenKrupp/EADS/Atlas* where the German government invoked Art. 346 TFEU to instruct the parties not to notify any part of a transaction involving naval equipment that concerned military secrets.

The civilian aspects of the merger have therefore remained to be notified to the Commission. The governments concerned have also informed the Commission that it would not be appropriate for the Commission to deal with the merger under the Merger Regulation.

[405] The Commission has taken the position that the Member State concerned must provide the Commission with sufficient information to verify that the conditions of the application of Article 346 have been met. This includes demonstrating that the transaction will not have adverse effects on suppliers of the undertakings concerned or intermediate and final customers (such as defence ministries) in other Member States.[511] Where the merger covers both military and non-military activities, the civilian aspects of the merger must still be notified to the Commission. In case M.528 *British Aerospace/VSEL* and case M.529 *GEC/VSEL*, the Commission accepted that the UK authorities should, on the basis of Article 346 of the TFEU, request British Aerospace and GEC respectively not to notify the acquisition of the military activities of VSEL. However, the Commission required that VSEL's civil activities be notified, even though they represented an extremely limited part of the operation.[512]

[406] Improper action under Article 346 of the TFEU can be challenged by the Commission or another Member State by direct action under Article 348 of the TFEU.

511 Article 348 of the TFEU provides that if measures taken in the circumstances referred to in Art. 346 have the effect of distorting the conditions of competition in the internal market, the Commission shall, together with the Member State concerned, examine how the measures can be adjusted to the rules laid down in the Treaty.

512 For these types of cases, in order to assess whether the concentration has a Community dimension, the total turnover of the parties (including turnover generated by their military activities) must be calculated.

Figure 4 Statistics for Cases Notified under the Merger Regulation: 21 September 1990–31 October 2023

21 September 1990 to 31 October 2023

I.) NOTIFICATIONS

	90	91	92	93	94	95	96	97	98	99	00	01	02	03	04	05	06	07	08	09	10	11	12	13	14	15	16	17	18	19	20	21	22	October 23	Total
Number of notified cases	11	64	59	59	95	110	131	168	224	276	330	335	277	211	247	318	356	402	348	259	274	309	283	277	303	337	362	380	414	382	361	405	371	281	9019
Cases withdrawn - Phase 1	0	0	3	1	6	4	5	9	5	7	8	8	3	0	3	6	7	5	10	6	4	9	4	1	6	6	8	7	10	12	7	9	8	4	191
Cases withdrawn - Phase 2	0	0	0	1	0	0	1	0	4	5	5	4	1	0	2	3	2	2	3	2	0	1	1	0	0	2	1	2	2	0	2	3	4	0	53

II.) REFERRALS

	90	91	92	93	94	95	96	97	98	99	00	01	02	03	04	05	06	07	08	09	10	11	12	13	14	15	16	17	18	19	20	21	22	October 23	Total
Art 4(4) request (Form RS)	0	0	0	0	0	0	0	0	0	0	0	0	0	0	2	14	13	5	9	8	6	10	13	11	16	13	16	13	8	12	15	18	12	8	222
Art 4(4) referral to Member State	0	0	0	0	0	0	0	0	0	0	0	0	0	0	2	11	13	5	9	6	7	10	12	9	14	12	11	14	6	9	17	12	9	7	195
Art 4(4) partial referral to Member State	0	0	0	0	0	0	0	0	0	0	0	0	0	0	0	0	0	1	0	0	0	1	0	2	0	2	4	1	0	2	1	5	2	1	22
Art 4(4) refusal of referral	0	0	0	0	0	0	0	0	0	0	0	0	0	0	0	0	0	0	0	0	0	0	0	0	0	0	0	0	0	0	0	1	0	0	1
Art 4(5) request (Form RS)	0	0	0	0	0	0	0	0	0	0	0	0	0	0	20	28	38	51	23	23	26	18	22	13	19	20	23	15	15	16	15	26	14	10	435
Art 4(5) referral accepted	0	0	0	0	0	0	0	0	0	0	0	0	0	0	14	26	39	49	22	26	24	17	22	11	19	19	22	15	15	16	16	26	14	10	422
Art 4(5) refusal of referral	0	0	0	0	0	0	0	0	0	0	0	0	0	0	2	0	0	2	0	0	1	0	1	0	0	1	0	0	0	0	0	0	0	0	7
Art 22 request	0	0	0	1	0	1	2	1	0	0	0	0	2	1	1	4	4	3	2	1	3	1	3	1	1	1	0	2	3	2	1	2	2	3	48
Art 22(3) referral (Art 22. 4 taken in conjunction with article 6 or 8 under Reg. 4064/89)	0	0	0	1	0	1	2	1	0	0	0	0	2	1	1	3	3	2	3	1	2	2	2	1	1	1	0	1	3	3	1	2	2	3	45
Art 22(3) refusal of referral																1	1	0	0	0	1	0	1	0	0	0	0	0	0	0	0	0	0	0	4
Art 9 request	0	1	1	1	1	0	3	7	4	9	4	9	8	10	4	7	6	3	5	3	11	2	2	2	2	3	3	2	5	3	3	4	2	2	132
Art 9.3 partial referral to Member State	0	0	1	0	1	0	0	6	3	2	3	6	7	1	1	3	1	1	2	0	3	0	1	0	0	1	1	0	1	1	0	0	1	0	47
Art 9.3 full referral	0	0	0	1	0	0	3	1	1	3	2	1	4	8	2	3	1	1	2	1	4	2	1	0	0	0	0	0	3	0	4	4	0	1	53
Art 9.3 refusal of referral	0	1	0	0	0	0	0	0	0	1	0	0	0	1	0	0	0	1	0	1	1	0	0	0	3	3	1	1	1	0	0	0	0	0	15

III.) FIRST PHASE DECISIONS

	90	91	92	93	94	95	96	97	98	99	00	01	02	03	04	05	06	07	08	09	10	11	12	13	14	15	16	17	18	19	20	21	22	October 23	Total
Art 6.1 (a) out of scope Merger Regulation	2	5	9	4	5	9	6	4	4	1	1	1	1	0	0	0	0	0	0	0	0	0	0	0	1	1	1	0	0	0	1	0	0	0	56
Art 6.1 (b) compatible	5	47	43	49	78	90	109	118	196	225	278	299	238	203	220	276	323	368	307	225	253	299	254	252	280	297	327	353	366	343	334	384	354	259	8052
Art 6.1(b) compatible, under simplified procedure (figures included in 6.1(b) compatible above)	0	0	0	0	0	0	0	0	0	0	41	141	103	110	138	169	211	238	190	143	143	191	171	166	207	222	246	280	302	283	278	309	291	216	4789
Art 6.1 (b) in conjunction with Art 6.2 (compatible w. commitments)	0	3	4	0	2	3	0	2	12	16	26	11	10	11	12	15	13	18	19	13	14	5	9	11	12	13	19	18	17	10	13	7	10	3	351

IV.) PHASE II PROCEEDINGS INITIATED

	90	91	92	93	94	95	96	97	98	99	00	01	02	03	04	05	06	07	08	09	10	11	12	13	14	15	16	17	18	19	20	21	22	October 23	Total
Art 6.1 (c)	0	6	4	4	6	7	6	11	11	20	18	21	7	9	8	10	13	15	10	5	4	8	10	6	8	11	8	7	12	8	8	7	8	5	301

V.) SECOND PHASE DECISIONS

	90	91	92	93	94	95	96	97	98	99	00	01	02	03	04	05	06	07	08	09	10	11	12	13	14	15	16	17	18	19	20	21	22	October 23	Total
Art 8.1 compatible (8.2 under Reg. 4064/89)	0	1	1	1	2	2	1	1	3	0	3	5	2	2	2	2	4	5	9	0	1	4	1	2	2	1	1	0	4	0	1	0	0	2	65
Art 8.2 compatible with commitments	0	3	3	2	2	3	3	7	4	7	12	9	5	6	4	3	6	4	5	3	2	1	6	2	5	7	6	2	6	6	3	4	2	5	148
Art 8.3 prohibition	0	1	0	0	1	2	3	1	2	1	2	5	0	0	1	0	0	1	0	0	0	1	1	2	0	0	1	2	0	3	0	0	2	1	33
Art 8.4 restore effective competition	0	0	0	0	0	0	0	2	0	0	0	0	2	0	0	0	0	0	0	0	0	0	0	0	0	0	0	0	0	0	0	1	0	1	6

VI.) OTHER DECISIONS

	90	91	92	93	94	95	96	97	98	99	00	01	02	03	04	05	06	07	08	09	10	11	12	13	14	15	16	17	18	19	20	21	22	October 23	Total
Art 6.3 decision revoked	0	0	0	0	0	0	0	0	0	1	0	0	0	0	0	0	0	0	0	0	0	0	0	0	0	0	0	0	0	0	0	0	0	0	1
Art 8.6 decision revoked	0	0	0	0	0	0	0	0	0	0	0	0	0	0	0	0	0	0	0	0	0	0	0	0	0	0	0	0	0	0	0	0	0	0	0
Art 14 decision imposing fines	0	0	0	0	0	0	0	0	1	4	1	0	1	0	1	0	0	0	0	1	0	0	0	0	1	0	0	1	1	2	0	1	0	1	16
Art 7.3 derogation from suspension (7.4 under Reg. 4064/89)	1	1	2	3	3	2	4	5	13	7	4	7	14	8	10	6	2	3	6	5	1	3	2	1	1	1	0	5	5	1	3	3	4	2	138
Art 21	0	0	0	0	0	1	0	1	0	1	1	0	1	0	0	0	2	1	0	0	0	0	0	0	0	0	0	0	0	0	0	0	1	0	9

9 SUBSTANTIVE ASSESSMENT

9.1 Significant Impediment to Effective Competition

[407] Article 2(3) of the Merger Regulation provides that a concentration will be incompatible with the Internal Market if it 'would significantly impede effective competition, in the Internal Market or in a substantial part of it, in particular as a result of the creation or strengthening of a dominant position'. Article 2(2) provides that concentrations which do not have such an effect shall be declared compatible with the Internal Market.

[408] This compatibility test involving analysis of whether a SIEC exists was introduced in 2004. The test was introduced as a means by which the Commission could protect against all the detrimental effects on competition which can occur as a result of consolidation, as recognised by economic theory.[513] Such an increased economic approach to the assessment of concentrations (thereby moving away from the dominance test) nevertheless preserves the jurisprudence of the Community Courts and the decisional practice of the Commission by making an explicit reference to the creation or strengthening of a dominant position.

[409] In making its assessment, the Community Courts have indicated that the Commission must carry out a prospective analysis. This requires a thorough analysis of the specific circumstances of each case in order to assess the overall impact of a concentration on competition. The likely situation in the absence of the concentration therefore provides the standard against which any merger analysis will be concluded. Such a position is referred to in the Horizontal Guidelines as the 'counterfactual'.[514]

[410] As the General Court pointed out in Airtours, 'if there is no significant change in the level of competition obtaining previously, the merger should be approved because it does not restrict competition'.[515] When the Commission carries out a prospective competition analysis, as it must in the case of a merger yet to happen, the past behaviour of the market will provide the foundations upon which it must substantiate, and against which it must test its conclusion as to the future probabilities of the impact of the concentration.[516] However, identifying the relevant counterfactual may also require the Commission to distinguish changes on

---

513 Before this reform, one of the main criticisms which was made to the Commission was its apparent inability to protect against consumer harm resulting from unilateral effects, that is, *'the tendency of a horizontal merger to lead to higher prices simply by virtue of the fact that the merger will eliminate direct competition between the two merging firms, even if all other firms in the market continue to compete independently'*, Carl Shapiro, Mergers with Differentiated Products, 10 Antitrust 23 (Spring 1996).

514 Horizontal Guidelines at para. 9.

515 Case T-342/99 *Airtours v. Commission* [2002] ECR II-2585, at para. 82 *'if there is no significant change in the level of competition obtaining previously, the merger should be approved because it does not restrict competition'*.

516 Case T-5/02 *Tetra Laval BV v. Commission* [2002] ECR II-4381.

the market which are expected to be caused by the merger from changes that cannot be viewed as merger-specific because they would have taken place in the absence of the merger.[517]

[411] In carrying out such an assessment of whether the concentration is compatible with the Internal Market, the Commission is required to take into account the following factors (Article 2(1) of the Merger Regulation):[518]

(a) the need to preserve and develop effective competition within the Internal Market in view of, among other things, the structure of all the markets concerned and the actual or potential competition from undertakings wherever located;
(b) the market position of the undertakings concerned and their economic and financial power, the opportunities available to suppliers and users, their access to supplies or networks, any legal or other barriers to entry, supply and demand trends for the relevant goods and services and the interests of the intermediate and ultimate consumers; and
(c) the development of technical and economic progress provided that it is to the consumers' advantage and does not form an obstacle to competition (these concepts are to be understood in the light of the principles enshrined in Article 101(3) of the TFEU).

[412] The above-mentioned appraisal criteria are reflected in the information requested in the Form CO with regard to the affected markets. However, they represent a mere checklist of factors to be considered by the Commission and are not exhaustive. They do not, in themselves, determine the outcome of the case. The impact that such criteria may have on the Commission's determination under Article 2 of the Merger Regulation varies from case to case. Also, following Recitals 28 and 29 of the Merger Regulation, the Commission has published three important documents which provide guidance as to the Commission's appraisal of concentrations: the Market Definition Notice; the Horizontal Merger Guidelines; and the Non-Horizontal Merger Guidelines. These documents form the framework for the Commission's analysis. Although they do not have the force of law, they can be relied on against the Commission itself and notifying parties are entitled to expect the Commission to follow its own guidance and to explain the reasons for any material departure from its published position.[519]

[517] Case M.5181 *Delta Air Lines/Northwest Airlines.*

[518] Recital 23 to the Merger Regulation also states that the Commission must carry out its appraisal of compatibility within the general framework of the achievement of the fundamental objectives referred to in Art. 2 of the Treaty, including that of strengthening the Community's economic and social cohesion, referred to in Art. 158. Consequently, the Commission may be prepared to consider matters such as the effect of a concentration on employment in the less developed regions of the Community in assessing compatibility.

[519] Case T-119/02 *Royal Philips Electronics NV v. Commission* [2003] ECR II-1433.

9.1.1 Horizontal Guidelines

[413] The Horizontal Guidelines provide a valuable and important analytical framework illustrating the Commission's approach in applying the SIEC test of compatibility. The Commission emphasises that *'most cases of incompatibility...will continue to be based upon a finding of dominance'*.[520] This appears to imply that in practice the SIEC test will result in little change, but the Horizontal Guidelines adopt a distinction between unilateral and coordinated effects to explain the varieties of competitive harm which may result from an anticompetitive concentration. This distinction equates broadly to distinguish: transactions which allow the merging parties to increase prices or reduce output unilaterally, thereby leading to price increases or reduced output for their competitors (unilateral effects); and transactions that facilitate tacit collusion on prices or output among the merging parties and their major competitors (coordinated effects).

9.1.2 Non-horizontal Guidelines

[414] In November 2007, the Commission published its guidance on vertical and conglomerate mergers. The Commission follows the view that vertical and conglomerate mergers are generally *'less likely'* to lead to a SIEC, particularly since they do not lead to any loss of direct competitors. The Non-Horizontal Guidelines accept that vertical mergers generally have a pro-competitive impact particularly as regards cost savings and the creation of efficiencies. Nevertheless, such benefits must be specified and verified as required by the Guidelines. The Market Definition Notice is described in further detail below.

9.2 Dominance

[415] Although no longer the central concept of EU merger control, the dominance test explicitly remains as a primary instance of competitive harm. The wording of Articles 2 and 3 of the Merger Regulation emphasises that a SIEC can result, *'in particular'* from the creation or strengthening of a dominant position. This wording was adopted in order to preserve the guidance that can be drawn from past judgments of the Courts and maintain a certain level of consistency with the standards of competitive harm which have been applied by the Commission and the Courts in assessing the compatibility of concentrations with the Internal Market while also allowing the Commission to prohibit certain concentrations on oligopolistic markets that are liable to result in a SIEC despite not giving rise to the creation of strengthening of a dominant position.[521] Accordingly, the new substantive test should not be seen to challenge the type of competitive assessment which was

520 Horizontal Guidelines at para. 4.

521 *See* Case T399/16 *CK Telecoms UK Investments v. Commission*, paras 86–90.

previously conducted by the Commission. A SIEC will generally result from the creation or strengthening of a dominant position according to the Merger Regulation[522] and the Horizontal Guidelines.[523]

[416] The Merger Regulation does not provide a definition of dominance. Instead, the Commission employs the definition given by the ECJ in Article 102 of the TFEU cases.[524] Consequently, the term *'Dominant Position'* means a position of economic strength enjoyed by an undertaking which enables it to have an appreciable influence on conditions under which competition can develop. The undertaking must be able to act to an appreciable extent independently of its competitors and, ultimately, of its consumers.

[417] The relevant question is therefore whether the merger increases the market power of the parties to such an extent that they will have the possibility of acting independently of their competitors, customers and ultimately their consumers. In accordance with standard economic theory, the Commission will assess whether it would be possible for the undertaking to increase prices or restrict output following the implementation of the concentration. Additional concerns include whether the company is able to establish a 'gate keeper' role enabling it to control entry to a market; the negative impact on reduced consumer choice over time; increased scope for predatory pricing; and negative effects of refusal to deliver to third parties.[525]

[418] In contrast with cases under Article 102 of the TFEU, the assessment of dominance in merger cases is forward-looking since the objective of merger control is to prevent the creation or strengthening of a dominant position. As a result, assessments under the Merger Regulation involve analyses of market forecasts and how competition is expected to develop in the future. The relevant forecast period generally applied by the Commission is five years. However, the actual relevant forecast period used in any given case will depend on the specific market.

[419] A finding of incompatibility can depend on a position of dominance being created or strengthened in the Internal Market or a substantial part of it. There is little authority on what constitutes a substantial part of the Internal Market. Where dominance exists only in a regional or local market or in a Member State, it is reasonable to argue that the Commission would have no reason for finding the concentration to be incompatible under the Merger Regulation.[526] This also appears to have been recognised through the changes made in 1997 to the Article 9 referral

[522] Recital 26 of the Merger Regulation.

[523] Horizontal Guidelines at para. 4.

[524] Case 27/76 *United Brands Company and United Brands Continental BV v. Commission* [1978] ECR-207, case 85/76 *Hoffman La Roche v. Commission* [1979] ECR-461 and case T-102/96 *Gencor v. Commission* [1999] ECR II-753.

[525] Cases M.833 *The Coca-Cola Company/Carlsberg A/S*; M.469 *MSG Media Service* and M.490 *Nordic Satellite Distribution*.

[526] In some cases the Commission appears to examine the effects of concentrations in areas which do not constitute a substantial part of the Internal Market (case M.804 *Auchan/Pao De Acucar*). Some of these cases could be explained on the basis of chains of substitution, meaning that the area forms part of a wider geographical market or that its competitive effects would be more widespread.

procedure. Such changes strengthened the power of a Member State to obtain referrals for concentrations which affect competition on a distinct market within that Member State and which do not constitute a substantial part of the Internal Market.

[420] In its assessment of whether the transaction will significantly impede effective competition, the Commission looks at a number of different factors, including in particular the parties' market shares, which thereby results in a precise definition of the relevant market.

9.3 The Importance of Market Definition

[421] The identification of the relevant market or markets affected by the transaction is clearly fundamental to whether a SIEC will exist. As the ECJ noted in case M.308 *Kali + Salz*, *'a proper definition of the relevant market is a necessary pre-condition for any assessment of the effect of a concentration on competition'*. The Horizontal Guidelines also stress the importance of market definition in order to assess the competitive constraints facing the merging entity. The aim of the concept of market definition is to identify and define the boundaries of competition between firms and between products. Such boundaries will be described with reference to two elements. The first relates to the product under consideration (the relevant product market), and the second relates to the geographic territory within which competition takes place (the relevant geographic market). Furthermore, such assessment is essentially prospective and takes into account imminent developments in relation to both the product and geographic markets.[527]

[422] Using those two parameters, market definition may rule out competition concerns. This was illustrated by case M.3216 *Oracle/Peoplesoft* where the only product market definition which the Commission regarded as supportable showed that the market comprised seven firms rather than three, a feature which ruled out the possibility of coordinated effects. By contrast, in case M.1524 *Airtours/First Choice*, the Commission defined the market as including only 'short-haul' foreign package holidays, thus excluding 'long-haul' operators such as Kuoni and Virgin, and establishing that the effect of the bid by Airtours for First Choice was to reduce the number of major UK travel groups from four to three. Likewise, geographic market definition was decisive for the clearance decision in case M.4734 *Ineos/Kerling*, where the merged entity would have had market shares in the market of suspension PVC which were presumptive of dominance in the UK, and approaching a monopoly in Scandinavia. However, having opened Phase II proceedings, the Commission concluded that the geographic market was not national but EEA-wide, based on trade flows, low transport costs, broadly comparable prices across the EEA and the buying habits of customers, illustrated when Ineos' UK plant had to be shut

[527] *See* the position expression by Competition Commissioner Joaquin Almunia in Policy Objectives in Merger Control, Fordham Competition Conference, New York, 8 Sep. 2011, Commission press release SPEECH/11/561.

down for a time. This meant that the new firm had a 'moderate' market share in the EEA and faced several major competitors, leading the Commission to clear the merger without issuing a statement of objections or requiring remedies.

[423] The Commission has published a Market Definition Notice setting out its principles for defining relevant markets in all competition cases.[528] On 26 June 2020, the Commission launched a public consultation to assess whether the Market Definition Notice should be updated in light of market developments since its publication in 1997. Responses to the consultation identified a number of significant trends that affect the way that markets work, including digitalisation, the rise of innovation-driven markets and globalisation. In particular, the growth of multisided platforms, digital ecosystems and online retail has introduced additional complexities that are not accounted for in the Market Definition Notice. Further, the Commission's prohibition decision in *Siemens/Alstom*,[529] in particular, sparked political pressure for a broader geographical view of market definition as the parties argued that the proposed transaction was required in order to better compete with rivals outside the EEA, particularly from China. In response to the prohibition, the German, French and Polish competition authorities have specifically called on the Commission to introduce more flexibility to better take into account competition at a global level and to protect European interests.[530] Further, respondents to the consultation suggested that supply-side substitutability and potential competition should be given greater weight, or the Market Definition Notice should be updated to clarify the distinction between the two concepts in the context of dynamic markets.

[424] On 8 November 2022, the Commission published the draft revised market definition notice and launched a further public consultation inviting comments on the draft. The proposed changes provide updated guidance on various aspects of market definition, including placing a greater emphasis on non-price elements including innovation and quality, which the Commission states will be equally as valid as the current SSNIP test that it acknowledges can be difficult to apply, particularly to multisided platforms due to the impact of network effects. On multisided markets, the draft notice also explains that the Commission may either define multisided platforms as separate markets, or define the products/services offered by the platform as a whole, and that this decision will depend on the level of substitution that is possible between the different sides of the platform. The draft notice also provides more specific guidance on the application of market definition to after-markets, bundles and digital ecosystems, innovation markets with significant investment in R&D (particularly in relation to pipeline products) and markets in which there is price discrimination or significant differentiation, as well as considering the forward-looking nature of market definition in markets expected to undergo structural transition (e.g., through regulatory or technological change).

[528] Notice on the definition of the relevant market for the purposes of Community competition law, OJ 1997 C 372/5 of 4 Dec. 1997.

[529] M.8677 *Siemens/Alstom*.

[530] *'Modernising EU Competition Policy'* (4 Apr. 2019), *see* https://www.bmwi.de/Redaktion/DE/Downloads/M-O/modernising-eu-competition-policy.pdf?__blob=publicationFile&v=4.

Other proposed updates include widening the possible scope for identifying supply-side substitutability and identifying alternative methods for calculating market shares aside from sales volumes (e.g., by capacity, production volumes or, in some markets, the number of downloads). Interested parties had until 13 January 2023 to submit comments on the draft notice, and the Commission aims to have a new market definition notice in place in the second half of 2023.

[425] Under the Market Definition Notice, the two basic principles involved are described as *'demand substitutability'* (i.e., the range of products which are viewed as substitutes by the customer) and *'supply-side substitutability'* (i.e., the degree to which other undertakings are able to supply or capable of producing acceptable substitutes).

[426] In assessing substitutability, the Commission advocates the US test of whether the parties' customers would switch to readily available substitutes in response to a hypothetical small (in the range 5% to 10%), permanent relative price increase in the products being considered. This is commonly known as the 'SSNIP' test (small but significant non-transitory increase in price).[531] If such an increase is not profitable because of the resulting loss of sales to closely related products, such additional products, services and areas are included in the relevant market. This is repeated until the range of products included in the market is such that small, permanent increases in relative prices would be profitable[532] (i.e., consumers would not switch to another product, and instead pay the increased price for the deferred product in question).

[427] It should be noted that the purpose of market definition is to define what might be termed an 'antitrust market' for the purpose of the Commission's investigation. Therefore such market will not necessarily be the same as the 'business market' in which an undertaking believes it operates. The reason for this is that from a business perspective, markets will generally be delineated by the products sold to a customer. Accordingly, if adopted in the context of competition law, such a focus would lead to overly narrow markets. Without going to such extent, the Commission will nevertheless generally adopt a narrow view of the market, particularly in the Phase I procedure where there is little time and often little information upon which to form a definitive analysis. This means that the Commission often identifies markets with a very small turnover or specialist or niche markets, particularly in relation to pharmaceutical cases.

---

531 Also known as the hypothetical monopolist test. It is also recognised by the Commission that this test has limitations when applied to a monopolist able to change monopoly prices. An increase in price from a monopoly price would suggest higher substitutability than actually exists. In this case, prices other than prevailing market prices would have to be taken into account.

532 For example, in order to establish whether product X constitutes a distinct economic market, assume that firm A has a monopoly in the supply of that product. If, in response to A raising its prices by a significant amount, customers switched to product Y supplied by undertaking B in such numbers as to make the price increase unprofitable, products X and Y must be in the same market. The test is repeated until all the substitutes for product X and all the actual and potential competitors of undertaking A have been identified. A similar method is used to establish the limits of the relevant geographic market.

[428] In many cases, the Commission does not commit itself to a particular market definition where it is not necessary to do so. This is due to the fact that the great majority of notifications raise no significant threat to competition (i.e., where there are no affected markets or where the parties' aggregated market shares do not lead to a SIEC even on the narrowest possible market definition). In such cases, the Commission will often content itself with the comment that *'exact market definitions may be left open'*, or similar, although the Commission must then at least briefly explain its reasoning for reaching this conclusion so as to enable concerned persons to ascertain the Commission's reasoning and ensure that said reasoning is open to review by the EU judicature.[533] In circumstances where the definition of the market is crucial for the assessment of compatibility, an economic analysis prepared by expert economists is advisable in order to support the parties' arguments. Firms of economists are usually employed in cases which reach the Phase II investigation or in difficult Phase I cases which entail remedies and long pre-notification discussions with the Commission. The Commission will also use the expertise of its Chief Economist, as well as resources available from the experts in other services, particularly in DG Economic and Financial Affairs and DG Internal Market. In this respect, the parties are encouraged to refer to the Commission's Best practices for the submission of economic evidence in merger cases which provides useful guidance on the Commission's practice with respect to market definition based on economic evidence.

9.3.1 Relevant Product Market

[429] The Implementing Regulation defines the relevant product as comprising 'all those products and/or services which are regarded as interchangeable or substitutable by the consumer, by reason of the products' characteristics, their prices and their intended use'.

[430] In assessing the relevant product market, above all, the Commission relies on demand-side substitutability. Supply-side substitutability is generally used to analyse competition in markets already defined by reference to demand-side factors which have been identified as a form of potential competition when assessing the effects of the transaction on the market. Supply-side substitutability is only taken into account in defining markets where its effects are equivalent to those of demand substitution in terms of effectiveness and immediacy.[534] Suppliers must be able to switch production to the relevant products and markets in a very short time without incurring significant additional costs (in terms of assets, additional investment, or time delays) or risks in response to small but permanent changes in price. Supply-side substitutability is therefore typically important in product markets

[533] *See*, for example, Case T394/15 *KPN BV v. Commission*, where the Commission's approval of the *Liberty Global/Ziggo* transaction (case M.7000) was annulled by the General Court as the result of a successful appeal by a third party, KPN, on the basis that, in leaving open the market definition as to whether the wholesale supply and acquisition of premium TV channels could be further segmented by film and sport channels, the Commission had failed to fully state the reasons why the proposed transaction did not raise any competition concerns in this regard.

[534] Market Definition Notice at para. 20.

where companies market a wide range of qualities or grades of one product which, though not substitutable from the point of view of the consumer, will constitute a single market as most suppliers are able to offer various qualities immediately. Even then, in cases where there are no significant obstacles to supply-side substitution, markets characterised by local specificities (such as the availability of a local presence to provide after-sale services) may still be assessed at a national level.[535]

[431] As a first step, the Commission identifies a possible field of substitutes based largely on the physical characteristics and functionality of the products. The starting point for this is in practice the market definition provided by the parties. Products that have the same characteristics are more likely to be in the same market. In certain cases, however, the Commission has defined physical characteristics very narrowly. For example, in case M.794 *Coca-Cola/Amalgamated Beverages*, the Commission defined the relevant market as cola-flavoured carbonated soft drinks and rejected the parties' arguments that the market comprised all commercial beverages based on the functionality of the product.[536] Likewise, in *Nestlé/Ralston-Purina*, the Commission defined separate markets for wet and dry pet food because of their different nutritional characteristics.[537] In other cases, the Commission has taken a much broader view of physical characteristics. For example, in case M.1355 *Newell/Rubbermaid*, the relevant product market was defined as home storage products, systems and food storage containers. The Commission stated that any narrower market definition would have been misleading as to the relevant competitive dynamics of the market. Products that have similar end-uses are also likely to be in the same market although in many cases this is not a determining factor. For example, in the *Coca-Cola* case, although all carbonated drinks may be used to quench thirst, the Commission specifically identified a separate market for cola-flavoured drinks. In addition, the Commission has often grouped several products together in one market on the basis that the suppliers of these products offered the whole range to the same customers.[538] A similar analysis was used, although reaching a different conclusion, in the merger between the respective coffee businesses of Douwe Egberts and Mondelez where the Commission noted that portions of coffee to be used in single-serve machines are put into sealed pads, pods or capsules, and each single-serve machine requires a specific type of consumable. The Commission concluded that each type of consumable belonged to a separate product market. A consumer cannot buy Nespresso-compatible capsules and use them in a Senseo machine or vice versa. Once a consumer has committed to a particular system, he or she is also committed to the type of consumable he or she buys. Accordingly, the Commission considered that each type of single-serve consumable constitutes a distinct product market.[539] In its initial assessment, the Commission

[535] Case M.10431 *Ali Group/Welbilt*.

[536] Industries where the Commission has not accepted supply-side substitutability in terms of product market definition include branded consumer industries that involve lead times (in terms of advertising to build up a brand, product testing and distribution) before the product can be sold.

[537] Case M.2337 *Néstlé/Ralston-Purina*.

[538] In case M.1047 *Wienerberger/Cremer & Bremer* (different kinds of plastic and cast iron pipes) and case M.970 *Thyssen Krupp Stahl/ITW Signode/Titan* (steel and plastic strapping).

[539] M.7292 *DEMB/Mondelez/Charger OPCO*.

also takes the relative pricing of products into account as wide-ranging price differentials usually indicate that different markets are applicable. For example, in case M.190 *Nestlé/Perrier*, the Commission found that the 200% to 300% difference in retail prices was incompatible with a single product market for soft drinks and mineral water.[540]

[432] As a result, having identified a possible field of substitutes, the Commission then attempts to assess how customers will react to changes in the relative price of the products.[541] Notwithstanding the emphasis in the Market Definition Notice on the use of the SSNIP test, this has not figured significantly in Commission decisions. Usually, data on prices and sales volumes is difficult to obtain in sufficient detail or over a sufficient period to provide empirical support for the SSNIP analysis. Instead, methods used by the Commission include:

- surveying customers to gauge their views on market definition and in particular their reaction to a hypothetical price increase in the product concerned;[542]
- looking at evidence relating to substitution in the recent past where there have been changes in price (all being equal) as a result of, for example, market shocks and launches of new products;[543]
- quantitative measures to assess patterns of substitution. These include (i) econometric and statistical approaches to elasticity and cross-price elasticity,[544] (ii) analysis of price movements over time,[545] (iii) analysis of causality between price series and (iv) analysis of similar price series, and their convergence;[546] and
- marketing studies (particularly in consumer product markets) and consumer surveys on usage patterns. Normally, these documents will be obtained from

540 *See also* case M.3056 *Celanese/Degussa/JV* where the Commission concluded that isomers n- and iso-butyric aldehyde were not part of the same product market because of price differences of 15%–40%.

541 The Commission considers that differences in product characteristics and intended use alone are regarded as insufficient to show whether two products are demand substitutes as this will depend on how customers value their characteristics.

542 For example, *see* case M.430 *Procter & Gamble/VP Schickedanz (II)* where the Commission used consumer survey results and market price data to show that, contrary to the arguments of the notifying party, sanitary towels and tampons were separate product markets. Although the products performed the same function they did not share the same characteristics and significant price changes in the one product relative to the other were not sufficient to induce most consumers to switch.

543 In case IV M.430 *Procter & Gamble/VP Schickedanz (II)*, the Commission took note of the fact that when a new brand of sanitary towel entered the market, there was a decline in sales of other sanitary towels but not in tampons, thereby concluding that tampons and sanitary towels were in separate product markets. Also in case M.1939 *Rexam/American National Can*, the Commission considered whether beverage cans made from aluminium formed a separate market from beverage cans made from steel and where the price of the main input, aluminium sheets, had changed substantially. The price of aluminium cans did not increase and instead the price of aluminium cans was sensitive to changes in the prices of steel beverage cans. Accordingly the Commission concluded that beverage cans made from steel and aluminium were part of the same product market.

544 Case M.2498 *UPM-Kymmene/Haindl*.

545 Case M.619 *Gencor/Lonrho*.

546 Case M.214 *DuPont/ICI*.

customers, competitors and other third parties active on the market via Article 11 requests.

[433] In some circumstances, the structure of supply and demand may lead to the identification of separate product markets where an approach based on physical characteristics, functionality and even price may suggest the opposite. Product markets may also be narrowed according to distinct groups of customers who are subject to price discrimination. This will usually be the case where it is possible to clearly identify which group an individual customer belongs to at the moment of sale, where trade among customers between different groups is not feasible. For example, in case M.4381 *JCI/FIAMM*, the Commission concluded that separate product markets existed for the supply of car batteries to vehicle manufacturers in the original equipment market and the supply of batteries to the replacement market. In several airline cases, the Commission has accepted separate markets for business travel (*'time sensitive'* passengers) and leisure travel (*'price sensitive'* passengers).[547] Several distinctions have also been drawn in the real estate sector[548] and in markets that supply internet services.[549] Barriers to entry for a given market and demand costs may also have a significant effect on market definition. These include regulatory barriers or other forms of state intervention, as well as constraints arising in customers' markets such as the need to incur significant capital investment in production processes, training, and loss of output in order to switch to alternative input. In case M.126 *Accor/Wagons-Lits*, motorway restaurant services were considered to constitute a distinct service market because of the different conditions under which motorway restaurants are regulated and operated. In case M.9706 *Novelis/Aleris*, the Commission concluded that flat steel products used in automotive bodies were separate from the market for aluminium automotive body sheets ('Aluminium ABS') because the lightweight properties of aluminium ABS provided an advantage over steel in helping customers to comply with increasingly strict CO2 regulations.[550] In the pharmaceutical sector, the Commission has drawn a distinction between prescription (ethical) and over-the-counter medicines, and, within these categories, distinct product markets according to the Anatomical Therapeutic Classification of medicines.[551] In case M.4180 *Gaz de France/Suez*, the Commission distinguished between customers who could choose their electricity supplier and those who did not have that possibility due to state regulation.[552] Finally, when a transaction involves products and services that are new or subject to continuous technological development, defining the relevant markets can also prove to be a challenging exercise as the traditional tools for market definition, such as the SSNIP test, may not be appropriate.[553] For example, the SSNIP test,

[547] *See* among others, cases M.5181 *Delta Air Lines/Northwest Airlines* and M.5440 *Lufthansa/Austria Airlines*.

[548] Case M.2025 *GE/BTPS/MEPC* and case M.1637 *DB Investments/SPP/ÖHMAN*.

[549] Case M.1069 *WorldCom/MCI (II)*.

[550] Case M.9706 *Novelis/Aleris*.

[551] *See* cases M.5253 *Sanofi-Aventis/Zentiva* and M.5502 *Merck/Schering-Plough*.

[552] *See also* case M.1853 *EDF/EnBW*.

[553] Case M.7217 *Facebook/WhatsApp*.

which is designed to assess to what extent products and services are currently substitutes to each other, is unlikely to capture the changes in substitutability brought by technological developments that may occur in the next two to three years (i.e., the time span relevant for the assessment of a merger). The increased prevalence of multisided markets is a particular challenge, with some respondents to the consultation on the Market Definition Notice suggesting that the SSNIP test needs to take into account the feedback effects of multisided markets, whereby the interconnected nature of users on different sides of the market results in indirect effects when changes are made to one side. Also, the SSNIP test cannot as such be applied with respect to digital products or services that are offered for free because price is generally not the main parameter of competition. Respondents to the Market Notification Definition consultation also raised this point and suggested alternative tests that could be introduced to take account of non-price parameters, such as a small but significant non-transitory decrease in quality or a small but significant non-transitory increase in cost.

[434] Product market definition was also a key element in the Commission's prohibition of the contemplated merger between Deutsche Börse and NYSE Euronext.[554] Indeed, the Commission's decision was largely driven by the conclusions reached on market definition where two main issues arose. First, whether different types of derivative products were in distinct markets. Second, whether exchange-traded derivatives competed with derivatives traded over the counter without the involvement of a regulated trading venue. With respect to the first question, the Commission identified different markets for each type of assets (single-stock derivatives, interest rate derivatives, equity index derivatives, etc.). As regards the second issue, the Commission rejected the parties' contention that exchange traded derivatives competed on the same market as over-the-counter traded derivatives. In its re-assessment of *Liberty Global/Ziggo* transaction,[555] the Commission concluded that the market for the wholesale supply and acquisition of premium pay-TV sports channels should not be further segmented by the two channels it comprised. In its assessment, the Commission considered whether access to certain sports events should be considered an 'essential' competitive factor, which it defined as *'an input that forces out of the market (or prevents market entry of) those which do not have it'*. The Commission concluded that access to certain sports events were not an essential competitive factor since a number of premium sports events are substitutable among themselves and having access to specific events was not a requirement to operate on the market. The Commission's reconsideration decision was appealed to the General Court by a third party, KPN, who claimed the Commission had erred in its application of market definition by ignoring market feedback that Ziggo's product was a 'must have' and therefore not substitutable with two other premium pay-TV sports channels.[556] The General Court dismissed KPN's appeal in full and concluded that, while it might be commercially desirable for television

[554] Case M.6166 *Deutsche Börse/NYSE Euronext*.

[555] Case T-691/18 *KPN v. Commission*.

[556] Case T-691/18 *KPN v. Commission*.

wholesale suppliers and retail television service providers to be able to offer a certain product to its subscribers in parallel with others, they considered such premium pay-TV services to be equally attractive, and the Commission was therefore entitled to consider them interchangeable when defining the market and there was no need to further segment the market.

[435] The outcome of two recent appeals of the Commission's application of product market definition to the General Court provides some additional clarification as to market definition application. In case M.8900 *Wieland/Aurubis Rolled Products/Schwermetall,*[557] the Commission conducted its competitive assessment both at the overall rolled products level and at the high-end segment of the market, based on the *'high degree of differentiation in terms of product performance, knowhow and technology, specifications of customers, intensity of competition and pricing'*. Wieland appealed the Commission's prohibition decision, alleging that the Commission applied a flawed concept of a high-end sub-segment, for which Weiland argued it provided neither a definition nor a clear-cut delineation.[558] However, the General Court confirmed the Commission's approach to market definition and concluded that different competitive dynamics were at play, specifically characterised by production contains linked to the growing demand for high-end rolled products, and the Commission was therefore justified to focus its analysis on the high-end rolled products segment in which the parties' activities overlapped. In case M.8713 *Tata Steel/ThyssenKrupp,*[559] the Commission concluded that hot-dip galvanised steel and electrogalvanised steel likely constituted separate markets and further distinguished a separate market based on the end-user, in this case, hot-dipped galvanised steel for automotive customers. ThyssenKrupp appealed the Commission's application of market definition to the General Court, alleging that the Commission failed to take account of demand and supply-side substitutability and thereby wrongfully omitting electrogalvanised steel from the market definition, as well as missing out the interchangeability of galvanised industrial and automotive products.[560] The General Court confirmed the Commission's approach to market definition, noting the lack of supply-side substitutability between hot-dipped galvanised steel and electrogalvanised steel and that the two are only substitutable in only one direction from a demand-perspective. ThyssenKrupp has appealed the General Court's application of market definition to the ECJ, arguing that the General Court wrongly upheld narrowly defined markets of automotive hot-dip galvanised steel and laminated steel for packaging.[561]

[436] Other appeals of the Commission's market definition application that are pending before the General Court should also provide further clarification in this area, in addition to the proposed changes to the Market Definition Notice. In case T-709/22 *Illumina v. Commission*, whereby Illumina is challenging the Commission's market definition on the basis that it erroneously creates an artificial distinction

[557] Case M.8900 *Wieland/Aurubis Rolled Products/Schwermetall.*

[558] Case T-251/19 *Wieland-Werke/Commission.*

[559] Case M.8713 *Tata Steel/Thyssenkrupp/JV.*

[560] Case T-584/19 *Thyssenkrupp v. Commission.*

[561] Case C-581/22 *Thyssenkrupp AG.*

between the development and commercialisation stages of the relevant early cancer detection tests, finds substitutability among different types of tests at the putative development stage, and finds innovation substitutability between certain multi-cancer and single-cancer early detection tests.[562]

9.3.2 Relevant Geographic Market

[437] Once the relevant product market has been defined, it is then necessary to define the geographic area affected by this market. The Market Definition Notice defines the relevant geographic market as a defined geographical area in which the product or the service concerned is marketed and where the conditions of competition are sufficiently homogeneous for all economic operators, so that the effect on competition can be evaluated rationally. On this basis, the Commission has considered all local, national, regional, Community and worldwide markets.

[438] The Commission exercises considerable discretion in deciding which factors are influential in any particular case, and rarely highlights any single characteristic as determining the relevant geographic market.

[439] The Commission first takes a preliminary view of the relevant market on the basis of a wide range of factors, the most important of which appear to be: comparative prices between areas;[563] trade flows and patterns of shipments;[564] comparison of active manufacturers, suppliers and customers; the distribution of their market shares; and the ongoing process of market integration in the EU. In doing so, the Commission will analyse in each case whether the process of market integration leads to European-wide markets or whether it will do so with sufficient certainty in the foreseeable and immediate future. Next, it applies a similar economic analysis to that used for the product market, namely, whether a notional increase in price would cause customers to switch orders to suppliers in other areas, as well as other quantitative tests used for the product market definition. Lastly, the Commission investigates practical impediments or barriers that might tend to isolate markets. These include the following factors: transport costs; national demand characteristics (such as preferences for national brands, language, culture and lifestyle); entry barriers (such as requirement for a local presence); conditions of access to or costs of setting up a distribution network; various regulatory barriers such as price regulation, legal monopolies, exclusive rights and tax regime; and technical standards. During its investigation, the Commission attaches considerable importance to the views of customers and competitors regarding the scope of the relevant geographic market.

[562] Case T-709/22 *Illumina v. Commission*.

[563] *See* cases M.6663 *Ryanair/Aer Lingus III*; M.6850 *Marine Harvest/Morpol* and M.7155 *SSAB/Rautaruukki*.

[564] The Commission has rejected the Elzinga-Hogarty test, commonly used by US antitrust authorities, to determine the geographic market. According to that test, where exports or imports exceed 10% of production or consumption respectively within a particular territory, that area is to be considered as belonging to a wider geographic market. The Commission concluded that the test fails to measure mutual interpenetration between the territories concerned: two-way trade is as important as the absolute level of imports or exports.

[440] While prior decisions are not legally binding on the Commission when assessing new concentrations and while there are instances where the Commission has not hesitated to diverge from well-established Commission practice even in mature and basic industries,[565] in practice, the Commission precedents often carry significant weight, and it may be difficult for the parties to convince the Commission to depart from prior conclusions regarding geographic market definition, in particular if those conclusions are recent.[566] At the same time, the move towards deregulation and privatisation of traditionally state-owned industries, as well as advances in manufacturing processes and new technology are increasing the minimum efficient scale of the operation of businesses. As a result, suppliers may no longer be confined to supplying the local vicinity or the territory of just one Member State. In its revised Market Definition Notice, the Commission explains that competitive conditions in distinct geographic areas may converge over time to the point where they are sufficiently homogeneous as to consider previously separate geographic markets as part of the same geographic market. This was the case in contrast to the Commission's 2001 *Metso/Svedala*[567] and 2020 *Outotec/Metso*[568] decisions, with the earlier decision concluding that the market for crushers was defined as EEA-wide but global in the latter. In particular, geographic market definitions in industries such as telecommunications, broadcasting and energy in particular are quickly evolving.[569]

Local Markets

[441] In the food and retail sectors, the tendency is to define markets as being local on the basis that customers are drawn from a local catchment area.[570] The Commission considers that the geographic market for the landfilling and incineration of hazardous waste is a catchment area of 300 km from the relevant treatment site,[571] and in the cement sector, the Commission considers that cement sales are made within a maximum distance of 150 km or 250 km from the production facility.[572] In the metal scrap recycling sector, the Commission recently considered the

[565] Case M.7155 *SSAB/Rautaruukki* where the Commission considered that there was a geographic market for steel products comprising Norway, Sweden and Finland, departing from previous decisions where it considered the market for steel products to be EEA-wide.

[566] Case M.6447 *IAG/BMI* where the Commission relied on decisions in more than fifteen prior cases to define the market in the passenger airline industry.

[567] Case M.2033 *Metso/Svedala*.

[568] Case M.9585 *Outotec/Metso*.

[569] In electricity markets, while still considering that certain markets are national in scope such as production or distribution, the Commission has changed its approach with regard to the market for the trading of electricity where it now takes the view that such a market can be transnational depending on the interconnection of national power exchanges. *See* M.4180 *Gaz de France/Suez*.

[570] In case M.2115 *Carrefour/GB* (retail supermarket), the Commission noted that *'supermarkets draw customers from a local catchment area'*. *See also* cases M.3905 *Tesco/Carrefour* (retail supermarket) and M.5112 *REWE/Plus Discount* (retail supermarket). In the beer sector, *see* case M.4999 *Scottish & Newcastle assets/Heineken*. In the chocolate sector *see* M.7408 *Cargill/ADM Chocolate business* where the Commission ultimately left the exact geographic market definition open but conducted its market analysis on the basis of catchment areas of about 500 km in distance either from the parties' plants or from the parties' customers.

[571] Case M.9969 *Veolia/Suez*.

[572] *See* cases M. 7009 *Holcim/Cemex West*; M.7054 *Cemex/Holcim Assets* and M.7252 *Holcim/Lafarge*.

geographic market to be the distance within which the parties travelled to purchase or sell 80% of the scrap.[573] Local markets are also generally found for the distribution of energy as a result of local networks,[574] for infrastructure management[575] and for airline routes or bundles of routes.[576]

National Markets

[442] The Commission has found national markets to exist on the basis of very high costs of transport and import,[577] regulatory barriers such as in the insurance, retail, corporate banking,[578] and pharmaceuticals[579] sectors, markets such as telecommunications that are not yet fully liberalised,[580] and energy where production is still essentially national (due to network and pipeline constraints and since production companies are still active primarily on a national basis).[581] Other relevant factors include: different consumer preferences and habits, particularly in broadcasting and television;[582] different prices and distribution systems;[583] difficult technical conditions of competition and requirements;[584] different market shares and languages;[585] location and identity of suppliers and purchasers;[586] and supply conditions which come with particularly *'just in time'* requirements.[587] However, many national markets are developing into wider markets as a result of the benefits of the single market programme, the EU public procurement regime and the ongoing creation of the single market.[588]

Regional Markets

[443] The Commission has also found regional markets crossing national borders in cases concerning cultural and linguistic requirements,[589] energy,[590] PVC,[591] and

---

[573] Case M.10249 *Derichebourg Environnement/Groupe Ecore Holding.*

[574] *See* case M.1532 *BP Amoco/Atlantic Richfield* (transport of unprocessed natural gas through offshore pipelines) and M.4180 *Gaz de France/Suez* (distribution of electricity for residential customers).

[575] Case M.4466 *HTA/CDPQ/BAA Budapest Airport.*

[576] *See* cases M.5440 *Lufthansa/Austrian Airlines;* M.5364 *Iberia/Vueling/Clickair* and M.5181 *Delta Air Lines/Northwest Airlines.*

[577] Case M.4381 *JCI/FIAMM* (aftermarket for car batteries).

[578] *See* cases M.5384 *BNP/Fortis* (retail banking); M.5509 *Crédit Agricole/CACEIS* (retail banking); M.4811 *Cetelem/Findomestic* (financial leasing) and M.5129 *Delta Lloyd/Swiss Life Belgium* (insurance).

[579] Cases M.7275 *Novartis/GlaxoSmithKline Oncology*; M.5778 *Novartis/Alcon*; M.5502 *Merck/Schering-Plough* and M.4423 *Merck/Serono.*

[580] Case M.1439 *Telia/Telenor* (cable TV telecom services), case M.1838 *BT/ESAT* (end-to-end network services) and case M.1795 *Vodafone Airtouch/Mannesmann* (telecommunications).

[581] Cases M.4180 *Gaz de France/Suez* (electricity and gas) and case M.5467 *RWE/Essent* (electricity).

[582] Case M.4600 *TUI/First Choice* (package holidays).

[583] Cases M.4842 *Danone/Numico* (production and sale of food products), case M.4147 *Linde/BOC* (bulk industrial gases) and case M.4972 *Permira/Arysta* (manufacture of pesticides).

[584] Case M.4519 *file:Lagardère/Sortfive* (TV).

[585] Case M.5250 *Porsche/Volkswagen* (cars).

[586] Case M.4381 *JCI/FIAMM* (OEM car batteries).

[587] Case M.2862 *Kone/Partek* (installation and maintenance of elevators).

[588] The liberalisation of the electricity market was a significant factor in establishing a finding of no dominance in case M.1882 *Pirelli/BICC* despite market shares of between 75% and 95%.

[589] Case M.4404 *Universal Music Group/BMG Music Publishing.*

steel products.[592] The Commission has also explored a geographic market distinction between Northern and Southern Europe, in relation to commodity steel, based on a differentiated pattern of supply as a result of differing supply and demand characteristics that could not be explained by transport costs alone, ultimately concluding that the market was EEA-wide but with strong indications of geographic differentiation.[593]

West European/EEA Markets

[444] The Commission has found West European/EEA markets to exist on the basis of: EEA-wide purchasing;[594] products traded with a European-wide marketing strategy;[595] services provided to multinational clients requiring service in several countries;[596] substantial trade flows between countries;[597] the effect of EU legislation such as public procurement rules; the inability of non-EEA suppliers to step in with a credible product[598] or to address EEA demand due to lack of track-record, regulatory requirements or transport costs;[599] the geographic reach of networks;[600] short delivery times[601] and the effects of deregulation on industries such as telecommunications and energy.[602]

World Markets

[445] There are relatively few cases where the Commission has ultimately decided in favour of a worldwide market. In general, trade patterns are crucial in judging whether the Community or Western Europe is part of a wider market including, for example, Eastern Europe, Asia or the US.[603] The Commission has found world markets in relation to products that can be easily transported, processed to

590 Case M.4180 *Gaz de France/Suez* (trading of electricity).

591 Case M.6905 *Ineos/Solvay/JV* where the Commission considered a market comprised of North Western Europe plus Austria, Finland, Italy and Switzerland.

592 Case M.7155 *SSAB/Rautaruukki*.

593 Case M.8444 *ArcelorMittal/Ilva*.

594 Case M.3680 *Alcatel/Finmeccanica/Alcatel Alenia Space & Telespazio* (satellite equipment).

595 Case M.4381 *JCI/FIAMM* (car batteries for OEMs), and case M.5142 *Bosch/Mahle/JV* (turbochargers).

596 Case M.1016 *PriceWaterhouse/Coopers & Lybrand* (audit and accounting services).

597 Cases M.3564 *Aster 2/Flint Ink* (off set printing plates) and M.4734 *Ineos/Kerling* (polyvinyl chloride and caustic soda).

598 Case M.7061 *Huntsman Corporation/Equity interests held by Rockwood Holdings*.

599 Case *M.10078 Cargotec/Konecranes*.

600 Case M.672 *BP/Sonatrach* (natural gas transportation) and case M.1882 *Pirelli/BICC* (production and sale of power cables).

601 Case M.8713 *Tata Steel/Thyssenkrupp/JV* (steel).

602 Case M.1845 *Time Warner/AOL* (online music delivery) and case M.1795 *Vodafone Airtouch/Mannesmann* (mobile telephony).

603 Even if low levels of international trade lead the Commission to conclude that separate geographic markets exist, it may nonetheless find that the potential for imports from markets outside may act as a constraint on its market power. In case M.315 *Mannesmann/Valourec/Ilva* the Commission concluded that the relevant market did not include Asia but that if the merged company raised its prices in Europe significantly, this would attract imports from Japanese steel producers which, having established a pattern of trade and commercial relationships with European customers, would be difficult to displace.

world standards and traded.[604] These include: certain money markets, foreign exchange,[605] reinsurance and asset management services because of the need to pool risks on an international basis;[606] commercial shipbuilding;[607] database management systems;[608] travel services;[609] global telecommunications services and satellite services for multinational corporate customers;[610] and aircraft in aircraft components.[611]

9.4 Anticompetitive Effects

9.4.1 Non-coordinated Effects

[446] In its assessment of mergers, the Commission follows an effects-based approach that tries to anticipate the possible anticompetitive consequences of mergers. To this end, the Commission may take account of not only the competitive conditions that prevail at the time of the proposed transaction but also future changes to the relevant market conditions that can be reasonably predicted. In the section below, we will first deal with cases where such anticompetitive consequences do not entail any coordination between the rival undertakings as regards price or the other features of competition, i.e., so-called non-coordinated effects. Within this category, it is useful to distinguish between horizontal, vertical and conglomerate effects. The Commission provides guidance as to its assessment of the first type of effects in its 2004 Horizontal Merger Guidelines. Later, in 2008, the Commission also published Non-Horizontal Merger Guidelines which cover both vertical and conglomerate effects.

9.4.2 Horizontal Mergers

[447] Horizontal mergers, i.e., those that happen between actual (or potential) competitors active at the same level of the production or distribution chain, have accounted for the vast majority of the transactions filed and challenged under the Merger Regulation. In assessing horizontal mergers, the Commission assesses

[604] Cases M.4985 *BHP Billiton/Rio Tinto* (aluminium and copper) and M.6765 *Precision Castparts/Titanium Metals* (titanium).

[605] Case M.4912 *Calyon/Société Générale/Newedge* (banking).

[606] Case M.1043 *BAT/Zürich* (insurance).

[607] Case M.4956 *STX/Aker Yards*. The Commission also opened an in-depth investigation in case M.9162 *Fincantieri/Chantiers de L'Atlantique* on the basis of concerns about the global cruise shipbuilding market, although the transaction was ultimately called-off.

[608] Case M.5529 *Oracle/Sun Microsystems*.

[609] Case M.5123 *Autogrill/World Duty Free*.

[610] Case M.1069 *WorldCom/MCI (II)* (telecommunications): case JV.15 *BT/AT&T* (telecommunications), case M.1185 *Alcatel/Thomson* (manufacture of aircraft and spacecraft); case M.437 *Matra Marconi Space/British Aerospace* (space systems) and case M.532 *Cable & Wireless/Schlumberger* (advanced telecoms services for international groups).

[611] Case M.877 *Boeing/McDonnell Douglas* (manufacture of aircraft and spacecraft); case M.3621 *Snecma/Sagem* (engines) and case M.2220 *General Electric/Honeywell* (aircraft and engines).

mainly the unilateral effects stemming from the transaction, i.e., transactions that allow the merging parties to increase prices or reduce output unilaterally, thereby leading to price increases or reduced output for all companies active in the same market. In analysing such possible effects, the Commission uses a market-based approach that seeks to predict the effects of a transaction on the existing parameters and dynamics of competition. In doing so, the Commission compares post-transaction competitive conditions with those that could be expected to prevail in the absence of the transaction (i.e., the so-called counterfactual).[612]

[448] In 2004, in an effort to increase transparency and provide guidance as to how the Commission assesses horizontal concentrations, the Commission published its Horizontal Merger Guidelines. These guidelines identify two situations that may give rise to unilateral effects that significantly impede effective competition:

- concentrations that create or strengthen the dominant position of a single firm, which typically would have a larger market share than its closest competitor following the transaction; and
- concentrations in oligopolistic markets which lead to the elimination of important competitive constraints that the merging parties had been able to exert on each other, combined with a reduction of competitive pressure on the remaining competitors, even when there is little likelihood of coordination between the members of the oligopoly.[613]

[449] For its assessment of horizontal mergers, the Commission proceeds in the following systemic way. It first defines the relevant product and geographic markets which are concerned by the transaction. Following this first step, the Commission then considers the following elements in its assessment:

- the parties' market shares and concentration levels on the relevant markets;
- the likelihood that a merger would have anticompetitive effects in the absence of countervailing factors, such as buyer power;
- the likelihood that entry would maintain effective competition;
- the likelihood that efficiencies would act as factor counteracting the harmful effects on competition which might otherwise result from the merger; and
- whether the conditions for the failing firm defence exist.[614]

[450] Not all of these elements will always be relevant or applicable to each and every horizontal merger, and it is also generally not necessary to analyse all the elements to the same level of detail. In assessing the unilateral effects of a merger, the Commission will focus on the loss of competition between the merging firms. In doing so, market shares play a central role. The move towards an effects-based analysis implies, however, that market shares will never be the Commission's sole

612 *See* cases M.5549 *EDF/Segebel*; M.5335 *Lufthansa/SN Airholding (Brussels Airlines)*; M.5727 *Microsoft/Yahoo! Search Business* and M.5655 *SNCF/LCR/Eurostar*.

613 Horizontal Guidelines at para. 25, and *see*, for example, case M.9829 *Aon/Willis* on the discussion about the lack of countervailing buyer power even in cases of large corporate customers.

614 Horizontal Guidelines at para. 11 and *see* below.

instrument to identify a SIEC. However, they will remain the starting point in every merger assessment.

The Relative Importance of Market Shares

[451] Based on the product and geographic markets identified, the Commission will start its analysis by looking at the market shares which the undertakings concerned hold on the relevant market. This allows the Commission to assess whether, post-transaction, the parties will be able to exercise or increase market power. For these purposes, it is necessary to aggregate the market shares of all undertakings which, following the concentration, would be under the control of the same undertaking within the meaning of Article 3(3) of the Merger Regulation. The market shares of the parties are generally calculated on the basis of the value of sales, as this is considered to constitute an accurate reflection of market power. However, parties are required to provide market share information in the Form CO in terms of both value and volume of sales. This is because in certain cases, the volume of sales may provide a fairer reading of the parties' market shares. In some industries (in particular in basic industries), a company's market position may be better reflected by the share of capacity that it controls. Accordingly, the Commission may pay more attention to this parameter of competition than to sales-based market shares.

[452] While the Horizontal Merger Guidelines describe market shares merely as *'useful first indications'*, in most cases, market share figures will strongly influence the outcome of a merger review. From this perspective, the Horizontal Merger Guidelines provide useful guidance regarding the applicable range of market shares which will be considered as problematic by the regulator. Accordingly, the Commission has moved away from the 40% threshold, traditionally taken to be indicative of dominance, to refer to a 50% threshold as possible *'evidence of the existence of a dominant market position'*.[615] The Commission has taken the view that market shares of this level can lead to competition concerns but are not themselves necessarily indicative of market power.[616]

[453] At the same time, a safe harbour generally exists for transactions which lead to a combined market share of 25% or less, as set out in paragraph 18 of the Horizontal Merger Guidelines and Recital 15 of the Merger Regulation. However, in all cases, it is important to assess market shares in the context of a market's characteristics and the effect of competition on it. Furthermore, it is also important to make a dynamic assessment of market power by analysing a transaction's likely effect in the years following the transaction. Decisions under the Merger Regulation therefore normally involve predictions in relation to how markets will develop where a concentration is to be permitted and, for many reasons, the past may be an unreliable proxy for the future. From this viewpoint, the key factors which should be

[615] Horizontal Merger Guidelines at para. 17, and *see* case T-221/95 *Endemol v. Commission* [1999] ECR II-1299 at para. 134 and case T-102/96, *Gencor v. Commission* [1999] ECR II-753 at para. 205 as well as M.10249 *Derichebourg/Ecore,* M.9820 *Danfoss/Eaton Hydraulics* and M.9343 *Hyundai Heavy Industries Holdings/Daewoo Shipbuilding*.

[616] Cases M.6101 *UPM/Myllykoski and Rhein Papier* and M.5898 *Saint-Gobain/Maxit*.

taken into consideration include the position of remaining competitors and entry conditions in the market under scrutiny, as opposed to the parties' market shares.[617] These factors are considered more likely to realistically illustrate the existence of market power held by an undertaking with a high market share. This is true in particular in fast-moving digital markets such as the market for consumer communications apps. For example, in its *Facebook/WhatsApp* decision, the Commission recognised that market shares fluctuate very rapidly, sometimes even within weeks or months. Accordingly, past market shares were found to not necessarily represent the effective competitive force of market players at the time of the Commission's decision or within the two- to three-year prognosis period that the Commission normally considers to assess the future effects of a merger.

[454] Another key factor in assessing market shares for horizontal mergers and joint ventures is the increment in market share resulting from the concentration and the gap between the merged entity and its closest rivals.[618] Where the increment is limited, there is typically room to argue that the effects of the proposed transaction are equally limited. That said, even a relatively small increase in market share may be considered sufficiently harmful to competition to warrant a prohibition where the transaction strengthens an already pre-existing strong market position. This may be the case, for example, where an undertaking is clearly dominant in an oligopolistic market and acquires a direct competitor that – despite being substantially smaller – was acting as a maverick in the market, thereby effectively constraining the larger players' market behaviour. While this was the situation in case M.430 *Procter & Gamble/VP Schickedanz (II)*, the Commission has stated that an increase of less than 1% would not typically constitute a strengthening of a dominant position. In general, it appears that the Commission considers increases of less than 5% not to have the effect of strengthening a dominant position. In case M.10249 *Derichebourg/Ecore*, for example, the Commission conducted a filtering exercise to identify prima facie problematic markets by looking only at those where the transaction parties had combined market shares of more than 50% or where a combined share of more than 40% was increased by an increment of at least 5%. In case M.890 *Blokker/Toys 'R' Us*, an increase in market share of only 4% was sufficient for the Commission to prohibit the concentration because 'the potential of the acquired business [was deemed] much greater than [was] reflected in its actual market share'.[619] Such a possible discrepancy between market share and competitive potential may be relevant in particular in digital markets, which have recently become the Commission's focus for a more vigilant antitrust enforcement under its new DMA[620] or its guidance on the application of the referral mechanism set out in

[617] Cases M.6132 *Cargill/KVB*, M.6126 *Thermo Fisher/Dionex Corporation* and M.6007 *Nokia Siemens Networks/Motorola Network Business*.

[618] It is also common for the Commission to use indices of pre- and post-merger market shares such as the Herfindahl-Hirschman Index in order to quantify how a transaction changes the level of market concentration.

[619] Case M.890 *Blokker/Toys 'R' Us*, para. 88.

[620] Regulation (EU) 2022/1925 of the European Parliament and of the Council of 14 Sep. 2022 on contestable and fair markets in the digital sector and amending Directives (EU) 2019/1937 and (EU) 2020/1828.

Article 22 of the Merger Regulation.[621] Here, so-called killer acquisitions may have to be assessed less in light of market share additions than in terms of how they may result in the elimination of an important independent innovator or the accumulation of competitively significant assets (such as raw materials, infrastructure, data or IP rights). Nonetheless, as stated above, the increment in market share resulting from the merger and the gap between the merged entity and its nearest rivals will often give the Commission a clear enough picture of the markets affected in order to enable it to move quickly to a Phase I decision on compatibility or to otherwise express serious doubts.[622]

[455] Typically, the Commission will use the following steps in its assessment of market shares to determine whether a horizontal merger will significantly impede effective competition:

- identify the aggregate share of the merged entity;
- consider whether the increment is sufficient to cause concern. The target undertaking is unlikely to be able to represent an effective competitive constraint if it has no significant market presence. Generally, this will be the case if its market share is under 5%, although caution must be applied to this rule of thumb when the acquirer commands a very high market share, as was emphasised by the Commission in case M.4842 *Danone/Numico*.[623] In that case, Numico had a market share of between 70% and 80% in the Netherlands, whereas Danone held less than 5%. Nonetheless, the Commission confirmed that '*under these market conditions, the removal of competition, however weak it may be, could be detrimental*';
- compare the merged entity's market share with that of its rivals: if it becomes the clear market leader, becomes more than double the size of its nearest rival, or faces competition only from firms with shares below 5%, the Commission will almost certainly move beyond a mere analysis of market shares and examine the competitive market conditions in more detail;[624] and
- where there are significant rivals remaining to compete with the merged entity (albeit not matching it in terms of market share) and where the merged entity has less than half the market share, the Commission will usually issue an unconditional clearance decision, and often does so without any explicit

[621] Commission Guidance on the application of the referral mechanism set out in Art. 22 of the Merger Regulation to certain categories of cases, C(2021) 1959 final.

[622] Case M.5086 *BAT/Skandinavisk Tobakskompagni*.

[623] Case M.4842 *Danone/Numico*.

[624] Case 85/76 *Hoffman La Roche*: '*An undertaking which has a very large market share and holds it for some time by means of the volume of production and the scale of the supply which it stands for – without those having much smaller market shares being able to meet rapidly the demand from those who would like to break away from the undertaking which has the largest market share – is by virtue of that share in a position of strength which makes it an unavoidable trading partner and which, already because of this secures for it, at the very least during relatively long periods, that freedom of action which is the special feature of a dominant position.*' [1979] ECR 461. *See also* cases M.5141 *KLM/Martinair*; M.5747 *Iberia/British Airways* and M. 6281 *Microsoft/Skype* where the Commission approved the acquisition resulting in a combined share of 70%–80% on the market for video calling services due to strong competition from rivals such as Facebook and Google which, despite their low market shares, had strong consumer brand with a robust monetisation model derived from online advertising.

consideration of whether the concentration might lead to a SIEC through its coordinated effects.[625]

[456] It is worth noting that very high market shares may be considered as tolerable in markets where the merged entity is subject to strong competitive restraints which limit its freedom to act or where such market shares derive from a limited amount of contracts which are regularly procured (so-called bidding markets where competition is *for* the market rather than *in* the market).[626] In case M.9820 *Danfoss/Eaton Hydraulics*, however, the Commission clarified that parties are unlikely to claim that market shares in bidding markets are not indicative of market power unless the relevant markets are 'winner-takes-all' markets, i.e., markets where a bidder either wins to supply the whole market or does not supply at all, where there are no incumbency advantages and where demand is sufficiently lumpy and where, therefore, market shares are bound to be volatile over time.[627]

[457] Similarly, high market shares in fast-moving and evolving markets may also not necessarily reflect market power as they may be volatile. This reality was recognised by the General Court in its judgment in *Cisco v. Commission*: 'the consumer communications sector is a recent and fast-growing sector which is characterised by short innovation cycles in which large market shares may turn out to be ephemeral. In such a dynamic context, high market shares are not necessarily indicative of market power and, therefore, of lasting damage to competition'.[628] Similar considerations underpinned the Commission's conditional Phase I clearance in case M.10431 *Ali Group/Welbilt*, where the Commission dispelled concerns about the transaction parties' high market shares in light of observed volatility and lumpy demand where the high shares were the result of sizeable but occasional orders. Another key consideration in that case was the expected growth in the market and the absence of barriers to entry which had the potential of attracting new competitors in the foreseeable future.

Closeness of Competition

[458] Another key factor in applying the SIEC test is the closeness of the competition between the parties to the concentration.[629] Where it emerges from the analysis of market shares that the merging parties may be significant competitors, the Commission will examine the closeness of the competition between them in more detail. This is regarded as the key to determining whether a SIEC will result from the merger as a consequence of the loss of that competition.

[459] In assessing the closeness of competition, the Commission relies first and foremost on its own Horizontal Merger Guidelines. While in the first instance appeal judgment of the Commission's decision in case M.7612 *Hutchison 3G UK/Telefónica UK*, the General Court had faulted the Commission for 'confusing

[625] *See* the 'Anticompetitive Effects' section below.

[626] Cases M.6203 *Western Digital/Viviti Technologies* and M.6214 *Seagate/HDD Business of Samsung Electronics*.

[627] *See also* case M.10575 *Bouygues/Equans*.

[628] Case T-79/12 *Cisco Systems and Messagenet v. Commission*, 11 Dec. 2013, para. 69.

[629] Horizontal Guidelines at paras 28–30.

three concepts, namely the concept of a 'significant impediment to effective competition', which is the legal criterion referred to in Article 2(3) of Regulation No 139/2004, the concept of 'elimination of [an] important competitive [constraint]', referred to in recital 25 of that regulation, and the concept of elimination of an 'important competitive force', used in the contested decision and based on the Horizontal Guidelines,[630] the EU's highest Court recently reversed that judgment, largely vindicating the Commission's approach. When referring the case back to the General Court, the Court of Justice did note, however, that companies can be considered close competitors even if their products are not particularly close substitutes as long as they are closer substitutes than the other market players' products.[631]

[460] In judging the closeness of competition between merging parties, the Commission has considered a wide range of factors including: business models (case M.4193 *L'Oreal/The Body Shop*);[632] brand position and strength (case M.3942 *Adidas/Reebok*);[633] pricing strategies (case M.7000 *Liberty Global/Ziggo*);[634] product range or portfolio (cases M.4257 *Smithfield/Oaktree/Sarah Lee*,[635] M.5253 *Sanofi-Aventis/Zentiva*,[636] M.6203 *Western Digital/Viviti Technologies*);[637] strength or focus in different geographic areas or localities (case M.4249 *Abertis/Autostrade*);[638] efficiency (case M.4057 *Körsnas/Assidomän Cartonboard*);[639] business structure (case M.4238 *E.ON/Prazská Plynárenská*);[640] market segment focus (case M.4615 *Merlin/Tussauds*);[641] and perhaps most importantly, customer overlaps (case M.4502 *Lite-On/PBDS*)[642] as they may be reflected in bidding data[643] and diversion ratios (these ratios measure the number of customers switching from one competitor to another – cases M.6497 *Hutchison 3G Austria/Orange Austria*, M.6992 *Hutchison 3G UK/Telefónica Ireland*, M.7018 *Telefónica Deutschland/E-Plus*, M.7612 *Hutchison 3G UK/Telefónica UK*, M.9706 *Novelis/Aleris*). Moreover, the closeness of competition between the parties may be less relevant where both face significant competitive constraints from elsewhere, as in case M.2522 *SCA/Cartoinvest*.[644] In that case, the Commission found that brand market shares in tissues of between 80% and 90%

[630] Case T-399/16 *CK Telecoms UK Investments v. Commission*, para. 173.
[631] Case C-376/20 *CK Telecoms UK Investments v. Commission*, para. 189.
[632] Case M.4193 *L'Oréal/The Body Shop*.
[633] Case M.3942 *Adidas/Reebok*.
[634] Case M.7000 *Liberty Global/Ziggo*.
[635] Case M.4257 *Smithfield/Oaktree/Sarah Lee*.
[636] Case M.5253 *Sanofi-Aventis/Zentiva*.
[637] Cases M.6203 *Western Digital/Viviti Technologies*.
[638] Case M.4249 *Abertis/Autostrade*.
[639] Case M.4057 *Körsnas/Assidomän Cartonboard*.
[640] Case M.4238 *E.ON/Prazská Plynárenská*.
[641] Case M.4615 *Merlin/Tussauds*.
[642] Case M.4502 *Lite-On/PBDS*.
[643] In case M.9969 *Veolia/Suez*, for example, the Commission assessed how often the transaction parties participated in the same tenders compared to other competitors and how often they lost a bid to the other party as opposed to other competitors.
[644] Case M.2522 *SCA/Cartoinvest*.

did not result in a SIEC because of the fierce pressure from own-label retailer brands which had commoditised the market.

[461] Also, where one of the merging parties is not yet present on the market but is expected to emerge as a significant effective competitor in the future, the Commission will take this factor into account and focus on the loss of potential competition. The potential competitor must be considered likely to enter the market within a reasonably short period of time or to have strong incentives to do so.[645] A good illustration of this type of analysis can be seen in the Commission's appraisal of concentrations in the field of both human and animal pharmaceuticals. In these cases, the Commission not only assesses the existing portfolios of the pharmaceutical companies but also takes into account the companies' respective pipeline of products and in particular the drugs which are in Phase III clinical trials.[646] In one case, *Novartis/GlaxoSmithKline Oncology Business*, the Commission went even further and took into account for its analysis of potential competition treatments which were being tested in Phase I and II clinical trials.[647]

Mergers with a Recent Entrant

[462] It is particularly unlikely that the market share of a recent entrant will be an adequate indicator of its true competitive potential. A merger with a recent entrant may therefore raise concerns even if the latter's market share at the time of the transaction is insignificant. In such a situation, the Commission often has to rely on the evidence relating to the firm's likely potential.[648]

[463] An example of such an assessment can be seen in case M.1672 *Volvo/Scania* where Volvo was the market leader in the Irish market for city buses. Although other manufacturers encountered barriers to entry, Scania had managed through one contract to enter the market and gain a market share of 32% in one year (at the expense of Volvo). The Commission prohibited the transaction, *inter alia*, based on the fact that the merger would have removed this newly introduced competitive constraint from the market.

Anticompetitive Increase in Buyer Power

[464] Even in transactions which do not give rise to either coordinated or non-coordinated horizontal effects, anticompetitive effects can arise where the merging parties' increase in buyer power allows them to potentially restrict competition and innovation from third parties. In the *Liberty Global/Ziggo* transaction, the Commission considered that Liberty Global could use its increased buyer power to hamper or eliminate over-the-top TV services (OTT) innovation (Netflix is an example of an OTT provider). In this case, although Liberty Global and Ziggo's cable activities did not overlap geographically, both companies acquired the same audio-visual content and TV channels from TV broadcasters for inclusion in their respective

[645] Horizontal Guidelines at para. 58, and cases M.5675 *Sygenta/Monsanto's Sunflower Seed Business*; M.5421 *Panasonic/Sanyo* and M.5188 *Mars/Wrigley*.

[646] *See* cases M.7277 *Eli Lilly/Novartis Animal Health* and M.7645 *Mylan/Perrigo*.

[647] Case M.7275 *Novartis/GlaxoSmithKline Oncology Business*.

[648] Horizontal Guidelines at para. 37.

retail pay-TV offerings. The Commission found that if the merger were to go ahead, Liberty Global would indeed enjoy an increase in buyer power by which it could weaken the Dutch market structure by insisting upon more and more onerous agreements with TV broadcasters, restricting their ability to offer their content online via an OTT service. In order to alleviate these concerns, Liberty Global committed to no longer enforce any existing carriage agreements for TV channels and associated content that restrict the ability of TV broadcasters to offer their content online.[649]

Other Relevant Factors

[465] While the above-mentioned factors constitute the starting point of any competitive assessment, the Commission tends to consider additional factors, especially in horizontal mergers that involve significant overlaps and relatively high market shares. Two of these additional factors will be briefly discussed here.

[466] The first *one* relates to the ability and incentive of the merged entity's rivals to react to and defeat a price increase by expanding their output. To this end, the Commission has started employing a so-called pivotality theory of harm which analyses the extent to which total production capacity in the hands of the merged entity's competitors would post-transaction be sufficient to cover the entire market demand. If a certain share of demand could not be met by the merged entity's rivals, the merged entity would be considered 'pivotal' and as such enjoying market power. After all, the merged entity would be 'de facto the only supplier for the remaining part of demand that cannot be served by rivals'.[650] Indeed, when market conditions are such that the competitors of the merging parties are unlikely to increase their supply if prices increase, the merged entity *may* have an incentive to reduce output, thereby raising market prices.[651] Conversely, when market conditions are such that rival firms have enough capacity and find it profitable to expand output sufficiently, the Commission is unlikely to find that the merger will create or strengthen a dominant position or otherwise significantly impede effective competition.[652] Output expansions are generally deemed unlikely when competitors face binding capacity constraints or if existing excess capacity is significantly more costly to operate than capacity currently in use.[653]

[467] These general principles have been applied – either explicitly as a pivotality theory or in the form of the Bertrand-Edgeworth model – to a number of Phase II cases such as, e.g., the *Outokumpu/Inoxum* review.[654]

[468] In that case, the Commission assessed if the merged entity's rivals would have the ability and incentive to expand output to such an extent that a price increase would be unprofitable. With the merged entity's rivals having a spare capacity exceeding 20%–30% of the market, the Commission ultimately found that

[649] Case M.7000 *Liberty Global/Ziggo*.
[650] Case M.9706 *Novelis/Aleris*, para. 529.
[651] Horizontal Guidelines at para. 32.
[652] Horizontal Guidelines at para. 33.
[653] Horizontal Guidelines at para. 34.
[654] Cases M.6471 *Outokumpu/Inoxum*; M.6905 *Ineos/Solvay JV* and M.9706 *Novelis/Aleris*.

these rivals were likely to have the *ability* to expand output sufficiently to make a post-merger price increase unprofitable. However, the Commission ultimately concluded that these rivals would not have the *incentive* to expand their output. This conclusion was essentially based on the premise that the pre-merger price competition was not intense and was unlikely to intensify post-merger. Pivotality concerns were central also to the Commission's decision to prohibit case M.9343 *Hyundai Heavy Industries Holdings/Daewoo Shipbuilding*.

[469] The second *factor* that the Commission will pay close attention to – especially in complex horizontal mergers involving homogenous products – relates to margins, which according to the Commission *may* be indicative of market power. As such, the Commission's chief economist considers margin analysis '*an essential ingredient*' to the Commission's merger assessment.[655] In case M.9820 *Danfoss/Eaton Hydraulics,* for example, the Commission noted that the merging parties' '*[ability] to generate relatively high margins [...] indicate[d] limited constraints from other competitors*'.[656]

9.4.3 Conglomerate Mergers

[470] Conglomerate mergers involve transactions where firms operate on different but related product markets and whose relationship is neither horizontal nor vertical.[657] In practice, conglomerate mergers are less likely than horizontal mergers to give rise to competition concerns because, except where they lead to the elimination of a potential competitor, they do not normally entail a loss of direct competition between the merging firms in the same relevant market. The Commission regards them as being able to lead to a SIEC where they result in 'portfolio power', regardless of the lack of any increase in market share in any relevant market.[658] Portfolio effects arise when the combination of complementary activities of two companies leads to a company that is 'more than the sum of its parts'. In other words, the merged company is in a far superior competitive position than its size may actually reflect.

[471] The Non-Horizontal Merger Guidelines explain the circumstances in which the Commission, based on its experience under the EU merger regime and the guidance of the ECJ and General Court in the *Tetra Laval*[659] and *General Electric*[660] cases, considers that conglomerate mergers may pose risks to competition.[661] The Non-Horizontal Merger Guidelines identify mergers between companies active in

[655] https://www.reuters.com/article/us-eu-m-a-antitrust/eu-antitrust-official-sees-competition-threat-if-mergers-lead-to-high-margins-idUSKBN1E613Z.

[656] Case M.9820 *Danfoss/Eaton Hydraulics*, para. 869.

[657] These are, for example, mergers between suppliers of complementary products.

[658] Form CO requests market data for any market where any party holds a market share of 25% or more. In practice, the Commission focuses only on markets directly related to markets affected by the concentration.

[659] Cases T-5/02 *Tetra Leval v. Commission* [2002] ECR II-4381 and C-12/03 P, *Commission v. Tetra Laval BV* [2005] ECR I-987.

[660] Case T-210/01 *General Electric Company v. Commission* [2005] ECR II-5575.

[661] Non-Horizontal Merger Guidelines at paras 91–121.

closely related markets as the focus of the Commission's attention to ensure that there is no likelihood of foreclosure through extending market power held in one market to other markets. This may be achieved by means of tying, bundling or other exclusionary practices (usually referred to generally as 'leveraging'). Such practices will not be feasible in the case of a conglomerate merger where the merging entities operate in markets which have little or no relationship with one another, hence the Commission's focus on 'closely related markets'. In its assessment of conglomerate mergers, the Commission examines three things: (i) whether the merged firm will be dominant and be able to foreclose its competitors; (ii) whether the merged firm will have the incentive to foreclose the market; and (iii) if it pursued a strategy of foreclosure whether the merged entity would have a market position resulting in a SIEC.

[472] There are three main types of conglomerate effects: technical and contractual tying; pure bundling; and mixed bundling.[662] In its *General Electric*[663] judgment the General Court distinguished between these three practices: (i) pure bundling occurring when sales are tied by means of a purely commercial obligation to purchase two or more products as a bundle; (ii) technical bundling where sales are tied by means of the technical integration of the products (this includes cases where the merging parties can limit the interoperability between their products and the products of their competitors);[664] and (iii) mixed bundling where a number of products are sold as a package on more favourable terms than if the products are purchased separately. Such practices are likely to arise only where real opportunities exist to implement them, for example, where two related products tend to be bought by the same customer or are designed so that they only function properly in combination.

662 Bundling takes at least two forms: first, there is the *pure* (or tying) bundling, which occurs when the products in question are not offered on a stand-alone basis. Bundling may also take the form of technical bundling, when products are designed and engineered in a way that means they cannot physically be separated, or will not function properly if used with competitors' products. Second, there is *mixed* bundling, where products remain available on a stand-alone basis, but are offered as a package on discounted terms, i.e., it costs less to buy the package than the two items separately. This is clearly possible when the merger involves complementary products.

663 Case T-210/01 *General Electric Company v. Commission* [2005] ECR II-5575.

664 Cases M.5529 *Oracle/Sun Microsystems*; M.5669 *Cisco Tandberg* and M.5984 *Intel/McAfee* where the Commission identified serious concerns regarding the possible bundling of central processing units (CPUs) and chipsets (where Intel holds a dominant position) on the one hand with McAfee's security solutions, on the other hand. In particular, the Commission was concerned that, as a result of the proposed transaction as initially notified, other companies' security solutions might have suffered from a lack of interoperability with Intel CPUs and chipsets or from a technical tying between the latter and McAfee's security solutions. The Commission was also concerned about possible effects on Intel's competitors if McAfee solutions were no longer compatible with non-Intel CPUs and chipsets. In order to address the Commission's concerns, Intel committed, among other things, to ensure that vendors of rival security solutions will have access to all necessary information to use functionalities of Intel's CPUs and chipsets in the same way as those functionalities used by McAfee. Intel also committed not to actively impede competitors' security solutions from running on Intel CPUs or chipsets. Finally, Intel also committed to avoid hampering the operation of McAfee's security solutions when running on personal computers containing CPUs or chipsets sold by Intel's competitors.

[473] Case M.3687 *Johnson & Johnson/Guidant* concerned the acquisition by Johnson & Johnson of Guidant, a supplier of surgical devices for coronary and endovascular applications. In its review, the Commission assessed the potential foreclosure effects resulting from bundled sales of complementary cardiology devices. The Commission analysed whether post-transaction, Johnson & Johnson would: (i) have the ability to bundle its products; (ii) have the incentive to do so; and (iii) whether such strategies could effectively lead to a foreclosure of competition. The Commission concluded that such effects were unlikely given that package sales in the cardiology devices sector were not a common feature of the industry, tendering procedures for single items were widespread due to the desire of hospitals to have a dual sourcing policy, and most importantly, competitors could also engage into a bundled sales strategy. The Commission took a different view when it looked into the conglomerate effects that case M.9660 *Google/Fitbit* gave rise to. After finding that the merged entity would be able to degrade interoperability between rivals' wrist-worn wearable devices and the Android OS they need to interact with, the Commission concluded that wearable original equipment manufacturers (OEMs) – in particular those that are not also integrated smartphone OEMs – would have very limited counterstrategies. Since about 50% of the wrist-worn wearables market were considered to depend on the Android OS, a possible foreclosure strategy was deemed to have a significant detrimental effect on competition. The existence of effective counterstrategies had already been critical in the M.5114 *Pernod Ricard/V&S* case where Pernod Ricard acquired the Swedish state-owned beverage business V&S.[665] Horizontal overlaps led to a commitment to divest several spirit brands but the Commission dismissed conglomerate concerns raised by complainants, referring to the strength of the spirits portfolios held by rivals such as Diageo, to the fact that the merged firm had few genuine 'must-stock' brands, and to market retailers' ability to de-list products if leveraging was attempted. These factors showed that no SIEC could result even if the merged entity did try to engage in bundling.[666] In case M.5932 *NewsCorp/BskyB*, the Commission investigated whether NewsCorp would be able to bundle pay-TV subscriptions with print, online and tablet application subscriptions for its various UK newspapers. BSkyB was the leading provider of pay-TV in the UK. The Commission ultimately considered that the transaction would not result in a SIEC. With respect to bundling with print subscriptions, the market investigation revealed that

665 Case M.5114 *Pernod Ricard/V&S*.

666 In case M.938 *Guinness/Grand Metropolitan*, the Commission also discussed the portfolio power theory at length. The merger brought together two portfolios of brands which appeared complementary. In Europe, Guinness was strong in gin but lacked a leading vodka brand whereas GrandMet was strong in vodka but lacked a leading gin brand. Moreover, both parties were strong in whisky but in different countries. The European Commission assessed the effect of including strong brands (i.e., 'must-stock' brands) belonging to separate markets in a range of drinks and found that their inclusion could give each brand greater strength on the market than if it was sold individually. It concluded that this would lead to portfolio power which could strengthen the competitive position of the portfolio's owner on several markets, regardless of the lack of increase in market share in the individual spirit categories. In order to alleviate that concern, the merging parties committed to divest two Scotch whisky brands on a Europe-wide basis and to end their distribution agreement for one rum brand in Greece.

price is only one, and not the main factor determining readers' choice of and loyalty to a newspaper. Furthermore, no such bundling had been attempted before. Finally, tabloid papers such as The Sun were found to not offer any subscriptions to their print editions. Moreover, the low subscription rate to newspapers of 6% of overall UK circulation and of 25%–33% for quality titles was found to indicate that the subscription model did not appeal to a majority of readers. With respect to bundling with online news, the vast majority of newspapers' online editions – apart from most News Corp titles – as well as other news sources were at the time free of charge, and there was no evidence that this would dramatically change in the foreseeable future. For these reasons, the Commission excluded that competition concerns in the newspaper publishing sector would arise from the transaction.

[474] Given that mergers which do not involve increments of market shares are less likely than horizontal mergers to give rise to competition concerns, the factual burden of proof on the Commission to prove that such a transaction will lead to a SIEC is therefore high. This is illustrated by the *General Electric* case,[667] where the General Court found that the Commission had not established that GE would engage in leveraging practices promoting the sale of Honeywell avionics products at the expense of those of Honeywell's competitors with sufficient evidence and certainty. The General Court also emphasised the need for the Commission to fully examine the disincentives of such behaviour. One disincentive is the possible illegality of such practices under Article 102 of the TFEU and the potential liability to sanctions and damages claims, which the ECJ held the Commission was bound to take into account in its *Tetra Laval* decision[668] [M.9564 LSEG/Refinitiv at 2355].

[475] For some years now, the Commission has been quite aggressive in its pursuit of conglomerate cases. In 2016, the Commission examined four deals in close succession for potential conglomerate effects: *Dentsply/Sirona* (dental equipment and consumables),[669] *Worldline/Equens/Paysquare* (payment software and relevant machines),[670] *Microsoft/LinkedIn* (computer operating systems and social networking services/app)[671] and *Broadcom/Brocade* (computer processors and interface cards).[672]

[476] The Commission requested remedies from the parties in each one of these deals, whereas the US authorities cleared the *Worldline* and *Microsoft* cases unconditionally. In *Microsoft/LinkedIn*, the Commission assessed conglomerate effects in five distinct technology markets. In four out of these five markets (Customer Relationship Management software solutions, online recruitment services, productivity software and enterprise communications services), the evidence did not show anticompetitive foreclosure. In one market, professional social networking services, the Commission was not able to exclude serious doubts of conglomerate effects and

[667] Case T-210/01 *General Electric Company v. Commission* [2005] ECR II-5575.

[668] Case T-5/02 *Tetra Leval v. Commission* [2002] ECR II-4381.

[669] Case M.7822 *Dentsply/Sirona*.

[670] Case M.7873 *Worldline/Equens/Paysquare*.

[671] Case M.8124 *Microsoft/LinkedIn*.

[672] Case M.8314 *Broadcom/Brocade*.

obtained a remedy (essentially providing for certain interoperability guarantees and access to certain Microsoft data).

[477] This trend continued with the review of *Qualcomm/NXP* (baseband chips and near-field communication and secure elements chips),[673] *Essilor/Luxottica* (eyewear and ophthalmic lenses),[674] *Bayer/Monsanto* (pesticides and seeds),[675] and *Dow/DuPont* (where the Commission required major remedies including the divestiture of DuPont's global R&D activity to address the concern that the transaction would significantly reduce 'innovation competition' for pesticides)[676] all of which were subject to a Phase II in-depth investigation in the EU (varying from six to nine months). By contrast, the *Qualcomm/NXP* deal was cleared in one month by the US authorities, and although the review of the *Essilor/Luxottica* transaction took longer, it primarily focused on raising rivals' costs and not bundling concerns. In *UTC/Rockwell Collins*, the Commission extensively investigated a significant number of vertical and conglomerate links, including in reaction to complaints received in the course of the merger investigation.[677] These concerns mainly related to the transmission of data from the aircraft and the possibility of the merged entity to bundle or tie different systems of the aircraft, in particular engines and avionics. Overall, the Commission concluded that UTC did not hold a sufficient degree of market power in aircraft engines to enable the merged entity to engage in practices leveraging its position in engines to foreclose rivals in avionics. The Commission also noted that commercial bundling was not a regular feature of the industry and that customers, mainly the airframers, control the procurement process in order to maintain a sufficient level of competition (including by breaking up bundled offers). In case M.10792 *Philip Morris International/Swedish Match*, the Commission dispelled conglomerate concerns by highlighting two key observations: first, the merging parties' competitors were found to offer must-have brands. Customers' loyalty to these brands was considered sufficiently strong to defeat any bundling/tying strategy that the merged entity could possibly engage in post-merger. Second, since customers were conducting separate contract negotiations for different product categories, the Commission saw limited scope for the merged entity to leverage its market position from one category to another.

9.5 Vertical Mergers

[478] As is the case with conglomerate mergers, concentrations between companies at different stages of the supply chain (i.e., suppliers and their distributors or customers) are also capable of leading to a SIEC despite the lack of any increase in market share in any relevant market. Rather, in vertical mergers, the concerns for competition result from potential foreclosure effects where rivals may lose access to

[673] Case M.8306 *Qualcomm/NXP.*
[674] Case M.8394 *Essilor/Luxottica.*
[675] Case M.8084 *Bayer/Monsanto.*
[676] Case M.7932 *Dow/DuPont.*
[677] Case M.8658 *UTC/Rockwell Collins.*

suppliers or customers.[678] As the Non-Horizontal Merger Guidelines set out, the risks to effective competition from a vertical merger stem from the potential for the merged firm to foreclose the market. This means the potential to deny essential products or services to its competitors (input foreclosure) or access to customers (customer foreclosure). Such ability will depend on: (i) the market power of the merged firm; (ii) the importance of the input it supplies in the upstream or downstream market (judged both by how essential it is and what proportion it accounts for of the cost of the product supplied in that market); and (iii) the possibility of timely and effective counter-measures from competitors and customers.[679]

[479] With respect to the prerequisite that the merged firm should enjoy market power, the Non-Horizontal Merger Guidelines provide that competition concerns are unlikely to arise where the merging companies' shares in the upstream or downstream markets are below 30% and where the post-merger Herfindahl-Hirschman Index is below 2000.[680]

[480] The Commission has identified concerns about such foreclosure effects in its analysis of several concentrations in the telecommunications and media industries, particularly where one or a few firms may be able to control access to markets and especially where technology is evolving rapidly. In case M.1845 *Time Warner/AOL*, the Commission was concerned that a merger between one of the largest media companies and a significant internet access provider would have dominated the emerging market of online music delivery. This was because the merged entity would have been able to dictate conditions for distribution of audio files on the internet. The concentration was cleared on condition the parties severed links between AOL and Bertelsmann, another media company.

[481] In *Google/DoubleClick*, the Commission commenced a Phase II investigation in order to scrutinise complaints that Google would use DoubleClick to discriminate in favour of Google's advertising intermediary, AdSense.[681] The concentration did not involve any horizontal issues because DoubleClick did not supply advertising space and Google did not offer ad-serving technology to third parties. The Commission dismissed third parties' complaints and issued a clearance decision without requesting remedies. It found that neither Google nor DoubleClick could exercise significant market power in their respective markets. It also found that customers did not face significant costs or obstacles to switching to the alternatives to Google and DoubleClick, as evidence of actual switching was demonstrated. There was also no evidence to support the suggestion that network effects in online advertising would lead customers to gravitate towards the merged firm, particularly as 'multi-homing' (i.e., participating in more than one online

[678] Form CO requires details to be supplied where any member of the merging groups has at least a 25% market share in a market upstream or downstream of another market in which any member of the other merging group is present.

[679] For a detailed analysis following the Non-Horizontal Merger Guidelines *see* case M.4942 *Nokia/ NAVTEQ*.

[680] Non-Horizontal Merger Guidelines at para. 25. *See also* case M.6765 *Precison Castparts/Titanium Metals*.

[681] Case M.4731 *Google/DoubleClick*.

advertising network) was a feature of the market and ad-serving technology fostered interoperability between ad-networks. Having concluded that the merged firm would not have the ability to foreclose competitors or partake in bundling practices, the Commission nevertheless went on to examine whether it would have the incentive to do so. It found that this was not the case for a number of reasons including the fact that contractual obligations to customers prevented discrimination by Google. In any case, such behaviour would be quickly detected by customers who would switch to other suppliers and exclude Google's subsidiary, AdSense, from their list of online advertising intermediaries, thereby damaging its reputation and business volumes.[682]

[482] In case *Google/Motorola Mobility*, the Commission considered whether Google would be likely to prevent Motorola's competitors from using Google's Android operating system. The Commission's investigation showed that Android helps to drive the spread of Google's other services. Consequently, given that Google's core business model is to push its online and mobile services and software to the widest possible audience, the Commission considered that Google would be unlikely to restrict the use of Android solely to Motorola, a minor player in the EEA as compared to operators such as Samsung and HTC. The Commission also examined whether Google would be in a position to use Motorola's standard essential patents to obtain preferential treatment for its services, including search and advertising. The Commission found that Google already had many ways in which to incentivise customers to take up its services and that the acquisition of Motorola would not materially add anything in this regard.[683]

[483] Case M.9660 *Google/Fitbit* is another example where the Commission closely assessed the vertical relationship between the parties (i.e., Google's supply of Android app stores (Google Play) and Fitbit's activities in the downstream market for wrist-worn wearables). Here, the Commission found the merged entity to have the ability and incentive to implement a bundling strategy as a means to foreclose rival smartphone and/or wearable OEMs. However, the projected effects of such a strategy on competition were found to be insufficient to warrant enforcement action because they could not significantly impede effective competition in the market. Key to this finding that a foreclosure strategy could not significantly impede effective competition in the market was the observation that rivals could effectively respond to a potential move by the merged entity to restrict distribution of wearable companion apps through the Google Play store – for example, by preinstalling wearable companion apps on mobile devices, or by offering them through a third party's or the OEM's own app store.

[484] In case M.9564 *LSEG/Refinitiv* that the Commission conditionally cleared after an in-depth Phase II investigation, foreclosure concerns centred on concerns about rivals' access to critical data. To assess the merged entity's incentives to foreclose, the Commission relied on a quantitative vertical arithmetic analysis that

682 *See* cases M.4747 *IBM/Telelogic, Thomson/Reuters;* M.4942 *Nokia/NAVTEQ;* M.4874 *Itema/BarcoVision*; M.4854 *TomTom/Tele Atlas* and M. 7353 *Airbus/Safran/JV.*

683 Case M.6381 *Google/Motorola Mobility.*

showed that downstream gains would more than outweigh any financial losses that an upstream foreclosure could result in. The Commission also noted that LSEG had previously engaged in foreclosure strategies which was considered an indication of what could be expected post-merger.

[485] The foreclosure effect of a vertical merger may also entrench a dominant position, particularly where the parties are already vertically integrated. This would thereby raise barriers to entry to potential competitors needing to enter more than one market in order to have a credible presence. In a number of consumer markets, the Commission has placed great emphasis on the importance of distribution systems and outlets where strong incumbents may have economies of scale and scope, as well as the potential to develop new channels when the end-user is constrained by cost or regulatory factors. In case M.4180 *Gaz de France/Suez*, the Commission was concerned that the merged entity's dominant position in the market for the wholesale supply of gas in France and Belgium would prevent (actual and potential) competitors from developing their business in the market for the production of electricity in Belgium. Indeed, given that the vast majority of electricity generation plants are gas-fired, the Commission determined that the merged entity would have had the ability to raise the production costs of its competitors in the relevant electricity markets. This would be achieved by increasing the price of gas, a market where the merged entity was already dominant. Given the vertical integration of Gaz de France and Suez which would supply its electricity plants with its own gas, the merged entity would have therefore been able to gain an uncompetitive advantage over its competitors in the electricity markets. To solve those concerns, the parties offered remedies in both the electricity and gas markets.[684]

[486] In case M.10078 *Cargotec/Konecranes*, the Commission's foreclosure concerns were compounded by an expectation that the transaction would eliminate an important independent customer and that this loss was bound to undermine rivals' scale, thereby giving the merged entity further room to increase margins or sales/ market share.

9.5.1 Concentrations and the Harm to Innovation Theory

[487] The Merger Regulation establishes a legal framework in which the Commission must investigate not only price or output effects but also effects on innovation. Indeed, the SIEC test covers all aspects of a loss of competition, including harm to consumers resulting from hampering future innovation and innovation competition. This concern is recognised both in the Commission's Horizontal Merger Guidelines and Non-Horizontal Merger Guidelines.

[488] The Commission's Horizontal Merger Guidelines state that one of the effects to be analysed in merger control is '*the effect on innovation*', putting the competitive harm caused by a reduction of innovation on an equal footing with

[684] Case M.4180 *Gaz de France/Suez*. For further examples of the Commission's practice with respect to vertical concentrations, please also *see* cases M.6410 *UTC/Goodrich* and M.6314 *Telefónica UK/Vodafone UK/Everything Everywhere/JV*.

price increases, or a reduction of output, choice or quality of goods and services.[685] According to the guidelines, the aim of the Commission's merger control is to prevent mergers that would be likely to deprive customers of these benefits, including innovation. Consequently, the loss of innovation can be at the heart of the anticompetitive effects of a concentration. The Horizontal Merger Guidelines specify that if a merger combines two important innovators, or eliminates a firm with promising pipeline products, the transaction can eliminate an important competitive force and thus lead to a significant impediment of effective competition against which the Commission should intervene.[686] The innovation potential of the merging firms is taken into account regardless of the current market position of the parties to the concentration.[687] This allows the Commission to scrutinise transactions that involve firms that are not actually present in a given market but are potential competitors, and firms that are developing products for a new intended use that are likely to compete in new product markets.

[489] For a concentration with a potential competitor to raise serious competition concerns, it is in principle necessary to show, first, that the potential competitor currently acts as a significant competitive constraint, or that there is a significant likelihood that, absent the transaction, it would grow into an effective competitive force in the foreseeable future. This is more likely in particular when the market is already concentrated, as in a market with many actual competitors a potential entrant is, in principle, less likely to be a significant competitive constraint.[688] Second, it needs to be established that there are not enough actual or potential competitors to maintain the necessary competitive pressure after the merger. In particular, barriers to entry must be high enough to exclude the existence of several other potential competitors, but the merging firm potentially entering the market must be well positioned to overcome these barriers, for instance, as it is present in an adjacent or vertically related market or already has specific entry plans.

[490] The Commission's Non-Horizontal Merger Guidelines provide a similar framework for assessing innovation effects in the context of vertical or conglomerate mergers. The guidelines acknowledge that one of the effects to be analysed in merger control is the effect on innovation.[689] They also state that concentrations involving innovative companies that are likely to expand significantly in the near future will be extensively investigated even when the post-merger market share is below 30%.[690] Non-horizontal concentrations may involve foreclosure scenarios that hinder innovation by other market players, for instance, when a competitor would likely lose access to the merged entity's product that is needed for it to innovate and remain in the market.

[491] Up until not long ago, the Commission mainly considered a concentration's effects on innovation in cases involving the pharmaceutical sector. Nowadays,

685 Paragraph 8 of the Horizontal Merger Guidelines.
686 Paragraph 38 of the Horizontal Merger Guidelines.
687 Paragraphs 20b and 38 of the Horizontal Merger Guidelines.
688 Paragraph 37 of the Horizontal Merger Guidelines.
689 Paragraph 10 of the Non-Horizontal Merger Guidelines.
690 Paragraph 26 of the Non-Horizontal Merger Guidelines.

however, the Commission's focus on innovation is much broader and an important factor in its enforcement policy.[691] This has led to the emergence of new theories of harm aimed at capturing negative effects of concentrations on overall innovation, outside individual product markets. Indeed, while in its earlier decisions relating to innovation, the Commission had analysed situations where one or both of the merging parties were developing products that overlapped with the other's current or pipeline products,[692] the Commission now also analyses the merging parties' research plans, taking into consideration (i) products that are in the very early stages of development,[693] (ii) overlapping lines of research,[694] as well as (iii) the parties' overall capability to innovate in certain innovation spaces.[695]

[492] When the Commission prohibited Illumina's (already implemented) acquisition of GRAIL (case M.10188), it noted that the transaction parties were '*engaged in an innovation race to develop and commercialise early cancer detection tests*' and that while there was '*still uncertainty about the exact results of this innovation race and the future shape of the market [. . .] protecting the current innovation competition [was] crucial to ensure that early cancer detection tests with different features and price points will come to the market*'. It is worth noting that the Commission took an equally prospective view on the future incentives of the merged entity to engage in an anticompetitive foreclosure strategy: '*While Illumina's sales of [next generation sequencing ("NGS")] technology to GRAIL's rivals represent a small proportion of its sales and profits, NGS-based early cancer detection testing is expected to expand rapidly and to become highly lucrative. Based on predictions, by 2035 this market would reach more than EUR 40 billion per annum, on a global basis. Given this enormous market potential and the ongoing close innovation competition in the development of early cancer detection test, the Commission considered that Illumina would have an incentive to foreclose GRAIL's rivals already today, despite benefitting from this action only at a later stage.*'

[493] The Commission's decision in case M.10188 *Illumina/GRAIL* follows a string of other high-profile cases over the last few years in which the innovation theory of harm took centre stage – despite repeated criticism about its unclear boundaries and criteria. In the *General Electric/Alstom* case, for example, which brought together two of the four 'full technology' firms able to produce large and very large industrial gas turbines worldwide, the Commission was concerned that the merged entity would discontinue some of Alstom's existing products and a pipeline product. The Commission was also concerned that the transaction would adversely affect innovation more generally in the gas turbines market as the removal of

[691] *See* in particular the speech from Commissioner Vestager 'Competition, the mother of invention' of 18 Apr. 2016 at https://ec.europa.eu/commission/commissioners/2014-2019/vestager/announcements/competition-mother-invention_en ('*One of the simplest defences against innovation is to buy up rivals that create innovative products. That's why, when we look at high-tech mergers, we don't just look at whether they might raise prices. We also assess whether they could be bad for innovation*').

[692] *See* cases M.8401 *J&J/Actelion*; M.8060 *Abbott Laboratories/St Jude Medical* and M.7975 *Mylan/Meda*.

[693] *See* cases M.7275 *Novartis/GlaxoSmithKline's Oncology Business*; M.7278 *General Electric Alstom* and M.7932 *Dow/DuPont*.

[694] *See* cases M.7932 *Dow/DuPont*; M.7963 *ChemChina/Syngenta* and M.8084 *Bayer/Monsanto*.

[695] *See* cases M.7278 *General Electric Alstom*; M.7932 *Dow/DuPont* and M.8084 *Bayer/Monsanto*.

Alstom, considered as the best in class in terms of technology and innovation, would reduce the competitive pressure on the two remaining competitors to invest significantly in innovation. The Commission ultimately cleared the transaction subject to a comprehensive remedies package consisting of the divestment of existing gas turbine technology, Alstom's pipeline technology, servicing agreements, engineers as well as two test facilities for Alstom's turbines. This package was designed to strengthen the purchaser's (Ansaldo Energia) ability and incentive to further improve the divested Alstom technology, thereby ensuring that innovation would continue in this sector.

[494] In the *Dow/DuPont* transaction, the Commission articulated even more clearly its theory based on harm to overall innovation. While the Commission's investigation identified problematic overlaps between the parties' existing products and the parties' respective development pipelines that they were either in the process of launching or intending to launch on the market with a high probability, the Commission also had strong concerns regarding the possible effects of the merger on overall innovation at the industry level. In this respect, the Commission determined that innovation is a key element of competition in the crop protection business, that competitive rivalry is an important driver of innovation and that the parties were two of only five companies worldwide which had sufficient R&D capabilities to discover, develop and launch new active ingredients in Europe. In light of these findings, the Commission was concerned that the concentration would reduce the parties' innovation incentives resulting in reduced innovation competition in several innovation spaces as well as at the industry level overall. In order to obtain clearance, the parties offered to divest substantially all of DuPont's global crop protection R&D organisation which included a large number of pipeline products.

[495] In its conditional clearance of Bayer's acquisition of Monsanto (case M.8084), the Commission further refined its approach to assessing potential harm to innovation competition, clarifying that its particular focus lies on factors such as the number of competitors, the existence of high barriers to entry, the closeness of competition in the innovation space and its importance for driving innovation in the industry, the likelihood of discontinuation, delay and reorientation of R&D efforts. In light of such an assessment, the Commission cleared the acquisition of Monsanto by Bayer only subject to a large remedies package designed to address, among other things, the Commission's specific concerns related to harm to overall innovation. The remedies include Bayer's global R&D organisation for seeds and traits as well as Bayer's research activities to develop a challenger product to Monsanto's glyphosate. They also cover certain Monsanto assets, which in future would have competed with a Bayer seed treatment against nematode worms.

9.5.2 Concentrations and Big Data

[496] As digital and technology markets evolve quickly, the collection of large volumes of data (often referred to as 'Big Data') has become an increasingly important topic in antitrust enforcement. The importance of data to the competitive process (be it in terms of interoperability and access to data or the continued consolidation of data in the hands of a few companies) is one of the Commission's top policy priorities today and a key focus area of its merger control mandate.[696]

[497] Commissioner Vestager has addressed Big Data in the context of concentrations on a number of occasions. Among others, Commissioner Vestager stated that '*companies need to make sure they don't use data in a way that stops others competing*' and that '*data could be an important factor in how a merger affects competition*'.[697] Accordingly, transactions involving the aggregation and integration of large datasets have been attracting close scrutiny.

[498] By way of illustration, in the context of Microsoft's acquisition of LinkedIn (case M.8124 *Microsoft/LinkedIn*), Commissioner Vestager warned that the Commission would assess whether '*the data purchased in the deal has a very long durability and might constitute a barrier for others, or if they can be replicated so that others stand a chance to enter the market*'.[698]

[499] One of the questions the Commission thus looked at was if LinkedIn's data was essential to compete in downstream markets in which Microsoft was active. If that had been the case, Microsoft would have been able to foreclose its competitors in these downstream markets by denying them access to LinkedIn's data. In this transaction, the downstream market under review was the one of customer relationship management solutions, which were being enhanced with features based on artificial intelligence and machine learning and thus needed to be fuelled with significant volumes of data. The Commission closely reviewed LinkedIn's data and, ultimately, concluded that this data was not an important input for customer relationship management solutions and that other datasets could be used by customer relationship management suppliers. Against these considerations, the Commission ultimately dismissed potential input foreclosure concerns.

[500] In the context of Apple's acquisition of Shazam (case M.8788 *Apple/Shazam*), Commissioner Vestager noted that '*Data is key in the digital economy*' and that the Commission '*must therefore carefully review transactions which lead to the acquisition of important sets of data, including potentially commercially sensitive ones, to ensure they do not restrict competition*'. This is what the Commission did and after thoroughly analysing Shazam's user and music data, the Commission '*found that their acquisition by Apple would not reduce competition in the digital music streaming market*'.

---

[696] On 22 Nov. 2018, Commissioner Vestager set out how she intends to approach the digitisation of the economy as well as her enforcement priorities. Of particular relevance, she stated the following: '*Data can be a source of business opportunities and new ideas. However, if only a few companies control essential data, other competitors may find it impossible to access the market. And when there is no competition, consumers get a worse deal*' (https://ec.europa.eu/commission/commissioners/2014-2019/vestager/announcements/competition-and-fairness-digital-society_en).

[697] *See* https://ec.europa.eu/commission/commissioners/2014-2019/vestager/announcements/big-data-and-competition_en.

[698] *See* https://biglawbusiness.com/eus-vestager-exploring-need-to-probe-deals-with-valuable-data/.

[501] Case M.9564 *LSEG/Refinitiv* showed that the importance of an input for downstream products is not necessarily a function of said product's 'cost factor relative to the price of the downstream product'.[699] Indeed, while the trading data in question represented only a small cost factor, the Commission's investigation revealed that this data was nonetheless suitable to carry a foreclosure strategy because of its omnipresence and systemic criticality for customers' downstream operations.

[502] Concerns about an increase in market power as a result of rivals' foreclosure from critical data lay also at the centre of the Commission's Phase II clearances in cases M.9660 *Google/Fitbit* and M.10262 *Meta/Kustomer*. In the latter case, the Commission's concerns were compounded by a worry that the transaction could increase lock-in effects for users Meta's large ecosystem. In both cases, concerns about an outright blocking or a degradation of access, for example, through limiting interoperability with competitors' products, were ultimately remedied by the parties' commitments to provide competitors for ten years with free and non-discriminatory access licences. These access remedies represent a notable exception to the Commission's general preference for structural remedies/divestitures.

[503] Considering that case M.9660 *Google/Fitbit* concerned the collection of users' health and fitness data for, among others, advertising purposes and that it, therefore, raised compliance questions under the EU's General Data Protection Regulation (GDPR),[700] it is worth noting that the Commission refused to include an assessment of such issues in its merger control analysis. According to the Commission, such issues are more appropriately dealt with under specialised legislation and in dedicated procedures: '*the assessment of the effects of the Transaction under the Merger Regulation in the present proceedings is predicated on the assumption that the Parties could lawfully combine their datasets. Should such assumption prove to be incorrect, the assessment of the effects of the Transaction under the Merger Regulation would be the same, but the Parties remain accountable for any breach of GDPR or the e-Privacy Directive, as transposed in Member States' laws*'.[701]

9.6 Coordinated Effects

9.6.1 Collective Dominance

[504] The Merger Regulation also applies to the creation or strengthening of a collective dominant position where some members of the dominant group are not party to the transaction in question.

[699] *See* Non-Horizontal Guidelines, para. 34.

[700] Regulation (EU) 2016/679 of the European Parliament and of the Council of 27 Apr. 2016 on the protection of natural persons with regard to the processing of personal data and on the free movement of such data.

[701] Case M.9660 *Google/Fitbit* at para. 411.

[505] The Commission first applied this approach in cases M.190 *Nestlé/Perrier*, M.308 *Kali + Salz/MdK/Treuhand* and M.619 *Gencor/Lonrho*.[702] It was confirmed by the ECJ and General Court in *Kali + Salz, Gencor/Lonrho* and finally *Airtours/First Choice*.[703] In *Kali + Salz*, the ECJ recognised that the Merger Regulation extended to collective dominance, but did not clearly define the standard of proof required to establish collective dominance. It held that the Commission had failed to prove that the acquisition of the former East-German potash producer MdK by Kali and Salz would create or strengthen a position of dominance. Further guidance was however provided by the General Court in *Gencor/Lonrho*. First, the Court accepted that market characteristics such as market transparency, homogeneity of the product, market maturity and multi-market contacts could be used in identifying whether the markets in question are prone to oligopolistic dominance. Second, it upheld the Commission's analysis as to how the operation would have changed the competitive relations between the competitors and thereby made anticompetitive behaviour more likely. Third, it concluded that structural links were not necessary for a finding of collective dominance, although confirmed that where they exist, they will be considered as important to the assessment of collective dominance.

[506] The General Court's judgment in *Airtours/First Choice*[704] annulled the Commission's prohibition decision regarding the merger. The decision sets out the key elements necessary to justifiably form a conclusion that a position of collective dominance is created or strengthened as a result of a concentration.

[507] The main focus of the Commission's analysis in the assessment of oligopolistic dominance is therefore the likelihood of tacit coordination, i.e., that in highly concentrated markets, it is very likely, if not inevitable, that the remaining firms will

---

[702] Joined cases C-68/94 and C-30/95 *France v. Commission* [1998] ECR I-1375 and case T-102/96 *Gencor/Lonrho* [1999] ECR II-753. The Court concluded that failure to apply the Merger Regulation to collective dominance would be incompatible with Art. 3(g) of the TFEU which sets out the Treaty aim of a system of undistorted competition.

[703] Case T-342/99 *Airtours v. Commission* [2002] ECR II-2585.

[704] In April 1999, Airtours (now MyTravel), had launched a hostile bid for First Choice, which was then in the process of emerging as a vertically integrated rival in the UK foreign package holiday market in competition with the three well-established incumbents, MyTravel, Thomson Travel Group (now part of the German group, TUI) and Thomas Cook. Had the bid been successful, those three groups would have held over 70% of the UK short haul foreign package holiday market. Despite a history of competition in this market and a 1997 report from the UK Monopolies and Mergers Commission (now the Competition Commission), which concluded that the market was *'broadly competitive'* the [European] Commission considered that subsequent consolidation and further vertical integration had altered structural conditions so radically that the loss of First Choice as an independent, and apparently somewhat maverick competitor, would result in the three remaining vertically integrated travel groups sharing a position of collective dominance in the UK market. This was the first case in which the Commission had attempted to use the Merger Regulation to prohibit or impose conditions on a merger which would still leave three competitors in the market. This also occurred at a time when there was undoubtedly political pressure from the then Competition Commissioner, Karel van Miert, to demonstrate that the Merger Regulation was not toothless where consolidation in oligopolistic markets was concerned which fell short of creating a monopoly or duopoly. In 2002, however, the General Court annulled the Commission's prohibition decision, finding that the Commission had not established that a position of collective dominance would result if Airtours acquired First Choice to the necessary standard.

recognise their interdependence and adapt their behaviour in order to achieve joint profit-maximisation. Tacit coordination in this context means that the undertakings do not actually enter into restrictive agreements or concerted practices that would infringe Article 101 of the TFEU.

[508] The Horizontal Merger Guidelines, reflecting the General Court's views in the *Airtours*[705] case, detail the Commission's approach to collective dominance and the conditions which must be established[706] as follows:

- First, firms must be able to observe each other's behaviour in the market with regard to the key parameters of competition, namely price and output. The market must be transparent enough for competitive initiatives to be readily identifiable.
- Second, there must exist a credible mechanism available to punish a firm which deviates from the uncompetitive norms of behaviour which the oligopolists have come to expect of each other. Moreover, the effect of triggering the punishment mechanism must not be such as to cause significant or long-term economic harm to all the firms in the market. If this were to be the case, retaliation would not be a practical proposition because of its relative effect on prices and profits across the whole market.
- Third, the coordinating firms as a collectively dominant group must be immune from effective constraints on their behaviour from other players in the market and from their customers which may be capable of destabilising the oligopoly.

[509] It should however be noted that in the *Impala* judgment,[707] the General Court indicated that the Commission must carry out a concrete analysis and not a prospective one when assessing the existence of a collective dominant position. Although the three conditions as set out in the *Airtours* case must still be fulfilled, *'they may be established indirectly on the basis of what may be a very mixed series of indicia and items of evidence relating to the signs, manifestations and phenomena inherent in the presence of a collective dominant position'*. In particular, market transparency could be presumed when, in the absence of alternative reasonable explanations, there is a close alignment of supra-competitive prices over a long period, in the face of falling demand.[708]

[510] In its assessment of collective dominance, the Commission commonly takes the following issues into account:

(i) The structural features of the market, to establish whether the market is prone to oligopolistic dominance. In this respect, it considers various factors (some of which are listed below), and the importance of these factors will depend on each specific case:

---

705 Case T-342/99 *Airtours v. Commission* [2002] ECR II-2585.

706 Horizontal Guidelines at para. 41.

707 Case T-464/04 *Impala v. Commission* [2006] ECR II-2289, which was further appealed to the ECJ in case C-413/06 P *Bertelsmann and Sony Corporation of America/Impala* [2008].

708 Case M.5020 *Lesaffre/GBI UK*.

- few market players holding collectively a high market share;[709]
- identifiable members of the oligopoly;[710]
- strong similarities between the oligopoly members in terms of market shares, financial resources, corporate size and structure and similar cost structures;[711]
- low price sensitivity;
- stagnant or moderate growth in demand;[712]
- homogeneous products, in particular commodity products and similar product lines, or standardised pricing of products;[713]
- market transparency;[714]

709 In case M.1016 *PriceWaterhouse/Coopers & Lybrand*, the Commission stated that collective dominance involving more than three or four suppliers was too complex and unstable to persist over time. However in its later M.1383 *Exxon/Mobil* decision, the Commission found nationwide oligopolies of four than four members to constitute a collective dominant position. It also indicated that it would be unlikely to investigate collective dominance issues if a merger were not to lead to an overall market share in excess of 50%. In case M.5907 *Votorantim/Fischer/JV* the three major suppliers of orange juice would have accounted for 80% to 90% of the market. In case M.5950 *Munksjo/Arjowiggins (Decor and Abrasive Businesses)* three suppliers of decor paper would have accounted for 80%–90% of capacity.

710 The companies constituting the oligopoly must be distinguishable from the next smallest competitors in the market. In case M.1016 *PriceWaterhouse/Coopers & Lybrand*, the Commission held that the market share gap of less than 10% between the smallest company of the 'oligopoly family' and the next smallest competitor in the market would make it impractical for the merged entity to pursue a strategy of duopolistic dominance.

711 The Commission has generally concentrated more on similarities in cost structures such as reducing incentives to charge different prices in the market. *See* in particular, Joined cases C-68/94 and C-30/95, *France and Others v. Commission* [1998] ECR I-1375 where large imbalances of market share between the undertakings concerned were considered to make the existence or creation of a collective dominant position highly unlikely. In case M.1313 *Danish Crown/Vestjyske Slagterier*, the Commission found that economic links, such as similar cost structures increased the possibility for competitors to coordinate their activity. Also *see* cases M.2201 *MAN/Auwärter* and M.4980 *ABF/GBI Business*. In case M.6093 *BASF/Ineos/Styrene/JV* the Commission excluded tacit collusion where the transaction would create substantial asymmetries in affected EEA chemical markets.

712 In cases M.1225 *Enso/Stora* and M.1016 *PriceWaterhouse/Coopers & Lybrand*, the Commission identified growth in demand as a destabilising factor in oligopolies and a stimulus to market entry and competition. In general, collective dominance has been found in markets with growth rates of only to 2%–4%. However, in markets with high barriers to entry it would be possible for collective dominance to exist with a higher growth rate. *See also* T-342/99 *Airtours* [2002] ECR II-2585. *See also* case M.5867 *Thomas Cook/Öger Tours*.

713 In case M.1882 *Pirelli/BICC*, the Commission concluded that the significant service element attached to individual projects constituted a factor against a finding of collective dominance. *See also* cases M.2389 *Shell/DEA* and M.2498 *UPM Kymmene/Haindl*. In case M.6203 *Western Digital/Viviti Technologies* the Commission excluded any tacit coordination on the market for hard disk drives post-transaction due to the multitude of products within a given market as well as the frequency of price negotiations with customers.

714 In order to monitor and respond to the actions of competitors, the market should be transparent on key issues such as price and quantities. In case M.1524 *Airtours/First Choice*, the development of holiday programmes on an incremental basis from season to season was found to create transparency. Conversely, in case M.1882 *Pirelli/BICC*, the Commission found that collusion was unlikely due to low price transparency for LV/MV products which resulted from the absence of meaningful list prices and varying customer defined specifications. In case M.7000 *Liberty Global/*Ziggo, following its in-depth investigation, the Commission concluded that certain elements, such as the degree of transparency, suggested that the Dutch retail telecoms markets may be conducive to coordination –

- lack of technical innovation or mature technology;[715]
- deterrence mechanism;[716]
- capacity levels (in some cases, the existence of excess capacity may render a market less conducive to collective dominance,[717] in other cases, however, excess capacity may indicate collective dominance as it represents an effective threat of retaliation);
- lack of external restraints such as countervailing buying power;[718]
- barriers to entry;[719] and
- structural and economic links between the undertakings concerned.[720]

---

also before the concentration. In case M.6471 *Outokumpu/Inoxum* the Commission excluded coordinated effects in the relevant market for cold roll steel products in the EEA because prices at customer level were agreed bilaterally between producers and buyers and were not public. *See also* cases M.1741 *MCI WorldCom/Sprint*; M.4753 *Antalis/MAP* and M.5755 *Schneider Electric/Areva T&D*.

715 Product innovation is regarded as making markets unstable and unpredictable by changing the conditions of competition and therefore making it more difficult to establish collective dominance. In case M.2097 *SCA/Metsä Tissue*, the Commission took account of the fact that technical innovation is relatively moderate in the tissue market (due to the long life of tissue machines) and concluded that it takes time to have a strong influence on competition.

716 This is in line with economic theories which illustrate that retaliation mechanisms (i.e., to punish firms who deviate from an implicit agreement) are an essential requirement for tacit coordination to be sustainable. However, this should be interpreted in light of the fact that retaliation can take many forms ranging from complicated mechanisms to a simple conversion back to competitive behaviour. In the *Airtours* judgment (case T-342/99 *Airtours v. Commission* [2002] ECR II-2585), the General Court noted that one potential retaliatory measure was the possibility for the other oligopolists to react at a downstream level of their vertically integrated operations, namely the distribution level, by discriminating against the holidays of the deviant oligopolist. *See also* the Horizontal Merger Guidelines at para. 55.

717 In case M.1517 *Rhodia/Donau Chemie/Albright & Wilson*, the Commission stated that collective dominance may be negotiated if it can be established that there are overcapacities which allow for the breaking up of parallel anticompetitive behaviour. Also *see* case M.1663 *Alcan/Alusuisse*.

718 Countervailing buyer power can play an important factor in collective dominance cases. In case M.1629 *Knorr-Bremse/Rexroth*, for example, the Commission concluded that the transaction was unlikely to give rise to anticompetitive coordinated effects within the remaining duopoly because customers were deemed sufficiently capable of controlling their suppliers. That said, the Commission has only rarely accepted that buyer power is significant enough a force to prevent the creation or strengthening of collective dominance positions. In case M.9829 *Aon/Willis*, for example, the Commission found that even large corporate customers would be unable to constrain their suppliers simply because of the lack of sufficient choice of supply.

719 Where a market is contestable or entry barriers are low, it is more difficult to establish collective dominance. This has been an important consideration in past collective dominance cases. For example, in case M.737 *Ciba-Geigy/Sandoz*, the Commission found a duopoly with market shares of between 70% and 80% in Greece and Spain. However, because entry barriers were so low, duopolistic dominance was not considered likely. Similarly, in case M.1313 *Danish Crown/Vestjyske Slagterier*, the Commission concluded that potential competition would be restricted partly because of the existence of exclusive supply obligations imposed on farmers who were members of cooperatives.

720 Structural and commercial links include cross-shareholdings (case M.2567 *Nordbanken/Postgirot*); production arrangements including swap agreements (case M.3314 *Air Liquide/Messier*); marketing arrangements (case M.308 *Kali + Salz/MdK/Treuhand*); joint ventures in the relevant or closely related product or services market (case M.1313 *Danish Crown/Vestjyske Slagterier*) and cross-distribution between competitors (case M.1524 *Airtours/First Choice*). *See also* cases M.5549 *EDF/Segebel* and M.6348 *Arla Foods/Allgauland*. The Commission has started assessing more systematically the impact of common ownerships of rivals by investors. As early as February 2018, Commissioner

(ii) Past behaviour by the merging firms and their competitors. To this end, the Commission will assess whether the transaction parties or their competitors have previously engaged in coordinated conduct – either in the relevant markets or in similar or related markets. If so, the question will be whether such past conduct is indicative also of future market behaviour or whether, for example, recent developments make coordination less likely in the future. To this end, the Commission will take into account, for example, variations in price, output and market shares over time, in order to assess the extent to which the industry is competitive. In case M.3314 *Air Liquide/Messier*, for example, the Commission took into account that the product markets in question had previously been subject to anticompetitive collusion that had been sanctioned under Article 101 of the TFEU. Where competition in the market is already muted, the change resulting from a merger would normally only need to be small in order for it to create a position of collective dominance.[721]

[511] The conditions found to be conducive to coordinated effects and collective dominance have been revisited by both the General Court and the ECJ in the litigation surrounding the Commission's first compatibility decision in case M.3333 *Sony/BMG*.[722] While the General Court quashed the Commission's original *Sony/BMG* clearance, that judgment was later overturned by the ECJ. According to the ECJ, despite seemingly applying the *Airtours* criteria (which neither Courts questioned or modified), the General Court had failed to identify a realistic monitoring mechanism consistent with a plausible theory of tacit coordination. The ECJ's judgment thereby reasserts the Commission's margin of discretion in applying the established *Airtours* coordinated effects criteria, but emphasises the need for an approach to be adopted which is rooted in the practicalities of the industry and market under review.

9.6.2 Coordinative Aspects Within Joint Ventures: Article 2(4)

[512] Article 2(4) of the Merger Regulation provides that to the extent that the creation of a joint venture constituting a concentration (i.e., a full-function joint venture) has as its object or effect the coordination of the competitive behaviour of the

Vestager explained that it is becoming more common for the same investors to hold shares in different companies in the same industry (*see*, e.g., Speech of 16 Feb. 2018, *Competition in Changing Times*). This has been an enforcement policy of the Commission throughout 2018 as the Commission still tries to understand what kind of impact common ownership has on the competitive dynamics. The Commission closely looked at that during, e.g., the *Bayer/Monsanto* review (Case M. 8084 *Bayer/Monsanto*). *See also*, case M.10153 *Orange/Telekom Romania* where the remedies that were attached to the Commission's clearance resulted in the divestment of a minority shareholding in one of the merging parties' competitors. The Commission had raised concerns that that shareholding could be used by the merged entity: (i) to obtain competitively sensitive information about a key competitor, (ii) that related veto rights could be used to undermine that competitor's future viability and (iii) that the shareholding could disincentivise future investments into the competitor's business, thereby undermining its ability to competitively constrain the merged entity in the future.

721 *See*, for example, case M.190 *Nestlé/Perrier*.

722 Case T-464/04 *Impala v. Commission* [2006] ECR II-2289, appealed to the ECJ in case C-413/06 P. *Bertelsmann and Sony Corporation of America/Impala* [2008].

undertakings that remain independent, such coordination shall be appraised in accordance with the criteria of Article 101(1) and (3) of the TFEU. This is with a view to establishing whether or not the operation is compatible with the Internal Market. A risk of coordination can arise from several factors: first, the joint venture may be producing a key input for its parent companies which may facilitate the coordination of downstream prices if sourcing from the JV results in an alignment of the parent companies' costs; second, the joint venture may act as a conduit for competitively sensitive information between the parents, for example, in forecasting their input requirements based on their future expansion plans; and third, any management seconded to the joint venture may disclose information about its parents' separate and competing activities.

[513] In making its assessment, the Commission takes the following into account:

(i) Whether two or more parent companies retain to a significant extent activities:
   - in the same market as the joint venture;
   - in a market which is downstream or upstream from that of the joint venture; or
   - in a neighbouring market closely related to such a market.

(ii) Whether the coordination, as a direct consequence of the creation of the joint venture in itself affords the undertakings concerned the possibility of eliminating competition in respect of a substantial part of the products or services in question.

[514] The establishment of the joint venture remains subject to the SIEC test set out in Article 2(1)–(3) of the Merger Regulation. However, to the extent that it brings about cooperative spill-over aspects as a direct consequence, these will be assessed according to the criteria of Article 101(1) and (3) of the TFEU.[723] The Commission will apply both tests within the strict procedural deadlines of the Merger Regulation. However, where the Commission decides to grant an exemption under Article 101(3) of the TFEU, it will not be limited in time.

[515] The investigation of spill-over effects of coordination between the parties essentially involves:

(i) The identification of the markets on which the coordination may take place (the market of the joint venture or markets where both parents are active).

(ii) The identification of the significance and nature of the parents' activities in those markets.[724]

(iii) The determination of whether the joint venture allows coordination between the parents (causal link between the creation of the joint venture and the coordinative effects).

---

723 Recital 5 of Regulation 1310/97.

724 Cases M.3141 *Cementbouw/ENCI/JV*; M.4596 *Wärtsilä Technology/Hyundai Heavy Industry/JV* and M.5942 *Lloyds TSB Bank/Svenska Handelsbanken/Dyson Group*.

(iv) The determination of the risk of coordination between the parents on markets where they are both active, i.e., whether they would have the ability and incentive to coordinate and whether, if they did, it would be effectual.[725]
(v) The assessment of whether their coordination would eliminate competition.

[516] It should be noted that, so far, the Commission has not yet prohibited a merger on this basis, and has granted conditional authorisation in four cases, of which two progressed to Phase II.[726] Case M.3099 *Areva/Urenco* provides a detailed examination of coordinative effects which also demonstrates the close relationship that may often exist between collective dominance and coordinative effects.[727] The concentration concerned the creation of a joint venture to research, design and manufacture centrifuges for the enrichment of uranium, a downstream market where both parents were active. Areva and Urenco were the only two EU suppliers of enriched uranium, having together approximately 80% of sales. Non-EU producers were unable to constitute an effective competitive constraint because of Euratom quotas (in the case of Tenex of Russia) and near-obsolete high-cost diffusion enrichment processes (in the case of the US company, USEC). The Commission found that the establishment of the joint venture would result in Areva and Urenco enjoying joint dominance in the EU market for the supply of enriched uranium. It also identified risks of coordination as a result of the influence that the joint venture board would have on each parent's capacity decisions, the structural link itself, and the increased scope for the exchange of competitively sensitive information. Despite the importance of a secure supply of enriched uranium indigenous to the EU, and continued technological development in the centrifugal enrichment process and equipment (benefits which the Commission doubted were merger-specific), the Commission accepted a panoply of remedies to remove the risks of coordination and the strengthening of a position of joint dominance. The Commission thereby avoided any potentially contentious analysis of the efficiencies and benefits of the joint venture in order to justify a declaration of compatibility. The commitments accepted by the Commission as conditions of its compatibility decision involved complex structural and behavioural provisions designed to create independent directors on the board of the joint venture. These included 'Chinese walls', a governance structure, and confidentiality obligations on management to ensure that the joint venture did not serve as a conduit for information between its parents.

[517] The Commission's analysis in previous cases examined under Article 2(4) of the Merger Regulation has broadly followed the same lines. In assessing whether there is a coordinative effect, the Commission has to show that such an effect is 'likely'. A coordinative effect does not arise simply as a result of the presence of two

[725] In case M.1732 *Sydkraft/Hew/Hansa Energy Trading* the Commission dismissed the risk of coordination in energy trading because it could not feasibly have had an effect on the APXenergy exchange market because of the market's transparency and price sensitivity.

[726] The two Phase I decisions are cases M.1327 *NC/Canal+/CPDQ/Bank America* and JV.22 *Fujitsu/Siemens*. The Phase II decisions are JV.15 *BT/AT&T* and M.3099 *Areva/Urenco/ETC JV*. Another Phase II case was withdrawn, case JV.27 *Microsoft/Liberty Media/Telewest*.

[727] Case M.3099 *Areva/Urenco*.

or more parent companies on the market of the joint venture or on related markets. Other factors commonly taken into account by the Commission include:

- the structure of the markets, in order to determine whether they are likely to create a relationship of interdependence between the parent companies, and the effect of the joint venture on the structure of these markets.[728] Factors include: the number and strength of competitors;[729] any existing structural links between the parent companies; the existence of barriers to entry to the market; whether the market is one in which technological innovation is rapid and therefore new competitors are likely to enter;[730] the existence of significant buyer power;[731] and whether the market is price sensitive;[732]
- whether there are economically meaningful incentives for coordination.[733] For example, where one of the parents is a new entrant into the candidate market, price coordination is unlikely[734] or where the parent companies concentrate on different types of customer – i.e., one concentrates on sales to consumers and the other on sales to professionals – they are unlikely to seek to coordinate their behaviour;[735]
- the relative size of the market on which the joint venture is active and the markets on which a coordinative effect may take place (the Commission has previously considered that where the candidate market is much larger than the market of the joint venture, it is unlikely that coordination will take place on the candidate market as a result of the joint venture);[736]
- whether the creation of the joint venture would in fact give the parent companies the means to coordinate their behaviour, i.e., whether there is a causal link between the creation of the joint venture and the coordinative effect that may occur. The Commission has therefore considered issues including the following: coordination occurring by other means than through the joint venture;[737] different distribution channels making coordination unlikely;[738] the joint venture not being a significant customer or supplier of the parent companies;[739] the direct connection between the technology used by the joint venture and the parents' businesses in the candidate markets;[740] and the

[728] Case JV.22 *Fujitsu/Siemens*.
[729] Case JV.25 *Sony/Time Warner/CDNow*.
[730] Case JV.44 *Hitachi/NEC-DRAM*.
[731] Case JV.40 *Canal+/file:Lagardère/Canalsatellite* and case JV.36 *TXU Europe/EDF London Investments*.
[732] Case JV.28 *Sydkraft/HEW/Hansa Energy Trading*.
[733] Case JV.39 *Bertelsmann/Planeta/NEB*.
[734] Case M.1327 *NC/Canal+/CDPQ/Bank America*.
[735] Cases JV.54 *Smith&Nephew/Beiersdorf/JV* and M.2334 *DMData/Kommunedata/e-BOKS JV*.
[736] Cases JV.1 *Telia/Telenor/Schibsted*, JV.29 *Lafarge/Ready Mix*, JV.24 *Bertelsmann/Planeta/BOL Spain*; M.5968 *Advent/Bain Capital/RBS Worldpay* and M.6315 *Hochtief/GeoSea/Seluga Hochtief Offshore JV*.
[737] Case JV.37 *BSkyB/Kirch Pay TV*.
[738] Case JV.21 *Skandia/Storebrand/Pohjola*.
[739] Case JV.5 *Cegetel/Canal+/AOL/Bertelsmann*.
[740] Case JV.6 *Ericsson/Nokia/Psion*.

lack of an effect on potential entry by the parents into the market of the joint venture due to licence restrictions;[741] and
- even where the joint venture may give rise to a coordinative effect, the Commission will very carefully examine whether it is likely that such a coordinative effect will be appreciable. Generally, where the parent companies' combined shares of the candidate markets are low, the Commission will consider that there is no likelihood of an appreciable coordinative effect.[742] In one case, the Commission considered that any restriction was not likely to be appreciable where the parties had a 27% market share of one candidate market, notably because they would remain subject to strong competition.[743]

9.7 Countervailing Factors

[518] The presence of indicators which raise significant anticompetitive effects does not necessarily lead to the conclusion that the merger is incompatible with the Internal Market. Following the Horizontal Guidelines, we will analyse four factors in more detail below which are capable of counteracting the potential harm to consumers which such indicators would otherwise point towards.

9.7.1 Potential Competition and Entry on the Market

[519] The Commission will assess to what extent potential competition is a competitive constraint.[744] The Commission examines whether the potential competitor's entry is probable, and whether it will be able to compete meaningfully and effectively, and within a time frame short enough to deter the merging parties from exploiting their market position. However, the existence of a mere possibility to enter the market is insufficient. Potential competitors may take the form of both new competitors and competitors competing in closely related product or geographic markets.

[520] The Horizontal Guidelines summarise the characteristics required for an entry to be considered competitive: likelihood; sufficiency; profitability; and timeliness. As the Commission noted in case M.4104 *Aker Yards/Chantiers de L'Atlantique*[745] potential entry must be *'likely, timely and sufficient'* to deter any anticompetitive effect

741 Case JV.17 *Mannesmann/Bell Atlantic/OPI.*

742 Case JV.19 *KLM/Alitalia.*

743 Case M.2079 *Raytheon/Thales/JV.*

744 For example, in case M.222 *Mannesmann/Hoesch*, the parties had a combined market share of 70% but the Commission did not confirm a finding of dominance due to the significant potential competition. Similarly, in case M.781 *Schering/GEHE Jenapharm*, the parties had a market share of 60% but the Commission did not confirm a finding of dominance due to strong actual and potential competition in addition to innovation in the market. Also, in case M.6671 *LBO France /Aviapartner*, the Commission attached great importance to the ease of entry into landside cargo handling services markets at Brussels and Roissy CDG airports where the parties held combined market shares of 50%–60% and 70%–80% respectively.

745 Case M.4104 *Aker Yards/Chantiers de l'Atlantique.*

of a merger.[746] Deterrents to such entry include: sunk costs (i.e., costs irrecoverable on exit); the scale of entry required; barriers to entry; customer switching habits; and the reaction of incumbents. These factors are equally relevant when the Commission is assessing whether a concentration removes a likely entrant and so impedes competition significantly, as it did in case M.3440 *ENI/EDP/GDP*.[747]

[521] The likelihood of entry on a market essentially requires an assessment of the barriers to entry. These are, for example, regulatory barriers, economic barriers (the need to build up brands and distribution), access to technology, access to data,[748] or high R&D costs. In all cases, the Commission attaches particular importance to the existence of sunk costs as a significant barrier to market entry.[749]

[522] While entry barriers may take a number of different forms, the Horizontal Guidelines classify them into three main types:

(1) legal and regulatory barriers (legal barriers);[750]
(2) technical advantages (technical barriers);[751] and
(3) reputational/incumbency advantages (specific barriers).[752]

[523] In assessing the significance of entry barriers in a particular market, the Commission takes not only existing conditions of competition into account, but also developments in the market that will change conditions for market entry in the future (such as impending legislation).[753] This may of course include the transaction itself.[754]

[524] According to the Horizontal Guidelines, the appropriate time frame for the analysis of potential competition and entry as a constraining factor depends on the characteristics and dynamics of the market in question. However, entry is normally only taken into consideration if it occurs within two years.[755] In case M.1693 *Alcoa Reynolds*, the Commission dismissed two reported Greenfield projects and a number of brownfield projects as likely competitive constraints on the merged entity. This was due to the fact that the Commission considered the implementation of

---

746 Horizontal Guidelines at paras 69–75. Case M.5075 *Vienna Insurance/EBV.*

747 Case M.3440 *ENI/EDP/GDP*. The application to the General Court to annul the decision was dismissed: case T-87/05, *EDP – Energias de Portugal SA v. Commission* [2005] ECR II-3745.

748 Case M.10262 *Meta (Formerly Facebook)/Kustomer*.

749 Case M.623 *Kimberley-Clark/Scott Paper*, case M.430 *Procter & Gamble/VP Schickedanz (II)*.

750 Cases M. 6497 *Hutchison 3G Austria/Orange* Austria; M.5364 *Iberia/Vueling/Clickair*; M.5335 *Lufthansa/SN Airholding (SN Brussels)*; M.5141 *KLM/Martinair* and M.1940 *Framatome/Siemens/Cogema/JV.*

751 Cases M.5611 *Agilent/Varian* and M.4180 *Gaz de France/Suez* M.2416 *Tetra Laval/Sidel.*

752 Cases M.6281 *Microsoft/Skype* and M.2824 *Ernst & Young/Andersen Germany.*

753 Case M.5181 *Delta Air Lines/Northwest Airlines.*

754 Case M.784 *Kesko/Tuko.*

755 Horizontal Guidelines at para. 74. *See also* case T-282/02 *Cementbouw v. Commission*, judgment of 23 Feb. 2006, which indicates the two-year period for a new entrant to build a new bricks works and Case M.10078 – *Cargotec/Konecranes,* where the Commission considered a 2–3 year timeframe as appropriate to enter the reach stacker market.

these projects to be uncertain, partly because they were unlikely to be operational within two years. A number of factors may influence how quickly entry may take place in the market. For instance, entry may be difficult or impossible in the short term because customers are bound to suppliers either explicitly, by long-term contracts[756] or implicitly because they purchase the products very rarely. Entry may also be prevented because it requires developing products,[757] building production facilities[758] or regulatory approval to be obtained.[759]

[525] In recent years, there have been a number of cases where the parties argued that their proposed transactions were needed to better compete against rivals from Asia and in particular from China. In the *Siemens/Alstom* transaction[760] it was argued that Siemens' acquisition of Alstom was essential to compete with Chinese CRRC, the largest train maker in the world. But Commissioner Vestager said that neither in the business of signalling systems nor in the high-speed train sector was the arrival of Chinese competitors in the European market expected 'in the foreseeable future'. The Commissioner reminded that 90% of CRRC business remained inside its home market of China and that CRRC had not sold any high-speed train beyond its borders, and finally that no Chinese supplier has participated in a tender for signalling in Europe. The Commission went on dismissing this argument and further blocking the transaction on 6 February 2019. Similarly, in case M.8947 *Whirlpool/Nidec*, the Commission rejected the parties' argument that Chinese suppliers posed a competitive constraint. Rather, the Commission's assessment revealed that Chinese rivals had so far failed to make a significant entry into the market as regarded products that required more advanced technologies and R&D investments. The Commission ultimately cleared that transaction subject to conditions after a Phase II investigation. In case M.9706 *Novelis/Aleris*, too, imports from China were considered too small to effectively constrain competitors in Europe. Importantly, the parties failed to prove that Chinese suppliers had the capacity to expand production and to increase their imports into Europe when sales to North America and in China itself generated higher prices. Similarly, in case M.10078 – *Cargotec/Konecranes*, the Commission rejected the parties' arguments that Chinese players had successfully entered the EEA reach stacker market and ultimately concluded that their entry was not significant, despite clearing the transaction.

9.7.2 Buyer Power

[526] The Commission assesses the strength of customers' buying power as a means of constraining the merging parties, although it must be said that it rarely alleviates significant competition concerns. This analysis of countervailing buyer

[756] Case M.4180 *Gaz de France/Suez*.
[757] Case M.3354 *Sanofi-Synthélabo/Aventis*.
[758] Case M.4381 *JCI/FIAMM*.
[759] Case M.3687 *Johnson & Johnson/Guidant*.
[760] Case M.8677 *Siemens/Alstom*.

power assesses whether buyers have other means to counter a potential increase of prices through their bilateral relationships with the supplier, thereby replacing the disciplining force of competition that is lost by the merger.[761] The Horizontal Guidelines provide five examples of buyer power: (i) the ability to credibly resort to alternative sources; (ii) the ability to sponsor entry or expansion upstream; (iii) the ability to credibly threaten to integrate vertically; (iv) the refusal to buy other products from the same supplier; and (v) the ability to delay purchases.[762]

[527] The Commission is more likely to assume that buyers will have an appreciable constraining effect on the concentration if the buyer structure is concentrated, as opposed to the situation where the buyers are large, sophisticated and resourceful undertakings. In case M.1225 *Enso/Stora*, the proposed operation resulted in a concentrated supply situation with the merger parties achieving market shares of above 60% for liquid packaging board used for applications such as milk and juice cartons. However, they also faced a very concentrated buyer structure since Tetra Pak was the main buyer accounting for more than 60% of these purchases. This was considered to prevent the creation or strengthening of a dominant position.[763] In case M.6765 *Precision Castparts/Titanium Metals*, the demand-side of the market for rotating grade titanium was highly concentrated, essentially comprising the major engine OEMs (such as UTC, Rolls-Royce, GE/Safran), Airbus and Boeing. In particular, four OEMs accounted for close to 80% of Titanium Metals' sales of titanium rotating grade products, and three OEMs accounted for approximately 70% of PCC's sales of titanium engine rotating components. The Commission considered that implementing an input foreclosure was likely to be a risky and ultimately costly strategy for the merged entity given that, *inter alia*, OEMs can leverage one supplier against another by switching or threatening to switch suppliers in relation to those upstream and/or downstream purchases where they face sufficient choice of suppliers. Overall, the Commission took the view that the OEMs' bargaining power in the aerospace industry constituted a significant constraint on the merged entity's ability to foreclose access to titanium inputs. While the automotive industry has often been referred to as a classic example of one that possesses buyer power, the Commission was not convinced when faced with this argument during its M.9706 *Novelis/Aleris* investigation. Since the merged entity was considered 'pivotal' and as such an unavoidable trading partner for customers (including those large automotive OEMs), the Commission found that countervailing buyer power was limited and set to diminish further as a result of the transaction. An additional factor in this conclusion was the high barriers to switching that customers were found to face. In M. 10153 *Orange/Telekom Romania Communications*, the Commission found the wholesale leased lines market would have a constraining effect on the merged entity due to the significant buyer power of large telecommunications companies.

[761] Case M.6765 *Precision Castparts/Titanium Metals.*
[762] Horizontal Guidelines at paras 64–67.
[763] *See also* cases M.3732 *Procter & Gamble/Gillette* and M.3512 *VNU/WPP.*

9.7.3 Efficiencies

[528] In several cases, parties have raised arguments as to efficiencies created by the transaction (such as cost savings) as constituting issues which must be taken into account in the effects assessment of the concentration. The evaluation of efficiencies is not a formal part of the assessment in the Merger Regulation. Article 2(1)(b), which sets out the criteria by which a transaction should be assessed, does however refer to the interests of the intermediate and ultimate consumers and the development of technical and economic progress resulting from a concentration.

[529] The Horizontal Guidelines clearly refer to the fact that the Commission must consider any substantiated efficiency claim in its overall assessment of the concentration. Consequently, the Commission *'may decide that, as a consequence of the efficiencies that the merger brings about, there are no grounds for declaring the merger incompatible with the Internal Market pursuant to Article 2(3) of the Merger Regulation. This will be the case when the Commission is in a position to conclude on the basis of sufficient evidence that the efficiencies generated by the merger are likely to enhance the ability and incentive of the merged entity to act pro-competitively for the benefits of consumers, thereby counteracting the adverse effects on competition which the merger might otherwise have'*.[764]

[530] The Horizontal Guidelines set out three conditions which must be met where efficiencies are to be taken into account. The efficiencies must:

- benefit consumers;
- be merger-specific;[765] and
- be verifiable.[766]

[531] The Commission also stresses the need for efficiencies to be proven as timely, advantageous and unachievable by other means than through the concentration.

[532] Efficiencies appear to have been a relevant factor in case M.3570 *Piaggio/Aprilia* where the Commission cleared a merger between the two leading European manufacturers of scooters. The clearance was awarded on the basis of an undertaking provided to the effect that the merged entity would supply its most advanced 50cc engine to any competing producers of motorbikes or scooters which expressed an interest. In doing so, the Commission pointed out that Piaggio's acquisition of Aprilia (which was in severe financial difficulties) would enable it to achieve greater economies of scale and to extend its product range. This would enable the merged entity to compete more effectively with Japanese producers

[764] Horizontal Guidelines at para. 77.

[765] Case M.6166 *Deutsche Börse/NYSE Euronext.*

[766] In case M.4006 *Inco/Falconbridge* the Commission concluded that the substantiated efficiencies were not merger-specific because they could be largely achieved through a joint venture between the parties. Although the parties had never agreed previously on the complex value sharing issues presented by a joint venture in nickel mining and processing, the Commission took into account Inco's joint ventures with other undertakings to demonstrate that such difficulties were not unbearable. *See also* case M.6166 *Deutsche Börse/NYSE Euronext.*

active across the globe. Additionally, the preservation of at least one EU manufacturer of motor scooters to compete with Japanese firms may well have played a part in the Commission's decision to accept this unusual remedy.[767] Efficiencies claims regarding the elimination of double marginalisation were also accepted and played an important role in the clearance of the *Orange/Jazztel* transaction. Prior to the merger, Jazztel bore the cost of wholesale access to Orange's mobile infrastructure in order to provide mobile communication services to its retail customers. The transaction reduced Jazztel's variable costs in the provision of mobile services, as it eliminated the wholesale margin that Jazztel was paying to Orange for access to its mobile network. The Commission considered these cost savings to be: (i) verifiable due to the availability of data to calculate costs, prices and margins; (ii) merger-specific, since there were no realistic alternatives or less anticompetitive ways to achieve a similar result; and (iii) likely to benefit consumers since these were variable cost savings and as such are likely to be passed on, to a certain extent, to end customers.[768]

[533] In the *Deutsche Börse/NYSE Euronext* and the *Hutchison 3G UK/Telefónica Ireland* cases, the Commission concluded that the verifiable merger-specific efficiencies resulting from the proposed transaction would be insufficient to outweigh the projected anticompetitive effects resulting from the transactions.

9.7.4 Failing Firm Defence

[534] The Merger Regulation makes no explicit reference to the 'failing firm' doctrine, and none of the factors mentioned in Article 2(1) of the Merger Regulation accommodate it. However, any assessment of the competitive impact of a concentration must take into account the degree to which the alleged failing firm is, at the time of the transaction, or would continue to be, an effective competitive force in the market. Accordingly, the Commission has accepted that a 'failing firm' argument could be relevant to the causation requirement in Article 2(2) of the Merger Regulation. In other words, a merger can be cleared where it does not in and of itself cause a SIEC.

[535] The ECJ approved this approach and its application to the *Kali + Salz* case.[769] The case concerned a proposed joint venture between Kali + Salz AG and Mitteldeutsche Kali AG (MdK). The latter was an East-German state-owned company, which was making large losses. It was proposed that MdK would be converted into a private company and Kali + Salz would receive 51% of the shares and voting rights. The transaction created a near-monopoly for the supply of potash in Germany and resulted in a company with 60% of the European market. However, the case was ultimately cleared since it was considered that a prohibition would have

[767] Case M.3570 *Piaggio/Aprilia.*

[768] Case M.7421 *Orange/Jazztel.*

[769] Joined cases C-68/94 & C-30/95 *France v. Commission* and *SCPA & EMC v. Commission* [1998] 4 CMLR 829.

led to the same market outcome as a clearance. Following this judgment, the Horizontal Guidelines briefly set out the principle under which the 'failing firm' doctrine is recognised, and point to three criteria as 'especially relevant' for its application namely:

(1) the failing firm would exit the market imminently because of its financial difficulties;
(2) there is no less anticompetitive alternative to the notified proposal; and
(3) in the absence of the merger, all the assets of the failing firm would exit the market.

[536] The 'failing firm' defence was successfully invoked in case M.2314 *BASF/Pantochim/Eurodiol*. In this case, the target companies Pantochim and Eurodiol were heavily indebted as their parent company was undergoing bankruptcy proceedings under Belgian law. Options such as a restructuring plan or other potential purchasers were found to be unrealistic and therefore the Commission accepted that the companies would be forced out of the market in the case that BASF did not acquire them.

[537] In the vast majority of the cases where the 'failing firm' defence has been argued, the Commission has rejected it and has furthermore indicated on numerous occasions that it does not intend to increase its scope of application.[770] The Commission's approach in its initial prohibition of the merger between Olympic and Aegean Airlines in 2010 perfectly illustrates its reluctance vis-à-vis this mechanism and the difficulties in implementing it in practice.[771] In the *Olympic/Aegean Airlines* case, the parties explained to the Commission that if not taken over by another undertaking Olympic Air would in the near future be forced out of the market because of financial difficulties. However, after a careful assessment of all internal documents submitted by the parties, the Commission considered that it could not be concluded that Olympic Air was underperforming against its business plan and revised budget. The Commission added that the airline had started to implement restructuring measures which should improve the airline's financial results in the short/medium term. Accordingly, based on the evidence contained in its file, the Commission concluded that Olympic did not meet the criteria of a failing firm in that it was unlikely that Olympic would be forced out of the market in the near future because of its financial difficulties if not taken over by another undertaking. Further to the Commission's prohibition decision, the parties have approached the Commission once again in 2013, and on 9 October 2013 the Commission approved the merger of the two Greek air carriers after the Commission's in-depth investigation had shown that Olympic Air would be forced to exit the market in the near future due to financial difficulties if not acquired by Aegean Airlines.[772]

[770] Speech of Nadia Calvino, Deputy Director-General for DG COMP indicating that the '*Commission would not depart from its policy on failing firms*', March 2009.

[771] Case M.5830 *Olympic/Aegean Airways*.

[772] Case M.6796 *Olympic/Aegean Airways II*.

[538] Alongside, the more traditional failing *firm* defence, merging parties have also approached the Commission with failing *division* defence arguments whereby not all the assets of the failing firm would exit the market. This was the case in *JCI/FIAMM*, where the merging parties claimed that FIAMM should be regarded as a failing firm, or at least a failing division.[773] However, despite FIAMM being on the verge of bankruptcy, the Commission was not prepared to apply the concept of the failing firm defence since it considered that the third statutory criterion was not fulfilled: it was not certain that all of the assets of the Italian company would exit the market absent the merger. In its approval decision however, the Commission demonstrated some flexibility by taking into account FIAMM's financial situation and requesting less extensive remedies than what would have normally been deemed necessary to restore normal competition. Accordingly, while not recognising the existence of a failing *firm as such*, through this case, the Commission acknowledges the possibility of the parties being successful in presenting a failing *division* defence arguments (i.e., where only a certain part of the company would be exiting the market absent the completion of the transaction). The Commission confirmed this position in the *Nynas/Shell/Harburg Refinery* case, where purchaser Nynas was successful in arguing that the oil-refinery assets owned by Shell would close if the proposed transaction was not approved.[774]

[539] More recently, the Commission confirmed its legal position regarding the application of the second criteria of the failing firm defence (i.e., there is no less anticompetitive alternative to the notified proposal) in its *ArcelorMittal/Ilva* decision.[775] The Commission noted that there was another consortium that participated in the tender for Ilva's assets, and had submitted a binding offer. ArcelorMittal submitted that due to the delays incurred and the degradation of Ilva's assets in the meantime, it would be unlikely that the alternative bidder would still be in a position of acquiring Ilva. The Commission however considered that in the assessment of the failing firm defence in the context of a bid, it should be determined whether the relevant criteria were fulfilled at the time of the bidding.

[540] The Commission also considered that it was not required to run a detailed assessment of this alternative bid as long as this was deemed a suitable alternative at the time of the adjudication. Similarly, in a similar fashion, the Commission considered that the third criterion, on whether the assets would leave the market in absence of the transaction, was not met at the time of the tender award. The Commission took the view that this criterion is to be assessed on the basis of objective elements such as the considerable value of the assets as reflected in the asset valuation of Ilva's assets in the bidding process.

[541] Despite the economic fallout from the COVID-19 crisis, the Commission has so far not accepted a related failing firm defence. In case M.9582 *Siemens Gamesa/Senvion/Ria Blades*, the argument was summarily rejected because the Commission

[773] Case M.4381 *JCI/FIAMM*.

[774] Case M.6360 *Nynas/Shell/Harburg Refinery*.

[775] Case M.8444 *ArcelorMittal/Ilva*.

considered that in case of a bankruptcy the target's assets would remain in the market.[776] Similar considerations drove the Commission's arguments in case M.9489 *Air Canada/Transat*. While the parties ultimately abandoned the transaction after a protracted Phase II investigation, the Commission stressed in its subsequent press release that it had analysed the COVID-19 crisis' impact on the parties and their airline competitors but that it had concluded that in the long-run Air Canada and Transat would likely remain actual or potential competitors.

9.8 Ancillary Restraints

[542] Articles 6(1)(b) and 8(2) of the Merger Regulation provide that a decision declaring a concentration compatible with the Internal Market also covers *'restrictions that are directly related and necessary to the implementation of the concentration'*. Until 2001, the Commission's normal practice was to require the parties to provide information so as to allow it to assess which restrictions were considered to be ancillary to the concentration and clear these restrictions under the same procedure as the concentration. However, in July 2001, the Commission published a Notice changing its policy which was subsequently replaced in 2005 by an updated Notice on restrictions directly related and necessary to concentrations: the Ancillary Restraints Notice. Restrictions which are directly related and necessary to the concentration still automatically benefit from the clearance of the transaction. However, pursuant to the Ancillary Restraints Notice, the Commission no longer assesses the restrictions during the merger procedure. Instead, companies are required to make their own assessment as to whether restrictions are covered by the merger decision or by a relevant block exemption. The Commission has only retained a limited role with respect to the assessment of restraints which raise novel or unresolved questions giving rise to 'genuine uncertainty'.[777] In practice however such questions are rarely presented to the Commission, and when such applications have been made, the Commission has generally declined to consider the parties' submissions on the ancillary character of the restraint in question as part of its assessment under the Merger Regulation.[778]

[543] The Ancillary Restraints Notice provides guidance on which provisions concluded in the context of mergers may be considered *directly related* and *necessary* to the implementation of the concentration, and which may therefore benefit from a decision declaring the concentration compatible with the Internal Market. Restrictions must be the inevitable consequence of the concentration itself and subordinate in importance to the main object of the concentration. In order to be considered necessary to the transaction it should be clear that without the restriction, the concentration could not be implemented or could only be implemented under more uncertain conditions, at substantially higher costs, over an appreciably longer period, or with considerably less probability of success. In assessing the

---

776 The Commission unconditionally cleared that case nonetheless in Phase I.

777 Ancillary Restraints Notice at para. 2.

778 Case M.6127 *Atos Origin/Siemens IT Solutions & Services*.

necessity of the restriction, the Commission will take not only its nature into account, but also whether it is proportionate, i.e., that its duration, subject matter, and geographic field of application do not exceed what the implementation of the concentration reasonably requires.[779] If alternatives are available, the option chosen must objectively be the least restrictive of competition by applying the proportionality standards set out in decisions made by the European Courts and the Commission.

[544] The Ancillary Restraints Notice sets out the principles applicable to the most common clauses in acquisitions and joint ventures as set out below.

9.8.1 Non-compete and Confidentiality Clauses

[545] A non-compete clause should be no wider than necessary to protect the goodwill and know-how transferred as regards the products and services covered, geographical scope, duration, and the parties to be restrained. This includes both physical assets and intangible assets (such as goodwill and know-how). Where the transfer in question involves both goodwill and know-how, non-compete clauses are generally justified for periods of up to three years.[780] When only goodwill is included, this period is reduced to two years. Longer durations may be justified in circumstances where it can be shown that customer loyalty to the seller will persist for more than two to three years or where the nature of the know-how transferred justifies additional protection.[781] The geographical scope of a non-compete clause must normally be limited to the area in which the seller offers the relevant products or services before the transfer and must remain limited to only the products transferred, although this includes improved versions or updates (and services forming the economic activity of the undertaking transferred).[782] Confidentiality clauses can be accepted for periods of longer than three years taking into account the companies' interests in protecting business secrets.[783] Provisions which restrict the vendor's right to purchase or hold shares in a competing company may be considered directly related and necessary to the implementation of the concentration provided

[779] Ancillary Restraints Notice at para. 13. *See*, for example, case M.496 *Marconi/Finmeccanica* where a transfer of activities from one joint venture parent to the other was not considered necessary to the implementation of the concentration.

[780] *See* cases M.2305 *Vodafone Group plc/Eircell*; M.2077 *Clayton Dubilier & Rice/Italtel* and M.1127 *Nestlé/Dalgety*.

[781] For example, in case M.1980 *Volvo/Renault VI*, the Commission accepted a non-compete provision of five years as a result of the high degree of customer loyalty in the truck market and the long life cycle of heavy trucks, the Commission accepted a term of three years. In case M.1160 *GKN/Brambles/SKP* the Commission reduced from seven to five years the duration of a non-competition clause.

[782] In case M.1979 *CDC/Banco Urquijo/JV* a non-competition clause was accepted only as regards the joint venture's banking activities in Spain and rejected for other territories. The scope of a non-competition clause can, however, be extended to areas where the vendor was planning to market before the transaction, provided that it had already invested in making the move, and to products and services either not yet marketed or at an advanced stage of development at the time of transaction.

[783] Case M.2355 *Dow/Enichem Polyurethane*.

that they do not prevent the vendor holding shares for investment purposes only.[784]

[546] Obligations between parent undertakings in a joint venture may be justifiable where, for example, they reflect a need to fully utilise a joint venture's assets to enable the joint venture to assimilate know-how and goodwill provided by its parents. In addition, obligations may be justified to protect the parents' interest in the joint venture against competitive acts such as the parents' privileged access to the know-how and goodwill transferred to or developed by the joint venture. As a general rule, such clauses can be accepted for periods of up to five years.[785] However, the Commission considers that non-compete clauses lasting over three years need to be justified by the parties.[786] However, non-compete obligations between the parents and the joint venture extending beyond the lifetime of the joint venture will never be regarded as directly related and necessary to the implementation of the concentration. The geographical and product scope of the non-compete obligation must be restricted to the area of the parent's activities prior to the establishment of the joint venture (or the geographical areas which the parent companies were trying to enter at the time of the transaction) and the economic activity of the joint venture. The duration of confidentiality clauses may exceed five years depending on the circumstances of the case.

9.8.2 Licence Agreements

[547] Licences and similar rights of know-how between the acquirer and the vendor are a common feature of sale and purchase transactions and will be considered to be necessary to the implementation of the concentration where they are limited to the same fields of use as those of the undertaking transferred. They need not be limited in time and can range from being simple or exclusive in order to protect the value of the business transferred.[787] However, territorial limitations on the right to manufacture in relation to the territory of the transferred activity in addition to restrictions which protect the licensor rather than the licensee would usually not be considered as necessary to the implementation of the concentration, and would therefore not be permitted.

[548] Licences granted by parent companies to joint ventures will generally be considered directly related and necessary to the implementation of the concentration regardless of whether the licence is exclusive or limited in time. However, the licence must be restricted to a particular field of use which corresponds to the activities of the joint venture. The same would apply in respect of licences granted by the joint venture to its parents or in the context of a cross-licence agreement.

[784] Case JV.40 *Canal+/file:Lagardère/Canal Satellite* and case M.1832 *Ahold/ICA Förbundet/Canica*.

[785] *See* among others case M.4912 *Calyon/Société Générale/Newedge*.

[786] Case M.2243 *Stora Enso/Assidomän/JV.*

[787] In case M.2268 *Pernod Ricard/Diageo/Seagram*, Pernod Ricard (who had obtained the 'Seagram' brand) granted an indefinite licence to use the Seagram name to Diageo (who had obtained the 'V.O' brand) in order not to weaken the brand 'Seagram's V.O.', allowing Diageo to continue to use the brand 'Seagram's V.O.'.

Licences between the parent companies would not be considered directly related and necessary to the implementation of a joint venture.

9.8.3 Purchase and Supply Obligations

[549] Obligations necessary to maintain existing purchase or supply links between the vendor and acquirer may be considered directly related and necessary to the implementation of the concentration where they are needed to ensure the continuity of the supply of products necessary for carrying out the activities retained by the vendor, or taken over by the acquirer for a transitional period.[788] Obligations must be on arm's-length terms, limited in scope and be unlikely to prevent effective competition or to foreclose markets. Obligations as to unlimited quantities or concerning 'preferred' supplier or purchaser status are presumed unnecessary to the implementation of the concentration and would need to be justified on a case-by-case basis. In addition, there is no general justification for the imposition of exclusive purchase or supply obligations unless exceptional circumstances exist, such as the absence of a market or the specificity of the products in question.[789] The duration of any purchase or supply obligation must be limited to the period necessary for the replacement of the relationship or dependency in the market. It is normally accepted that a supply or purchase obligation can last for up to five years. In exceptional cases, a longer duration may be acceptable, at least for purchase or supply obligations aimed at guaranteeing the quantities previously supplied.[790] Service and distribution agreements would be regarded under the same principle as supply arrangements.

[550] A wide variety of purchase and supply relationships between a joint venture and its parent companies have been accepted where these are necessary to ensure that the joint venture can establish itself as a viable entity in the market. Generally, such arrangements will not constitute acceptable ancillary restraints if they are to last for more than five years. Other factors which are indicative of an obligation being ancillary include the arrangement being at arm's length and at market prices.

[551] Restraints which are not considered to be directly related to and necessary for the implementation of the concentration are not per se illegal but are not automatically covered by the Commission's merger decision. These clauses could instead be justified under Article 101(3) of the TFEU or, alternatively, they may fall within the scope of a block exemption regulation. For example, licence agreements

---

788 Case M.2355 *Dow/Enichem Polyurethane*.

789 Case M.1536 *Wind/Enel STC* where the Commission accepted an outsourcing agreement whereby Wind would provide telecommunications services to Enel on an exclusive basis. One of the arguments for accepting the agreement was that it would allow Wind to become a competitor of Telecom Italia, the largest player on the Italian market. *See also* case M.1053 *Mannesmann/Philips* where the Commission stated that preferred supplier clauses may have the same effect as exclusive supply obligations to the extent that they affect supplies from competitors.

790 Case M.550 *Union Carbide/Enichem* where the Commission accepted an initial duration of seven years.

which contain restrictions on competition may fall within the Commission's block exemption on the transfer of technology, Commission Regulation 772/2004.[791]

9.9 Parallel and Successive Concentrations

[552] The issue of priority regarding the assessment of the transactions arises when two concentrations taking place in the same market are notified to the Commission at the same time, or within a very short time period from one another, thereby resulting in overlapping assessments of the economic impact of the two transactions. When faced with such successive notifications, the Commission follows a 'priority rule' whereby it analyses the first transaction notified on its own merits and without regard to the second, while analysing the second transaction in light of the market structure created by the first transaction. The application of this priority rule has led to debate, in particular since notifying parties are not fully in control of when a formal notification is submitted to the Commission (given how pre-notification discussions with the Commission take place), and are therefore arguably unable to affect their priority.

[553] The Commission faced a situation where it applied its priority rule in its assessment of the *Seagate/Samsung HDD* and *Western Digital/Viviti Technologies* cases. On 23 November 2011, the Commission cleared Western Digital's acquisition of Hitachi's hard disk drive (HDD) business, renamed Viviti Technologies, under the Merger Regulation.[792] The Commission's clearance decision was subject to commitments to divest its production plant and related facilities for the manufacture of 3.5 inch HDD. The Commission's investigation into the *Western Digital/Viviti* transaction ran in parallel with another transaction in the same field: Seagate Technology's acquisition of Samsung's HDD activities. Seagate's acquisition was cleared on 19 October 2011 after an in-depth investigation, but without commitments.[793]

[554] The Commission, in application of its priority rule, analysed the notified transactions on the basis of the situation which applied at the time of notification. The Seagate transaction which was notified one day prior to the Western Digital transaction was therefore analysed independently of the Western Digital transaction, while the latter was analysed taking into account the outcome of Seagate's acquisition.

[555] The Commission had followed a similar approach when it assessed two transactions taking place in the satellite navigation market: *TomTom/Tele Atlas*[794] and *Nokia/Navteq*.[795] TomTom notified its proposed acquisition to the Commission

[791] Commission Regulation No. 772/2004 on the application of Art. 101(3) of the TFEU to categories of technology transfer agreements, OJ 2004, L 123/11.

[792] Case M.6203 *Western Digital/Viviti Technologies*.

[793] Case M.6214 *Seagate/HDD Business of Samsung Electronics*.

[794] Case M.4854 *TomTom/Tele Atlas*.

[795] Case M.4942 *Nokia/Navteq*.

four months before Nokia filed its own notification to the Commission. Accordingly, the Commission's review of the *TomTom/Tele Atlas* case did not take account of the second transaction which had been publicly announced by Nokia. In contrast, the Commission's assessment of the *Nokia/Navteq* transaction considered TomTom/Tele Atlas to be a vertically integrated competitor. Both transactions were ultimately cleared unconditionally following a Phase II investigation.

[556] A similar situation arose when the Commission assessed two concurrent transactions in the copper industry: *KME/MKM*[796] and *Wieland /Aurubis Rolled Products/Schwermetall*.[797] KME was the first to formally notify, filing its acquisition of rival MKM on 4 June 2018, while Wieland Werke followed just a week later on 13 June 2018 with its acquisition of certain assets from Aurubis. The first transaction was cleared unconditionally in Phase I, whereas the second deal was blocked by the Commission following the rejection of a number of remedies put forward by Wieland. The Commission's 'priority policy' means that the market was already significantly more consolidated when it reviewed the second transaction as opposed to the market landscape of the first transaction, however, the Commission noted that the effect of taking the KME/MKM merger into account in the competitive assessment of the Wieland transaction was neutral in this instance, since any potential positive effect of the KME/MKM merger and any negative effects resulting from more concentrated market would offset each other. Wieland appealed the Commission's decision and the General Court dismissed the appeal in its entirety on 18 May 2022.[798]

10 APPEALS TO THE COURT

10.1 Decisions That Can Be Challenged

[557] The Merger Regulation envisages formal decisions of the Commission at various times during the procedure. Indeed, there are numerous types of decisions which may be taken under the Merger Regulation, many of which are subject to review by the Community Courts, namely the General Court and the ECJ. In application of Article 263 of the TFEU, all Commission decisions that produce legal effects can be challenged before the EU courts by the addressees of the decision or any other party concerned directly and individually. On the other hand, preparatory measures including a statement of objections cannot be challenged. Judicial review of merger decisions by the General Court is based on the same principles of judicial review of other Commission acts, as set out in Article 263. Importantly, the General Court does not hear the appeals of merger decisions on their merits, substitute its findings for the Commission's conclusions or take decisions on the Commission's behalf. In *Tetra Laval*, the ECJ concluded that the General Court's

[796] Case M.8909 *KME/NKM*.
[797] Case M.8900 *Wieland/Aurubis Rolled Products/Schwermetall*.
[798] Case T-251/19 *Wieland v. Commission*.

annulment of the Commission's decision did not go beyond judicial review into a hearing on the merits, as the Commission had contended.[799]

[558] There is now a considerable body of jurisprudence specific to merger decisions and the EU merger regime. To date, appeals have been made against some seventy or more Commission merger decisions. In approximately a quarter of them, the Commission's decision has been annulled, at least in part (with the latest being the General Court's annulment on 28 May 2020 of the Commission's prohibition of the proposed acquisition of Telefónica Europe Plcby CK Hutchison Holdings Ltd).[800]

[559] Examples of findings in merger cases that are capable of appeal include a finding of dominance,[801] the correct calculation of turnover,[802] whether control has been acquired solely or jointly,[803] whether the Commission has correctly refused to clear a merger in the light of commitments offered by the parties,[804] whether the obligation to cooperate with Member States has been complied with,[805] the use of Article 22(3) referrals,[806] and infringement of general principles of EU Law such as the right of defence,[807] adequate reasoning, legal certainty and the protection of legitimate expectations,[808] and whether a concentration was implemented before the standstill obligation.[809] In practice, the Community Courts require a high standard of proof before they will be willing to disagree with the substantive reasoning of a Commission decision. This is particularly the case with regard to economic questions such as dominance and the effect of the concentration on competition.[810] In *Kali + Salz*, the ECJ found that the Commission had failed to establish the necessary legal standard of facts required to support the finding of collective dominance.[811] More recently, the General Court appears to have adopted the approach that *'the Commission had the onus to provide convincing evidence to support its conclusions that the merger entity would probably behave in the way foreseen'*.[812]

[560] In a judgment of 11 December 2013, the General Court dismissed Cisco Systems' application for annulment of the Commission's *Microsoft/Skype* unconditional

799 Case C-12/03P *Commission v. Tetra Laval BV* [2005] ECR I-1113.

800 Case T-399/16 *CK Telecoms UK Investment v. Commission*. The Commission lodged an appeal of this decision with the ECJ on 7 Aug. 2020.

801 *See* case T-342/99 *Airtours v. Commission*.

802 Case T-3/93 *Air France v. Commission* [1994] ECR II-121.

803 Case T-125/97 and T-127/97 *Coca-Cola v. Commission* [2000] ECR II-1733.

804 Case T-125/97 *The Coca-Cola Company v. Commission* [2000] ECR II-1733.

805 Case T-88/94 *Société Commerciale des Potasses et de l'Azote v. Commission* [1994] ECR II-401.

806 Case T-22/97 *Kesko Oy v. Commission* [1999] ECR II-3775.

807 Case C-265/17P *Commission v. United Parcel Service*.

808 Case T-2/93 *Air France v. Commission* [1994] ECR II-323.

809 Case C-746/21 P *Altice v. Commission* and Case T-609/19 *Canon v. Commission*.

810 *See*, for example, case T-102/96 *Gencor v. Commission* [1999] ECR II-753 and *Kesko v. Commission* [1999] ECR II-3775.

811 Joined cases C-68/94 & C-30/95 *French Republic v. Commission* [1998] ECR I-1375.

812 Case T-210/01 *General Electric Company v. Commission* [2005] ECR II-5575.

Phase I clearance decision.[813] In particular, the General Court rejected the applicants' submission that the Commission was subject to a higher standard when it decided against opening a Phase II investigation, and confirmed that the Commission was subject to an identical standard of judicial review irrespective of whether it approved concentrations in Phase I or in Phase II.[814] On 28 May 2020, the General Court annulled the Commission's decision to prohibit the acquisition of Telefónica Europe Plc by CK Hutchison Holdings Ltd.[815] This is the first time that the European Courts have expressly interpreted the application of the Merger Regulation to a concentration giving rise to non-coordinated effects on an oligopolistic market (so-called 'gap cases'). While the General Court accepted that the Commission can prohibit gap cases in circumstances where it can demonstrate a SIEC with a 'strong probability', being stricter than on a 'balance of probabilities' but less strict than 'beyond all reasonable doubt', the General Court concluded that the Commission had failed to meet the standard of proof in this case. The Commission is appealing this decision to the ECJ.[816] In a judgment of 22 June 2022, the General Court applied a different standard of proof in *Case T-584/19 Thyssenkrupp AG v. Commission*, when it concluded the Commission must '*show with a sufficient degree of probability, [. . .] that the transaction significantly impedes effective competition in the internal market*'. The General Court did not clarify whether 'sufficient degree of probability' meant the same as 'balance of probabilities'. However, by applying this standard, the General Court eased the burden of proof on the Commission with regard to demonstrating a SIEC.[817]

[561] On 20 October 2022, Advocate General Kokott added more colour to the standard of proof applicable to gap cases. She concluded that the General Court had erred in law when interpreting the standard of proof in *Case T-399/16 CK Telecoms UK Investment v. Commission*, by requiring a higher standard in concentrations giving rise to non-coordinated effects. According to Kokott '*in general terms, neither the type of concentration nor the complexity of assessing the plausibility of the possible effects of a concentration has, as such, an effect on the standard of proof required, which therefore remains the same in all circumstances*.'[818] The ECJ agreed,[819] setting aside the judgment and referring the case back to the General Court.

[562] Further, in its judgment of 16 March 2023 in *Towercast v. Autorité de la concurrence and others*, the ECJ expanded the scope of merger review rules by finding that concentrations that do not meet the Merger Regulation or national notification thresholds could still be subjected to *ex post* review pursuant Article 102 TFEU if they involve a dominant undertaking.[820]It is important to note that, unlike the ex

---

[813] Case T-79/12 *Cisco Systems Inc and Messagenet SpA v. Commission.*

[814] *See* paras 45–50.

[815] Case T-399/16 *CK Telecoms UK Investment v. Commission.* The Commission lodged an appeal of this decision with the ECJ on 7 Aug. 2020.

[816] Case C-376/20 *European Commission v. CK Telecoms.*

[817] Case T-584/19 *Thyssenkrupp AG v. Commission*, para. 280.

[818] Case C-376/20 *European Commission v. CK Telecoms*, Opinion of AG Kokott paras 46–67.

[819] Case C-376/20 *Commission v. CK Telecoms UK Investments*, para. 79.

[820] Case C-449/21, *Towercast SASU v. Autorité de la concurrence and others*.

ante merger control review established in the Merger Regulation, the Article 102 merger review would only be applicable where the acquirer already held a dominant position in the relevant market, and the acquisition would substantially impede effective competition on this given market. Overall, the judgment in *Towercast* confirms the recent trend of the Commission expanding the scope of its legal mandate to review concentrations that do not meet merger control notification requirements.[821]

10.2 Parties Who Can Bring an Action

[563] According to Article 263 of the TFEU, 'any natural or legal person may institute proceedings against an act addressed to that person which is of direct and individual concern to them, and against a regulatory act which is of direct concern to them and does not entail implementing measures'. Addressees of decisions, such as the parties to a merger prohibited by the Commission pursuant to Article 8(3) of the Regulation, do not have any problems of locus standi. The undertakings concerned, within the meaning of Article 1 of the Regulation, will clearly have a sufficient interest to bring an appeal. This will be the case even if, for example, a purchase agreement lapses before the proceedings are begun.[822]

[564] However, the position of third parties is not as straightforward because they must satisfy two conditions. First, a party has to show that the decision in question is of direct concern. A party may, for example, have a sufficient interest if it is affected by the terms of a commitment given. It does not matter that the commitment has not, in fact, been implemented or that its implementation is dependent on the undertakings which are the addressees of the decision.[823] Second, a party must show that it is individually concerned. It is the established rule of the Court that persons may only claim to be individually concerned *'if that decision affects them by reason of certain attributes which are peculiar to them or by reason of circumstances in which they are differentiated from all other persons and by virtue of these factors distinguishes them individually just as in the case of the person addressed'*.[824] As will be seen, the Court has regard to two matters when determining whether a third party is individually concerned by a Commission decision on the compatibility of a merger with the Internal Market. First, the extent of the third party's participation in the

[821] *See* Case T-227/21 *Illumina v. Commission*.

[822] As the General Court held in *Gencor*, the Commission's decision could have produced effects during the period that the agreement was in force and those effects are not necessarily eradicated by its repeal. An action for annulment is also admissible if it prevents the alleged illegality from being repeated in the future. *See* para. 41.

[823] Case 25/62 *Plaumann & Co. v. Commission* [1963] ECR 95. *See also* the position of EMC/SCPA in the *Kali und Salz* case (above), paras 54–58.

[824] In *Kali und Salz*, the ECJ held that a party was directly concerned because it risked the loss of its sales network and the termination of certain distribution arrangements. Joined Cases C-68/94 & C30/95 *French Republic v. Commission* [1998] E.C.R. I-1375, paras 49–52.

Commission's administrative procedure, and second, the effect on the third party's market position.[825]

[565] The position of competitors was thoroughly reviewed in the content of the *BaByliss* case.[826] The Commission argued that the application of *BaByliss* was inadmissible because the undertaking was not an actual competitor of the parties to the concentration and had not produced good evidence even of its status as a potential competitor. The General Court, however, found that the merger between SEB and Moulinex was clearly of direct and individual concern to the applicant and pointed to a number of factors in support of its finding. These included: BaByliss' participation in the Phase I proceedings; its position as a leading player in personal care products generally; its intention to enter EU markets, albeit that its entry had been delayed and was to be confined to France (not an affected market within the Commission's decision because of the Article 9 referral back to the French authorities); and its attempts to buy Moulinex from the French administrators.

[566] The position of competitors is also well established in airline mergers. Consequently, the General Court had little difficulty in finding that EasyJet had standing to challenge the Commission's decision on the merger of Air France and KLM because EasyJet was already a competitor and thus individually concerned.[827]

[567] Customers with standing may also appeal Commission decisions (or intervene in the appeal procedure) although this has occurred only rarely in practice. In 2010, the General Court confirmed that the Belgian consumer group, Association Belge de Consommateurs Test-Achats which had appealed the Commission approval decision in case M.5549 *EDF/Segebel* was entitled to be heard in EU merger proceedings, provided that the concentration relates to goods or services used by the final consumers.[828] Finally, it should also be noted that third parties directly affected by a Commission decision adopted during the merger control proceedings also have a standing to appeal such a decision (e.g., in the event that the Commission imposes a fine, a periodic penalty for failure to respond to an RFI).

10.3 Procedure

[568] Applications to review merger decisions must be initiated according to the normal deadlines for the review of Commission acts. Actions for annulment carry a time limit of two months from notification of the decision, which is non-extendable. The procedure before the General Court then follows four stages, namely written pleadings, preparatory enquiries, the hearing (oral procedure) and the judgment.

825 Case T-177/*04 EasyJet Airline Co Ltd v. Commission* [2006] ECR II-1931, at para. 35.

826 Case T-114/02 *BaByliss SA & DeLonghi SpA v. Commission* [2003] ECR II-1279, paras 87–117 which concerned a challenge by a potential competitor and purchaser of Moulinex to the Commission's clearance in Phase I, subject to commitments, of the rescue acquisition of Moulinex by SEB.

827 Case T-177/04 *EasyJet Airline Co Ltd v. Commission* [2006] ECR II-1931.

828 Case T-224/10 *Association Belge de Consommateurs Test-Achats v. Commission.*

[569] Following modification of the Rules of Procedure of the General Court ('the Rules of Procedure'),[829] an expedited procedure process came into effect in 2001 to improve the efficiency of judicial control, particularly in relation to merger cases.[830] Under the revised system, the General Court is authorised to suspend its normal rules of priority for dealing with appeals cases, and therefore expedited cases may jump the queue. The written procedure is normally then limited to the application and the defence stages only. The pleadings must be brief and concise, with greater emphasis being placed on the oral hearing before the Court.[831]

[570] The expedited procedure is not exclusive to appeals against merger decisions, and is available where *'the particular urgency and the circumstances of the case requires the Court to give its ruling with the minimum of delay'*. Nevertheless, delays in merger appeals had been fiercely criticised prior to such modification. Since its introduction, a number of merger appeals made to the General Court have been granted such treatment, and the aim of reaching a judgment in under twelve months has normally been achieved. For example, case T-310/01 *Schneider* shows that urgency will count more in favour of an application than complexity will against it. In this case, judgment was delivered ten months after the application, despite the fact that the complexity of the facts and the issues raised must have put the case at the limit of eligibility for expedited treatment.[832] Procedural complications, such as issues of confidentiality, may still lengthen the process.[833] As of 2018, the record stands at seven months.[834]

[571] The most obvious candidates for expedited treatment in the field of mergers are cases such as *Schneider* and *Tetra Laval*. Both involved completed public bids where the embargo, in Article 7(3) of the Merger Regulation, on implementing the merger did not apply. Almost as urgent are cases where the deal has been closed but cannot be implemented because of Article 7(3), resulting in a period of uncertainty for the acquired undertaking. This prevention from consummating the transaction may have for consequence that the undertaking loses key customers or employees and may possibly even lead to precisely the loss of competition which the Regulation is designed to avoid. These commercial and financial advantages of the procedure will normally weigh strongly in favour of an application for expedition. Bringing an application under Article 263 of the TFEU does not apply to 'stay' the

[829] OJ 1991 L136/1 Corrigendum, OJ 1991 L317/34; as amended by OJ 1994 L294/17, OJ 1995 L44/64, OJ 1995 L172/3, OJ 1997 L103/6 (Corrigendum OJ 1997 L351/72), OJ 1999 L135/92, OJ 2000 L322/4, OJ 2003 L147/22, OJ 2004 L132/3, OJ 2004 L127/108, OJ 2005 L298/1, OJ 2006 L386/45, OJ 2008 L179/12, OJ 2009 L24/9, OJ 2009 L60/3 and OJ 2009 L184/10.

[830] This was one of the proposals in the Commission Report of 28 Jun. 2000.

[831] Article 76a of the Rules of Procedure of the General Court.

[832] Case T-310/01 *Schneider Electric SA v. Commission* [2002] ECR II-4071. The General Court refused the first application for expedition and granted a renewed application for expedition only after the applicant cut down its pleading. The Commission also extended the period it had set for Schneider to dispose of its controlling shareholding in Legrand until after the General Court had delivered judgment.

[833] Particularly where the proceedings are brought by a third party *see*, for example, Case T-464/04 *IMPALA v. Commission* [2006] ECR II-2289 (20 months).

[834] Case T-87/05 *EDP Energias de Portugal SA v. Commission* [2005] ECR II-3745. *See also* Case T-417/05 *Endesa v. Commission* [2006] ECR II-2533 (7½ months).

operation or the effect of the decision in question. Nevertheless, under Articles 278 and 279 of the TFEU, the Court may order that a Commission decision is suspended or prescribe interim measures if it considers that the circumstances so require.[835]

[572] An application for interim relief is conditioned on fulfilling two conditions. First, the applicant must have lodged an admissible annulment action against the decision. Consequently, where the main action is ultimately inadmissible, the application for interim relief must also fail. Second, the request for interim measures must state the circumstances which give rise to urgency and the pleas of fact and law which establish a prima facie case for the interim measures applied for. In merger cases, interim measures applications almost always seek the suspension of a Commission decision pending final judgment by the courts.

[573] Merger cases to date illustrate that the burden on a third party seeking to halt a merger by challenging the Commission's decision is substantial. The Court must avoid 'grave and irreparable' damage being suffered, but is subject to the requirement that measures under Articles 278 and 279 must be of a provisional nature in the sense that they must not prejudice the final judgment in the case. The applicant's interest in having the operation of the contested decision suspended must be weighed against the public interest in implementation of decisions adopted under the Merger Regulation and the interest of third parties affected by suspension of a decision. The General Court confirmed that interim measures may be granted only where there is strong evidence of serious and irreparable damage, and that therefore an application based on mere assertions that remain hypothetical and unsubstantiated statements will fail.[836]

[574] In case of the annulment in whole or in part of the Commission's decision, Article 10(5) of the Merger Regulation specifically provides that the Commission should re-examine the concentration with a view to adopting a new decision (as of 31 December 2018, the EU courts have annulled eleven Commission prohibition decisions). The new appraisal takes place on the basis of a new notification or a supplement to the original if the passage of time has rendered the original notification factually incomplete or because of changes in market conditions. Where no such changes have occurred, the parties must certify this fact without delay. The period for the new decision then begins from the receipt of either the new or updated notification or the certification that allows the Commission to proceed on the basis of the original notification. It is implicit from these procedural rules that the Commission is to assess the concentration in the light of the circumstances prevailing at the time of the new notification. It would be unusual if the Commission was unable to take account of subsequent developments, for example, in the markets concerned. Article 10(5) puts the matter beyond doubt, stating that the '*concentration shall be re-examined in the light of current market conditions*'.

[835] The CFI has rejected applications for interim measures in several cases including case T-96/92 *R CCE Grandes Sources v. Commission* [1995] ECR II-1213 and *CCE Vittel and CE Pierval v. Commission*, case T-322/94 *Union Carbide v. Commission*, case T-342/00 *Petrolessence SG2R v. Commission*.

[836] Case T-411/07 *R Aer Lingus Group plc v. Commission*, 2008 ECR II-411.

[575] Appeals to the ECJ lie as a right stemming from the judgments of the General Court, and must be brought within two months of the notification of the General Court decision appealed against. Such appeals may be brought only on points of law, under Article 256 of the TFEU. In effect, this means as recently stated by the ECJ, that the General Court has exclusive jurisdiction: first, to the facts, except where the substantial inaccuracy of its findings is apparent from the documents submitted to it; and second, to assess those facts.[837] Consequently, the ECJ has no jurisdiction to establish the facts or, in principle, to examine the evidence which the General Court accepted in support of those facts. Provided that the evidence has been properly obtained and the general principles of law, the rules of procedure in relation to the burden of proof, and the taking of evidence have been observed, it is for the General Court alone to assess the value which should be attached to the evidence produced to it. Except where a clear sense of the evidence has been distorted, such an appraisal does not constitute a point of law which is subject to review by the ECJ.

10.4 Possible Action for Damages

[576] A possible consequence of the annulment of a Commission prohibition decision may be a damages claim brought against the Commission. While the Merger Regulation is silent on this point, Article 340(2) TFEU provides a means of redress for damage wrongly inflicted by an EU institution. To support such a claim, three conditions must be met:

(1) the Commission's conduct was unlawful;
(2) actual damage has been suffered; and
(3) there is a causal link between the unlawful conduct and the damage.

[577] With respect to merger control decisions, the standard of proof is particularly demanding for damages claims. As the Courts have consistently pointed out in actions for the annulment of Commission merger control decisions, the Commission enjoys a broad margin of discretion when assessing the competitive effects of mergers notified under the Merger Regulation. Given the breadth of its discretion, only the most egregious errors leading directly to a loss would seem capable of meeting the evidential standard. To date, only very few claims for damages have been brought under the Merger Regulation, the first by Schneider following the Commission's prohibition of the *Schneider/Legrand* transaction,[838] and the last by ASL Aviation Holdings and ASL Airlines (Ireland) Ltd (ASL) in relation to the Commission's prohibition decision in the *UPS/TNT* case.[839]

[837] Case C-413/06 *P Bertelsmann AG and Sony Corporation of America v. Impala, Commission and Sony BMG*, 10 Jul. 2008.
[838] Case M.2283 *Schneider/Legrand.*
[839] Case M.6570 *UPS/TNT. Express.*

[578] In the *Schneider* case, the Court of First Instance (CFI) ruled for the first time that a merging party can be compensated (at least in part) for losses sustained as a result of the illegal prohibition of its merger.[840] The Court pointed out that, for the Community to incur non-contractual liability, there must have been an unlawful conduct on the part of the Community's institutions, with the standard of review being whether there was a *grave and manifest disregard* of the limits of their powers of assessment.

[579] Such a manifest disregard of powers will occur where the acts or omissions of the Commission which cause damage cannot be explained by the 'objective constraints' of the merger control procedure. In other words, the Commission is allowed some margin of manoeuvre in its dealings with the notifying parties, but only insofar as its actions are justified or explained by the time constraints of the market analysis procedure or any technical problem arising from that analysis which would require additional scrutiny.

[580] The Court found that there had been such an infringement of Schneider's rights of defence on the facts since the Commission's Statement of Objections had not allowed Schneider to adequately assess the Commission's competition concerns, in particular with regard to the issue of the leveraging of dominance in certain related national markets.

[581] This had deprived Schneider of the possibility of offering appropriate remedies that were capable of reducing or eliminating the Commission's competition concerns. There was no objective justification nor explanation for this infringement of the rights of defence.

[582] The Court, therefore, concluded that the illegality, whose existence and character were not disputed by the Commission, resulted in an obligation on the Commission to compensate for the harmful consequences of that illegality. However, such compensation was very limited in scope as it covered only the expenses incurred by Schneider in respect of its participation in the resumed merger control procedure. The final amount awarded by the Court to Schneider was EUR50 000.

[583] In any event, by identifying the threshold at which point the Community incurs non-contractual liability for unlawful conduct as a situation where there was a 'grave and manifest disregard' of the limits of the authority's powers of assessment, it follows that the Commission may be exposed to a successful claim for damages under the Merger Regulation only in exceptional circumstances. A failure of assessment or reasoning is unlikely to be considered sufficiently serious to find the Commission liable for non-contractual damages.

[584] The Court will have the opportunity to apply these principles in the *UPS* case.[841] In December 2017, UPS brought a claim for damages following a judgment rendered by the General Court annulling a Commission decision prohibiting

[840] Cases T-351/03 and C-440/07P *Schneider v. Commission*.
[841] Case T-834/17 *United Parcel Service v. Commission*.

the acquisition of TNT by UPS.[842] UPS is seeking roughly EUR1.7 bn for damages sustained as a result of the Commission's prohibition decision and the subsequent acquisition of TNT by FedEx. A separate but related damages claim has also been brought by ASL, who had planned to buy TNT Airways, a unit of TNT, at the time of the UPS negotiations. However, the transaction did not go ahead, and ASL alleges that this was a direct result of the Commission's prohibition decision in the *UPS* case.[843] ASL ultimately purchased TNT Airways in 2016 when Fedex acquired TNT. At the time of writing, both cases were still ongoing.

11 LINKS TO MAIN EU LEGISLATIVE TEXTS

[585] These are links to the main EU legislative texts to which many references are made in this chapter.

- Merger Regulation:
  https://eur-lex.europa.eu/legal-content/EN/ALL/?uri=CELEX:32004R0139.
- Implementing Merger Regulation:
  https://eur-lex.europa.eu/legal-content/EN/TXT/PDF/?uri=CELEX:32023R0914&qid=1696000059339.
- Consolidated Jurisdictional Notice:
  https://eur-lex.europa.eu/LexUriServ/LexUriServ.do?uri=OJ:C:2008:095:0001:0.

[842] The General Court judgment (Case T-194/13 *United Parcel Service v. Commission*) was since upheld by the Court of Justice (Case C-265/17 *Commission v. United Parcel Service*).

[843] Case T-540/18 *ASL Aviation Holdings and ASL Airlines (Ireland)/Commission*.